THE REMORSELESS ROAD

SINGAPORE TO NAGASAKI

JAMES McEWAN

D0474983

For the men of
Nos. 36 and 100 Squadrons
Royal Air Force, Royal Australian Air Force
and Royal New Zealand Air Force
who flew the Vildebeests;
for those who survived captivity
with me at Ohama;
and for those
whose journey ended there.

First published in the UK in 1997
by Airlife Publishing Ltd

This edition published 2001

British Library Cataloguing-in-Publication Data
A catalogue record for this book
is available from the British Library

ISBN 1 84037 301 6

Printed in England by MPG Books Ltd, Bodmin, Cornwall

Airlife Publishing Ltd
101 Longden Road, Shrewsbury, SY3 9EB, England
E-mail: airlife@airlifebooks.com
Website: www.airlifebooks.com

CONTENTS

Acknowledgements

In compiling this account I have been able to enlist the assistance of men who served with me at the time, and have confirmed – or where necessary amended – my own records, which the circumstances rendered fragmentary. They have also filled in gaps in my own knowledge of some events in which I was not directly involved. To all my former comrades in Singapore, Java and Ohama my debt is heavy, and I thank them for their steadfastness, companionship and support during those distant and ill-starred, but crowded and eventful, days.

In particular, my debt to Elwyn Cummins, whom I interviewed on his return from Endau, and to Charlie MacDonald, the details of whose story I had from his own lips only many years later, is heavy and is here warmly acknowledged. Likewise I owe much to the late John Blunt, and to Peter Atherton, Ivor Jones, Syd Sanders and Scotty Thomson, all Australian aircrew, and to Tom Lamb, a pilot in the RAF. In several important instances they alone were in a position to report at first-hand on events, particularly in the Endau disaster, in which they were desperately involved.

In the 1920s and 1930s Douglas Brodie and I served with Butterfield & Swire in China, and marched as comrades in the Shanghai Scottish. Now he lives less combatantly in Vancouver in Canada. There his son and daughter-in-law, John and Heather Brodie, enlisting the resources of modern technology, with which they are familiar, typed and prepared my manuscript for publication. To them this volume, in a very practical sense, owes its existence. It was an exacting task, undertaken quite voluntarily. It has put me greatly in their debt; and earned for them my deep gratitude.

FOREWORD

A three-and-a-half-year spell, at an earlier period, in China, during which I acquired an acquaintance with the language together with my Edinburgh degree, saw my translation, early in 1941, from my teaching post in George Watson's College in Edinburgh to a direct commission in the Intelligence Branch of the Royal Air Force Volunteer Reserve. For practical training in the techniques of operations I was sent to the Operations Room at Leuchars Air Base, on the east coast of Scotland; and in the autumn of that year I was posted to the RAF Station at Sungei Patani, which is on the mainland of Malaya, a little north of Penang Island and near the Siamese border. But I was destined never to see Sungei Patani, the Japanese anticipating my arrival there by a matter of days; and I was diverted to Singapore, where I arrived, the auspices being adverse, on Friday, 13 January 1942. Sungei Patani being by this time, unavailable to me, I was posted as Intelligence Officer to Nos. 36 and 100 Squadrons, who were flying Vildebeest torpedo-bombers and operating out of Seletar Air Base in the north of the island.

The period which follows, whose drama and aftermath are related in Parts One and Two of this book, provided some of the most melancholic pages in British and Imperial history. In a fierce air battle, fought above the little town of Endau on the east Malayan coast, the two squadrons lost half their aircrews along with half their aircraft. In a military catastrophe which was soon to climax with the fall of Singapore and with its consequences for both the British Empire and the whole future of white men in the East, it is inevitable that blame is apportioned – and rightly so, though not exclusively should it fall on the heads of those who were in Singapore and Malaya at the time at the cutting edge. One inescapable consequence is that this reproachful contagion spreads to taint others who only did their duty, fearlessly and sacrificially.

Withdrawn hurriedly to Palembang in Sumatra, the survivors continued the struggle in the Dutch East Indies. Detached from my squadrons, I was then posted to Air Headquarters, at Sime Road, in the centre of the island, where I remained till the night of 10/11 February when, carrying secret papers, I flew to Batavia (now Jakarta) in Java, in the Catalina that brought General Wavell on his last visit to the island before its fall.

When, in March 1942, Allied resistance in Java collapsed, about 1,200 men of the RAF and the RAAF fell into enemy hands. From various points on the island these men had by August of that year been assembled in a camp called Makasura, about six miles south of Batavia. They were divided into three groups of about 400 men each, preparatory to dispatch overseas. The first group marched out of Makasura in fairly good heart, believing they were on their way to Siam where they would be billeted in hill stations, the mountain climate being healthier for Europeans than the sweltering plains of north Java. Thus was the infamous Death Railway euphemised. Whatever substance this early rumour possessed soon dissipated and they were diverted to Japan. On the voyage north disease, mostly dysentery, took a heavy toll, many of the men dying. On their arrival in the Bay of Tokyo, the survivors were manifestly in no condition to be dispatched to the coal-mines in Hokkaido, which was their intended destination, and they were dispersed among various camps in the Tokyo area.

The last of the three groups was sent to Sandakan in north Borneo for employment in the building of an airfield. To make good the wastage caused by death and disease, fresh drafts of prisoners were from time to time introduced. As the war drew towards its close the Japanese, fearing invasion of the island by Australian forces, marched the survivors from the coast to an inland village called Ranau. On the way all were either massacred or died from the rigours of the journey. Had not seven Australians managed to slip off undetected into the bush, nothing about their fate would ever have come to light. Of the 400 men who left Java, not one survived.

On 21 October 1942 the second group (of which the author was a member) boarded the *Yoshida Maru*, a seedy coaster, in Batavia and sailed for Singapore, where they arrived four days later. There, during a further four days, they were subjected to various forms of ill-usage and humiliation before being put aboard the *Singapore Maru*, which sailed on 29 October for Japan. On 13 November the vessel put in to Takao, now known as Kaohsiung, in south Taiwan where she underwent certain structural modifications in order to accommodate a further 600 Japanese troops. During the passage of the Formosan Strait very severe typhoon conditions were encountered, and in the over-crowded holds the situation of the prisoners swiftly deteriorated and soon became appalling. Not till 27 November did the *Singapore Maru* reach Moji in north-eastern Kyushu, where the men were to be disembarked. This vessel was later to acquire some notoriety and engaged the attention of the War Crimes Commission in the Far East (see Appendix Two). Of the proceedings, the curious will find a condensed report in Lord Russell's book *The Lords of Bushido*.

It is about the men who lived and fought through these tragic episodes in history– those who survived, and those who now lie in their thousands in nameless jungle graves or beneath eastern seas – I now write, and honour. It is their faces I see and voices I hear, with all the clarity of fifty-plus years ago.

JAMES McEWAN
EDINBURGH

A Note on Place Names

The task of the geographer has been made much more difficult by the headlong flight from Empire which marked the period following the Second World War. Nowhere has the process been more conspicuous than in South-East Asia, where many of the emergent nations have displayed a great eagerness to rid themselves not only of foreign domination but also of the place names which they considered a humiliating reminder of it. In their place they restored, wherever they existed, the original native names that they had superseded. Thus, Batavia became Jakarta.

For my part I have adhered to the forms which were adopted by the British and Dutch settlers and which contemporary usage made familiar. In very few instances is the divergence so marked as to raise in the mind of the reader any real doubt about the place referred to.

Map of Dutch East Indies
including Java

PART ONE

PASSING BELLS BY ENDAU RIVER

The warriors lie
Cut off in their joy.
All the valiant band has fallen
The proud ones beneath the ramparts

From The Wanderer
in *The Exeter Book*

TO EASTERN WAR

A t 11.00 a.m. on Sunday, 3 September 1939, the writer was standing on the deck of the Cunard liner *Laconia*, then at anchor in Belfast Lough. He was out of touch with events. Now homeward-bound, for the last few weeks he had been on vacation in the USA. Scorning lifts, he had hiked from Burlington in Vermont down through the Green Mountains to Albany at the head of the Hudson. He had slept, at times on straw, in primitive youth hostels, which were then an innovation in the States. Beside him on the deck were two groups of girls, one German and the other French, tourists like himself. One of the German girls had placed a battery-powered radio precariously on the ship's rail. Presently from this instrument there issued a voice. It was a thin voice, sounding disembodied. Britain, announced the speaker (for it was Neville Chamberlain, the Prime Minister) and Germany were now at war. Breaking out around him, loud sobbings signalled in female hearts a surrender to despair.

To answer his country's need the writer had little to offer. For the rough business of war his profession of English master at George Watson's College in Edinburgh furnished him with no training. He did, however, possess one esoteric aptitude, a legacy from an earlier sojourn in China: he could speak Mandarin. China was already locked in a mortal contention. Issuing from the Horned Isles, Japanese invaders had annexed Manchuria. They had penetrated deep into the central and southern regions. Long a possibility, an assault upon British and Dutch dependencies in the south had now become a threat. To retain as an effective ally in the possible extension of hostilities this vast, dismembered, but defiant empire would demand succour. In these circumstances an ability to speak Chinese would undoubtedly prove an asset.

But for a chance to exploit his linguistic capability he had to wait till the spring of 1941. Sensing that their day had come, the Japanese were poised for embroilment in the southern regions. Offering his services to the RAF, he was granted a commission in its Volunteer Reserve. Basic training began immediately at Loughborough College in the English Midlands, to be followed by practical instruction at Leuchars Air Base near St Andrews in Scotland. Fit now for service, he was posted to Sungei Patani. An RAF station on the Malayan mainland, opposite Penang Island and near the Thai border, it was at the time a hotbed of international espionage and intrigue, where the survival of an inquisitive British intelligence officer could neither be guaranteed nor expected, and was unlikely to last long enough for him to lament its brevity.

But he was spared calamity by the appearance of the Japanese on the scene only a matter of days before his arrival. Diverted to Singapore, he arrived there – the auspices being bleak – on Friday, 13 January 1942. He was then posted as intelligence officer to Nos. 36 and 100 Squadrons, which were operating out of Seletar Air Base on the north of the island. Highly trained and resolute airmen, they were equipped with obsolete Vildebeest torpedo-bombers and assigned the duty of monitoring, and eventually engaging, any Japanese landing on the east coast of the peninsula.

Joining them, he was privileged to share their comradeship and record their fate.

The author, James McEwan.

Vickers Vildebeest Mk II aircraft of 100 Squadron, RAF. *(Philip Jarrett Collection)*

Vildebeests of 100 Squadron flying line-abreast over Singapore in the mid-1930s.
(Philip Jarrett Collection)

THE VALIANT BAND HAS FALLEN

Jock Forbes was one of the pilots. He had the taut, muscular torso of the classical athlete. His too was the hair, clustering in tight curls round the head, and the straightest of noses. Tanned by prolonged exposure to the tropical sun, his skin had taken on the bloom of burnished bronze. But it was not the purple ether of Attic heavens that had nurtured his boyhood years but the sullen, and often rainy, skies of Antrim in Northern Ireland. It was this, also, which provided the clue to the soft lilt in his voice. Despite this, as his name made clear, his forebears had originally come from Scotland. This identity of ancestry had probably much to do with the selection of the crew who flew with him in his Vildebeest. His navigator, who had the good clan name of Charlie MacDonald, hailed from Hobart in Tasmania. In his gun-turret sat Jock Grant, also Australian but of Scottish extraction.

In the Mess Jock Forbes belonged to that small, yet significant, coterie who were Scots. Though separated in youth from the lone shieling on the misty island, he had managed to acquire – how I do not know (or, if I ever did, now forget) – a fair smattering of the Doric, which he would on occasion air with the exuberance affected rather by the exiles than by those to the manner born. From time to time, on meeting in the Mess or the hangars, we would pause for a moment to exchange some badinage in our 'mither tongue'. A venial foible, it gave us both much pleasure, recalling as it did shared joys, now obscured by the mists of distance and war, 'o' hame and infancy'. What our comrades who happened to be within earshot made of these exchanges we never paused to consider. In their unenlightened ears it must have sounded as outlandish as a rhapsody of Ossian.

As Tim Rowlands led the first sortie in to the attack on the enemy vessels at Endau, his starboard flank was covered by a Vildebeest in whose cockpit sat Jock Forbes and behind him his Scottish-Australian crew. But before they ever reached their targets, being intercepted by a powerful force of Navy O fighters, they came under very heavy fire. Hit in the upper arm by a cannon-shell, Charlie MacDonald received a grievous wound. Another shell, striking Jock Grant in one of his legs, mangled the flesh and shattered the bone. From the barrage only the pilot escaped injury. But his aircraft had not shared his good fortune, being riddled with shell-holes. Missiles had also severed some of the struts which anchored the wings, which, now, with their support impaired, began to flap with the rhythmic, ungainly motion of a great bird in flight. Gone now was any hope that the aircraft would ever be able to make it back to base. The immediate concern of the pilot was to bring it down to forest-top level and so defeat the determined efforts of his assailants to shoot him down.

It is idle to speculate on what, in those desperate moments of battle, was passing through the mind of Jock Forbes. Most likely it seems that his intention was to seek some clearing, or open road, in the jungle wide enough to admit the passage of a Vildebeest, and thus provide his crew with an opportunity to escape. But, nursing his crippled aircraft over the tree-tops, the pilot must have despaired of ever finding the gap he sought since on all sides stretched the jungle, unbroken and limitless. But at length, through the thick lattice of forest boughs beneath him, he was able to detect a straggling, brown thread which denoted the presence of a road. This he followed as offering the last opportunity to avoid crashing into the tree-tops.

This resurgence of hope was to achieve fulfilment. At length he arrived at a gap in the forest where the trees retreated sufficiently to expose the road beneath. But the opening seemed scarcely large enough to admit something with the wing-span of a Vildebeest. To add to his problems he exercised only limited control over his machine, some of the control wires having been shot away with the struts. But in this extremity he had to rely on his flying skills, aided by a measure of good luck; and success, surprisingly, crowned the attempt when, dropping through the gap, the crippled aircraft made a bumpy landing on the forest road. What, however, from the air the trees had concealed was that, right ahead of the landing, the road passed in a narrow cutting through a low ridge. Despite desperate efforts on the part of the pilot to bring his machine to a halt before making contact with this obstacle, it plunged into the cutting whose banks, being steep and constricted, caught the tips of both wings and wrenched them from the fuselage.

Disembarked hastily from the invasion fleet, a company of Japanese scouts had in the meantime been dispatched to scour the neighbouring roads in an effort to locate any British forces that might be in the area. These men had probably been watching the Vildebeest as it made its lumbering passage over the tree-tops and, finding it wedged in the cutting, made towards it, breaking into a run nearer the aircraft. Anchored with his shattered leg in his turret, Jock Grant watched the developments. As the enemy got near, he turned his machine-gun on them, thereby ensuring that with the liquidation of some of the enemy, he was inevitably ensuring his own. To the motives and movements of Jock Forbes during this time much mystery still attaches. This much is certain: since, alone among the crew, he had escaped injury, if anyone was to make a break for it, he was most likely to succeed. What is equally evident is that he made no effort to do so. Climbing down, very deliberately, from his cockpit, and turning his back on the advancing Japanese, he set off, with slow, measured stride, along the road that led through the cutting. It almost seemed that from his mind fear and his future had taken their leave and that, regarding his fate as inevitable, he was prepared to meet it without taint of the craven. If this, indeed, was his conclusion, we shall never know what reasoning led him to it; and to unravel the events which were immediately to follow must remain the domain of speculation.

For the next reliable information about what happened to him we must admit the passage of a week or two till such time as, accompanied by Japanese guards, a batch of British prisoners was being marched along a road in the vicinity of Mersing. Among their number was an Australian airman called Graham McCabe, who has left an account of the proceedings. Shot down into the sea during this same sortie, he had been picked up by the Japanese, presumably to extract information from him. Arriving on the outskirts of the town, the party came to a bridge. At this point the guards interrupted their march to take their charges aside to inspect an open grave in which lay the bodies of several Australian soldiers and two British airmen. All had been beheaded. The identification of one of these airmen caused McCabe no problem, Jock Forbes and he being comrades in the same squadron. About the other airman he could not speak with the same assurance though he had little doubt that it was the body of Jock Grant.

There remained the third member of the crew, Charlie MacDonald. When the Vildebeest plunged into the cutting, in his mind at least there was no doubt what he should do. No sooner had the aircraft shuddered to a halt than, leaping from his seat, he began a desperate effort to scale the bank. But some formidable obstacles opposed his attempt. The slope was steep. The earth was friable and sodden. He had a shattered arm. But matching his efforts with the challenge of the task, he succeeded in making it to the top. With this initial impediment now behind him, he made off into the bush with all possible speed. But as he left the scene he heard a desperate cry rising from the cutting: it was the voice of Jock Grant, and the word was, 'Don't'. For his act of courage exacting a bloody revenge, the enemy was dispatching the wounded gunner with the bayonet. Three days of desultory wandering in the bush found Charlie MacDonald no nearer his goal of escape or refuge than when he had embarked upon the search. He was now reconnoitring a *kampong*, lurking under cover and waiting an opportunity to slip unobserved into one of the huts in search of food. It was at this moment of stealthy surveillance that there hove into view a group of men apparently bent on the same purpose as himself. Sauntering leisurely down the main street, they were peering into each hut as they passed. While the odd assortment of clothing they wore provided no reliable clue as to their identity, their stature and pigmentation established them to be European. One of them, a tall man, had a huge crop of fiery red hair, which was standing on end. Their appearance thus banished from Charlie's mind all fear that they might betray him to the enemy; and, thus assured, he decided to break cover. A premonitory whistle alerted them to his presence, whereupon contact was made. He now discovered that they were British sailors, survivors from the destroyer *Thanet*. Dispatched from Singapore to engage the enemy forces at Endau, the vessel had been sunk in action. Being sailors, and their work being with the sea, the men were ill-equipped to make a success of survival in the Malayan jungle. Indeed, so comprehensive was their inadequacy, that it would probably have gone ill with them had they not thus by chance fallen in with this resourceful navigator. Their knowledge of their whereabouts extended little further than the fact that they were stranded on the Malayan peninsula, from which plight they would find it difficult to escape. It was an ignorance which our navigator was spared.

The encounter was immediately followed by a council-of-war. Here it was decided that survival was most likely to be achieved by an association of his navigational skills with their nautical ones. For this collaboration to bear fruit what was obviously needed was a boat. But, fecund though it might be in other respects, the Malayan jungle was not noted for providing boats. To find what they were looking for, they had to reach the sea. This, after some wandering, they did, arriving on the coast in the vicinity of Mersing where, drawn up on the beach and abandoned, providentially, it seemed, for their use, was a junk. A professional inspection by the sailors pronouncing it to be seaworthy, they decided to appropriate it for their own use. As an initial destination they decided to make for one of the small islands, which are numerous in this coastal region of the South China Sea. They chose one of the smallest and least conspicuous of them, hoping that the dense jungle growth with which it was covered would conceal both themselves and their junk from prying, and possibly disaffected, eyes. On landing, they found it uninhabited, which disposed of another risk: no natives were here to give away their retreat to the enemy. By their reckoning, their stay on the island would last several days at the least. This would give them time to reconnoitre, to study the traffic on the surrounding seas and assess the dangers of continuing their voyage. To their surprise, their sojourn on the island did not extend beyond the first day. Expecting to see evidence of Japanese naval activity, they found the nearby waters deserted. Thus reassured, they hauled their junk from concealment, and, climbing back on board, put to sea.

Their subsequent passage down the coast of Johore proved uneventful and in due course they arrived in the eastern approaches to the Straits of Johore. Here, being picked up by a British patrol vessel, they were taken to the island of Pulau Ubin. At this point the collaboration between airman and seamen, which had proved so fruitful for both parties, was, having served its purpose, dissolved with cordial expressions of thanks and goodwill. Charlie MacDonald took himself off to the barracks of the Gordon Highlanders at Changi.

From the moment when, in the heat of battle over Endau, the shell had ripped through his upper arm, Charlie had had little opportunity to attend to his wound. Now the consequences of neglect were all too evident, and of what they portended Charlie himself had a good idea. Had he needed any confirmation it was provided forthwith by the two doctors who examined him. Gangrene had already set in, and so extensive had been its progress that what was now at stake was not so much his arm as his life. At first the medical men seemed not to be primarily concerned with saving his arm: in a case of mortification as advanced as this, what was obviously called for was amputation. But before resorting to this ultimate therapy, they decided to try an experiment. Into their hands had just come some samples of a new drug called sulphonamide, or M&B 693. Of its use they had no experience, and of its curative powers no more knowledge than was conveyed in the accompanying literature. But advance publicity had vested it with a potency which at the time stopped short only of the phenomenal, especially in cases of gangrene like this. To this happy decision Charlie MacDonald owes certainly the retention of his arm, and in all probability of his life as well. In application, the drug fell nothing short of the remarkable properties with which it had been credited. First to subside was the pain, followed shortly by the inflammation. Then the suppuration declined. The threat that the infection would invade his chest receded. So remarkable was his restoration to health that the period of expected convalescence shrank from weeks to a matter of days. Presently he reached the stage when he was pronounced fit enough to exchange Changi Hospital for the Transit Camp at Bukit Timah. There more rural surroundings, removed from the stresses of town and hospital life, would favour a more speedy restoration to active service.

But hardly had he settled in his new quarters when further threat forced upon him renewed migration. On 8 February, under cover of darkness, the Japanese, crossing the Straits, were soon within striking distance of Bukit Timah. Singapore itself was the only possible destination for a further retreat.

A Fugitive in the Islands

Singapore was being blasted and was ablaze. Its citizens were perishing in their thousands. In the meantime desperate efforts were being made to evacuate some of the most vulnerable among them while a route of escape still remained open. On Thursday, 12 February, the final convoy was due to put to sea. Its departure would witness the extinction of the seaborne exodus.

In addition to various tankers and lesser craft, the nucleus of the convoy consisted of three medium-sized, passenger-carrying vessels of which the largest was the *Empire Star*. On board her, embarked as passengers, was a party made up of the last European nurses on the island. There was no doubt what fate was likely to be theirs were they to fall into the hands of the enemy. From Hong Kong had come reports of rape and butchery by the Japanese soldiery of hospital nurses. Appointed as a medical officer to the vessel for this hazardous voyage was a young doctor who, for several years, had practised in the city. On the outbreak of the war he had been granted a commission in the medical branch of the Royal Navy Volunteer Reserve. He was also, incidentally, my cousin. His name was Edward Thomson.

Sweeping swiftly round the docks, a rumour that the final convoy was on the point of putting to sea started a wave of panic among the roving bands of deserters and refugees, who thronged the jetties. Among them were many drunk and desperate. Seeking a vessel to board they were not averse to using force to achieve their end. Of these a group of Australians appeared at the foot of the gangway of the *Empire Star*. Denied admission, they charged into the vessel, shooting dead a British officer who attempted to restrain them. That same night the convoy sailed, but encountered unexpected delay in negotiating passage through the minefields. But that difficulty overcome, they proceeded without serious interruption till noon of the following day, by which time they had been spotted by Japanese reconnaissance planes, and subjected to relentless bombing attacks. Several tankers were set on fire and sunk, while the *Empire Star* sustained some direct hits with consequent loss of life and casualties. Nonetheless, the vessel succeeded in reaching Batavia; and after a brief stay and some temporary repairs she renewed her voyage to arrive in due course at Fremantle in Western Australia.

By 13 February – a day that will go down in Singapore history as 'Black Friday' – it was abundantly clear that the city was in its death-throes. Seeing no prospect either of relief or escape, some army units, having lost their nerve and their will to fight, were not too distressed by this forfeiture to begin to desert their posts. By the morning of Sunday, 15 February, rumours were rife among the upper echelons of the military establishment that the ceremony of formal surrender would take place at four p.m. that day.

Marooned in Singapore was a group of officers whose prospects were bleak. Members of Dalforce, the Chinese Volunteer Unit, they had distinguished themselves in battle, but had failed to make good their escape with the main body on the previous night. Were they to fall into the hands of the enemy, their nationality and their actions consigned them to an end too painful to contemplate. With these as nucleus – but including also some senior members of the executive – an escape party was formed whose efforts were greatly assisted by a naval commander who, in the first instance, provided them with essential charts to assist their passage through the mine-fields, and was subsequently instrumental in procuring for their use a boat, the *Kembong*, which was a sixty-foot motor launch in the service of the Straits Fisheries. A decision was taken to restrict the escape party to twenty-five, and to exclude the wife of one of the fugitives whom another member of the party had misguidedly endeavoured to include. The vessel being hurriedly provisioned for the venture, a final selection for the escape party was made.

From confinement in his underground retreat near the post office, the imminence of surrender had released Charlie MacDonald, and in a mood of casual enquiry, he made his way down to the docks, where he was confronted with scenes of unbridled anarchy. It was while he was there, but in what circumstances we do not know, that he fell in with some members of the *Kembong* party. On their expressing some doubts about the navigational skills among its members, he promptly offered them his services, claiming that, as preparation for an expedition of this nature, nothing could be more rigorous than navigating a bomber by night over the featureless Malayan jungles. At first it appears they were inclined to spurn his overtures, possibly having reservations about his wounded arm and his total lack of documentation to support his claim. But in the chaotic conditions then prevailing on the docks, their search for an alternative navigator, on which they had confidently embarked, ended in failure, and Charlie was co-opted as a supernumerary member of the crew. To supplement the mine charts, and a few others which they had managed to obtain, Charlie set out in search of some more general charts, meeting with no more success than the others. But the expedition led to the acquisition of a document of some interest. To chronicle this ill-starred day in the history of Singapore, the local newspaper, *The Straits Times*, surmounting all obstacles, had succeeded in producing a crisis edition, of which he obtained a copy. This proved of immediate use in establishing the earliest day of sailing, while being of later interest as a souvenir.

Eight o'clock was decided upon as the hour for departure: it was by then virtually dark, and there remained most of the night to get well away from Singapore before dawn would expose them to greater risk of detection and capture. During the boarding of the launch, severe problems were encountered, the jetty being crowded by army deserters while the vessel lay about 500 yards off shore. When a small boat was procured to serve as a ferry, and embarkation got underway, the watching deserters threatened to rush the vessel, the crisis averted only through one of the escapees declaring loudly that this was a special mission! In this way, the embarkation was allowed to proceed to its end, and, under a smoke-filled sky, with a lurid back cloth provided by the blazing oil tanks on Blakang Mati Island, and the city itself in flames, the small group slunk away in their frail craft on their hazardous venture with the furtive bearing of thieves in the night.

During the hours of darkness the crossing of the Straits was accomplished without incident and, breaking over the Sumatran coast, the dawn found the *Kembong* anchored briefly at the entrance to the channel that separates the large island of Bengkalis from the mainland. It is into this channel that the River Siak, which crosses the island from the mountain barrier in the west, debouches, and it was up this river that the *Kembong* now made its way, coming about noon to the town of Bengkalis.

It had been an oil town, with all the disincentives to lingering which this implies. From the Dutch the party now learned that another escape group from Singapore had preceded them and had gone on up-river the previous day, a course which they were strongly urged to follow without delay. Before leaving, they took on board a party of Australians. Caught up in the desperate fighting to hold the line at Batu Pahat, on the other side of the Strait, they had been cut off by enemy infiltration in their rear. For a time they had attempted to carry on the fight, supplied by drops from the air. One of the Vildebeests engaged in this operation was, by a strange coincidence, none other than Charlie MacDonald's own machine. Deciding to make a break for it, they secured a small boat in which they managed to cross the Strait to Sumatra. But this exhausted their efforts, the crossing of the distant western mountains, which had featured in their vague original plans, being, of course, far beyond their powers; they needed to be taken under somebody's wing. Two further launches, laden with military personnel, arrived on the scene, and the three decided to set off in convoy in the evening on a night voyage to the next town upstream, which was Pekan Bahru, and which is about a hundred miles from the sea. The Dutch had provided the *Kembong*, which was to lead the way, with a pilot. But in the darkness, on a winding, shoal-clogged river, navigation proved difficult and the vessel ran aground. But, towed off by the launches, she was able to continue upstream, surviving the shoals and other hazards of the tortuous channel till, about noon, she arrived at Pekan Bahru. This was as far as the vessel could go, and the hundred miles or so, which still separated them from the coll on the western mountain barrier would have to be negotiated by road. The three vessels, having served their purpose, were handed over to the Dutch.

It was late afternoon when three large buses arrived to take the combined groups; and they set off. Day was ebbing by the time they reached the foothills of the western range, and the climb began. Above them towered a line of volcanic peaks. The road was bad and progressively became worse as they climbed, differing little in places from a watercourse, which in the rains it would undoubtedly become. In recurring S-bends it scaled the gradients. Never far away was the possibility of mechanical failure or a sudden subsidence in the road which would plunge them with their vehicles into the yawning gulf beneath. But, against the odds, nothing untoward occurred and shortly after midnight, they reached the coll. Dismounting from their buses, the fugitives now learned that the hill-top small town was called Pajakumbuh and to their joy and relief they found an empty train standing in the station. It was not due to leave till daybreak, so in the meantime they crowded into its compartments to snatch some brief hours of sleep.

As dawn broke, the train set off on the steep descent of the mountain range.

A remarkable feat of railway engineering in its own right, the track passed in the descent through some breathtaking scenery, to appreciate the beauty of which would have required a time somewhat less turbulent. Arriving at length at the foot, they continued on towards the sea; and shortly before noon they pulled into the station at Padang, a large port on the western Sumatran coast. Hoping to be restored to some approximation to normality in life, they were immediately confronted with a situation which the strenuous efforts of the Dutch authorities had failed to bring under control. From every small port on the east coast of the island, along every road and path that led west, the refugees had flocked in their terrified thousands, fleeing from the alien hordes whose odious reputation had preceded them, to converge on Padang. Many nations, and every walk of life, were represented, excepting only the humblest, the poverty and helplessness of their situation denying them the chance of escape from it. United in their dread of the Japanese invader, they fled blindly, inveigled by the mirage of a waiting ship and the safety which the ocean alone now could provide. Under the pressures to which they had been subjected, law and order had collapsed, or functioned only intermittently. Municipal services had disintegrated under demands they had never been designed to meet. In some instances even military discipline – less predictably and venially – had foundered. Unfamiliar with the Indonesian (and Muslim) practice of using bottles of water for personal hygiene, many had persisted in their use of toilet- and, in its absence, newspaper, and had choked the drains. Before a senior British officer had appeared the distraught mayor of the town reported that British soldiers, in broad daylight and seemingly without shame, were fornicating with native girls in the town park, to the great affront of the citizens.

It was into this chaotic situation that Charlie MacDonald and his companions were discharged, being directed to the New Hotel, which they were assured was the best in town. There they found refugees of many races and occupations, saddest of all being the women and children, most of whom had lost, or had lost contact with, their menfolk. Everything was in short supply, especially news of the war; more often it was not available at all. The one surprising exception was currency – Dutch guilders – of which they were invited to avail themselves. Responding without enthusiasm to the invitation, they stuffed wads of notes into their pockets and handbags, dubious of ever finding anything on which to spend this largesse.

Meanwhile senior British officers in Padang had been in communication with British Headquarters in Batavia about the possibility of evacuating the large British contingent marooned in the city, and had received an encouraging response. Next morning hopes were justified when the promise appeared about to be fulfilled. Drafts were prepared for immediate evacuation, and shortly after noon they were marched to the station to entrain for the port, which was a few miles distant. They arrived there just in time to witness HMS *Danae*, a British light-cruiser, making her way into the harbour. Embarkation was conducted with great dispatch, and no sooner were the five hundred or so evacuees safely on board than the vessel put to sea to vanish with all possible speed into the approaching night. Her destination was the small port of Tjilatjap, which is about midway along the south coast of Java. The voyage was completed without misadventure, and on the afternoon of the second day out the *Danae* entered the crowded harbour of Tjilatjap and promptly discharged her passengers.

From Tjilatjap, Charlie MacDonald made his way to Bandoeng. This is a charming city, which lies in a vast caldera high among the peaks of West Java, and isolated from the unhealthy low-lying valleys. In consequence, in an island long notorious for the virulence of its fevers, it enjoys a climate which is claimed to approach perfection. Shortly after his arrival in the town, Charlie fell in with Ivor Jones. The rear gunner of a Vildebeest, he was among the few to survive the second sortie against Endau. Both being Australians, and comrades in Malaya, they decided to join forces. For a spot in which to recuperate after their hectic experiences nowhere more idyllic than Bandoeng could be found, but if they were to survive, they had to resist the insidious temptation to squander precious days in this mountain paradise. Alive to the danger, they decided that, as at Padang, the solution to their problem was a boat. Once they found a boat, it would not be hard to prevail upon some of their countrymen to throw in their lot with them. The plan would be to sail it from island to island along the Indonesian archipelago that led to Australia, travelling by night and lying up in some creek by day. But boats were not things that were readily available in their mountain retreat. Obviously they had to get out of it. The west end of the island had been ravaged by war; and there was little chance of finding a boat there. But its eastern end, and in particular its south coast, had been spared the worst of the fighting, and offered some hope. So they set off to explore the south coast. The further they travelled, the more remote appeared success. On the beaches, what met their disconsolate gaze was not boats but the funereal ashes of boats. In an effort to appease the Japanese, whom the islanders were already coming to look upon as their future masters, they had put a torch to everything on the beaches that would burn. Sullying the white sands, piles and patches of wood ash indicated the places where the ardent arsonists had been at work. Their plans in disarray, the two would-be escapees sadly retraced their steps.

It is at this point that, for the time being, Ivor Jones withdraws from this narrative. But, if we remain with Charlie MacDonald, we find him a couple of days later back at the place where he had first set foot on Java. In the short interval since he had last seen it, the port of Tjilatjap had taken a cruel battering. Its wharves were cluttered with the scarecrow skeletons of burned godowns, while sunken shipping clogged its channels. Contemplating this depressing spectacle, Charlie ruefully concluded that from Java there was no escape: on these ravaged wharves his dogged battle with adversity had, belatedly, to admit defeat.

It was at this dark moment when his fortunes had arrived at their nadir that his eyes were greeted by a spectacle that inspired joy and challenged credulity. Into the wreck-littered harbour there now sailed, slowly and warily, two foreign ships. The first of these was the *Kota Khedi*. A Straits vessel, she was now an armed merchant-cruiser. Her mission was to evacuate the survivors of No. 205 Squadron. These were the men who had flown the Catalinas out of Seletar up to the time when a Japanese fighter attack had put an end to their operations by the destruction of their machines at their moorings in the Seletar creek. The embarkation was carried out with great dispatch, and no sooner was the last man on board than the vessel put to sea, making for Colombo. The second vessel was the *Aboukir*. Her purpose was to embark the survivors of the American 19th Bomber Group, who flew Liberators. These were the first men from the Allied air forces to engage the eastern Japanese convoy on its way to the invasion of East Java. Again the men were embarked with haste, and, the task completed, the *Aboukir* negotiated her way out of the harbour, her destination Fremantle in West Australia.

But here we must go back a moment or two in time to the point when, evacuation completed, her officers were preparing to haul up the gangway. At its foot there now appeared an Australian airman. He had a dejected look and, admittedly, was not looking his best. He told them that he had been the navigator of a Vildebeest torpedo-bomber. In an air battle in Malaya, his machine had been shot down by Japanese Navy Os. He was the only survivor of the crew; that was why he was now on his own. In the engagement he had received a very serious wound in the arm, but happily that was pretty well healed now. Since then he had been on the run. But he could see no way of ever getting out of Java. On the other hand, if he could only get back to Australia, he was confident that his war experiences could be put to good use in the training of future aircrews. In the circumstances, would they be prepared to consider adding his name (incidentally, it was Charlie MacDonald) to their supplementary passenger list? The boarding officers were much taken by his tale. There was, they concluded, much sense in what he said. Indeed, this was the kind of man who deserved all the help they could give him. So, with no more ado, he was invited on board, and he climbed up the gangway.

It would be stretching a point to claim that, when he boarded the *Aboukir*, Charlie MacDonald took final leave of his problems and perils. Suffice to say that he survived them, and the vessel duly made it to Fremantle. Death and captivity, which had dogged his heels, had finally to admit defeat. Hobart in Tasmania, which he had quitted to serve his country so long ago, was to see him once more.

CARNAGE IN THE *KAMPONG*

The first day after my arrival in the Transit Camp at Bukit Timah, which was in the middle of the island, the Adjutant's office was clearly too swamped with the papers of the many men who had just disembarked from the convoy to have any time to devote to my impossible posting to Sungei Patani. But on the second day – Thursday, 15 January – I succeeded in having a brief word with him. He had an arresting presence. His face was thin and ascetic, and his manner somewhat aloof and sacerdotal. On my entrance to his office, he was engrossed in a tall pile of posting-papers and nominal-rolls that cluttered his desk. But he raised his eyes from them and, in a very remote and desiccated voice, asked me my name. Yes, he had seen something about a McEwan somewhere . . . and Sungei Patani as well? . . . he rummaged through his papers. Ah yes! Here it was! I was a little late for Sungei Patani; it was somewhat out-of-bounds now. But they would manage to fix up something for me in a day or two. In the meantime, perhaps I would care to go down to Singapore, to Records, and let them have my particulars? Transport was going down that very afternoon with the Hurricane pilots. Perhaps I might care to join them? He gave me the hour.

The appointed time found me at the guardhouse, where I had been preceded by a light truck – but I could see no sign of my promised Hurricane companions. The Corporal driver said his instructions made no mention of any others beside myself: if it was the Hurricane pilots I had in mind, they had already gone. They had been summoned that very morning to Seletar. So I jumped in beside him, and we set off. He was an essentially English-looking youth, finely boned, with a frank and almost boyish face, and very different from the more rugged and stocky build of my fellow countrymen in the north. About him there was no trace of the martial or the aggressive; even the loose ill-fitting uniform he wore hung awkwardly on his thin frame. Markedly dialectal, his voice had a pleasing cadence, and pointed to an origin somewhere in the English Midlands. He was, I thought, the kind of sensitive young man whose spirit might be exposed to much bruising in Singapore.

We had got no further than the main gate when the siren began its sinister warbling, which brought his foot urgently to the brake pedal. Might it not be better, he suggested, for us to 'hang up for a little' till we could see how the wind was blowing? But, fresh to this scene, I could see no reason why everything should come to a halt just because the siren had gone – this was not the way that wars were won! So I suggested that we should carry on; I hung out of the side of the truck and kept a sharp look-out on the sky, and all he had to think about was just watching the road and driving as fast as he could. If things got too hot, I would call on him to stop, and we should dive into the nearest monsoon drain. We had not gone very far when the drumming of bomber engines could clearly be heard, even above the noise of the truck, and coming in from the north-west, from the direction of the Causeway. Though I was watching intently, I could see no evidence of hostile aircraft.

Being constantly directed to the sky, my eyes could not take much note of where we were going, except that we were getting there fast. All that I was vaguely aware of was that we had arrived in an unfamiliar part of the city, and were driving along a wide road, lined on both sides with opulent-looking houses. At length we drew up in front of a very imposing building. With my idea of a typical records office, nothing could have provided a starker contrast. Double-storeyed, with splendid, white walls, it stood in its own landscaped garden, which was enhanced with scattered parterres aflame with flowers. From its air of restrained elegance and seigneurial dignity one might conclude its owner to be some government nabob, or wealthy merchant with a refined taste for architecture and gardening. Dismounting from the truck, I walked up the path to the main entrance. The door stood wide open and unguarded. The whole place was deserted, with no one to say nay to me as I walked in. Looking curiously into some of the rooms, I found them tenantless as Egyptian tombs, long since despoiled by robbers. On the desks papers lay about, just as they had been dropped from fleeing hands. Nothing had been put away. Nothing was locked. I could have helped myself to as many documents as took my fancy. As far as I could see, I could even have set fire to the place, and got away with it.

Baffled by this extraordinary encounter with Records, I retraced my steps through the garden back to the truck. There I found the Corporal, leaning back against the engine cowling and anxiously scanning the southern sky. He said that a dog-fight was going on up there. He had been watching aircraft as they dodged in and out among the clouds. I explained that I had found the office deserted. The staff had simply vanished, where I had no idea. The Corporal then told me that they might not have vanished just as inexplicably as I imagined. He pointed to a low turf-covered mound in the middle of the garden. Following his finger, I could see a slit in the ground, and through it some eyes were watching us. I decided to go over to investigate. On nearer approach, I realised that the opening gave access to an underground shelter. There were more of them, too, scattered about on the lawn, and camouflaged, like this one, by the flower-beds. Crouching on some steps that led underground was a Sergeant. A surly and uncompromising man, he had been rendered tetchy by watching my exploration of the deserted office, while he and his colleagues, who might have been expected to be there, were skulking in their underground retreats. Declaring that he was under orders to remain in the shelter till the all-clear sounded, he left no doubt that he was not prepared to come out to attend to such a trivial matter as my particulars. Declining to resort to persuasion where it was certain to meet with rebuff, I handed him my record book, asking him to forward it to me at the Transit Camp office once he had recorded my details. When I got back to the truck, I found the Corporal still intently watching the sky; excitedly, he pointed out to me where the dog-fight was being pursued. Now I could see the aircraft dodging in and out among the clouds. He said that though he had been watching the fight all the time I had been speaking to the man in the shelter, so far he had seen no aircraft shot down. But clearly this was no place to loiter, and without more ado, we jumped into the truck and set off for the Transit Camp.

On the way down I had been so absorbed in scanning the sky for enemy aircraft that I had lost all sense of location, and now, on the way back, I had no idea of where we were. As we left the town I could, however, see right ahead of us a long, steady gradient that led towards a low ridge, through which the road passed by way of a deep cutting. At each side, silhouetted clearly against the sky, stood an immense cedar, their outward branches sweeping away in soaring curves while their inner ones met and intertwined high above the road to form an arch, so that it looked like one of the *tottori*, or monumental arches, which the Japanese erect above the ceremonial avenues by which their Shinto shrines are approached. As we advanced up the hill, the noise above our heads increased dramatically, indicating that the dog-fight was now being joined at a much lower level. Clearly the Corporal's time for 'hanging up' had arrived. Stretching as far as I could out from the side of the truck, I scanned the sky, but still could see nothing. I called to the driver to stop. Responding instantly, he swung his vehicle on to the verge. Leaping from our seats, we scuttled towards the monsoon drain that ran alongside the road, and plunged into it.

We barely had time to squat down in the bottom when what sounded like a huge object went screaming across the sky, very low down. It just cleared the top of the cedars and plunged from sight behind the ridge. There followed a blinding flash, as if the sky had been set on fire, and a thunderous explosion. The walls of the drain seemed to shiver and shake. Soon a column of smoke began to pile up in whorls behind the cedars, and our ears caught the crackling of flames. Though naturally anxious to be on our way and out of this danger zone, we still considered it too hazardous to venture out as there might be other bombs to follow. So we remained where we were, crouching down in the drain, for possibly five minutes. It might have been as much as ten: it was very difficult to think of time with all this convulsion around us. The raging of the fire became louder, and the smoke billowed higher and higher into the sky. At length the threat of further bombs seemed to have receded and we thought that the time had come to climb out of the drain. We thumped off the worst of the red earth which clung to our uniforms, and climbed back into the truck. Starting very cautiously, the driver proceeded up the slope to the summit. Once he arrived there, he stopped for a moment or two so that we could survey the scene. We could now see that lying along the keel of the little valley which lay at the foot of the slope was a *kampong*. The bomb had seemingly landed on that part of it that lay furthest from the road, and many of the huts were already well alight. Being tinder-dry, the bamboo and *atap*, from which they had been constructed provided ready fuel for the flames. Though it had not long been started, so violent was the conflagration that it could not be very long before the whole *kampong* was consumed. A macabre curiosity held us as we watched its progress. It was all so inevitable. As one after another of the huts caught fire there was a preliminary spluttering and crackling before the bamboo poles, which provided the uprights, began to burst with reports like rifle fire. Once released, the flames leapt with an angry hiss high in the air. Slithering to its thin foundations, the hut, with a whimper, was consumed. A little pause would follow as the flames crept to their next victim. With a fire on this scale, there was nothing we could do to halt its progress. All we could do was watch fearfully and helplessly.

At length we decided to go down and see at closer quarters what was happening at the foot. Braking gently, the Corporal let the truck free-wheel gently down the slope till it reached the *kampong*, where we stopped and dismounted. Though it was no more than a matter of minutes since the bomb had dropped, a lorry had appeared from somewhere – it must have just happened to be here at the time – and it was standing on the road, almost – though not quite – blocking it to through traffic. Having been unhinged, the back door of the lorry was hanging down, and from the burning *kampong* several older Chinese men were dragging bodies and loading them into the lorry. By the time we arrived and looked into it, possibly half a dozen had already been loaded, the last having just been thrown in, and they were back among the burning huts, probing for more. They worked in silence, no one speaking, and showing no emotion. It was as if what they were engaged upon was nothing more than a routine job.

The last two bodies hoisted into the lorry were those of an old woman and a very young girl. The old woman's blouse had been ripped from her body by the force of the blast, leaving her breasts exposed, withered and mangled. Stamped on her sad, shrivelled face was the grotesque agony of her dying. About the age of the little girl I could not be certain – possibly about seven or eight, and certainly still a child. Lying on her side, she had one arm tucked naturally under her head, while the other stretched across and rested on the old woman's shoulder. Her slender figure was enclosed in a small, tight, white blouse, while on her legs was a pair of black, floppy trousers. Gathered behind her head, her hair was tied with a piece of red knitting-wool to form a pony-tail. It is strange how stark tragedy has the power to etch indelibly on the memory even the most trivial of details. Thus it is that, even today, as clear as at that poignant moment, I can still see her felt-soled, cheap slippers, which had a few coloured flowers, rather like daisies, embroidered artlessly round the toes. Her face was quite unmarked, making it hard to believe she was in fact dead. Could it be that some terrible mistake had been made? While she was still sleeping, or having lost consciousness, could she have been confused with the dead and loaded into the lorry? It was a scene hard to look at, and harder still to accept. This macabre juxtaposition of the beginning of life with its withered close epitomised the unquestioning harvest of death. It left both the Corporal and myself in shock. For a while we stood, both of us, gazing at the bodies, not saying a word, mute spectators at the mindless havoc of war. At length, his voice mingled with the crackling of the fires, the Corporal broke the silence.

'Some catch it pretty rough!' he said. The gap between the speech and emotion proving unbridgeable, I expressed my agreement. Then he added: 'It makes you think, sir. It makes you think!'

Two of the Chinese came back along the path, dragging the body of a man. He was very old and thin, his face shrivelled and distorted like that of the old woman. They indicated to us that they wanted us to stand back from the lorry while they hoisted the body into it. Then they turned away, and went back to the *kampong* to search for more. Just beside the road, and not far from where we were standing, a large hut went up in a sudden roar of escaping flame. Tossed high in the air, a shower of sparks fell thickly about us. The Corporal and I looked at each other, reading each other's thoughts. If some sparks were to land on the Bedford, what was to hinder it from going up just like the hut? The place had the fascination of a morgue, but it could dispense with spectators like ourselves. We could not do anything to help, and we would probably be an embarrassment to those who could. As one, we leapt back into the driving seat and, with some difficulty, the Corporal edged his truck round the lorry. Once on the unobstructed road, he set off at high speed for the Bukit Timah camp.

Three days later, which was Sunday, 18 January, I went over as usual to the Adjutant's office to make my enquiries about news. I found him at his desk. He told me that a signal had just come in about me. I was posted as Intelligence Officer to Nos. 36 and 100 Squadrons, torpedo-bombers. They were stationed out at Seletar on the island. What, I asked him, were they flying?

'Vildebeests,' he said.

I had never even heard of them.

Early on Monday, 19 January, I was driven in a truck from Bukit Timah camp, which is in the middle of the island, to the air base at Seletar, which is beside the Johore Strait on its northern rim. On my arrival in the Officers' Mess I was received most civilly by the Station Adjutant. We discussed generally the nature of my duties and the circumstances of the Mess, after which, having recorded my particulars, he led me along the corridor of the north wing of the building to show me my bedroom. No sooner had I entered the room than I became aware of some articles of a personal nature, including a hairbrush on the dressing-table, which showed that the room was already occupied. About this the Adjutant was most apologetic, explaining that the emergency had placed upon the available accommodation demands that could be met only by asking officers to share rooms for the present.

There was, however, one thing which might persuade me to overlook the inconvenience: like myself, my room-mate was a Scotsman, the Station dentist. Granted he hailed from Manchester, which was a bit away from the Highland hills, but he was as Scottish as myself, a fact to which his name of Graham bore witness. Something else might help to soften the blow of shared tenancy: his picture, hanging there on the wall! That could not fail to bring some consolation to my homesick heart.

'Go over,' he said, 'and have a closer look at it!'

A watercolour, it hung just above the dentist's bed. It showed a Highland landscape, with a burn tumbling with carefree abandon between rocky banks. In the foreground was a splendid specimen of that most Highland of trees, a silver birch, gazing at its reflection in the mirror of a wine-dark pool, tinctured by the peat. Beyond the stream was another, worthy to be its companion, a rowan, or mountain ash, its branches drooping and bejewelled with its clusters of crimson berries. Behind them, climbing steeply to the bare, grey hills, were the heather-clad slopes with, above them and outlined against the sky, their jagged crests. Here and there through the purple tapestry the underlying rock heaved its ashen bosses. Here were all the hackneyed elements for a sentimental Highland picture. Surprisingly, the one thing absent was sentimentality. What redeemed it was its starkness, and a certain austere beauty. My sensibility engaged, I examined the picture in detail. Nowhere could I see any evidence to indicate the painter. But I turned it over, and there on the back was this legend: AT KINLOCH AILORT, ALFRED WILLIAMS, 1897.

From boyhood, both on foot and by bicycle, I had trekked the lonely roads of the Scottish Highlands, but none of my jaunts had ever guided my steps to Kinloch Ailort's heather-clad braes. Nor, indeed, at that moment was memory able to attribute to it any but a vague location, somewhere perhaps in the far north-west, in Prince Charlie country, probably near Loch Shiel, where his statue was. But the Adjutant's intuition that the picture would engage my interest had hit the mark for, before my exile's eye, the very name summoned back from forgotten days agreeable images. Its melodious syllables echoed as an endless lullaby the babble of the hill burns, enshrining something of the enchantment of the northern places where the weeds and the wilderness still held dominion, resentful of the alien encroachment that threatened it from the south. Even as I gazed at the picture my pulse quickened, responding to childhood loyalties. Still, somewhere deep in the subconscious, the call of the wild inviolate places awakened atavistic yearnings.

THE MAN THE JAPS COULDN'T KILL

A big man, he was too ample of paunch and florid of countenance to fit the stereotype of the airman. A rumbling laugh indicated a conviviality of spirit. It was these aspects which, after my return with the Adjutant to the ante-room after being allocated my bedroom, first drew my attention to him, and presently by the fact that he seemed to be taking a peculiar interest in me. At length he came across to confront me.

'I'm Station Defence,' he announced loftily. 'Got a shelter?'

I told him that I had not got a shelter *as yet*, which was no cause for surprise considering that I had been on the Station no more than an hour or so. The search for a shelter could be appropriately conducted after I had seen to a few more immediate concerns such as unpacking my bags. This, with a dismissive wave of the hand, he brushed aside as nothing more than sophistry.

'Nothing,' he declared, – 'repeat *nothing*, – comes before a shelter! Come to think of it, I may have the very thing for you. Care to come out with me for a moment or two?'

Leading me down the steps of the Mess, he escorted me back along the road in the direction of the main gate. Presently we arrived at a large patch of grass, marking whose further border was a file of towering trees, between whose straight boles I could make out a group of white buildings. Only later was I to discover that these were the Sergeants' Mess. On arriving beside this open lawn, my companion stopped and, quitting the road, stalked across to a very low mound about twenty yards distant. Gazing down at it, he studied it ruminatively for a moment or two before calling me over to join him and inspect what I took to be a singularly uninviting slit-trench. Across its top had been laid several battens to support a few sheets of corrugated iron on which was piled the earth dug out in the excavation. At one end a roughly nailed wooden ladder afforded access to the dank and dark interior. With splendid rhetoric he expatiated to me on the virtues of the shelter.

'This,' with rampant assurance he informed me, 'is the safest shelter in the whole of Seletar. Indeed, if you had come a couple of days ago, it would not have been in my power to offer it to you. Up to then it was reserved for the CO, having been specially constructed for him. He gave it up only on being provided with a bigger – but I can assure you no better – one. To tell you the truth, I wouldn't mind having it for myself.'

I spared him the question of how he thought his ample bulk could be comfortably insinuated within its narrow compass, being troubled by the obvious gap that yawned between what I was asked to inspect and the encomiums he was lavishing upon it. I now asked him who was going to share the shelter with me.

'No one!' he said.

Then I asked what about the other officers.

'They,' he said, 'have got their own shelter. It's dug out of the bank on the other side of the road. You can't see it from here because of the bushes.'

Poised between doubt and indebtedness, I accompanied my benefactor back to the Mess.

Next morning – Tuesday, 20 January – I was on the point of rising from the breakfast-table when the siren sounded. For this daily disruption it seemed an odd hour – so odd, indeed, that I was inclined to put it down to a false alarm. But so unambiguous was the exodus which the other officers were making for the door that I hastily revised my assumption and tagged on at the tail of the queue.

'You've forgotten your tin hat!' warned a reproving voice as we arrived at the door. Indeed, in the haste, I had, and, retracing my steps, grabbed it from the peg where in solitary reproach it hung. Strapping it hurriedly on my head, I made for the door only to discover that my carelessness had cost me my companions, who had already gone to earth in their special shelters beyond the bushes. Having forfeited the fellowship of their shelter, I had to reconcile myself to the isolation of my own. Dashing along the road, I crossed the lawn and tumbled down the ladder into the slit-trench. Despite Station Defence's assurance that mine was to be a sole tenancy, I found I had been forestalled: at the far end, cowering in the darkness, were two shapes dressed in white gowns. Houseboys from the Mess; having no shelter of their own they must have heard that the CO was abandoning his, and could see no restraint upon assuming his tenancy. With their trespass now exposed, they displayed obvious anxiety lest I find their intrusion resented. But from me they had nothing to fear: in this hour of imminent danger, I welcomed their companionship.

In the early days of the war, at Mersing, which is on the east coast about eighty miles from Singapore, a radar station had been established which gave early warning of Japanese raids. This was especially effective if they came from Kuantan airfield, which had fallen into enemy hands. But, coming under threat from the unexpectedly swift Japanese advance down the peninsula, it had been dismantled and brought back to the island. Reliance for warning of impending attack was now limited to visual identification. Much thought had obviously been given to the siting of the Seletar look-out post to ensure maximum field of vision. Rising from the shore beside the Seletar Creek, it consisted of a tall and spindly tower constructed of lashed bamboo poles and topped by a small eyrie which was connected to loudspeakers strategically sited at various places on the aerodrome. The task of manning this vital post seemed to have been entrusted to a single man, his idiosyncratic Glasgow voice alone being heard over the loud-speaker system. Matching its dialectal singularity was the remarkable composure it displayed: even during the attack by enemy fighters which sank the Catalinas and peppered the look-out tower itself with some fusillades, the imperturbable voice maintained its running commentary. Being endowed with courage, its owner seemed also to be blessed with good fortune, for he continued to function in its eyrie at least till the surviving aircraft departed for Palembang. Now, huddled behind the Chinese in the slit-trench, I listened to the familiar voice, composed as ever, monitoring the invaders.

'I've picked them up!' he announced. 'They're coming in from the Causeway. I think there are twenty-seven of them. They're flying at about 25,000 feet, in three viks. They seem to be making for Sembawang.' [the aerodrome a little further to the west] 'Correction. They're past Sembawang. It must be Seletar now.' [a pause] 'They're closing in on the perimeter. Soon they'll be overhead. Take cover! *Take cover!*'

Torn between curiosity and fear, I edged a little up the ladder in my anxiety to have a look at the raiders as they approached. Just as the cautionary voice described, they were coming in from Sembawang. In the blue heavens, with not a cloud about, they showed up very distinct in their three viks. Now they were nearly above us. In the cockpit of the leading aircraft of the formation a green light flickered. Responding with well-rehearsed acknowledgement to the signal, all aircraft gave a simultaneous lurch as the bombs were released from their racks.

'Bombs away!' came the voice in final admonition from the loudspeakers. '*Bombs . . . away!*'

Abandoning the ladder, I squatted behind the Chinese, pressing my hands tightly over my ears to exclude the sound. As the bombs fell there broke over the aerodrome a fiendish discord of whistlings and shriekings. Sweeping across the aerodrome, a crescendo of explosions advanced in our direction, the earth responding in recurrent convulsion. Almost skimming our shelter, a huge object thundered past. Another followed – and yet another! A terrible roar split my ears and the earth trembled. Caving in before the blast, the side of our trench buried the three of us in clods and earth. As consciousness dwindled in the bedlam, I experienced a very vivid awareness that my end was upon me. Stunned and inert, I lay for a moment or two. Then, a measure of consciousness returning, I clawed desperately at the clods that buried my head and restricted my breathing. With an effort I succeeded in freeing first my hands and arms and then my shoulders. In the clods before me appeared a heaving other than my own. Digging feverishly with my hands I uncovered first one bleached and muddied Chinese face, and then another. Though paralysed with terror, they were at least alive. Renewing my efforts, I got their heads and shoulders free, allowing them to breathe.

Of one side of the trench no trace remained, to mark its departure only a sagging gap. No more than three feet from it was an enormous crater, in whose depths a bluish smoke was seething and giving off an acrid stench which, even in this extremity, was felt by the nostrils. Though the rim of the crater had burst into the slit-trench, so tenacious had been the blue clay beneath that, despite its thinness, it had withstood the terrible force of the blast. A little beyond the first stretched in line two similar craters. Gazing anxiously around, I sought help. But the scene that met my eyes was a wilderness, from which all evidence of human life had fled, or been erased. Almost on the point of abandoning all hope of outside assistance, my eye caught two airmen standing beyond the line of tall trees and gazing intently in my direction. Calling out as loudly as I could and waving my arms, I invited their help; disregarding my appeal, they continued to stand there, lost in contemplation. At length, waving their hands above their heads, they dashed off in the direction of the white buildings, from which presently they returned accompanied by others. Once again they paused to scan the scene puzzled, it seemed, as to whether I was a wounded airman in this world or a visitant from the next. Finally, their doubts apparently set at rest, they came charging towards me.

First to arrive beside my shelter was a Sergeant, who called out some message whose purport I could not grasp, showing that my hearing had suffered some injury. Then, from its louder repetition I made out that they had sent for a doctor. The first thing I needed was not, I protested, a doctor, but some help in getting out of this slit-trench. And I was not alone in extremity: there were two Chinese. I had no idea whether they were hurt or not, and turning round to see how they were faring, I was confronted with the spectacle of two deep and empty holes in the clods. All this I attempted to explain to the Sergeant. I had not seen them disappear and had no idea how they had gone. The Sergeant shouted out that, a moment or two before he had seen two house-boys, with dirty white coats, making it hell-for-leather for the main gate. These doubtless were my fugitive Chinese. If they could get along as fast as that, there could not be that much the matter with them. Gripping me by the shoulders and easing me out of the clods, some of the airmen restored me to the more solid bank. But presently summoned by the airman from the Mess, the Station doctor appeared on the scene. Though I was not aware of any obvious injury, apart from my affected hearing, the doctor warned me against complacency: there was no saying what internal injury I might have sustained, and neglecting it now would merely be piling up trouble for the future. I must go immediately to the Alexandra Hospital for a thorough check-up. For this purpose a truck was summoned; I was hoisted into it and driven away.

In the hospital I was handed over to a young doctor, who conducted a thorough examination. Having heard my account of events he appeared to be astonished that, apart from my ears, I seemed to have escaped serious injury. The healing of my ruptured ear-drums could be left to time and nature. If in a place so hectic as Seletar moments of quietude did intervene, I might devote them to reflection on my good fortune.

Discharged from the hospital, I returned to Seletar. For my reception a committee had assembled in the Mess, including, surprisingly, Station Defence, who gave no evidence of being put out by the hollow nature of the paeans of praise he had showered upon the slit-trench. They insisted upon my immediate return with them to the scene of my escape, having examined which they declared their unanimous opinion that a human being could not have been in that dismal trench when the bomb exploded and subsequently emerge alive. Thereupon they dubbed me 'The Man the Japs Couldn't Kill'. Often as I entered the dining-room for dinner, the unwelcome sobriquet rose as a concerted greeting from the tables. But it was pointless. Mine, at that time, was not a brow on which laurels could find natural lodgement. Besides, the Japs had time in which to put in hand a further test of my vaunted immunity to mischance. They also, as I was soon to discover, could look to an accomplice in an unsuspected quarter.

Just three days later I was seated at the dinner-table in the Mess when a Sergeant suddenly appeared at my side.

'You're wanted, sir,' he said, 'in the Ops Room,' adding, with a note of urgency in his voice, 'immediately!' This being, apparently, no ordinary matter, I collected my tin hat on the way and made for the door. But I was intercepted. In my path stood a fellow officer.

'Where are you off to?' he asked. I conveyed to him the instructions I had just got from the Sergeant. 'I thought that was what I heard him say,' he replied. 'But that's not the way to the Ops Room. Come with me and I'll show you a short-cut!'

The slit-trench, and its consequences, was still too painful a memory for me to rush into collaboration even with a colleague without some serious safeguards.

'I'll stick to the way I know,' I said. 'It may prove quicker in the long run.'

'Come with me!' he said peremptorily. Only that 'immediately' in the Sergeant's message can explain my tame submission. I followed my self-appointed guide out of the ante-room and into the corridor of the north wing of the building. It took but half a dozen steps to translate me from the subdued light of the ante-room into total darkness. I had entered foreign territory. I could see nothing. Even my guide was now a shadow, hurrying on and threatening to abandon me in his wake.

'Slow down a bit!' I besought him. 'I'm lost!'

He paid no heed. Turning about, he was presently swallowed up in the darkness.

'Right ahead!' I heard the retreating voice call out along the echoing corridor. 'Right ahead! You can't miss it!'

With hindsight I should, of course, have likewise turned round and groped my way back to the ante-room, and then taken the way by the main road as I had intended at the outset. But that peremptory 'immediately' was still drumming in my brain, emphasising the need for speed. Warily venturing a foot forwards, I explored the surface to see what it was made of. Hard and rough, it suggested concrete – at least substantial footing. This gave me some confidence and, sliding one tentative foot after another, I probed my way forwards. This preliminary success tempted me to injudicious haste, and my vigilance relaxed. Thrust forward, a foot suddenly discovered that there was nothing to support it. I made a desperate effort to retract it and regain my balance, which I had lost. But all to no avail. I was over the edge, and was falling.

At the north end of the Mess the ground fell away abruptly, and to compensate for this difference in elevation an additional ground floor had been added to the building. Linking it to the first floor, on which I had been shuffling in the darkness, there must at one time have been a stair, but where it was – or even if it still existed – I naturally didn't know. The end of the verandah on the first floor must also at one time have been protected by a balustrade, but it, as so much else, the bombs had removed. In the darkness I had stepped off the first floor and landed on the path beneath, where a slab of concrete, covering a manhole, provided me with the hardest of landings. Within the space of three days I had twice fallen victim to the foolish and irresponsible advice of a fellow officer. On striking the slab, my feet took the full shock of the impact, and I heard the very distinctive 'crack' of fracturing bones. For a while I lay helpless, but when I made an effort to stand I found that my left foot was very painful, whereas the right one, as soon as I exerted any pressure on it, just buckled over, forcing me back on my knees. Desperate, I called out for help, but between me and receptive ears walls and doors presented an impenetrable barrier. If I was ever to reach the Ops Room, it would have to be by my own unaided efforts.

The distance, as later inspection confirmed, was not great, and had I been uninjured, I would have covered it in a few minutes. But, such as it was, it threatened to defeat my most determined efforts. Having no idea of my surroundings, I crawled on my hands and knees, and did make a little progress though with still no end in sight. Had it not been for an adventitious event of no other consequence, I might have lain there till daylight brought discovery of my plight. But, issuing from a momentary opened door right ahead, a beam of light provided the stimulus to renewed effort; and, on the verge of collapse, I at last reached the Ops Room door. The Controller took a long, hard look at my feet, now grossly swollen and distorted.

'Well,' he said, 'you seem to have made a proper job of it this time. Not satisfied with the slit-trenches? There's only one thing for it now – right back to the Alexandra Hospital!' A truck was summoned, I was hoisted into it and driven away. Whatever duties I had been sent for to perform would now have to be consigned to other hands.

Beckoned a second time to inspect his wayward patient, the young doctor must have been intrigued by his penchant for adversity. With obvious tact, however, he refrained from all but casual enquiry into the circumstances in which I had come by my latest injury. But X-rays adopt a less sensitive attitude to feelings, and those that were now taken revealed multiple fractures of the metatarsals of the right foot, while the left had escaped with severe lesions. The doctor declared that the right leg would have to go into plaster to the knee and, more startling, its owner would have to go into a hospital bed till such time as there was evidence that the broken bones were knitting satisfactorily. My future suddenly looked bleak. Against this second proposal I summoned all the reasons and eloquence I could command.

'Whatever happens,' I pleaded, 'I must get back to Seletar. My duties there are vital. There's no one there to take my place if I'm to go into hospital!'

Busily the doctor continued applying the plaster to my leg while listening with notable forbearance to my heated harangue. Finally, when I had done, he observed that if I was as indispensable to Seletar as I was making out, then there was no question but that back to Seletar I should have to go. But there must be no misunderstanding about the decision I was making: one more of my seemingly inevitable 'accidents', especially if it happened before the bones had time to knit together, and I might find myself the unhappy occupant not of a hospital bed but of a wheelchair. It was up to me! In any case, let me come back in ten days (he trusted that I should not find it necessary to accelerate my return by a further mishap) and he would remove the plaster from my leg and have a look at the foot.

The driver taking my arm, I managed to get down the stairs and was driven back to Seletar. Worn out by the day's travail I went straight to bed, where I lay in deep dejection gazing across to Kinloch Ailort's mountain burn and its Highland trees, transmuted into glowing colours on the opposite wall. But even its potent anodyne failed to bring its normal balm to my bruised spirit. My mind was thronged with problems. For how, I wondered, was I, hobbling with this heavy plaster on my leg, ever to get about the station? How was I to answer an urgent summons to the Ops Room such as the one that led to my present infirmity? How, for that matter, was I ever to reach a slit-trench to enjoy the dubious protection with which the Seletar variety appeared to dispense? But by the time a troubled sleep had brought some peace to my weary brain, a vague plan had taken shape there, and, going next morning to the Adjutant, I put it to him.

'Have you by any chance,' I asked him, 'got on the Station such a thing as a bicycle – a common-or-garden push-bike?'

Across his face crept the broadest of smiles.

'Strange to relate,' he said, 'but I haven't the foggiest idea. I've never been asked the question before. But give me till tomorrow and I'll see what we can do for you.'

Next morning, summoned from the breakfast-table, I went out on to the verandah; and there I found, standing at the foot of the stairs, a Chinese. A beaming smile lit his face, while his hands gripped the handlebars of a brand-new, gleaming, blue bicycle. Though not all dispatched, my troubles were tamed. Modern, if modest, technology had come to lend a crutch to bolster the inadequacies of the human frame.

THE FLYING MEN

Whereas in the early days of the Malayan campaign the fighter pilots hailed, for the most part, from either Australia or New Zealand, the crews of the torpedo-bombers were, with a fine eclecticism, drawn from the four quarters of the Commonwealth, and indeed the Empire. But for a reason that was largely incidental the pilots tended to be English, their being nearer to the active theatres of war having provided them with superior facilities for training. A few, and these by no means the least accomplished, were volunteers: 'weekend flyers', their skills and zeal in mastering their exacting leisure pursuit earning them promotion from the Tiger Moths, on which they had done their training, to the altogether sterner cockpits of the Vildebeests.

In one field the Australians exercised a jealously guarded monopoly, and bold indeed would have been the man presumptuous enough to challenge it: the rear-turrets of the Vildebeests were acknowledged by all to be exclusive Australian territory, as indigenous to these Antipodean warriors as Bondi Beach itself. The vigorous outdoor life that many of them had led back home in their vast continent had toughened their bodies and sharpened their reflexes, leaving no doubt that, had facilities been available to them for training, they would have made excellent bomber pilots. From their colleagues in the two squadrons the Australians were set off by the distinctive, well-cut, blue parade uniforms they wore, which, being longer than the normal British equivalent, were dashingly flared. They also enjoyed the advantage of being furnished with black plastic buttons which, while looking smart, avoided the tedious chore of polishing. The Australians had created for themselves an image of being hard men, which, though never openly admitted, was clandestinely fostered. One consequence of this was that they went out of their way to pour scorn on all expressions of sentiment. As with the rest of the aircrews, danger and hardship were their constant bedfellows, but these they treated with disdain; and when the time came they fought in their machines with rare tenacity and courage. Even when dragged bleeding from their aircraft, they would as often as not be protesting that their wounds were really not that bad. Yet the hard exterior was often no more than a threadbare cloak to conceal something much more sensitive and vulnerable and beneath it there lurked the ingenuousness of a boy, along with his venial prejudices. They had an engaging habit of airing their opinions oracularly as if giving voice to axioms of unassailable veracity. They often indulged in much harmless leg-pulling and banter which, if taken seriously by the misguided, could prove infuriating. All made use of their unique outback jargon which, delivered in their peculiar Cockney-related drawl, was often shot through with marvellous vividness and colour.

Physically, the aircrews of both squadrons exemplified the finest qualities of their race. Almost all were above average height. Lean and hard men, bronzed by the tropical sun, many of them were singularly handsome. A few among them permitted their hair to exceed in length what then met with approval in the other services, but this was no more than an adolescent foible; subsequent excess in this line, extending to ribbon-tied pony-tails, would without a doubt have provoked their ribaldry and contempt. Off-parade dress of the aircrews while on the station – and less frequently off it as well – displayed a 'sweet disorder', and sooner would they have parted with their shirts than with their flying boots, which came to assume the significance of a badge of office. It was an affectation to be purchased only at a price, for in the hot and humid climate of Singapore, thick, padded wool was not a fabric of wear that added materially to the comfort of its wearers. They all wore very wide, and also very brief, shorts which revealed their muscled thighs and biceps. A carefree, exaggerated swagger was often associated with their gait. The spiritual and moral qualities of the aircrews matched – if they did not, indeed, exceed – their physical ones. I am convinced that, even by the time I first came to know them, they had already come to regard themselves in the light of expendable men. Yet this knowledge brought with it no visible despondency; if anything, it released in them an almost festal gaiety of spirit. Never have I known men who seemed to be more at peace with themselves and with the world. If as seemed probable, and for some even inevitable – life was destined to be brief – and probably bloody – what sense was there in hoarding what remained of it, or pining at its brevity? In this respect they revealed a curious kinship with the Japanese *kamikaze* pilots at a later stage in the war.

The two torpedo-bomber squadrons were, by common consent, the most highly trained and experienced in Singapore. They had also been the longest stationed there. No. 36 Squadron had come out in 1930, just before – and No. 100 Squadron in 1933, just after – the outbreak, in 1931, of the Sino-Japanese conflict. They represented an early attempt to adumbrate a theory, first propounded by Sir Hugh Trenchard as early as the mid-1920s, that the defences of the new naval base in Singapore could be safely entrusted to a tripartite force of aircraft: reconnaissance machines to locate an enemy; torpedo-bombers to attack it; and fighters to provide cover for the bombers. The more traditional view, which was espoused both by the Admiralty and the Chiefs of the Imperial General Staff, was that the new weapon had never been put to the test in the crucible of war, and till such time as it had, prudence favoured the retention of heavy static defences, which had proved their worth in many a conflict. But in the case of Singapore, the argument embodied a fatal flaw: it rested on the assumption that, to an enemy contemplating an assault from the landward (that is the Malay Peninsular) side, the jungle presented an impervious barrier.

For the Vildebeest torpedo-bomber, the paramount advantage claimed was its mobility and versatility. Unlike static defences, it need not be permanently anchored in Singapore Island, but could be moved about swiftly to any area where trouble threatened to erupt. So versatile was the Vildebeest reckoned to be that to it was assigned the dual role of torpedo-bomber to be launched against enemy warships threatening Singapore itself and harrier of hostile tribesmen on the north-west frontier of India. Even with the belated recognition that the Malayan jungle lacked the impenetrable qualities with which it had been attributed; and while the fifteen-inch guns might be doomed to silence and impotence in their casemates in Changi, the Vildebeest still retained its ability to operate against an enemy on the east coast of Malaya just as effectively as on the island of Singapore itself.

What rendered this impressive argument sterile was not so much its theory as the limitations of the only instrument available for its exercise. For this exacting role the Vildebeest had forfeited its adequacy. Its cruising speed, for instance, was around 82 mph and its sole armament two 30 mm guns. To confuse highly trained Japanese airmen flying in modern machines with Pathan tribesmen waging mediaeval war was to court disaster. To assume that the obsolete Vildebeests might accomplish what the two British battleships had so signally failed to achieve was to desert fact for fantasy. While over their target the Vildebeests had almost invariably to grapple with an aircraft which was certainly to be reckoned among the handful of supremely versatile and formidable fighting machines which the entire struggle threw up. The Japanese Navy O – later, and especially among the Americans, to be better known as the Zero – had a maximum speed of 358 mph, which put it on a par with the Spitfire, and its manoeuvrability was greater. It carried two 13.2 mm and two 7.7 mm guns. But most potent of all, and in the event its decisive weapons, were its two 20 mm cannon, which could cause deadly execution among slow British bombers. Even before it took to the Malayan skies, the Vildebeest was out-paced, out-gunned, and outclassed.

Passing Bells by Endau River

Ｗe were now far into January 1942. Still the relentless Japanese advance continued down the peninsula, maintaining an average of about ten miles a day. Soon it would reach its climax in Johore. Between it and the Straits was strung out the last British defensive position. Starting at Mersing on the east coast, it followed roughly a road that ran across the tip of the peninsula to reach the mouth of the Muar River on the west.

Even from the opening of hostilities the threat of a seaborne invasion of the east coast had been ever-present, the advantages to be gained from it being obvious. Tempting for General Yamashita was an attack on the island before British reinforcements had time to arrive, and to launch this with any real hope of success he needed additional armaments such as assault boats, siege artillery, munitions and stores of all kinds. To obtain these he had to rely on the railway from Siam. A long and tortuous route, it was slow at the best of times, and constantly exposed to sabotage. What would alter the position dramatically would be the possession of a port on the east coast, and there was one that met all the requirements. About the ideal distance from Singapore (eighty miles), Mersing was linked to it by a good road. Thoroughly alive to the threat which Mersing imposed, the British had fortified it. During the previous year, a force of Australians had ringed the town with a series of pill-boxes and strong points. But now the deteriorating situation on the west coast had seen the stripping of Mersing of a large part of its garrison to shore up the crumbling position in the west, where the well-established enemy tactic of infiltrating under cover of darkness waterborne troops behind the British lines had been meeting with its usual success.

A little further up the coast from Mersing is an estuary where the Endau River flows into the sea. About thirty miles up its course the Japanese had, before the war, worked a bauxite-mine, from which they shipped the ore down-river in barges to be loaded into freighters at the small port at its mouth. For this work they maintained a number of their nationals at the port; and doubtless by this time these would be reinforced by a network of spies and native sympathisers, both at the river-mouth and along its course as far as the mine. They would also maintain close contact with the aerodrome at Kuantan, a little further north, which they had occupied and were now using as their principal base on the east coast. Outside of the polar regions, this is one of the zones on earth most intractable to aerial photography. For days on end the most observant eye or advanced camera is reduced to the futility of the blind. The lateral mountain range, which forms the backbone of the peninsula, attracts to itself vast cloud-banks which can climb to a height of 30,000 feet or more, and filter off unpredictably to blanket the entire coast. Serious enough in themselves, these obstacles are intensified by the monsoon – and at that time it was blowing.

During these critical days as January was drawing to its close, the man entrusted with the task of surveying this coast and keeping track of Japanese activities was the Commanding Officer of the photo-reconnaissance unit. Lewis, a squadron leader, was a very big man, thewed like Hercules, with broad shoulders and very powerful, sun-tanned legs, which his shorts revealed. For his sole use had been assigned the best aircraft that was available, but it is an indication of the poverty of British resources at the time that this turned out to be a Buffalo. Stripped of every dispensable article of equipment, it had been tuned up in an effort to add a few knots to its modest speed, and equip it more adequately for its vital role. Lewis carried out his sorties usually in the early morning, this being, in this freakish climate, the time when visibility tended to be at its best. His flightpath followed the east coast, its purpose simply to look out for, and report, any signs of enemy activity on the neighbouring seas, but especially in the Mersing/Endau sector. It was obviously a very lonely mission, and just as clearly a dangerous one, to which fact several scars on his aircraft bore graphic testimony. What had saved Lewis from something even worse was his outstanding skills as a pilot.

By Friday, 23 January, the fate of the whole Mersing/Muar line hung precariously in the balance. If the enemy was to make his predicted descent on Mersing or Endau, he could not find a time more favourable to his purpose. Everything depended on the eyes and the camera of that lonely pilot in the morning skies. But during these fateful days, the climate was to furnish a decisive illustration of its fickleness. From south of Mersing even as far north as Kuantan, the whole coast was enveloped in a veil, murky beyond penetration. On his return from a sortie, neither Lewis nor his camera had anything to report. Whatever activities the Japanese might be pursuing in its concealment were beyond our ken. Then, with dramatic suddenness, things were to change.

When, at 9.30 a.m. on Monday, 26 January, Lewis entered the Ops Room at Seletar it was clear from his face that the period of waiting and uncertainty was at an end. The Japs, he reported, were at Endau! Over the small port, weather conditions for his purpose had been well-nigh perfect; and he was confident he had got some good photographs. A little north of the town he had located an enemy force which he estimated to consist of two cruisers, twelve destroyers, and two transports. They were making for the estuary, and clearly were intending to land troops there. Shortly before 8.00 a.m. he had sent off a sighting signal to the Air HQ, giving them the details.

For five consecutive nights the crews of 36 and 100 Squadrons had been heavily engaged over Johore, bombing Japanese troop concentrations and dropping medicine and supplies to hard-pressed British troops. On Wednesday, 21 January (to take but one instance) two Vildebeests did what an Australian major later reported as 'a fantastic job in bursting through to us at the bridge at Parit Sulong with medicines and bandages'. Vital, if exhausting, work, this was not that for which the men had trained so assiduously. Now when the moment for that at last arrived, they had not long returned from night operations; their machines were lined up on the runway, unfuelled and unarmed, and they themselves had not long retired to bed. Nevertheless the immediate effect of Lewis's news was to dispatch a message to the Messes putting all crews on immediate stand-by.

Being developed with urgency, Lewis's photographs were found to justify the excellence he had predicted for them. But having disposed of one serious problem, they promptly replaced it with another, no less intractable: they showed that the three-day complete fog blanket had allowed the enemy to approach its objective unobserved, and by the time that morning reconnaissance had detected their presence they had already arrived in water which was considered too shallow for the effective use of torpedoes. At Headquarters a conference was hurriedly convoked to consider the advisability of rearming the aircraft with bombs, which the crews' lesser training promised to be more effective in the conditions; or, despite the shallowness of the water, persisting with the torpedoes, for which the men had thoroughly trained. To their deliberations they admitted the commanders who would have to lead whatever sorties were decided upon. Finally, though not without some hesitancy, a decision was arrived at to use bombs. Presently an exploratory signal came through to Ops Room from Headquarters with a request for the numbers of aircraft that could be put into the air for an immediate strike against the enemy task-force at Endau. After consultation, the hangars reported that, though they required servicing, twenty-four machines were available, comprising twenty-one Vildebeests and three Albacores. Given time for rearming and refuelling, of these, twelve could be got ready without delay. With a further hour or two for servicing, work on another twelve should be completed. Despite redoubled efforts on the part of the fitters, however, noon had come and gone before the first twelve were ready to take to the air. Thereupon the operational order came through: all available aircraft were to be launched in an immediate attack on the enemy. The man who was to lead this first strike was then ordered to the Ops Room for briefing.

An Englishman, Tim Rowlands was a professional airman. Above the average height, he possessed the robust frame and the ruddy countenance of a man who had spent most of his days among fields. In the companionable atmosphere of the Mess, his was a laugh that was readily heard, as was the hearty greeting that was its inevitable precursor. But from his aspect all signs of levity had been erased, to be replaced by the tension and gravity which a decisive challenge, and its inescapable consequences, might engender. Entering the Ops Room, he stood to attention in front of the Controller's desk.

'Reporting for duty, sir!' he said, the voice clear and incisive.

Laconically, obviously at pains to stifle all traces of the histrionic, the Controller set out the broad lines of attack. The twelve Vildebeests would take off immediately for Endau. Accompanying them would be nine Hudsons. They had also asked Palembang (that is, Sumatra) for all bombers available there. Hurricanes and Buffalos would provide air cover to the limits of availability – exact details were not yet at hand. The Vildebeests would naturally select as targets the biggest vessels they could see, troop ships appearing to be the most likely. But decisions would be left to their own initiative; they would judge the position as they found it. The good wishes of all in the Ops Room accompanied them on their mission. To these, he was sure, could be added the good wishes of all the citizens in Singapore if they only knew of the venture on which the airmen were about to embark. There in the middle of the Ops Room stood Rowlands, alert, listening intently to every word that issued from the Controller's lips, and with every eye upon him. Isolated for the moment from his crews, he looked a very lonely figure, bearing a heavy load of responsibility. The briefing came to an end.

'Very good, sir!' he said as, turning on his heels, he made for the door, and was gone.

Presently the roar of engines revving-up announced that the sortie was taking to the air. The time would be about two o'clock. The northern sky into which they flew showed not a sign of cloud. Their mission would lack the great advantage of cloud cover. The first sortie had gone about an hour when a further signal arrived from Headquarters: all available aircraft were to be launched immediately in a follow-up attack. The hangars reported that twelve aircraft – nine Vildebeests and the three Albacores – were almost ready. Thereupon the commander of the second sortie was summoned to the Ops Room for briefing.

In any company and at any time Squadron Leader Markham would have engaged the attention of the curious eye. In his mid-thirties, he had a spare frame, and his look was ascetic and scholarly. Unlike Rowlands, he was not a professional airman, having done his training in his spare time as a member of the Malayan Auxiliary Air Force. From the ordinary airman the academic temper of his mind and training set him a little apart. Professionally, he was a civil servant, having served for about ten years as an officer in the Malayan Education Department, where his professional competence was held in high regard. In the Mess, rumour also had it that in pre-war Singapore society, where he was familiarly known by the nickname of 'Cyp', he and his wife were a very popular couple. As a pilot in the torpedo-bomber squadrons, Markham was regarded by those best qualified to pass judgement on him – i.e. his fellow airmen – as falling just below the highest class. This, of course, should occasion no surprise in view of the fact that he was an amateur operating among professionals. What had been responsible for his promotion over the heads of professionals to the command of a squadron was the flair and the general qualities of leadership which he displayed.

From those distant days a shadowy pageant drifts before the mind's eye, and I endeavour, fleetingly, to arrest its progress before it retreats inexorably into the eternal shades. It is night. In my little office in the hangars I am hunched over my board, writing up my report on a night sortie. Having returned from a raid over Johore, the airmen, interrogations now at an end, have retired to the Mess. I am on my own, but as I am soon to note, not quite alone for there in a corner, poring over a chart and utterly absorbed in some problem that is continuing to bother him, is Markham. On his intense, scholarly face, slimly framed by his closely cropped, light auburn hair, the dim light from the shaded bulb falls obliquely, accentuating its dramatic highlights. In the subtlety of the chiaroscuro, the effect is pure El Greco, or else Rembrandt in one of his reflective moods. At length, he raises his eyes and rolls up the chart. Then he comes across to where I am seated.

'Would you mind,' he asks in his typically quiet and shy way, 'letting me have a glance at what you've just been writing about us before you go over to Signals to send it off?'

It was on the shoulders of this scholar-airman that there now fell the task of leading the second sortie. A comrade-in-arms of Rowlands, and in bearing and discipline a compeer, he came into the Ops Room and, standing to attention, saluted. For the Controller there was little left to say, and of what there was, Markham already knew the gist. Attentive, he listened to the dispassionate voice and its laconic instructions. Without question or demur, he accepted the mandate that had been entrusted to his hands, about its implications neither Markham nor his crews could have entertained the slightest doubt. At Endau the enemy had, by this time, been thoroughly alerted; once bloodied, their pilots were eager to exploit their advantage. In the intense silence as Markham left the Ops Room, did that faint murmuring one seemed to hear proceed from the overwrought brain, or was it perchance an echo from a sandy arena in ancient Rome: '*Moriturus te saluto!*'

Seated, in the cockpit of his Albacore, Markham was revving up his engine preparatory to take-off when his attention was diverted to events which were taking place above Johore. Returning from the first sortie, a Vildebeest was making its way back to the airfield, the erratic nature of its flight bearing testimony to the fact that it had been mauled. So damaged, indeed, appeared its condition that a crash-landing was anticipated and the fire-picket was alerted. But with a struggle, the pilot did succeed in bringing his machine to earth and, after several lurching staggers, to a halt. Very intently, Markham had been watching events. No sooner had the machine come to a stop than, climbing down from his cockpit, he ran across the runway to have a word with the returned crew. What passed between them, naturally, was not recorded; but in its absence there can be little doubt about its nature. Hastening back to his Albacore, Markham climbed once more into the cockpit and led his sortie into the air. The time would be about four p.m.

From the reports of those who managed to come back from the air battles over Endau, it was difficult to piece together any coherent account of what had happened, shocked and often wounded men recounting that fragment of combat or disaster which their ordeal had branded indelibly on their consciousness. On their flight up the coast both sorties experienced the absence of cloud cover that had marked their departure, and over their targets the sky was clear and visibility unlimited. So slow were the Vildebeests that their fighter escort experienced the greatest difficulty both in making and in maintaining contact with them. Indeed most of the crews reported that, from first to last of the sorties, they had not sighted a single British fighter. Above Endau, a powerful force of enemy Navy Os was stacked and waiting for them. The engagement that ensued pursued such a violent course that, in most cases, the British pilots found it impossible to disengage from combat sufficiently long to enable them to select, and attack, a target. Nonetheless, making allowance for error in the heat of combat, claims were made for two direct hits on troop ships, and on a warship, though one of the bombs failed to explode. They also claimed, with less conviction, some damage to equipment and stores that had already been landed.

Leading the first attack with courage and unflinching resolution, Tim

Rowlands had been assailed by several enemy fighters, but he had been unde-flected from his target and was last seen plunging in flames into the sea. In command of the second sortie, Markham had displayed a courage and resolve akin to those of his comrade, and had shared his fate. Around them, the reports confirmed that the sky appeared to be streaked with flame, testifying to the destruction of other Vildebeests. Some uncertainty will, inevitably, continue to attach to the nature and the grim course of the action at Endau. But the statis-tics of the British losses admit of no ambiguity. Of the twelve Vildebeests that set out on the first sortie, five were shot down at the scene of action or failed to return to base. On the second sortie losses were even more severe: of the twelve aircraft engaged, no fewer than seven (five Vildebeests and two Albacores) did not return. The air battle at Endau was brief, bloody and decisive, and its consequences were far-reaching. On that bright, cloudless afternoon, the men of 36 and 100 Squadrons faced death fearlessly, and half of them met it. In the humming Allied factories the loss of aircraft could in time be made good; nothing could bring back these gallant, squandered airmen.

Throughout the night which followed (26/27 January), and on to the next day, the unloading of the enemy ships was pursued with great vigour, the arrival of nightfall seeing its completion with little serious disruption. With the two eastern ports now in enemy hands, and through them pouring all the reinforcements that General Yamashita had called for, the fate of Singapore passed from the sphere of doubt to become a certainty.

PER ARDUA AB ASTRIS

Three days after the disastrous air battles at Endau, the door of the Ops Room at Seletar was pushed open to admit a bizarre figure. He was, for one thing, much below the middle height. His jowls were shadowed by a sprouting black bristle, and in his eyes was a gleam which seemed to vary between a frown and a twinkle. Blistered from prolonged exposure to the tropical sun, his arms and knees were brick-red as well as being disfigured by the weals of leech bites. His uniform was in disarray, though the left breast of his tunic still displayed the half-wing of a navigator of the Royal Australian Air Force. His feet were thrust into a pair of flying boots whose size indicated that they had been made for a much bigger man, and had been lent to him. With every eye fixed on him, he stalked to the middle of the room. Halting there, he drew himself smartly to attention and, saluting, addressed the Controller.

'Reporting for duty, sir!' he said. The ironic analogy with the afternoon when the very same words were uttered here by Rowlands and Markham was lost on none. But in the event it was not misplaced for was not he numbered in that illustrious band, being one of their men, Elwyn Cummins, Pilot Officer of the Royal Australian Air Force, and navigator of a Vildebeest? One of two brothers hailing, I think, from Sydney, and both serving in the same squadron (though only one had participated in the Endau battle), he had last been seen as he climbed into his machine before it set off for Endau.

'And where,' the Controller asked him, making ineffectual efforts to dissemble his astonishment, 'have you blown in from?'

'Endau!' answered Elwyn.

'And how did you manage to make your way from Endau to Singapore?'

'Walked!' said Elwyn, the twinkle in his eye banishing the frown. As an answer it displayed the twin virtues of the terse and the true.

Prodded by the Controller, Elwyn went on to explain. The Vildebeests had arrived over Endau and found the Japanese ships strung out beneath. They were an inviting target. For any mission other than that on which they were embarked, weather conditions were perfect. The sky was cloudless and visibility unlimited. But stacked above the ships and waiting for them was a powerful force of Navy Os, having come, presumably, from Kuantan. Before they had had time even to select their targets, they were set upon. Leading the strike, Markham had drawn upon himself the brunt of the Jap attack. But he never wavered and, diving upon one of the ships, went down in flames into the sea. Presently his fate was shared by many of his comrades, arcs of flame in the sky tracing their passage to death. As the others, Elwyn's own aircraft, set upon by several enemy fighters, had taken heavy punishment. In an effort to shake off his assailants, his pilot had plunged down to jungle-top level where, following rehearsed tactics, he had zig-zagged among the tops of the trees, displaying superb skill and daring. Though the enemy had pushed home the pursuit with fanatical zeal, they failed to shoot him down. But he had not eluded his fate, merely postponed it. With his engine about to fail at any moment, it was clear that the end was near. At length the pilot had given the order to his crew to bale out.

Taking a quick glance down towards the jungle, which was scudding past just beneath his feet, Elwyn had not relished what he saw. Fearing that at this zero altitude his parachute would have no chance to open, he wavered. But there was no option, and he went over the side plummeting with his 'chute only partly distended, into the topmost branches of a tree, which rose high above the forest floor. Being pliant, its branches had cushioned his fall, swaying widely under the impact. For a time he hung there, shaken but miraculously unhurt, supported by the cords of his parachute. At length, using the knife which he carried as an element in his escape kit, he had cut some of the cords. Knotting them to form a rope, he had shinned down this to reach the ground in safety. With his back propped against the bole of the great tree whose other extremity had been the agent of his deliverance from probable death, the indomitable and resourceful navigator had settled down to take stock of his situation. Round him stretched the jungle. Virtually impenetrable, it abounded in dangers, only a few of which he had heard of, and even fewer was he able to recognise. Any thicket or tuft of grass he disturbed might harbour a venomous snake. Any branch he passed under would be sure to drip down upon him its loathsome seepage of leeches. Every river might provide a home for crocodiles. The bush would harbour unknown creatures of whose threat the first warnings he would be likely to receive would be delivered after he had fallen an unwitting victim to them. He had had neither maps nor compass, a cruel deprivation for a navigator, and he had had neither food nor water. It was a measure of the desperate nature of his predicament that the Japs, who could not be very far away, he had counted among the less immediate of his concerns.

At length, in that fertile brain, there had evolved a plan. The boldness of its concept might have led to its rejection by any less daring than its present exponent. At least, it offered the only hope of success. The key, he had determined, lay in his being able to find the Endau River, which he knew was hereabouts. Having secured this immediate goal, he would put on his Mae West and, pretending to be a corpse, float down its waters till he reached the sea. Then, having retreated beyond the reach of landing Japs, he would drift in gradually towards the shore till his feet regained dry land. After that, he would set off on foot for Singapore. For the success of his plan, two conditions had been essential: first, he would have to find a stream which, naturally, would lead him to the Endau River; and second, he would have to await the arrival of darkness as without it he could not hope to pass undetected through the Japanese forces already landed at the river mouth. His search for a stream had ended speedily and successfully when he found one which trailed sluggishly through the bush. Following this, he had encountered heavy undergrowth that clogged its banks, recurrently forcing him into mid-channel in his efforts to barge a way through. But his persistence had been rewarded, and at length he reached the broad waters of the Endau River. Tired with his exertions, he had sought out a shady nook on the fringes of the jungle where he might rest and await the arrival of night.

Then at length the swift evening had closed in, and presently the moon rose, being very near full and bright, making the river, by day a muddy waterway, now like a silver serpent winding through the jungle, its ill-favoured livery having undergone a magical change. Inflating his Mae West, Elwyn had waded out into the stream, before allowing himself to drift off with the current. Contrary to his expectations, the sensation had not been disagreeable. His progress steady and uneventful, at last he reached the estuary and the Jap camp on its banks. The makeshift camp and been crowded with soldiers. Clustered round their camp-fires, and surrounded by piles of equipment, they were eating rice out of their dixies. From time to time, as he drifted past, a soldier, pausing from what he was doing, would gaze out curiously at the bright-yellow life-jacket and its 'corpse' floating past. But, happily, not one of them had taken it into his head to carry his curiosity any further by getting a dinghy and paddling out to investigate, the consequence of which would have been Elwyn's final and fatal unmasking. Deciding to take no risks, Elwyn had allowed himself to be carried well out to sea before paddling gently down the coast, easing himself in towards the shore. At last his feet had touched solid ground. Removing his life-jacket, he had paused for a moment to study the lie of the land. Riding at anchor, their shapes clearly illuminated by the moonlight, were strung out the enemy ships. What a perfect target they had made! Why was it that at least a detachment of the Vildebeests – if not indeed the whole of the second sortie – had not held back and launched by moonlight? At least much of that slaughter of the cloudless skies would have been avoided; and in its place what havoc they might have caused among them! Further, might they not have sown some disruption among those soldiers with their rice dixies round their camp-fires? Surely there had been some failure in planning and tactics! But speculation would have to be deferred to a moment less harassed. So, boldly, he had set off on his long trek to Singapore. Doggedly through the hours of moonlight he had trudged on; and dawn, at last breaking over the lonely shore, had been able to detect no diminution in his pace.

At about noon that day he had come to one of those bizarre rock formations which are a feature of certain limestone regions of Malaya and neighbouring Siam. Rising high above the palm trees, and quite close to the beach, was a pagoda-like monolith. His curiosity engaged by this strange phenomenon, Elwyn had paused for a moment to gaze at it, eventually approaching more closely to inspect its character. Not till he was within its shadow, the bright light having hitherto dazzled his eyes, had he realised that standing on its top and eyeing him intently were two Japanese soldiers. They had rifles, and their fingers were on the triggers. What, he wondered, alerted to this imminent threat to his survival, could they be doing there? Were they look-outs? Had they been posted on this lofty observation post to report the approach of any hostile vessels from the south? Might there be still more of them further south along the beach, and might he already be cut off? He had been able to see no way of extrication from this predicament except (and it was a long shot) bluff! So, affecting the eccentric tin miner or the amateur geologist, he had taken to sauntering about for a while, picking up an odd stone here, or a shell there. These he would examine before discarding them, displaying in the meantime no disposition to be on his way as long as the surveillance persisted. At length their vigilance (unlike his own anxiety) had given certain indications of relaxing. Taking the risk, he had edged back gradually towards the beach, finally resuming his journey, and waiting expectantly for the bullet in the back which would seal his fate even before he could hear its report. But, inexplicably, the fingers on those triggers were never pressed.

As the sun advanced towards its noon-day fervency, so had mounted his suffering from hunger, exceeded only by his craving for water; on the baking sands of the beach, to which he had been confined in the interest of speed, were no trees or palms to screen him from its rays. All he was able to find in the way of food was a few unripe coconuts and bananas which he had plucked from wayside palms, while for water there was nothing but the few dubious streams which meandered across the sands, often towards extinction. In normal circumstances these were places he would have shunned as the plague, which would have been the likely consequence of their consumption. But even the spectres of cholera, typhoid and dysentery had not been frightful enough to deter him from scooping with his hands from a few of the runnels at the head of the cleaner-looking of the pools some water to slake his thirst. At least he had been spared further contact with the enemy; nor, apart from a few timorous Malay fishermen who fled his contact, had he encountered any Malays. Eventually he had reached the south-east tip of the peninsula where, in the neighbourhood of Bukit Chunang, he had fallen in with a British patrol. Having provided him with some supplementary clothing (including the out-size flying boots), they had brought him back over the Causeway and delivered him to Seletar.

This being the first eyewitness we had seen who was in a position to report on the ground situation at Endau, we subjected him to close questioning on all aspects of the fight as he had witnessed it. Was there a possibility, we wondered, that more of his comrades, having been shot down over the jungle, might at that moment be making their way, like himself, on foot? To support this possibility, Elwyn had little evidence to offer. All the aircraft he had seen shot down were over the target area – that is, the sea. Even if they did manage to escape from their burning aircraft, their crews were given little chance of survival. There did exist a possibility that the Japanese might have picked up some from the sea in an effort to extract information from them, but this was an eventuality about which we were not likely to hear much. Subsequent events seemed to corroborate this conclusion since we heard nothing more of other airmen who had been shot down and survived. But in this conclusion we were mistaken, for of the men shot down nine in fact did survive. But this was something we had to wait till the war was over to learn.

The destruction of one half of our Vildebeests in those few, tragic hours at Endau made it imperative to husband those that remained. Clearly Seletar was no longer a fit place for their retention, the daily rain of bombs, which by now had become incessant, making it virtually impossible to protect them from destruction on the ground. High Command had naturally been keeping their future under close review, and on Tuesday, 27 January (the day following Endau) a signal arrived from General Wavell's Headquarters in Java ordering the immediate transfer of all remaining aircraft to Palembang in Sumatra. From the general order an exclusion was made to permit the retention on the island of a few Hurricanes and Buffalos to serve as spotters for the guns. For a little while longer, each day just as dusk was falling, a lone Hurricane made a low circuit of the city and the northern sector of the island, its design being, presumably, to reassure those beneath that British aircraft had not taken a final leave of the Singapore skies. But in the ears both of the citizens and the armed forces the bombs provided a more urgent admonition. Denuded of aircraft, Seletar had been deprived of its function and its *raison d'être*, and a rumour was current that in a day or two the Army would march in and take over the aerodrome.

The departure of the aircraft from the runway was accompanied by that of the officers from the Mess and the few houseboys who had been brave enough to stay behind in the kitchen and provide for their domestic needs. The departure of the aircraft was carried out with an urgency that differed little from the frantic, officers being instructed to take with them only those basic articles deemed essential for survival, and to abandon the rest. These hurried hours transformed the bedrooms, hitherto models of orderliness, to a chaos of abandoned clothing and personal possessions. To the position of my colleague and myself there was now attached an unsuspected ambiguity. Having been posted from the Transit Camp as intelligence officer to 36 and 100 Squadrons, I never doubted that I should be accompanying them to Palembang. The Squadron Adjutant, however, insisted that, having been posted not to the squadrons but to the Ops Room, it was in the Ops Room that I should remain. To appeals, both from myself and from members of the squadrons, that that would leave the flying crews bereft of an interrogator, and the Ops Room with one they did not need, he remained obdurately deaf. How discreet of fate to withhold from me the knowledge that, but for this recalcitrant Adjutant, I should in all probability have been beside the Hurricane officer in the ambush at Palembang – and shared his fate. So, with feelings akin to those of mourners at a bereavement, we watched the Vildebeests take off for Palembang and in their wake the remaining officers in the Mess climb into their trucks for their journey to the docks and their promised ship for Palembang. Now we were on our own, the last two officers to live in the Mess, pensioners of a once noble fellowship – and now without a task or, possibly, a future.

Still at his desk in the Ops Room was the Controller, and with him were the two Australian navigators and one or two of the clerks. But all had taken the wise precaution of acquiring accommodation outside the station, the Mess being no longer a place for those who set any store by peaceful slumber. At first my colleague was disposed to follow their example, a proposition which, on reflection, we rejected, regarding our continued presence on the station as tantamount to a modest, if futile, gesture of defiance. In an effort to secure our bedroom, we piled three mattresses in front of our spare bed and another three on top, so that it might serve as an emergency shelter if time did not admit a hasty retreat to a slit-trench outside. To the problem of food we failed to find a satisfactory solution, making do with a few tins retrieved from the kitchen cupboards, and consumed without ceremony on the dust-deep, long refectory table in the dining-room. In the meantime the bombing maintained its daily, relentless momentum. Every morning and every afternoon the premonitory droning would fill our ears, and the formations would appear in the skies to discharge their baleful freight. They had adopted, and perfected, a form of pattern-bombing which had deadly effect. The four Singapore airfields had been designated prime targets by the enemy, but to Seletar, being the largest and now the home of the Hurricanes, they devoted a disproportionate amount of their effort.

Since the opening days of the war, the Officers' Mess had been the witness to some strange vicissitudes of fortune. Painted a bright ochre, and roofed with terracotta tiles, it was a conspicuous landmark, visible for miles, this garish image having been designed to ease identification by commercial aviators unfamiliar with the location. The modification of this conspicuous aspect, which the substitution of commercial by hostile airmen obviously demanded, had inexplicably been neglected. But the need for change was borne in dramatically upon those responsible for ignoring it by a daring act on the part of a furtive Japanese airman. Tagging on unnoticed at the tail of a returning and unsuspecting flight of Hurricanes, this infiltrator, his deception aided by a glowing twilight, managed to approach the aerodrome. Then, at the last moment peeling off from the flight, he swooped down over the Mess and released a bomb. Grazing the roof harmlessly, it plunged into the Sergeants' Mess beyond, causing many casualties and extensive destruction. Next morning a gang of coolies was hastily assembled and into the hands of each man was thrust a pail of tar and a brush, with instructions to obliterate every piece of light-coloured wall he could see. Throughout the day the men worked with a will, and by the time it reached its end the walls were as black as the night into which they stealthily retreated. The operation proved to be a complete success, emphasising the folly of its earlier neglect. Afterwards, though surrounded by bomb craters, and with its black walls showing a tetter of grey cavities from splinters, the Mess itself escaped a direct hit.

Ironically, the one thing in the whole aerodrome which was possibly the furthest removed from the conduct of war was that which most graphically displayed the evidence of its havoc. The little roundel of trees near the main gate, beside which had stood the sentry-box and its martial but ill-fated guardian, had suffered a cruel battering, several bombs having landed right on top of it to topple its trees over like a pleached hedge. Stripped of their bark and grotesquely naked, the stumps stuck up in the air like caltrops, suggesting that Death had not long ago passed that way – as, indeed, he had. Over my mind one place, however, exerted a macabre and irresistible fascination. On occasion, as I walked along the road on my way to the main gate or the Ops Room, an urge would seize me and, yielding to the unquenchable curiosity, I would cross the grass to gaze into the slit-trench where, with my two Chinese companions, I had so narrowly escaped death. Since that fearful day nothing much had changed, though a grey, viscid seepage, curdled on the surface, now partly filled the three holes in the clods where we had crouched. Scattered in the vicinity were the corrugated-iron sheets from the roof, twisted and colandered by the blast. As a *memento mori* nothing could have matched the bleak eloquence of its admonition.

But, wandering aimlessly over the station, we chafed at our inactivity. At the back of our minds lurked the fear that, unless we did something about it, we might linger on in Seletar in a limbo, forgotten and forsaken. So we had a word about it with the Controller, whom we found to share our concern, attributing our neglect to my ambiguous attachment both to the Ops Room and the squadrons. To resolve the problem he proposed to have a word with

Headquarters in Sime Road. The conversation confirmed his suspicions, Headquarters expressing surprise that we were still in Seletar and not with our comrades in Palembang. To rescue us from involuntary exile in Seletar, they proposed to send a truck to take us to Sime Road.

Sunday, 1 February was the day we took our leave of Seletar. The rumoured arrival of the Army had so far not materialised, and in this unreal hiatus the aerodrome looked a depressing wilderness, a tribute to the destructive power of concerted Japanese bombing. Only recently a hive of purposeful activity, now from its roads and workshops had departed the familiar figures in blue or khaki. The time had come to follow in their footsteps, and with mixed feelings of relief and sadness we welcomed the HQ truck when it came to collect us in the morning. Hoisting our kit on board, we climbed in beside the driver and with a lingering backward look drove out of the maingate for the last time.

THE BUNGALOW IN LORNE ROAD

Situated in the heart of the island, Air Headquarters occupied the keel of a narrow, tree-filled ravine which Nature herself seemed to have contrived for concealment. Consisting of a series of unpretentious wooden huts, they conveyed the impression of some minor industrial or commercial enterprise. The huts were segmented into self-contained units, each giving on to a verandah which ran the length of the building. Coming to the place inadvertently, the stranger would be unlikely to conclude from the exterior that behind this facade very important affairs were being conducted.

Arriving from Seletar, we drove up Sime Road, confronted with no evidence to suggest Headquarters buildings. At length we turned into a tree-lined drive which ended in a gravel terrace, at the far side of which was a sentry-box. The terrace occupied the rim of a ravine, down the steep side of which, and concealed by the dense foliage of the trees, descended a zig-zag series of stairs. Down these we climbed to make our first acquaintance with Headquarters. At the foot we were met by a Sergeant who showed us to the office of Wing Commander Marchbanks, the Head of the Intelligence Branch, who extended to us a warm welcome. After an exchange of preliminary information, he escorted us to the Junior Intelligence Office, which we were to occupy. Despite its smallness, it was admirably appointed to discharge the function for which it was designed. Its cabinets were stocked with reference books, maps, charts, aircraft profiles and all the material we might conceivably need. After the dishevelled existence which in the preceding weeks we had led at Seletar, this represented nothing short of affluence to our curious eyes, and could not fail to bring a measure of restoration to our bruised spirits. Yet from this plenitude one essential ingredient was missing, to restore which even Headquarters was impotent: in the skies above Singapore, the RAF no longer patrolled, and in its absence all the rest was shadow not substance. Nevertheless, it did serve to cushion our minds against the painful awareness of our redundancy.

Lunch brought a meeting with the other members of the establishment. They themselves had been spared all bombing and evinced an understandable eagerness to hear some first-hand reports from those who had. What they were anxious to have was details of what had happened at Seletar, hoping that from this they might be able to form an assessment of the likely effects of similar bombing on the crowded heart of Singapore city itself. During this very close inquisition, we were conscious of an air of calm dedication to duty among those who were directing air operations in Singapore.

During the afternoon Marchbanks came to our office to enquire about our arrangements for messing. My colleague, he said, presented him with no problem. During his earlier stay at HQ, he had billeted with a friend in Singapore, and had indicated his intention to renew the association. But he had heard nothing about what I had in mind. The question surprised me. I had always assumed that each station had its own living quarters for its officers. But, explained Marchbanks, to this general rule Sime Road proved an exception. Most of its officers, being of senior rank, preferred to make private arrangements for living in Singapore itself. However, in my own case, there should be no immediate cause for concern: I could come to live with him till such time as I had found my feet. His wife having left for Australia, he was living in a bungalow on his own. It was not far away, down in Lorne Road. I must have passed it on my way up. Even with my 'gammy' leg, it was well within my reach, providing I took my time in walking. He had a houseboy and an amah – both excellent – and we should manage comfortably enough.

At the day's end, I set off with Marchbanks to walk to his home in Lorne Road. But the absence of hindrances, which he had predicted, failed to take account of the association of the hale with the halting. The attempted co-ordination of our steps created unexpected fatigue on my part. None the less we persevered, like men walking on railway-sleepers, till at length we reached the crossroads and were within sight of our goal. It was now that I realised that the ground on all sides of the road junction was low-lying and marshy, and in consequence the road, which crossed it, was carried on a low embankment. A little along Lorne Road, however, the land rose, and it was here that the houses were built. They looked attractive buildings, each nestling in its garden. At the back the ground fell away to a low depression, beyond which rose an escarpment. It was buried in a dense tangle of brushwood, above which towered a file of gigantic trees. Their boles were pedestalled upon plinths of twisted roots. This marked the northern end of a low ridge which was densely overgrown with trees and brushwood and stretched down into the city to end in a bluff, which was called Fort Canning. Here was situated the Army Headquarters. Not far to the east of that was Government House itself.

Leaving the crossroads, we turned up Lorne Road. We had not gone far when, pushing open a gate, Marchbanks showed me into a very attractive garden. Over the lawn, scattered powder-blue tamarinds provided shade, and on it crescents of flowering poinsettias added colour. He then led me into the hall of the building. From this a passageway led along the back of the house to the drawing-room. Beyond it again was the kitchen. The drawing-room was floored with tiles to counter the heat, and on them some scattered Persian rugs conveyed an impression of refined affluence. A large room, it extended from back to front of the house to end in a colonnade of low, snuff-coloured arches, much in the Moorish mode, which gave on to the more select part of the garden. Under the arches were several cane chairs, well padded with floral cushions. Two of these we pulled to the garden's edge, and there we surrendered to their inviting comfort. Presently, dispensing, as far as I could see, with summons, the boy appeared with his tray and drinks. Wafted by the fitful breeze which the approaching night stirred to life in the garden, the air ebbed and flowed about us, scented with flowers, lulling our senses to a deceptive temptation to forget the dangers that were crowding round us. Savouring this present felicity, how hard it was to traverse back the few hours in time, and miles in space, to the bomb-pitted airfield at Seletar with the deserted Mess and the dusty dining-room, at whose refectory table we sought sustenance from the few tins retrieved from the kitchen cupboards. There we snatched by night a fitful rest on an iron bed. Beside it was another on which we had piled mattresses to scramble beneath if danger suddenly threatened. There were, of course, provided time allowed, the shelters behind the bushes which had been the officers' lairs. With ironic impartiality, their design fulfilled the functions both of a sanctuary and a sepulchre. Sipping the wine in my glass, I took note of the finely drawn features of my host. Surprisingly, despite the heavy burden of responsibility he carried on his shoulders, time and turmoil had failed to carve a furrow on that calm brow. When war with Japan drew near, he had been charged with the task of assembling material for an intelligence section. Working unremittingly, he had striven to introduce a measure of order into the confusion, which was the legacy of the squandered years. None could have had greater grounds for recrimination, but never once did I hear a word of grievance pass his lips.

As darkness drew its cloak over the city, we had dinner in the small dining-room which, being adjacent to the drawing-room, shared its view over the garden. With the pleasant meal approaching its end, the boy brought in for dessert a bowl piled high with the exotic and delicious fruits with which the tropics add allure to a twilight meal. In the mellow light from the table-lamp, we made our choice from lychees with their sweet, fleshy aril, luscious pawpaws, and that deceptive fruit which, beneath a forbidding exterior, conceals a succulent core – the hairy rambutan. Having dined, we retired to the cane chairs beneath the arches of the colonnade. Soon in our hands were the little, delicately tinctured blue cups from which, drifting upwards to our nostrils, rose the aromatic fragrance of Mocha's choicest brew. We talked long into the night. We talked about the war and its probable development. We discussed Intelligence, the scarcity and unreliability of our own, and the abundance and accuracy of the Japanese. Inescapably we voiced concern about the future. But from these graver issues, how agreeable it was to turn, from time to time, to recall life in the old Singapore – sybaritic and parochial though it undoubtedly was – before, in our ears, sounded the premonitory rattle of samurai swords above the northern horizon.

At length came the hour for retiring. Through the open French window of my bedroom, the warm, humid night-air wafted the fragrance of flowers. Undressing, I slipped under my mosquito net and crawled between the sheets. Having been freshly laundered and aired in the sun, they smelt sweet. Under my cheek, the cotton pillow was soft as a caress. For a little while I gazed dreamily through the French window into the garden. At length, the spectres of Seletar being, at least for the moment, exorcised, I fell for the first time in weeks into a deep and untroubled sleep.

THE OLD ORDER CHANGETH

The battle for Johore was going badly. Quilted with rubber plantations, jungle and swamp, the flat country was admirably adapted to the Japanese tactics of infiltration and ambush. One British brigade was lost; the artillery and transport of another two had to be destroyed to prevent their falling into the hands of the enemy. Two Australian divisions were reduced to a shadow of their former strength. While the retreat of battered and weary units continued to the Causeway, a decision was taken to advance the evacuation of all mainland forces to the island to the night of 30/31 of January. To protect this hazardous and very difficult operation, the Argylls threw a defensive cordon round the bridge-head, through which the retreating units made their way to the Causeway. First to make the crossing were the Australians, to be followed by the British and Indian units. When the operation was successfully completed, the Argylls abandoned their defensive ring and followed. Bringing up the rear were the last two surviving pipers of the regiment, the skirling notes of their pipes echoing along the Straits. The tunes they played were 'Hielan' Laddie' and 'A Hundred Pipers', whose notes had often sounded on more glorious fields, but never with more fervour. Fearing an enemy attack at this moment of heightened vulnerability, their Colonel urged upon the two men the need for haste. But to exhortation they appeared indifferent, their measured tread bearing witness that in them, at least, defeat had not stifled defiance. Meanwhile the engineers, busy preparing demolition charges at the side of the Causeway, chafed at what they regarded as time-consuming ceremonial. When the withdrawal was at length completed, the engineers blew a thirty-foot gap in the Causeway, an operation of limited success, though not devoid of symbolic undertones for by it Singapore announced the severance of the last links with her imperial past. The old, familiar world which she had known, and which blindly she had imagined was destined to last for ever, had come to an ignominious end.

The following day another symbol of the new order appeared in the sky above the Sultan's palace in Johore in the shape of a Japanese observation balloon. For this intruder I predicted an eventful, if brief, life, for a Hurricane, slipping down-sun out of a cloud-bank, or a well-directed shell from a shore battery, would soon put a stop to whatever mischief the observer in its basket was bent upon. But though we had no knowledge of it at the time, the spotter in the balloon was not the sole observer active in the area, for in the topmost attic in the palace was ensconced no less a personage than General Yamashita himself. Supreme Commander of Japanese forces in Malaya, he was presently to be familiar to a much wider public as 'The Tiger of Malaya' – destined, too, in the fullness of time to mount a scaffold in Manila, there to expiate atrocities committed by troops under his command in the Philippines, but especially in the city of Manila. And if that Hurricane burst of fire, or that shell straying somewhat from its target, had peradventure gone through his window, causing some disruption within, might it have altered appreciably the course of the campaign? Who is to say? But to general bewilderment and dismay, neither the Hurricane nor the shell was ever dispatched; and the balloon continued to float there, flaunting its immunity, with what effect upon the morale not only of the native population but of our own troops it is not hard to imagine. Even a dummy balloon on our side, had one (as it should have) been available, would have shown that to that audacious watcher we were not without riposte. Rumour had it that the reason behind the balloon's inexplicable immunity in blatant effrontery was our reluctance to jeopardise by the wanton destruction of his palace the support both of the Sultan and of his people at a time when it was imperative to retain both. There could be no doubt that orders had come from the highest quarter to spare the edifice all attack. But if this were the real reason behind the abstention, it was a benefit which hardly justified the heavy price at which it had been purchased.

One of the first instalments of this levy was demanded almost immediately. Directed by this spotter, the Japanese now began to open harassing fire against carefully selected targets on the island. Government House could scarcely expect to share with the Sultan's palace its immunity. Lying roughly in the direct line of fire from Johore, Lorne Road was now liable to collect any shells that fell short. Being likely to occur at any hour of the day, these barrages were particularly difficult to forecast, though experience soon taught us that breakfast and dinner were occasions when it paid to exercise extreme vigilance. These were the times when the enemy might assume that the residents would be at home for their meals.

WE RUN THE GAUNTLET

On the morning of Friday, 6 February, we were spared the usual disruption. After breakfast, Marchbanks and I set off to walk to Headquarters. But no sooner had we turned the corner from Lorne Road into Sime Road than, out of a cloudless sky, and without warning, shells began to fall thickly round us. Caught thus in the most exposed of places on top of the embankment, with no cover within easy reach, we made for the higher ground at the bottom of the golf-course, where we were fairly sure there was a monsoon drain. It was now that the reality of the handicap which my injured leg inflicted upon me made itself evident for, try as I might, the best I could achieve was an ungainly lope. Relieved of me, Marchbanks would have been able much sooner to reach safer territory. I urged upon him the need to carry on by himself, and leave me to follow in his wake as best I could. But this suggestion he brushed aside, saying that it would merely amount to replacing one target with two. He had just spoken these words when a shell came whistling over our heads, and we flopped instinctively to the ground. From the edge of the embankment which we had just passed came a sharp crack. But two steps had saved us. The missile had landed over the verge and not on the road. Flying upwards and outwards, the shards passed harmlessly, though very close, above our backs.

For a time we struggled on. Ringing in our ears were the recurrent blasts of exploding shells. It was manifest that we could never hope to last long in this barrage without being hit. If we were to survive at all, it was imperative that we find some kind of cover soon. Fortunately just then there appeared on the south side of the road a little row of Chinese graves. Each was marked by the traditional rounded headstone. Leading down to them was a little pathway, though it may have been no more than a drain. For a moment I paused, pondering whether it was deep enough for our purpose.

'Like a breather?' asked Marchbanks, aware of my hesitancy.

'I could do with one!' I said.

Thereupon we flopped down into it, sprawling out flat to provide as small a target as possible were a shell to fall near us. The protection it offered was very dubious, but it was the only thing within reach at the time.

Presently a slight lull occurred in the bombardment, and without waiting to satisfy ourselves that it was more than temporary, we scrambled to our feet and renewed our flight to the golf-course. Once we reached it, we soon found the monsoon drain we were looking for, and dropped into it. The barrage had not ceased, though the shells that did come over were more desultory, but falling with remarkable consistency on or near the crossroads. The point had clearly been ranged and the spotting was accurate. Equally clear was the fact that the Japanese had spies, monitoring our movements, and relaying this information to their gunners on the other side of the Straits. What they were aiming at was the elimination of some senior officers on their way to Headquarters. In this instance, they had come within an ace of achieving their intention.

At length, the firing dwindled and died. Clambering out of the drain, we resumed our journey to Headquarters. Our arrival there crowned our success, our bedraggled appearance showed at what cost.

After dinner I retired to my bedroom. The day was Friday, 3 February when my cabin trunk and valise, having been left in the *Warwick Castle*, finally caught up on me. My purpose was to collect a few things for my immediate use. But I had barely unfastened the lock on the cabin-trunk when the suspicion of a knock on the door suggested the presence of someone desiring entry, the suspicion hardening to certainty on its repetition. In response to my call to come in, there now sidled into the room the sveltest, frailest, loveliest little sliver of youthful amahood it had ever been my fate to gaze upon. Her long hair, falling half across her brow, gleamed blue-black with the sheen of lacquer. The eyes that shone beneath its sweep were lustrous, with a great warmth in them. Her features were small, but observed a perfect proportion with her body, her delicate skin displaying a rare synthesis of texture and colouring. She wore a white cotton blouse which was very tight-fitting, and a sarong that recalled a Menzies tartan, though its colouring was less demonstrative than the lichen-dyed Highland variety, and its sett more elusive. About her was a curious, almost translucent fragility which, in my China days, would have instinctively suggested a Sung vase from Hangchow, both possessing the same ethereal quality, impalpable, like Beauty a'tiptoe and about to retreat into the eternal shades. These, and her engaging shyness, were, I think, her chief characteristics. It was as if a Dresden shepherdess had suddenly become animate, as if a porcelain Galatea had been given breath. For a moment or two I gazed at her, reduced to silence by the spell of her beauty, and waiting for her to make known her purpose.

'Sirts makee washee?' she asked, her voice matching her figure, being wonderfully soft with a bird-like, fluting quality. The accumulation of soiled linen – the legacy of many laundry-less days – which her enquiry drew forth from my valise might well have daunted a heart any less resolute than hers. But she appeared little put out as shirts, vests and pants piled up in an intimidating heap on the floor.

'My makee washee!' she said. 'This night no can do. Perhaps tomorrow OK?'

I said that tomorrow would certainly do. I should be happy to have them done at any time, and I apologised for the size of the pile. Then, bending down, the frail little creature picked up a huge armful and took it off to the kitchen, returning later for the rest.

On the afternoon of the following day Marchbanks came to my office with a suggestion. He thought it might be in my interest to set off from HQ a little in advance of the others and make my way to Lorne Road in my own good time. I think he felt that my efforts to synchronise my steps with his was doing no good to my injured foot. No doubt he also had some anxieties about the possible renewal of the barrage in the evening, considering it wise for me to be under cover before it started. When, having negotiated the crossroads without misadventure, I was approaching the bungalow, I became aware of some small craters in the road which had not been there when we passed that way in the morning. So that cursed gun had been at it again! Once inside the garden I was further startled by the sight of the lawn: a shell had excavated one half of a flower-bed and, scattered like gouts of blood, poinsettias strewed the lawn. Worse still, the house itself had been hit, a shell having struck the wall between the door and the hall window. Sheared off by the impact, a slab of rough-cast lay shattered on the ground. Though fissured and gouged, the exposed bricks still stood, testifying to the robustness of its construction.

I had just hung my cap on the hall-stand when I heard a shuffle of slippered feet in the passage, and before me appeared the boy. The look on his face, eloquent beyond the compass of words, conveyed that something dreadful must have happened since we left in the morning. His cheeks were grey and sunken. His eyes, which were stained with weeping, stared from his face in a distracted manner. For a moment or two he remained standing there, his lips quivering, though no sound issued from them. I thought he was recoiling from the news he had to impart. But at length he made a great effort to pull himself together.

'*Tuan*,' he said. '*Tuan* . . .' Then his voice drifted away as if he could not bring himself to utter the fatal words.

'Amah . . . amah . . . have *die*!'

The words struck me like a hurled javelin. That gentle, endearing creature! Only the previous night she had carried my laundry to the kitchen! Now *have die*! Could fate, if none other, not have done something to protect one as innocent and hapless as she from what must have been a brutal death? The boy remained very still, watching my reaction.

'When,' I asked him, 'did amah die?'

'Afta' tiffin,' he said.

'Where?' I asked.

'Come, *tuan*,' he said. 'I take you look-see!'

Expecting to be taken to see something harrowing in the kitchen, I braced myself. But, changing in one deft movement his slippers for his heavier outdoor clogs, the boy led me out through the arches of the drawing-room into the garden. Then we walked down to where it ended, and then followed a faint track through the marshland that extended beyond. As I picked up my steps in his wake, I could see one or two shell-holes here too, which looked very recent, though some water had already seeped into them. Beyond the swampy hollow was the bank, with its line of great trees, one of which I could see had been hit, some of its branches hanging down like tatters on an old scarecrow. Following the boy, I climbed up the bank to the stricken tree, continuing on to the other side of it – that is, the one furthest from Johore whence the gun-fire had been directed. The base of the trunk rested upon a plinth of roots. Grotesquely tangled and interwoven, and some of enormous size, they twisted outwards over the ground to a great distance. At one point, however, the roots drew apart to form a curious little nook. No more than a yard square, it was carpeted with soft turf, and enclosed by the bole of the tree and the large roots. It was, one might have fancied, a place where youthful Dryads, spent with their frolickings, might retire to while away a languorous afternoon.

About a yard from the ground, however, and just above this little nook, the trunk was heavily trenched where a shell-splinter had gored the bark; beneath this, the bole and roots were splattered with crimson stains. In the centre of the patch of turf a ragged red-brown smear indicated where blood had seeped into the earth. At the sight, enquiry froze on my lips. In the presence of evidence so bludgeoning, any comment would be irrelevant, if not intrusive. Before me stood the boy, his eyes riveted to the spot, with one hand pointing forlornly at the discoloured earth. He did, indeed, make some effort to speak, but, in place of words, involuntary gulpings filled his throat. Soon, welling in his eyes, tears trickled down his cheeks. At length I asked him where the amah was now.

'Amah have die,' he repeated. 'Moto' ca' have take amah?' Then, pausing for a moment, he added: 'Amah no come back!'

'To the hospital?' I ventured.

'Amah no go hospital,' he said. 'Amah go . . .' Then, his eyes glazing again as if about to stream with tears, he stopped. 'P'haps amah go mama and papa.'

The phrase baffled me. Did he mean that the amah had been taken to her parents', and her own early, home? Or was this no more than a Malay euphemism for death?

In a heavy silence, punctuated by the uncontrollable sobbing of the boy, we made our way back to the bungalow. Once inside I asked him why the amah had gone to the tree in the first place. Would she not have been far better to have stayed in the bungalow? There was, of course, an excellent shelter which had just been constructed in the garden. But presumably they felt, even in danger as over-powering as this, that the taboos which custom had erected between master and servant were much too solemn to defy.

'Afta' washee makee finish,' the boy went on to explain, 'afta tiffin, plenty boom-boom-bang. Garden all break. P'haps homeside break too. Amah plenty frighten. Amah say: "Tree-side more better!" Amah go tree-side. Tree-side amah die.' I asked him why he had allowed the amah to go on her own to the tree; but he merely said: 'My belong kitchen,' by which he implied that as houseboy it was his duty to remain in the bungalow to look after it and its contents.

The tree, of course, should have provided the safest of shelters. Coming across the little refuge on an earlier excursion, the amah must have seen its possibilities as a retreat in a crisis. The shell that killed her must have struck a branch on the Singapore, that is, the safe, side of the tree, bursting on impact. It was a chance in a million which neither she – nor anyone else for that matter – could possibly have foreseen. Had she remained in the kitchen or, better still, gone to the new shelter in the garden she would have been spared. Her fear must have driven her desperate for protection, and she did what she imagined was for the best. Who was to warn her, or even to know, that it was for the worst?

A little later, on Marchbanks's return from HQ, I told him the pathetic story of the amah's death. As in my own case, it administered a great shock to him. Though he had known her for very much longer than I had, he knew surprisingly little about her, having inherited her from the previous occupants of the bungalow on taking over. He did not even know whether she came from up-country or from Singapore, though he suspected that Singapore was the more likely. For some time now I had been able only by a supreme effort of will to hold my feelings in control. But now the time had come for me to get away on my own for a little, and I went to my bedroom. There I found, arranged in neat little piles on my bed, all beautifully washed and ironed, the laundry which I had handed over to the amah the night before. It must have been the final task which she performed in her brief life. At this last, poignant testament to her devotion to duty – and in particular her service to me personally – in circumstances which must have been as harrowing as can be imagined, the last buttresses of my self-control swiftly crumbled; and stretched out, inconsolable, on the bed beside the laundered shirts, I gave myself up to the emotions of the bitter hour.

At the time a desperate war was being waged, and there was no way open to me to investigate where the amah had been buried. The tumultuous conditions then prevailing might well have consigned her to one of the vast communal death-pits for the victims of the bombing of the city. But even if she had been laid to rest in some more sequestered ground, and I had been able to find it, I should have been little likely to identify her grave: in the rigidly hierarchical community of Singapore, it was not to the meek and humble of the earth that remembrance was ostentatiously accorded. But at least I might have expected to find a posy of simple flowers there to mark the spot, laid by some humble and loving hand. For neither to caste nor rank do flowers find it necessary to pay homage, extending to all, including this elfin and innocent creature, who had so much in common with them, their fragrance and their loveliness. Now in some nameless grave, like so many thousands of others at the time, soon to be forgotten as if she had never been, the amah takes her rest, the hapless victim of a war she knew nothing about, quenched in one swift moment of terror, and snuffed out like a small candle in a nightwind.

THE SIEGE PERILOUS

Dawn on Sunday, 8 February broke over Singapore under a leaden sky, sagging with rain. After breakfast, which was undisturbed, we set off to walk to Headquarters. The journey was without incident till we reached the shoulder of the heights, which was well past the danger-point of the crossroads, when several whining arcs of sound, high in the heavens, announced the usual couriers of disruption on their way to Government House, there to dispel any false hope that their Sabbath peace was to be respected.

A little after midday the rain stopped, and under a clearing sky, heavy guns opened up abruptly from the other side of the Johore Strait. Starting somewhere in a noisy prelude near Johore Bahru at the north end of the Causeway, they worked eastwards with diminishing intensity in the direction of Palau Ubin, the large island at the eastern end of the Straits. Westwards from the Causeway, they sounded more subdued, but there was no doubt that this was a real bombardment and not just sporadic blasting at random targets. As the afternoon wore on, the intensity of the firing declined a little, though it never quite stopped, and the threat of renewal always remained. We therefore decided on an early return home in case we should again have to run the gauntlet of the barrage at the crossroads, which clearly could be raked at will. We reached home, however, without incident to find that the gun that had been the cause of so much distress had been silent, the boy reporting that, as far as he knew, no shells had landed anywhere near the house.

No sooner had we sat down to dinner in the evening than the barrage opened up again, and this time the noise was quite deafening. With the heavier detonations the whole earth gave a shudder, and even the little vase which held flowers on the table gave out, ironically, a responsive tinkle. Up beyond the golf-course, the darkness was shattered by exploding mushrooms of light; and the echoes of the detonations pursued each other along the ridge-top towards Seletar till lost in smothered growlings in the east. To this alarming accompaniment, we struggled on with our meal, the Wing Commander giving it as his opinion that this at last sounded like the softening-up preparatory to an attempt at invasion. But at length it all became too much to endure indoors and, breaking off the meal, we went out into the gardens to get a better view of the spectacle.

About ten o'clock the barrage rose in a frightening crescendo to its climax, its thunder rolling back and forth along the line of the Straits, while the flame, spouting from the gun muzzles, cast flickering reflections in the upper sky like a hideous Aurora Borealis. In concentration, loudness, and simple frightfulness, this far surpassed anything I had ever imagined. After a time, seemingly kindled on this side of the Straits, other fires added their contribution to the lurid glow. While we watched, fearfully, a deep reverberating roar sounded far to the east from somewhere in the vicinity of Changi, and drowning for a moment the more staccato barking of the Japanese artillery from the other side of the Straits. To it we listened with reviving confidence.

'That,' said Marchbanks, 'is the fifteen-inch guns opening up at Changi!'

But the sound came only at long intervals whereas the Japanese barrage continued without intermission.

As we stood waiting, in hope, for another burst from the east, something very large streaked across the sky high above our heads and, plunging among the trees over on the ridge towards Singapore, burst with a great flash. This was no light gun, such as had brought our earlier sorrow; frayed by my earlier experiences at Seletar, my nerves were becoming raw. I asked the Wing Commander if it was not time to try the shelter. He, however, gave the impression of being reassuringly cool.

'Whatever you think!' he said.

Our shelter had been dug on the east side of the garden, near the hedge which separated us from our neighbours. A broad, deep trench, it was roofed over with heavy beams on which was piled the excavated earth. On each side was a port-hole, and along each side of the floor two short posts had been driven into the earth, boards being nailed on them to provide a couple of seats. At a push, the shelter could possibly hold eight people, but at the moment it held only two, Marchbanks's wife having left, and the boy having chosen – in view of earlier happenings, we hoped wisely – to seek protection elsewhere. The bombardment continued unabated, the flashes of the guns being so bright that they fitfully lit up the interior of the shelter and threw our faces into strange relief so that they appeared daubed with red blotches. Marchbanks spent most of his time gazing through the porthole which faced north towards the Straits. But, changing his position for a moment to that which faced east, he said he thought he saw someone in the shelter next door. Joining him, and watching, I saw first one head and then another peer out timidly from the opening at its end, and then duck back quickly at every blast, waiting a little before venturing out again. At length a thin, frightened little voice drifted across to us, asking if we would mind very much if they came over to join us – just for company! Marchbanks extended to them a ready welcome and, climbing up the ladder, he went across to their garden and escorted them back to our shelter. They proved to be an English couple, elderly and very frail, with grey, pinched faces. The bombardment had reduced them to a state of abject fear, the husband scarcely uttering a word, while his wife was so distraught that from the moment she entered the shelter her voice did not desist for a moment.

'Singapore's a terrible place now!' she declared. 'It's all those soldiers about. They've ruined everything. They've taken over the place. These Australians with their big hats walk around as if they owned it. But I suppose that ours are every bit as bad . . .'

Only with difficulty did I manage to suppress my feelings of outrage. Those soldiers, whom she took pleasure in vilifying, were at that very moment sustaining the barrage along the northern shores of the island. They had come a very long way to get here to protect her, and the likes of her, and were getting nothing from it beyond the risk of death. In that aged and arid heart gratitude had atrophied. The vapouring of this venomous-tongued old woman lent substance to the legend of the luxury-loving settlers who resented the presence of the army as it spoiled their indolent, pleasure-loving way of life. It was a moment of tension when an angry word might well have been spoken – and inevitably regretted. But Marchbanks, displaying the understanding and magnanimity which played so essential a part in his nature, poured oil on the troubled waters. It might not, he suggested, be all the soldiers' fault: they were just not familiar with the Singapore way of life. After all, Japanese soldiers might be worse . . . That was as far as he got. She cut him off abruptly.

'Japanese soldiers, did you say? You don't mean to tell me that *Japanese* soldiers would dare to land on the island with all these Australians and British about?' Marchbanks said that you never could tell. They might make a try. 'Well, if they do,' she declared, 'they'll never frighten me!' Then in words which revealed the obliquity of her mind, she added: 'The trouble with soldiers is that you could never invite *people like that* into your home!'

Some time after midnight there was a slight lessening in the intensity of the bombardment, though the glow in the sky increased from the burning *kampongs* on the nearer side of the Straits. A great arc of fire selvaged the northern shore of the island; and almost in the middle of it a double pillar of black smoke rose high in the sky, seeming to come from the naval base, and suggesting that some oil-fuel tanks had been fired. It was now essential that we should get some sleep, if we were to get any at all, though this would mean abandoning the relative safety of the shelter. To the prospect of returning to their home or their shelter the elderly couple reacted testily, and in an effort to postpone separation, resorted to every wile. Would we not, they finally suggested, care to join them for a drink? But this long, exasperating vigil had, in Marchbanks's mind, at last succeeded in putting patience to flight. It was late, he told them firmly, and they had to go home. So he led them away, the husband's lips sealed as ever, while from his wife's poured protestations as prodigal as when she first arrived.

Returning to my bedroom, I considered for a thoughtless moment undressing and going to bed. But a grumble of artillery from the other side of the Straits drove that folly from my mind. Taking off only my shoes, I stretched out on top of the sheets. But it was an unruly night, and my sleep was spasmodic.

When, next morning, we arrived at Headquarters, we found that the atmosphere there was tense, though it was very difficult to get any definite information about what was happening. One thing, however, was clear: under cover of darkness the Japanese had indeed succeeded in crossing the Straits and had established some kind of a bridge-head on the island. The shelling had apparently knocked out our forward defences along the shore. The Australians had taken the brunt of the attack on the positions they held west of the Causeway. Reports were coming in of bitter hand-to-hand fighting, but reserves were being rushed up to contain the threat.

About mid-morning a few of us, with no duties to perform, were sitting in the small Station canteen, not drinking, but just eager for news, when a strange RAF officer entered the building. I thought he seemed a little unsteady on his feet, and his face was unnaturally grey. Without saying a word he went across to a chair and slumped heavily into it. Someone who seemed to recognise him asked him what had brought him over from Tengah, which was the aerodrome lying further to the west. He answered that he had come with an urgent message, and was returning immediately. Just as dawn was breaking, Japanese soldiers had suddenly rushed the perimeter of the aerodrome. No one had any idea that they were near, and they might very well have taken it, but the RAF rallied just in time and were holding them when he left. The position was undoubtedly critical, but he believed that if they could get reinforcements rushed up in time, it could be held. Then he broke off speaking, and began to tremble as if a bout of malaria was coming on. He sat bolt upright, a hand on each knee, looking straight ahead of him, trying to control the tremor. Then he began to speak again, ruminatively, as if communing with himself as with the others in the canteen.

'Do you think,' he asked, 'that the docs will be able to do anything for him?' We all looked puzzled, while he cast his eyes round the room, appealing for reassurance. He did not seem to realise that we had not shared his experience, whatever it was. Someone asked him who it was that the doctors were to do something for. 'The man that was sliced down the back!' he said. It was hard to watch the intensity of his hidden distress without some details of its cause. The sweat stood out in beads on his grey forehead, revealing the turmoil that was going on within. 'The officer that was sliced down the back,' he said once more, this time very slowly, as if baffled by our failure to provide an answer. 'The RAF officer that the Jap hit in the back with his sword. His ribs were split open. I saw it myself. I tell you: I saw it *with my own eyes!*' Again he cast that careworn look round the small canteen. Could someone not tell him if the docs could do anything for him? One of the listening officers said that docs could do wonders these days. There was no saying how they might be able to patch him up. It was not much of an assurance, but it seemed to comfort him a little. 'Thank you!' he said. 'I wouldn't like to think they could do nothing for him.' Then he seemed restless, as if about to get to his feet, and muttered something about returning to Tengah immediately. They needed every man they could get at Tengah! Someone brought him a drink and he gulped it down quickly. Then, rising from his chair, he walked out of the canteen. I never saw or heard of him again.

Later in the afternoon an order was circulated through the offices that all classified papers were to be collected immediately and brought out for destruction, it being emphasised that this was merely 'a precautionary measure'. In our office we had little or nothing that would add appreciably to the knowledge that Japanese Intelligence already possessed, but what we had we collected and brought out. Then, with the others, we carried our bundles to a small plateau about halfway up the slope where several long pits had been dug. At the head of each stood an officer, holding in his hands a drum filled with caustic soda. As the documents were tossed into the pits, he shook some of the powder over them. Fire, of course, would have been a far surer and faster destroyer, but the trouble with flames or smoke, especially in unusual places, is that they attract attention, and this was something we were anxious to avoid at all costs. It was hard work, lugging the heavy bundles in the stifling heat up the steep slope. But our task was, at length, on the point of completion when a messenger unexpectedly arrived to announce that a decision had been taken to disperse the stocks of liquor, and that anyone who was free should come to collect his ration. Having no particular disposition for liquor at the best of times (and this was not one of them), I had no desire to collect my 'ration', but I joined the queue, curious to witness what might prove to be a unique occasion. Presently from the canteen there emerged an officer whose florid countenance and notable paunch suggested that temperance was a virtue he did not hold in high esteem. The cause of his jubilation was manifest in his hands, of which the right clutched a bottle of whisky, while the left held one of gin. As he passed by I asked him what he proposed to do with his loot, the moment not being particularly propitious for carousal.

'Do with it?' he bellowed throatily. '*Do with it*! I'll soon find something to do with it, even if I've to pour the lot down the drain. Besides, have you never stopped to consider what would be likely to happen if the Japs got their hands on this stuff?'

Rhetorical though the question was, the problem had naturally not escaped my attention; indeed, it was one of the reasons why I welcomed the decision to disperse the stocks. But this still failed to dispose of the question of how the officers proposed to deal with such a large haul of liquor, especially at a time when it would have been the height of folly to drink it. Though they stopped short of admitting it to me, I have a shrewd suspicion that some of them buried their booty in secret caches in the ravine, marking it down for future use. It would, no doubt, come in handy when the time arrived for the victory celebrations. Alas, the tides of war would wash most of them to shores too distant for them to honour this rendezvous. Others, Singapore and its baneful draught long since quaffed and now forgotten, would, on happier isles, raise purer chalices to their lips.

Twilight was now descending, swiftly as is its tropic wont on the island and my colleague and I decided to walk up to the heights of the golf-course to have a last look at the fires before turning in for the night, or for as much of it as would be vouchsafed to us. That high point commanded a very wide prospect over the entire battlefield. Daylight, draining from the sky, was giving place to the great glow from the burning *kampongs*, matching it in brightness but falling far behind it in awesomeness. It seemed hard to believe that in the space of one short day the Japanese should have been able to make such devastating inroads into our defences. It was also clear that in a very short time the tides of battle would be lapping at the foot of the ravine in which Headquarters lay.

We got back from the heights just in time to hear an announcement that all personnel were to attend an immediate conference. There we were addressed by a senior officer who told us that our term of service as airmen or administrators was now at an end, and that from now on we were to regard ourselves as infantry – no more and no less – and to act accordingly. The first step in our transformation would be the issuing to us of rifles and ammunition, which would be done immediately; they would try to get some additional weapons later on. We were to keep our rifles always beside us, ready for action, both by day and night. We did not need him to tell us that the time for their use might not be far off. For the time being we should be confined to the Station, and should have to sleep there. They would do their best to get some blankets for us, and we should have to rig up some makeshift beds in our offices. Sentries would be posted, who would maintain a constant look-out. For this, and for other duties, a rota would be prepared as soon as possible.

By the time the meeting broke up, darkness was settling over the island, its arrival anticipated by the gloom in the ravine. Collecting each man his blanket, we discussed what provision to make for the night ahead. Some had strong misgivings about sleeping in the offices at all, fearing that they were too exposed to sudden attack, especially since the enemy was sure to be well-advised by their Intelligence of the layout of the Station, and the importance attached to a sudden swoop on the senior RAF officers of the island. The difficulty was that there was no alternative place readily available, and we finally decided to sleep on the verandah, and not in the rooms, where we thought we could maintain a more effective look-out. Choosing our spaces, we rigged up our mosquito nets, and soon an intricate reticulation encumbered the verandahs, making it very unlikely that we should be able to see, far less intercept, an enemy creeping up upon us in the darkness. Each man slipped a clip of cartridges into the magazine of his rifle and laid the weapon beside his bed. Then, wrapping his one blanket round him, clearly inadequate protection from the hard floor, he used anything available – in most cases his shoes – for a pillow.

For hours, it seemed, I lay awake, troubled by the flickering light in the sky, and even more by my unquiet thoughts. But at length, under the compulsion of sheer exhaustion, my determination to remain watchful wilted and, pulling the blanket up to my brows, I drifted off into a fitful sleep.

KING'S MESSENGER

An urgent hand was at my shoulder and, opening my eyes, I descried the figure of a Sergeant kneeling on one knee beside my bed and holding up the flap of my mosquito net with the other hand. Insisting on getting an answer, he was repeating over and over again: 'Wakey, wakey! Wakey, wakey!' I told him that I was awake, and asked him what the trouble was. Japs? He said it was not Japs *yet*! But I was wanted up top-side in the Ops Room. The Controller wanted to see me immediately. I said that there must be some mistake. I had never spoken to the Controller in my life, and had not even been inside the Ops Room. So why should he want to see me in the middle of the night like this? The Sergeant must have got my name mixed up with that of one of the other officers sleeping round me. The Sergeant was not to be shaken in his conviction that I was the man wanted. The name given to him was definitely McEwan, and I was wanted *now*!

Though still convinced that there had been some mistaken identity, I crawled from my mosquito net and, groping for my shoes, put them on. Then I straightened and buttoned up my bush shirt. It was strange how raw the night mist was down here in the ravine, and I shivered involuntarily. With the Sergeant leading the way, I now climbed up the steps and, about halfway to the top, turned off along a path that contoured the slope to lead to a door which gave entrance into the hillside. Then, pushing the door open, the Sergeant ushered me in. The room surprised me by its size, its length and lofty ceiling seeming incompatible with a chamber that had been excavated from the escarpment. The light was dim, casting long shadows, though clearly illuminated on the wall facing me as I entered was a large chart of Singapore and Malaya, with two little flags stuck on to the island aerodromes, testifying graphically to the vanished – and vanquished – squadrons. No less eloquent was the Order of Battle board next to it, which was quite bare. At the far end of the room was a broad table, at the middle of which sat the Controller, his face illuminated by the broad, yellow cone of light that fell from a small green-shaded lamp on the table beside him. Apart from ourselves, he was the only person I could see in all the room.

The Controller was a man of a most arresting presence, his features ascetic – almost indeed gaunt – and his eyes untroubled. With them he regarded me closely as I advanced to the table where he sat, and saluted. When he addressed me his voice sounded very patrician, with grave, measured tones. In a different setting it might well have been the master in a college in one of the ancient universities; in a different age, the superior in a medieval monastery. He told me a decision had been taken to send me out. Two of us would be going: I would fly by Cat to Batavia, while Stephen would go by Hudson to Palembang. They had some classified papers for me to take with me. I could collect them just before I was ready to go. The Cat would be at Kallang at first light. For a moment I hesitated, not sure whether this was the end of the interview, but he did not enlarge upon it and, sensing my doubt, he added, with a kindly smile, that if he were I he would try to get in a little sleep before he set out. Opportunities might be limited for some time.

Turning on my heels, I took my leave and climbed down the stairs, my mind in a kind of trance, compounded of the hazy comprehension which its sleep-clogged condition admitted and the startling information that had just been imparted to it. Nothing could hold out richer promise than Batavia for, once in Java, I might be able to rejoin my old squadrons – unless, that is, they had other plans in mind for me. Nor did the fact weigh little with me that, for the time being at least, I should be free of the clutches of the Japs. Crawling back under my mosquito net, I stretched out on the hard boards. For a time I listened to the rhythmic breathing of the sleeping men. What, I wondered, had they to look forward to in the morning? Whatever it was, it was not likely to be pleasant. Meanwhile I made up my mind to lie awake till it was time to collect my papers and set off for Kallang.

Once again that hand was at my shoulder, its purport peremptory as ever. What was it this time? Surely it could not be the Controller again? But it was, and he wanted me *now*! Wearily I put on my shoes and followed the Sergeant submissively up the stairs. In the Ops Room, the Controller was still seated at his table just as I had left him, the scholarly face lit by the dim lamp. He said he was very sorry, but *it was off*! The situation had changed since I saw him last; and they had been forced to alter their plans. I would not be going out by Cat after all. Now I could go back and join my comrades and have a longer sleep. With the cruel words ringing in my ears, I left the Ops Room and climbed down the interminable stairs. How I envied the men quietly sleeping around me! No golden chances had been dangled tantalisingly before their eyes to be suddenly snatched away. At least there could be no more sleep for me now, my portion the pangs of a blighted hope.

For the third time this disordered night, that hand was at my shoulder. There was no need to enquire of the messenger the nature of his tidings. Meekly I put on my shoes and set off up the stairs in the wake of the Sergeant. In the Ops Room the same unnatural calm prevailed, the little green lamp burning with its dim light, so redolent of a wake, and behind it the quiet face lit by its beams. Crossing to the table I awaited the announcement of my fate. His voice as impassive as ever, the Controller announced that *it was on*! I was going out after all! The Cat would be at Kallang at first light. He held out his hand to me with a large envelope, bound with tape and sealed. These, he said, were my papers. They wanted me to take them with me to Batavia, and deliver them *in person* to the CO at HQ once I reached my destination. I would see to it, of course, that these papers never got out of my hands, *in any circumstances*. Did I understand? I said I understood, I would see his instructions carried out to the best of my ability. But could he tell me how I was to get to Kallang? And how much time I had? He said that transport would be waiting for me at the guard-house. As for time (he looked at his watch) they had been forced to cut it a bit fine. The change of plans had upset their timetable a little. But he was confident that I should manage all right. He wished me well on my mission.

Leaving the room, I hurried down the stairs. Beside the bed of my Seletar comrade, I knelt down, and, lifting up the flap of his mosquito net, shook him gently till he opened his eyes. It took a little time for my excited announcement that I was going off to Java to sink into his returning consciousness.

'Why Java?' he asked.

This was no time for explanations, however brief.

'Orders!' I said.

Then, grasping his hand, I took my leave of him. We had been through some rough times together at Seletar. We had stayed on when the aircrews departed, and managed somehow to survive the bombs. Now it was hard to abandon him to his unknown fate. In my perplexity of spirit I resorted to one of the half-dozen Japanese words I had picked up from him.

'*Sayonara!*' I said.

To his sleep-bewildered face the word brought back the old smile I had known so well at Seletar.

'*Sayonara!*' he muttered. 'Good luck in Java!'

Hurriedly I tucked the flap of his mosquito net back under the corner of his blanket. Then, casting a glance along the thicket of nets that cumbered the verandah, I took a silent farewell of their sleeping occupants, wishing them a peaceful goodnight. Then I set off up the stairs to the guard-house and my promised rendezvous with the waiting transport.

The gravel terrace I found, to my astonishment, deserted, with no hint of transport anywhere, the only sign of life being the sentry sitting in his box. To my enquiry about the transport which the Controller had said would be waiting for me, he returned a puzzled gaze; it was, he said, the first he had heard of it. As far as he knew, there was no transport within miles, everything on wheels having already been commandeered to take supplies up to the front lines. There was nothing for it, then, but a return to the Controller to see if his authority could whistle up something, so I set off for the stairs.

I had just reached their top when I was startled by a call from the sentry; looking back, I could see the shaded headlamps of a vehicle approaching up Sime Road. Arriving at its head, two thin pencils of light swung into the drive and approached the sentry-box. Running back from the stairs, I arrived in front of it just as a taxi drew up beside me. The door opened and an RAF officer stepped out. He went up to the shaded headlights and, taking from his pocket a handful of coins, counted out his fare into the extended hand of the driver. Then, a step into the darkness removed him from view, neither the officer nor his passenger apparently being aware of my presence almost by their side. A couple of steps and I was at the taxi; grasping the opened door, I called to the driver to take me to Kallang. He jumped into his driving-cab and, pretending not to hear me, grasped the wheel and revved up his engine. As I made to get into his vehicle, I repeated my instructions to drive to Kallang. Taking his foot from the throttle, he swung himself around in his seat. Then, turning on me a face filled with blazing anger, and with eyes closed in two sinister, oblique slits, he spat out his answer: 'Kallang no!'

It would be idle to belittle my astonishment. Nothing in my considerable experience of the Far East had led me to anticipate this kind of thing, and I had no precedent to guide me as to what his reactions might be under different kinds of treatment. Craven submission would, naturally, seal my fate, and in any case was quite out of the question. But might an angry outburst be any more successful? Trying to keep a cool head, while maintaining a firm grip on the taxi door, I lowered my voice to a menacing whisper.

'*Pigge* [Drive]. Kallang!' I said.

The eyes seemed to close completely. Nervously the lips twitched.

'Kallang no!' he repeated defiantly. 'I speak: *Kallang no!*'

Desperate ills call for remedies no less desperate. Time did not admit of wheedling or haggling, or bribery, even if I had had the means or the mind to resort to it. I had to get to Kallang with urgent documents and this was the only means at my disposal. So, still keeping a hand on the door in case he suddenly released the clutch in an effort to throw me off, I used my free hand to slip the hood from my revolver holster and drew the weapon. Then, ostentatiously cocking it, I uttered, very slowly and deliberately, the one word: '*Kallang!*' Fox-like, his eyes followed my every movement. For a moment or two he vacillated, and I feared he might decide to call my bluff. But in the end he capitulated. Giving his head a little nonchalant toss, he smiled wryly.

'OK!' he said. 'Kallang OK!'

The change had been sudden, and it had about it a touch of the theatrical. I feared he might have trickery in mind. However, I jumped into the vehicle, sitting in a corner where I could keep a watchful eye on him, while, conspicuous on my knees, reposed the ultimate instrument of persuasion in case any call for its services might arise. We drove down the drive and out into Sime Road. Once clear of the trees, I stole a hurried glance backwards towards the Straits. The whole shoreline seemed to be in the grip of a general conflagration. It had been frightening enough when we had watched it from the golf-course heights as dusk was falling. But now the black arch of night provided a proscenium for its more dramatic display. It was a spectacle which no potential victim could contemplate without fear and horror. Sadly I turned my gaze to the road ahead.

Presently we arrived at a place where the fairway descended to a sunken plateau which in all probability was one of the greens. On this, cavorting eerily in the dim light, appeared a group of weird figures. Clad in long white gowns, they gave the impression of witches engaged in a night coven. On nearer approach I realised they were Chinese houseboys, and what was engaging their attention was not the momentous events which were taking place not so far from them, but a football which they were dribbling over the turf with great zeal. While in China I never ceased to be amazed at the untroubled fortitude with which the citizens of that remarkable land would face up to calamities which others less dispassionate would find devastating. But my experience had never encountered anything to match this.

Once over the brow of the heights, and on the run down Sime Road, I became aware of a pearl glimmer in the eastern sky. It was not the dawn yet but its harbinger. Was there, I now wondered, time enough to make a flying dash into our bungalow in Lorne Road to retrieve some clothing? I had nothing but what I stood up in, and being beside the road the bungalow was designed to facilitate such an excursion. My great fear was that, once he got me out of sight in the house, what was to prevent this man whose behaviour had amply confirmed his unreliability from driving off and leaving me to my fate? It was a risk which in normal circumstances I should never have contemplated, but the present crisis, making a cool appraisal of the dangers impossible, drove me to resort to it. I asked the syce if he would mind stopping for a moment at our house. It was in Lorne Road, and would not detain him long. I quite expected him to refuse, and was pleasantly surprised when, with unexpected affability, he turned round and said: 'Lorne Road OK!' I pointed out the house when we came to it, and he drew up. With my clenched fist I beat on the door, and listened. Not a sound! Perhaps the boy, having heard that the Japs had landed, had fled, knowing full well what fate awaited him if caught in a European home. Then I rattled on the window beside the shattered wall. I heard a distant stirring and the sound of slippered feet approaching in the hall. Sleepily from behind the door came the boy's voice, and, recognising mine, he slid back the bolt on the door.

The face that greeted mine was heavy with sleep. Stammering a few embarrassed words, I rushed through to my bedroom. Everything was arranged meticulously, awaiting my return. Kneeling down, I unlocked my cabin trunk and began to rummage through its contents, making a rough selection of the items I considered it necessary to take with me. Shirts, of course, and underwear, stockings, towel – even though it was heavy and awkward to carry, my blue uniform. Then I uncovered, neatly folded and forgotten about at the bottom of my trunk, my Highland dress. I had packed it at the instigation of an English officer who had just returned to Leuchars from a tour of duty in Singapore. In Malaya, he assured me, the colourful garb of the Gael carried a cachet which far outweighed the inconvenience of its carriage. It was advice which it would have been in my interest to ignore. What was I to do about it now? Carefully – almost indeed reverently – I lifted out the items one by one: the Prince Charlie coatee; the silver sporran with the grey, seal-skin pouch; the green-and-white diced stockings; and the shoes with the silver buckles, with, of course, the McEwan tartan kilt. Playing for time, I asked the boy if he had anything I could carry them in, and after a hurried foray to the kitchen he returned with a small wooden handcase covered with wicker. It was the kind of thing that was once common enough, but which the supersession of Victorian modes of travel had removed from the contemporary scene. The acquisition of the means now provided the pretext for the retention of the dress. Improvidently, perhaps, but with a romantic flourish, I packed the items into the bottom of the case and on top of it my blue uniform. There followed my shirts and underwear, my shaving and washing things, and a few extras, mementoes for the most part. The case was now bulging. Kneeling on the lid, I forced it down so that I could coax the hasp over the staple and then secure it with the toggle. The seams groaned and stretched but, surprisingly, held. Now I was ready to go.

With the boy at my side, I hurried back along the passage to the door. Then came the moment of leave-taking. None I ever experienced caused me more pain; for what could I say to this faithful servant who had so loyally stood by us? I did the best I could, muttering a few disjointed phrases. The other *tuan* would soon be back to look after things. I had been ordered away, and had to obey orders. He had done much for me, and I was grateful – the home, the chow, the handcase – but I could not bring myself to mention the poor, murdered amah. No longer could I bear to look into that betrayed and woebegone face, those open and honest eyes. Opening the door, I ran along the garden-path towards the road, almost afraid to raise my eyes lest I should find the road deserted and the taxi gone. But, to my inexpressible relief, I found the taxi still waiting.

'Kallang OK!' called out the syce as I jumped in, and he set off.

As we drove down the sharp slope of Lorne Road, my mind became engaged with a new fear. By this time, every main road into Singapore would be sure to be controlled by roadblocks, manned by detachments of troops. How would these men regard me, travelling not by official transport but by common taxi, at this ungodly hour, their suspicion liable to be increased by this very unmilitary-looking hand-case which appeared to be my only luggage? Would they not find it necessary at least to hold me up till they had made some enquiries to establish my identity? And even the briefest delay might see that Catalina off to Batavia with an empty seat, and he who was intended to fill it, standing forlorn and forsaken on the runway.

At the foot of Lorne Road we turned into Thomson Road, continuing down which till we came to Bukit Timah Road, which we followed to its end beside the Kallang River. This skirted Chinatown, which was once the most densely populated quarter of Singapore. Here the evidence of destruction was on every hand, and on a vast scale. Piles of rubble lined the streets, though I could see no fires, there being nothing left to burn. Through the gaps in what had once been tenements I caught glimpses of downtown Singapore and the docks where great fires were still roaring, above them a great pall of smoke darkening the sky. The air that blew in through the taxi window was heavy with the acrid stench of burning rubber, coming from godowns which had been stacked with this commodity. Much to my surprise and relief, not once during the ride from Sime Road had we seen a roadblock, soldier or pedestrian. What we had been driving through was a city of the dead.

Having followed the river down to the sea, we rumbled, at length, on to the iron bridge. Crossing it, we turned down to the right. After a little, the syce brought his vehicle round in a wide arc and, drawing up, jumped down from his cabin to open my door. Could this be the same man who, but an hour or two earlier at Sime Road while I stood with my hand on my pistol, spat out his refusal to go to Kallang? Obstructed and desperate, I had at the time been filled with wrath. Now the sight of the pathetic figure, with a shoddy and shapeless cotton jacket draped limply over his scrawny chest moved my heart to compassion. Who were we arrogant foreigners, with few roots, and fewer loyalties, in his land, to order him about imperiously? I asked him what his fare was, being already familiar with standard tariff to the Raffles Hotel, and this was only a little further on. He asked for the usual daylight fare and I was taken aback, expecting some natural inflation in view of the hour and the abnormal circumstances of the ride. Into his hand I counted the dollars he asked for, adding a couple more 'for the King'. But had I emptied into his hand the entire contents of my wallet, adding a couple of dollars for every crowned head in the whole of south-east Asia, my bounty would have left undischarged the debt I owed him for getting me to Kallang in time.

'Thank you, *tuan*!' he said.

His voice sounded genial and friendly. From enemies we had become friends, linked in a common disaster, and playthings of the same grim destiny. Then, jumping back into his cab, he revved up his engine. With a crunch of rubber in rubble he made off towards the iron bridge, finally rumbling over it to be lost in the battered city.

In the face of manifold difficulties and palpable dangers – aided, too, by a generous measure of good fortune – I had, by reaching Kallang, accomplished the first part of my mission, – but with not a moment to spare. Low over the marshy estuary of the Kallang River hung a pearly mist. But it was dissipating, seething gently as it lifted into the cool air, though it half-hid the surface and deceived my eyes. But now that I could look closely at it, I saw that Kallang runway no longer existed as such, being just the shattered ruins of an aerodrome, having been bombed out of existence. In whatever direction I turned, all that met my eyes was crater after crater, churned up in the grey ashes with which the air station had been reclaimed from the sea. How, I wondered, was Stephen to get to Palembang? No Hudson could ever land on a slag-heap like this. At least a Catalina asked for nothing more than water, and Japanese capability, impressive as it had proved itself, stopped short of bombing craters in the South China Sea.

I was now faced with the problem of where, on the rim of this wilderness, the Catalina was likely to land: at the moment I could not even see the end of it, that being obscured by a low-lying bank of mist. So, picking my steps with care among the craters, I decided to walk out to the end to make an inspection. I had got about halfway to my objective when I suddenly became aware of a group of figures, looking a little ghostly in the mist. They were all in uniform, standing in a circle, and in a kind of huddle. They embraced the three services – army, navy and air force; there was even a glengarry among them. For the moment I was baffled by their presence here at this time of the morning – could they be getting out like myself, deserting the sinking ship? At least it seemed prudent to approach them and make my presence known. Then, as I got nearer, I realised with utter astonishment that what I was looking at was the whole High Command of Malaya! Their awareness of my presence almost coincided with my discovery of theirs, and I saw a head or two turn curiously in my direction, and a word of enquiry (or could it be caution?) seemed to be exchanged. When I got near to them, the General turned towards me, and I saluted. The salute he returned seemed to me a little shy – even, indeed, a little perfunctory. I winced with embarrassment at the very unsoldierly-looking wicker-case in my hand and, seeking concealment, I walked over to a great bollard which was nearby, a solid iron stanchion of obscure purpose which the bombs had spared, or failed to demolish. Secreting my case in its welcome shade, I sat down on top of it to take my bearings. Being neither conspicuous nor obscured, it provided a post for observation which could not have been bettered.

Lieutenant-General Percival was, of course, easily identifiable from the numerous photographs I had seen in the newspapers, but there was something essentially elusive about both his person and his personality. I had long come to regard great commanders as men of dominating character, striding about among their troops and moulding them to their will by sheer personality. But in

Percival's case this charismatic quality was not much in evidence, indeed he seemed to shun publicity, and at Seletar I never met an officer who had as much as seen him in the flesh. Now that I could see him, I could study him at leisure while he talked to the others beside him. He was, in the first place, thin, even to the point of emaciation, his baggy shorts emphasising the spindly nature of his legs. His face had an almost squirrel-like look, a closely cropped moustache failing to conceal incisor teeth, which protruded. His chin receded into a long and rather thin neck. I had been told he had a distinguished Staff College record, which would explain his present command, but this was not the kind of man, I felt, to fire retreating and demoralised troops with a new zeal for battle. What he lacked was dynamism, or at least the look which indicates its possession.

Air Vice-Marshal Pulford presented no problem in identification, for he was always in and out of the Ops Room at Seletar, where he invariably had a kind and encouraging word for junior officers like myself. The archetypal flyer, he was spare and wiry with a lean, aquiline face, sunken cheeks, and sharp, slightly hooded eyes. His head was long and narrow, with marked frontal development. He had a little, closely trimmed moustache, and a mouth usually twitched up at one side as if about to break into merriment. But the most distinguishing mark of his features was his ears, which stuck straight out curiously from his head, and now (as always) his cap was jauntily cocked over one of them. The glengarry, I now saw, was worn by a Colonel of a Highland regiment, but whether it was the Argylls or the Gordons I was unable to distinguish. There was also present, at the far side of the group, an Admiral, but I could not see him properly as he was partly obscured by the others. But it was almost certainly Admiral Spooner, who, along with Pulford, was soon to meet a lonely and tragic death on a malaria-infested island near Banka. A few aides completed the group.

What still eluded all understanding was the purpose of their presence here, all together, at this unseemly hour. Whatever it was, it certainly involved them in a heavy risk, for what was to prevent an enemy fighter from skimming in low over the water, obscured by the mist, and dropping a bomb among them, or raking them with a few bursts from his machine-gun? There was nowhere they could retreat for cover, other than a few waterlogged and mud-filled bomb craters. It was just within the bounds of possibility that the whole High Command of Singapore and Malaya could be wiped out by a stealthy marauder in a matter of moments.

Turning my eyes from the officers and looking out to sea, I suddenly became aware of two nozzles, spouting long pennants of flame, approaching eerily through the mist, with scarcely any noise. Then, looming gigantic in the half-light, the shadowy outline of the Catalina appeared, the jets of flame trailing as the pilot throttled back, and seeming to lap and flicker round the fuselage. Finally, the great machine touched down and, with engines purring softly, veered in towards the western corner of the runway, where it came to rest. My attention was so engrossed by the sheer expertise of the manoeuvre that I failed to take notice of the group of officers, and when, belatedly, I turned to look in their direction I found to my astonishment and alarm that they had gone. Almost immediately my ear caught the *putt-putt-putt* of an engine just started, and coming from a small motor boat which, being moored close under the bank, had escaped my notice. The officers having already embarked, an aide was busy untying the painter which secured the small craft to a wooden peg on the bank. Fear of imminent abandonment lent a strident note to my voice as I called to them to wait for me. Rather testily, the aide informed me that I had better 'look slippy'. Clutching my case, I ran over to the bank only to find that the boat had already cast off, and a widening gap appeared between it and the shore.

'Jump!' called out the aide peremptorily; seeing my hesitancy, he added, 'I'll catch you!'

The assurance failed to overcome my reluctance, or fear that my weak foot would never sustain the sudden jar of contact with the boat. But a renewal of exhortation, by this time laced with annoyance, finally overcame my misgivings; bracing myself, I launched myself across the gap, pushing my sound foot forward to take the shock of contact. But I need not have feared: even before my foot touched the thwarts, a powerful pair of hands seized me by the waist and held me as in a vice. Then the launch pushed off; the helm being put hard over, swivelled in a wide crescent under the giant wings before coming to a stop just beneath the now opened door. Looking up, I saw two figures framed in the doorway. One was that of the pilot; the other, silhouetted in anonymity, I did not recognise. They were engaged in earnest discussion, making arrangements for the Cat's return to Singapore.

'Well then, *exactly at midnight!*' observed the stranger as, turning round, he prepared to descend the ladder. The scales fell from my eyes. My doubt about the purpose of the officers at Kallang dissolved. It was General Wavell himself! The General's uniform was of an unfamiliar shade of powdered saffron, meticulously pressed, and his face had a friendly, relaxed look. His frame was portly, but he descended the ladder agilely enough and stepped into the launch.

A sudden spurt of its engine revived my worst fears. In a moment or two, unless I did something urgently, I should find myself back on the cratered runway, and the Catalina would be off to Batavia without me. For the second time, my voice no less apprehensive than before, I appealed to them to wait for me, explaining that I was going on the Catalina. Smiling indulgently, Air Vice-Marshal Pulford urged me to 'get a move on'. Being still, of course, in the stern of the launch, I was furthest away from the aircraft. But from man to man I was hustled along till I reached the bows and was within reach of the ladder. Gripping a rung, I climbed upwards. At the top a strong hand shot out and, gripping me unceremoniously by the collar, deposited me in a heap on the floor of the aircraft. This seemed the ultimate debasement. Beside it my wicker-case was a venial irrelevance – that is, if I had still had it. Thrust into my bush-shirt pocket, a nervous hand confirmed the continued presence of my sealed package. But I had parted company with my case. Anxiously thrusting my head through the doorway, I informed the departing launch of my loss. The throttle being suddenly shut back, the craft drifted to a stop. In the stern, where I had landed when I jumped in, stood Pulford. Bemused, he bent down and, groping among the feet, retrieved the modest object of my quest. Holding it aloft for general inspection, he asked if *this* was the *thing* that I was after. Every instinct I had pleaded for repudiation, but its contents were too valuable to me to contemplate forfeiture, and I reluctantly admitted ownership. From man to man it was passed along till it arrived at General Wavell, who, having just boarded, was still in the bows. Cradling it for a moment in his hands to gauge its weight, he looked upwards, his face wreathed in a broad smile.

'One . . . two . . . *catch!*' he called as he tossed it upwards. Soaring in a high arc through the open door of the Cat, the case returned to my welcome custody, whereupon the launch pulled away, a few bemused faces among its occupants exchanging smiles.

For a moment or two the pilot leaned over me in the doorway, watching the launch till it reached the shore. Then he shut the door. Sticking through the Perspex-bubble on the starboard side of the aircraft, and just at my shoulder, was a heavy machine-gun, and a belt of cartridges lay across the floor.

'You take charge of that!' said the pilot, indicating the weapon, as he made for the cockpit. But I had to confess to him that, never having undergone instruction in the operation of machine-guns, I was unable to use it. To his face the disclosure brought a look of incredulity and despondency.

'You mean to tell me,' he said, 'that you're in the RAF, and can't handle a machine-gun?'

My confirmation of the fact brought him no noticeable comfort. '*Tid 'apa!*' he observed resignedly. A Malay term, it sprang instinctively to native lips whenever things adopted their customary recalcitrance, and most of our men had added it to their vocabulary. Roughly rendered in English, it might read 'O, forget it!' or 'What's the use!' His disapproval having been aired, the pilot disappeared into the cockpit. Presently with a great roar the engines sprang to life, and a shuddering passed along the whole fuselage. Then the huge machine taxied round till it faced south. The throttle being opened up, the Cat, for a moment or two, appeared to paw the water in impatience to be on its way. At length, restraint being relaxed, it skimmed off, a white brocade of foam streaming in its wake. A gentle heave of the nose indicated the moment when it became airborne. Pulling up into the cool, empty skies that arched above the South China Sea, the aircraft set course for Banka and Batavia.

That same night the Catalina honoured its rendezvous. Stepping in the darkness down the cratered bank to embark, General Wavell lost his footing and, falling heavily, received serious injuries to his back. On his arrival in Batavia he had to go immediately into hospital. This was to be his last visit to the beleaguered island before its fall.

In this great and tragic drama I had been assigned a very minor role, but now it was nearing its end the time had come for me to step off-stage. Yet, before the year was out, I was destined to pass this way again, though on this occasion I was travelling in the opposite direction and was under different management. In my firmament storm clouds were swiftly gathering, and no star of hope shed its consoling rays.

PART TWO

TRESPASSERS IN EDEN
WITH THE
VILDEBEESTS IN JAVA

What though the field be lost,
All is not lost.

Paradise Lost
John Milton

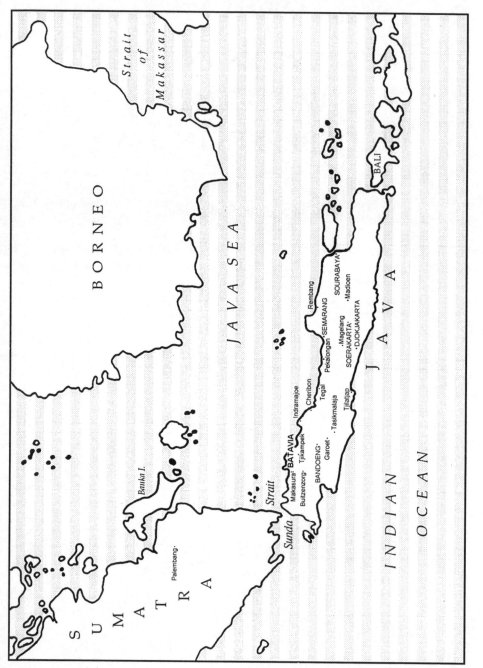

Java

THE BOY GUNNER

I crouched on the floor of the Cat with my shoulder hunched into the corner of the machine-gun bubble, watching the island appear to retreat as we climbed away southwards over the Riu Archipelago. From the air its most characteristic feature was its sheer insignificance, a little, flat diamond of land tacked on to the end of the Malayan peninsula, all signs of human activity of a peaceful nature concealed by the dense carpet of tropical vegetation with which it was covered. Of warlike activity there was evidence enough: in particular, along the northern shore that stretched from the Causeway to the western tip of the island, the clustering fires were so dense that it seemed a broad band all along the coast had been given over to the flames. At the other side of the island great fires raged in the dock area, though the town itself showed little evidence of burning, and there were several ships still at the wharves, one or two of them of considerable size, and none of them, as far as I could see, seriously damaged. Above the dockyard, as they had done since the Causeway was blown up, two dense, black columns of smoke stood up into the sky, reaching a great height. They came, as we thought, from the oil tanks, fired by Japanese bombing or shelling: happily, we did not know the truth, that they had been fired by our own men to deny them to the enemy.

Of the impregnable defences which, we had been told, made Singapore one of the most formidable fortresses on earth, neither from the air nor on the ground had I seen any evidence. Nor did the land –for the most part flat and soggy – lend itself to the creation of powerful fortifications. Possibly much of the widely publicised impregnability was no more than bluff, and when the Japanese called our bluff, and exposed it for what it was, our humiliation was so much more abject. Later, in the middle of the war, the Japanese took an Italian reporter from the *Gazetta del Popolo* on a tour of the southern regions; visiting Singapore, he reported as follows:

> Singapore was something like a nightmare to anyone who would think of attempting an assault against these well defended oriental territories of England. But visiting Seletar and the rest of Singapore Island, I wondered at first where all these fortifications were that the English had been for decades boasting about. The commander of Seletar [the naval base, presumably] said that the English had the ability to make the world believe that it is an impregnable fortress, but it was no better than a third-rate Japanese naval base.

And this – making due allowance for national self-esteem – may be no more than an adequate assessment of the position.

It is difficult to be sure that, looking back on it now, I am not enriching what were then my impressions with the benefit of hindsight. Yet I am confident that, as I looked down on the burning and beleaguered Singapore, I knew instinctively that this was a crossroads of history. The legend that European troops would always be superior to Asiatic, which had been sustained, with notable feats of arms, since the Battle of Marathon, could never hope to survive the events of the last weeks on the Malay Peninsula, and now on the island itself. The truly climacteric confrontation, however, had not taken place on land, but at sea off Kuantan; and when the *Repulse* and the *Prince of Wales* had been attacked, not by a sneaking submarine, but alerted and in broad daylight, by a few dozen Japanese bombers, and had gone down in an hour, nothing could be quite the same again. And yet, despite the shattering nature of our reverses, never for one moment did any of us in Singapore ever doubt that ultimately the Japanese would go down to resounding defeat. In their hour of arrogance and triumph, they had taken on too much. Against the vast industrial potential of the USA, not yet in gear, they would find that fanatical heroism was not enough, and they would be crushed by sheer weight of weapons. What would happen to us, in the meantime, was another matter.

The island now grew dim and distant and dropped out of sight, leaving only the grey sea beneath us, and the scattered archipelago, which stretched to a nebulous horizon with a sapphire gleam at its eastern edge. I shook my head a little to clear my eyes, strained with gazing at the distant island, and stretched my shoulder which was cramped from leaning into the curved Perspex of the gunner's bubble. Across the passage sat the other gunner, whom I had vaguely noticed when I entered the aircraft, but my senses had been so actively engaged elsewhere that I had had no opportunity to take notice of him. Now, to my astonishment, I saw that he was no more than a boy, and could not have been more than sixteen. His person embodied an ideal of Dutch boyhood, being tall, blond and blue-eyed. Bleached by the sun to an ashen silver, his hair clustered round his head in short curls, so that he had the aspect of a boy Apollo; and his boyishness was emphasised by a small nose which tilted slightly upwards and gave to his features a particularly frank and open look. He wore a white sailor-suit, like a Viennese choirboy, with blue stripes running across the chest and a white bib whose starched perfection betokened a mother's anxiousness that he should look neat. Even his trousers, which were curled up in the bubble, still retained their creases. For a little I watched him unobserved, his eyes fixed on the oval of sky he could see through his bubble, and his hands gripping tightly the stock of his gun.

I wondered what had prompted the Dutch authorities to entrust such a vital job to hands as innocent and untried as his. Could not one of the tough, seasoned Australians have been seconded from a Vildebeest turret? Granted his keenness, would he have commanded the veteran determination, and trained skill, to shoot it out coolly with a Japanese fighter, had one arrived on the scene? Perhaps it was a subtle trick to mislead, for an inquisitive eye prying into the machine at Batavia would be unlikely to conclude that with a gunner like this it could be engaged on any mission of importance. Then, seeing me watching him, he straightened up and smiled across by way of greeting. I asked him if he spoke English, but he looked embarrassed, moving his head from side to side. Then he said, 'OK!' and, after a little reflection, he added, 'England OK!'

I tried to find out if he came from Java, or whether he was indeed Holland-born, helping out the inadequacies of language with a few pantomime gestures. Spurred to childish emulation, he ran the index finger of the right hand along the distended fingers of the left. 'Nederland OK!' he said. 'Java OK! England OK! America OK!' Then he faltered, the outstretched finger poised in indecision. 'Aus-tral-ee-a OK!' he concluded, his brittle little peal of laughter echoing strangely in the great belly of the Catalina. He looked at me a moment appealingly, as if fearful I might disapprove. Then he repeated the pantomime with the other hand. 'Japan no, no, no, NO OK!' renewing his thin little mirthless laugh. How sad, I felt, that boyish hands like his should be habituated to the alien and destructive mechanism of a machine-gun.

We had reached almost the mid-point between Singapore and Banka when a faint glow in the aircraft announced the near approach of the dawn. Shuffling across the floor to the other side, I sat beside the youthful gunner, gazing at the eastern horizon. All the eastern sky was hung with a pastel so rare and delicate that it seemed scarcely earthly, and then a saffron flush appeared above the indigo ribbon that marked the horizon. Presently a little flicker appeared, as first one ray prodded upwards, then another followed, and soon a whole quiver of gleaming arrows pierced the eastern sky. Under them the vast grey table of the sea broke into lines of coruscating light whose animation was so human that they looked like the ranks of an immense *corps de ballet*, each girl wearing a crystal crown on her head. Fascinated, I sat beside the ash-haired gunner, watching this splendid display of the wonders of nature, disappointed that so few in these regions had at that moment the inclination to look at it. In the returning light, the islands beneath us now became transfigured, the fronds of the palm trees, which hung limp, still dark, and the boles jet-black. But in the coral shallows near the shore the water showed a tawny yellow, fading into opal beyond, and darkest cobalt in the deeps.

When we got to Banka we renewed our acquaintance with the débris of vessels of various sizes, and in various degrees of dereliction, clogging the narrow channels. Some lay on their sides, some stood upright, even with no more than the funnels above water, some were beached. In the clear water, their outlines showed up in surprising detail. In a little jade bay in the lee of an island we came upon a small steamer, listing badly, but whether beached, or anchored in shallow water I could not determine. As I watched her, I became aware of a dipping of one wing of the Cat, and the great aircraft went into a wide spiral, sweeping round, lower and lower, as she descended towards the sea. I could see no life on the deck of the vessel, or any other sign to justify the particular attention that was being accorded her. Was he preparing to put his 'plane down on the water in order to take somebody, or something, off? I was not to know, for the inspection broke off as suddenly as it had begun; now the Cat, her nose turned upwards, climbed again into the skies and resumed her flight towards Batavia.

Unlike the Riu Archipelago, near Singapore, which seemed to be largely uninhabited, the islands beneath us, even the smallest of them, seemed each to have its *atap* hut in the shade of a palm tree, and its numerous family. At our approach the children would rush out to the edge of the beach and hold their hands up to shade their eyes as they watched us pass, though their elders observed a greater caution, keeping the bole of a tree between themselves and us. Recent enactments in these waters had, it seemed, curbed their natural curiosity.

The further south we flew over the islands of the Banka Archipelago, the more stifling and sultry became the atmosphere in the fuselage of the Cat, conditions that usually presage thunderstorms; and soon I was aware of a darkening-over of the sky, and tatters of mist began to flick past the bubble, soon to be followed by occasional, but loud, spatterings of rain. I twisted my head round to gaze forward and there, across the southern horizon, stretched a great rampart of cumulo-nimbus, brown for the most part, with a very black base, though the flattened globes at its summits were silver-grey. Having heard unnerving accounts from pilots of experiences in this kind of cloud formation, I looked forward with some apprehension to our encounter with this obstacle, my anxiety increased by the fact that, having flown from Singapore at a comparatively low altitude, we were in no position to fly either over or round it.

The pilot maintained his course, the inside of the aircraft growing more heavy and oppressive each minute, with hanging veils of cloud swirling past the bubble with increasing frequency. Then came heavy splashes of rain in huge drops which whipped past the wings to crash against the Perspex of the bubble with the sound of pebbles. We struck the black wall of the cumulo-nimbus with an impact that sent a shudder through the whole of the Cat's fuselage; and for some moments everything was blotted out by black vapour which boiled and seethed round the turret. The rain descended in perpendicular rods, thick as arrow shafts, which sobbed and gurgled over the wing and along the side of the belly, while the propellers, striking the wall of rain, made a high-pitched note which could be heard above the general pandemonium outside. Now the aircraft began to shudder violently, seized in the anarchic forces of the turbulence, and I began to entertain fears for our safety. Looking across at the young gunner, I saw that he was holding on grimly to the handles of his gun, his body meanwhile being thrown across the floor by the jolting of the machine. Sustained by a youthful nonchalance, he seemed impervious to fear; and, when he saw that I was watching him, he stuck up one thumb and called out 'OK!', which greeting I was in no frame of mind to reciprocate.

We had been flying for some time through this bucking blackness, my mind too agitated to take much reckoning of time, when the Catalina gave a kind of lurch, or shudder – and there we were, soaring out in a serene, sunlit sky, the change incredibly abrupt. I cast a glance backwards at the black wall of cumulo-nimbus towering into the sky while the slipstream whipped the water, like giant's tears, from the wing fabric, obscuring my vision. A few patches of vapour, strung out here and there overhead, tossed down a few playful showers that pattered soothingly on the Perspex beside my head, as if to mock my earlier fears.

After we had been flying for about four hours, there appeared, far ahead of us, a great green forest, sleeping in majestic and primeval repose, Batavia hidden somewhere beneath its impenetrable covering of leaves. Gazing at it intently through his bubble, the young gunner at length gave a little chuckle of delight, and attracting my attention, called out, 'Java!', raising his thumb and giving it a little triumphant jerk at the same time. Even as we came in to land, the forest seemed unbroken, and Batavia, though a big city, remained completely concealed under the trees. As we approached land, two long, claw-like structures materialised out of the misty alliance of shore and water, stretching out into the Java Sea for a distance of perhaps a mile, leaving a narrow gap of about a hundred yards between them at the mouth. Gliding down, we touched water just inside the narrow entrance between the breakwaters, continuing on into the outer harbour, and ploughing a boiling furrow of white foam as we went. Now, for the first time since I boarded, I saw the co-pilot who, emerging from the cockpit, and opening a small locker, took out a canvas bucket attached to a long rope which he tossed into the sea. Instantly it filled, leaping and bouncing like a wild sea-creature in our wake. Gradually we lost speed, skimming gently, and then drifting, till finally we stopped. The pilot pulled in the bucket, and, emptying it, stowed it away. Soon, from the side of the breakwater, where it had been tied up, a little rowing boat pulled out, its occupant an old man, who caught a rope tossed to him from the Cat and tied it to a buoy. Our flight was over.

I shook hands with the youthful gunner exchanging with him words of farewell, which neither of us understood, though the sentiments were clear enough. Then, leaving him, I went into the cockpit where I found the pilot sitting with a log-book on his knee, into which he was entering data from his instruments. He looked at me enquiringly. I asked him if we were now free to go ashore, and he said that the co-pilot was going to the office in a little while and would take me with him. This, he explained, was only Tandjong Priok, the port of Batavia, the town itself being about six miles away. But it was easy to get to: I could take my choice of train, tramway or taxi, though he would recommend a taxi. I then said I wanted to ask him two things: first, why he went down to inspect the beached steamer at Banka. He looked at me blandly, saying that it was just for a look-see. But, I retorted, there were other vessels and he did not go down to have a look-see at them. He was in no way put off, explaining with a roguish twinkle in his eye that there were different kinds of vessels and different kinds of look-see. I took the point that General Wavell's pilot observed total discretion in all things, though I had imagined my uniform might have evoked a fuller confidence – and I had my own little secret, too, carefully stowed in my pocket. Then I asked him the second thing: was he not afraid for the Cat in the cumulo-nimbus – after all the wings were flapping and the fuselage was shaken badly in the turbulence. He said that every pilot experienced anxiety in cumulo-nimbus, but at times, such as this, you could not escape it, and he had great faith in the Catalina for she was a 'sound kite'. That was the end of our interview. I shook hands with him warmly, thanking him for bringing me down safely, and then, just to let him know that I was privy to more of his counsels than he suspected, I wished him well on his *return* trip. Suddenly he cocked up his ears.

'Ah, you've been listening, I see!' he said. For an answer I gave him a knowing smile, and, the co-pilot now appearing, I climbed with him into the little boat and we were rowed ashore.

We walked along the breakwater towards the inner harbour where some ships were tied up and unloading was taking place, cargo being carried by coolies to godowns which lined the road on the other side, and behind which rose a stately line of tall palms above a bank with plots of flowers. We had not yet gone halfway along the quay of the inner harbour when suddenly the air-raid siren began to wail, its unexpectedness accentuated by the peacefulness of the scene and the emptiness of the sky. Nevertheless its notes were the prelude to a scene of unimaginable confusion, a vast mob of coolies tumbling out of the ships and godowns and making for the shelter of the bank beyond. They were followed, at a distance, by their women and children, all screaming shrilly, and seemingly abandoned by their menfolk. It was a scene which filled me with alarm, and boded no good for the future.

I gave voice to my concern with the co-pilot, who clearly shared my anxiety. If this was what happened when there was a false alarm – as I was nearly certain this was – what might we expect during a real raid, when bombs were falling? The co-pilot explained that the Javanese were a highly volatile and unpredictable people, rushing like sheep wherever one led; and he could not see them standing up to concentrated bombing such as we had suffered in Singapore.

When we got to the end of the inner harbour, now quite deserted, he pointed out to me where the taxi-stand was, over in front of the harbourmaster's office, though he could not hold out much hope of my being able to engage a taxi. However, when I got there I found that there were several taxis, though only in one did a driver remain, the others having gone to earth along with the coolies behind the ridge. Pointing to my RAF cap, I said to this man, 'Batavia!' 'Koningsplein!' he answered, without a moment's hesitation, and, jumping into the vehicle, I was driven off.

At first we drove through the dock area, rattling over railway lines and boulder cobbles, till we came to the older part of the city, a place of straggling and senile streets, separated from each other by dirty brown canals in place of roads. The houses tended to be wooden, with the attractive dilapidation of old age, and roofed with tiles with a warm, red patina. The siren had driven many indoors in panic. But some were still about, a lithe people, the women's sarongs emblazoning the earthen pavements. After a time we came to the banks of a broad, dirty waterway which suggested both a canal and a river, though I later discovered it to be the River Tjilliwong which connects the harbour with the new Batavia. To this unprepossessing stream the Dutch attach the felicitous name of the Molenvliet, or the Mill Stream, though only an imagination distorted by homesickness could confuse it with some of the more picturesque waterways of the Netherlands. For about twenty minutes we drove along the Molenvliet till we arrived at a much more impressive part of the city, some larger shops and more elegant buildings lining the roadway. The driver turned round to inform me that this was the Rijswijk, which means the Rice Town. At the end of this we crossed a bridge and, driving through a narrower lane, came upon a vast square lined by immemorial banyans in whose shade reposed mansions of great opulence. On the east side of the square we drew up in front of a large building above whose portals was inscribed KONINKLIJKE PAKETVAART MAATSCHAPPIJ, and whose intimidating orthography seemed in harmony with the general, patrician atmosphere of the place. Jumping from his cab, the driver opened the door and pointed to the stairs that led up to the entrance of this imposing building. The fare he asked for his services was naturally in gulden, but it appeared to me to be modest, and, having none of these coins, I tendered the equivalent number of Straits dollars, which being slightly higher in value evoked no question and he pocketed them readily. Then, with appropriate diffidence, I mounted the stairs.

The main office of the Royal Dutch Mail Packet Steamship Co. seemed, on my first entry, to be a vast and, with its tiled floors, an echoing place, an atmosphere of animated improvisation surrounding its large and widely separated desks. All the three services seemed to be sharing its facilities, and across one part of the counter, which bore the notice RAF ENQUIRIES, I addressed myself to the Flight Lieutenant on duty. He asked me breezily where I had come from and when I told him Singapore he asked what boat I was off. I replied that I was off no boat, having come by Cat. 'Oh!' he said, a little surprised, 'and when did you come off this Cat?' I told him about an hour before. 'Any others with you?' he continued, the catechism clearly indicating that he suspected something irregular in my arrival. 'I haven't seen any others this morning!' I told him there were no others – I travelled alone. 'How come you travelled *alone* on this Cat when there are so many others needing to get out of Singapore?' I indicated that the transport of personnel from Singapore scarcely came within my province, but I had papers to deliver to the CO personally.

'Can't be done!' he said peremptorily. 'The CO is far too busy to see anyone!'

'In that case,' I said, 'I'll just wait till he finds time to see me.'

It took two expeditions from the Flight Lieutenant to gain me admittance to the office of the CO, who clearly had been informed of my arrival by Cat, and shared his junior officer's dubiety about my means of travel. 'Come by Cat?' he said, before I could communicate to him the purpose of my visit. I said I did – not enlarging on the statement – but, apologising for my insistence on seeing him personally, I went on to explain that I had been given papers in Singapore with explicit instructions to deliver them to him personally whereupon I delivered the package into his hands, and left the room.

The Flight Lieutenant collected a pro forma on which he proceeded to record my service particulars. Then he asked how much money I needed. The question, both by its nature and its phrasing, borrowed so much from the unique that a ready answer escaped me; parrying defensively, I asked what the others were having. He mentioned a figure of such generous proportions that I compounded for it immediately, and, receiving the counted-out gulden, I signed the receipt with ready bravura. Surprisingly, this frail document got out of Java, being the last testament to my survival to be received at home for over two years. I was then dispatched to a side-counter to be 'kitted out', which process I found amounted to the issue of a knife, fork, spoon and aluminium mug. Thus panoplied against misfortune, I returned to the Flight Lieutenant. 'Now for a billet!' he said, scanning a long list of names and addresses that lay before him, and which, he said, belonged to Dutch families who had volunteered to receive British officers into their homes till more regular accommodation could be arranged for them. He ran his pencil down the page, hovering for a moment over a name, moving on a little, and then returning to it. 'Van der Ploeg?' he mused. 'Sourabaya Jalan?' He thought that might suit me and, writing the name and address on a piece of paper, he handed it to me. One of the taxis at the door, he said, would take me to the place. He asked me to let him know how I got on. It might take a day or two to get me fixed up with a job – probably it would be back to 36 and 100 Squadrons once they were re-formed in Java. In the meantime, could I look in twice a day just to keep in touch, and would I leave my telephone number? Apart from that, time was my own.

As I re-emerged into the splendour of this first Java morning, the bright sunlight dazzled my eyes so that it was through a diaphanous veil that I saw the line of taxis drawn up across the road. In the first, when I approached it, I found the driver with his cheek propped on his clasped hands, leaning against the back of the driving seat in that form of meditation which shares with sleep most of its characteristics except total unconsciousness. When I pushed my paper into his hands, he shook himself like an awakened dog and looked at it; then, muttering 'OK!', he motioned me to step into his vehicle and we drove off. Turning down to the south-east corner of the Koningsplein, we then drove along a main road running south-west, which I later learned was called Kramat. After about a mile this led to a garden suburb, or almost a detached township, called Meester Cornelis, a place of neat Dutch bungalows interspersed with huddled native settlements, and the last outpost of the city on the way to Buitenzorg and Bandoeng. Presently we came to a long, narrow canal lined with trees and a broad road on to which faced some fine bungalows. We drove down to its southern end where we crossed a small concrete bridge, quite Chinese in its little, graceful arch, and pulled up in front of a house, almost opposite it and not far from the end of the road. The building had a roof of warm terracotta tiles and a jutting-out section in front, before the window of which stood a remarkable tree. It was uncommonly thick in the bole, which supported a long cone of dense foliage resembling an ivy tod.

I dismounted, and walked through the little garden up to the front door which, as was the custom in Dutch Indonesia, stood wide open. Not sure how to announce my presence I waited a little, and presently a Dutch schoolboy appeared from the interior of the house. For a moment I looked at him in astonishment – he looked the very re-incarnation of the little gunner on the Catalina: the same blue-striped sailor-suit; the same short, fair curly hair; the frank and open countenance. Only in years could a distinction be drawn, for this boy could not have been more than about ten years old.

'Mevrouw van der Ploeg?' I stammered, reading from the paper in my hand.

'Spreekt u Hollandsh?' he asked.

I shook my head, and he ran off to the back of the house, from which he presently returned accompanied by his mother, a smiling and gracious Dutch lady. Her fluency in English immediately dispelled my fears and, extending her hand, she welcomed me to her home. We went into the drawing-room, which was the front room of the house, sheltered by the remarkable tree. The room was comfortably – indeed elegantly – furnished, its most arresting feature a picture of a narrow street in Nice, the tall yellow houses framing a glorious vista of the Mediterranean, luminously blue, the work, my hostess told me, of a Dutch painter. The large tree beside the window which had engaged my curiosity was, I now learned, a *tandjeong* tree, and they cherished it, shade being 'worth a lot in the tropics'. While we reclined in the comfortable chairs, the boy, without, as far as I could see, instruction, brought tea. The cups were filled and there interposed, almost by way of benediction, that silent moment before drinking, when there came skipping in from the back garden and, quite unaware of my arrival, a remarkable vision of childhood innocence. Seeing a stranger talking to her mother she stopped, full in the doorway, the light surrounding her head like a halo.

'This,' said Mevrouw van der Ploeg, 'is Tineke!'

The childlike beauty of Tineke borrowed nothing from any of the specious aids that ornament can offer, but rested its appeal solely upon simplicity. Her hair was parted at the left side and brushed in a silver swath across her forehead where, secured by a grip, it fell below the ears, curling into the neck. Beneath the sweep of this silver lock the brow was smooth and unclouded; her nose was small, with an engaging little tilt, while two wrinkles curved winsomely down to the corners of her mouth, deepening when she smiled. Her lips, as she stood looking at us, were slightly parted, the revealed teeth superb; and her skin had borrowed from the sun just enough tincture to enrich, but not coarsen, it, and was of that elusive shade which ivory acquires with age. Her eyes were large and gentian in colour, radiating an indefinable innocence. Her dress was simple, the cloth of a kind of Paisley pattern, though it was probably based on traditional *batik* motifs, with brown sun-flowers against a background of blues and greens. A crystal button secured it at the throat, and above it – her only ornament – was a simple, gold pin. The sleeves were gathered up in little rucks below the armpit. Shyly, Tineke came over to meet the 'Englishman', making the kind of curtsey that transforms observers into idolaters. Then we shook hands. Though bilingual in Dutch and Javanese, she had only a few words of English, but this imposed no barriers to friendship, and, her shyness soon melting, we managed over our frail little bridges of communication, partly lingual, partly mimetic, to make our meaning clear enough.

In the evening, Herr van der Ploeg came back from his office, a large, strongly built man who in his younger days had been athletic, but whose activities in this direction had been curtailed in Java, both by his professional duties and by the climate. He occupied a very high post in the government agricultural department, though the nature and importance of it I was not to discover till much later. His professional interests were scientific but he conversed with ease and deep knowledge about the arts and especially about the culture of Java. We had an excellent dinner, mostly of Javanese dishes, the majority of which I was encountering for the first time. Then we sat in the drawing-room, exchanging over coffee reminiscences mostly about Europe, though we did talk about Java, referring with surprising infrequency, to the war.

Soon came the children's bedtime, Tineke prefacing her departure with a repetition of her incomparable little curtsey. Jan – that was her brother's name – indulged in some boyish drollery which, I later discovered, was very typical and amusing. In my bedroom I was introduced to that indispensable appurtenance of Dutch colonial life, the 'Dutch wife', which is a long roll or pillow which you grasp between your arms and legs while sleeping and which markedly reduces the addiction to the itches and skin irritations which plague life in the tropics. One British custom, which I followed and which apparently was unknown in the Dutch dependencies, was to leave my shoes outside my bedroom door for the boy to clean. This, I learned long afterwards, had set up intriguing lines of enquiry on the part of the children. Had my shoes, they speculated, become so offensive to my nostrils that I could not bear to have them in my room beside me at night-time? One other sorrow and disappointment afflicted Jan alone, Tineke not being so personally involved in martial affairs: I was not, alas, a Hurricane pilot!

Out in the back garden was a tree, very insignificant in comparison with the lordly *tandjeong*, but dear to us for it was in the shade of its great profusion of oak-like leaves that we had our breakfast. Of all the hours of the day I always regarded this as the most precious, for the sun had not yet risen to that fierce intensity which, from noon onwards, made life in low-lying Batavia very disagreeable. Apart from the heat the afternoon also brought the rains, regular as clockwork and heralded by a faint rumbling of thunder distantly in the unseen hills about Bandoeng. Soon there came a darkening of the sky and the rolling of the thunder advanced with great rapidity. In Batavia, the vividness and ferocity of the lightning exceeded anything I have experienced elsewhere, and I never freed myself of the fear of being struck by it. The rain sluiced down in a solid cataract, turning the roads into torrents and any pedestrians brave enough to attempt them into drowned cats. But the mornings were different. These were pure felicity, and a deep contentment was ours at breakfast-time. Jan was a notable trencher-man, but Tineke ate sparingly, at times appearing listless, while her mother watched her solicitously. 'She never eats her breakfast well in Batavia,' she explained. 'It's the heat. How different it was when she was on holiday in Friesland!' Friesland? It loomed very large in Mevrouw van der Ploeg's imagination these days in Batavia. During the vacations from Java, they had gone to the island of Ameland which lies off the Frisian coast, where they had rented a wooden farmhouse. Each morning before breakfast, Jan and Tineke would go riding on their ponies along the dunes, Tineke's hair streaming behind her in the wind. When they returned to the farm, ruddy-cheeked and invigorated from their exertions, they ate their breakfast ravenously.

But now Tineke was listless, for these were distant days and the delectable island was inaccessible from the breakfast table beneath the tree in the garden in the Sourabaya Jalan. How long would it be till they were able to taste these joys again? Longer – far, far longer – than any of us at the time ever dreamed.

'A' Flight Vildebeests of 36 Squadron, RAF, in Singapore shortly before the commencement of hostilities. (*Philip Jarrett Collection*)

A Vildebeest of No.36 Squadron seen over Singapore in September, 1936. *(Philip Jarrett Collection)*

Jan van der Ploeg.

Tineke van der Ploeg.

THE CHURCH IN MEESTER CORNELIS

Sunday, 15 February, like the preceding Sunday, when the Japanese landed on Singapore Island, was, in Batavia a halcyon day which even the thunderstorms forbore to sully by issuing with their attendant deluges from their mountain stronghold in Bandoeng. In the afternoon we sat in the garden, enjoying the almost English blandness of the air. Mevrouw van der Ploeg said that they intended going to church for the evensong service, and wondered if I would care to accompany them, the children having asked her to approach me about it. The service being in Dutch, some of it naturally would escape me; but she thought I would understand enough to justify my attendance. Besides, this might be the last chance we had for a long time of going to church together as a family.

About mid-afternoon, therefore, we set off, walking north along Sourabaya Jalan under the trees and beside the canal till we reached its end. Here the trim Dutch bungalows gave way to nondescript native huts, and among these we made our way along children-thronged roads till we came to a cluster of very tall trees. This marked the end of a public garden, long and narrow in shape, with sentinel trees lining each side and a broad double pathway with a central strip of dwarf-palms and variegated bushes – the whole reminding me of the pleasance of a minor Bavarian schloss, without, of course, the dramatic backcloth of the Alps. Along this we walked leisurely, the children running on ahead, till we came in sight of the gleaming white walls and steeply-pitched black roof of the Lutheran church.

It was a striking edifice but recently built, the low walls unpierced by windows, a few vertical slits admitting, in the bright tropical light, a sufficiency of illumination. In the south-east corner where the south transept – in which was the main door – met the nave rose a tall campanile, which was also stark white. At its top was a clock, above which a stubby pyramidal roof supported a large weathercock. Something about it recalled to me the architecture of the old Norwegian stave-kirks, though there was nothing of their bare, rocky settings about the lush surroundings. Doubtless its kinship with traditional Dutch churches was stronger still, but I was less familiar with these. The interior of the church was marked by the same plain angular severity as the exterior. The walls were wainscoted in dark wood to a height of about six feet, the same wood being used for the pews. The simple wooden pulpit was in the middle of the long northern wall of the nave, and above it were the organ-pipes. As in many English country churches, the chairs had woven rush seats. The upper walls were of white, quite unrelieved by carving or decoration. Along with the very steep pitch of the roof, this gave to the building a peculiarly soaring quality, making it appear much larger than it really was.

By the time we entered, the church was already filled, most of the heads seeming to be flaxen, and many very young. We went to the family pew, which was down the right aisle, about the middle of the church, but soon it too was filled with visitors and I could not see where any latecomer would find a seat. The service, which followed was marked by a great piety and dignity, the Lutheran form of worship retaining sufficiently strong affinity with the Scottish Presbyterian liturgy to remove from me any consciousness of unfamiliarity. Contrary, however, to Scottish custom, the congregation remained seated for the singing of the psalms and hymns, while they stood for the prayers; like the Scottish church, the Dutch Lutheran has drawn heavily for its hymnology upon the musical heritage of the German Reformation, and in consequence most of the tunes were well known to me. While ordinary Dutch was naturally beyond my comprehension, I found that the readings from Scripture presented me with remarkably little difficulty, the English version being familiar, and many of the words – especially the basic and recurrent ones – bore a resemblance to Broad Scots, and of course to German, so marked that their meaning was quite clear.

At length we came to the Lord's Prayer which, I imagine, was intended to conclude the service; and the congregation rose to its feet. Reverently, and with bowed heads, they intoned the consoling words, easily familiar in Dutch: 'Onze Vader, die in de hemelen zijt, Uw naam worde geheiligd, Uw koningrijk kome ...' Then, at this most serene and sanctified of moments, something intrusive and infinitely irreverent took place. Fluctuating eerily over the city, and quite drowning the voices of the congregation, there rose the wailing of the air-raid sirens. A cold hand of anger and abhorrence clutched at my heart. Could anything more fittingly typify the actions of the Japanese than this? I took for granted that the congregation would now, in an orderly fashion and as speedily as possible, file out of the church and seek shelter elsewhere; the surrounding woods and gardens must have places of greater sanctuary. But, to my surprise, each stood just where he was, head still bowed.

Clearly the pastor had made no provision for a contingency like this, and stood ineffectually in the pulpit, having no idea what to do. Possibly he thought – and he may well have been right – that the worship of God took precedence over all human activities, even those designed to further personal survival. Against this, what defence might he tender in mitigation were a bomb to fall on this crowded church? At length, he stirred himself to address the congregation in a direct, personal way, laying aside for the moment his formal, liturgical tones. I whispered an enquiry to Mevrouw van der Ploeg about what he was saying, and she told me that he proposed to suspend the service for a little to allow those who wanted to to leave the church. There were shelters, he said, in the garden and he thought it better that the children should be taken there now. No one made the slightest move. No elder initiated the steps that would give the children a lead. I stole a quick glance round the church to see why they declined to leave but all that met my puzzled eyes was the field of flaxen heads, reverently bowed and apparently calm, though this was gently betrayed by a subdued sobbing that I heard coming from several places in the church. Now, too, I became aware of a tightening of the sleeve of my RAF tunic – it was Tineke's hand gripping it firmly in the hope, as if by some osmosis of the spirit, of gaining some consolation thereby.

Then there fell upon my ears another sound, muted as yet but quite distinct from the sirens – it was the faint drumming, coming from somewhere high up in the western sky, of bomber engines. At last, my anxiety giving way to indignation, I felt that the pastor would be driven to some action. Could he not see that he was merely inviting total destruction upon his assembled congregation. But still he stood, frozen into helpless immobility, and while I waited a shrill whine rose above the sound of the approaching bombers, and my spirits revived in an irrational surge of elation. It was a flight of Hurricanes going in to attack; I could not mistake *that* sound!

This in no way removed or even lessened our danger: a bomb jettisoned by a harassed bomber harboured no less destructiveness than an aimed one. Concentrated bursts of machine-gun fire directly above our heads now highlighted our peril, and the pastor must have been of this mind for, now at last galvanised into action, he solemnly raised one hand and, amid the uproar, resumed his prayer: 'Uw wil geschiede, gelijk in den hemel . . .' The words were swallowed up and lost in a shattering explosion that shook the church to its very foundations, to be followed by another. We did not know where the bombs had fallen – clearly not very far away, and over in the direction of the Konigsplein. Still the pastor held his hand high in the air, and when at last the echoes of the explosions had faded into silence he took up again the broken words, his voice quivering under the strain: 'Verlos ons van den booze. Want uw is het Koningrijk, en de Kracht, en de Heerlijkheid, in der eewigheid, Amen!' He sank to his knees. An eerie stillness filled the church, and the air outside. We could hear a faint murmuring of engines fading in the north, and the Hurricanes had gone.

Hurriedly, but in no panic, we rose to leave, the notes of the organ now rising up almost triumphantly to fill the high roof of the church. In the pews voices broke out in excited whisperings. We filed out on to the road, and with a word or a smile to friends walked across to the gardens. I saw more than one handkerchief pressed to dim eyes. Ahead of us, through the gardens, ran Tineke and Jan, their gaiety quite restored. How great a blessing it was, observed Mevrouw van der Ploeg, that children did not understand, or forgot so readily! Not so apt to consolation, I gathered, was her own mind. Clearly her mother's heart was wrung with deep anxiety for her children.

Deserted by the sun, the evening air now felt cool and refreshing on our cheeks, the sky above empty and clear apart from a few down-tatters of cloud, the only couriers we had seen this day from the Bandoeng mountains, which drifted lazily out towards the Java Sea. In the tallest tree-tops one or two awakened flying foxes glided, like ragged carpets, silently from branch to distant branch. Mevrouw van der Ploeg recalled the children to her side and, taking hands, we wandered slowly through the deserted ways of Meester Cornelis, under the lambent sky, back to our bungalow in Sourabaya Jalan.

LAD WI' THE PHILABEG

On the afternoon of Monday, 16 February, an hour or two after the fall of Singapore had been announced on the radio in Batavia, my entrance into the Koningsplein office was observed with unexpected interest by two officers – one RAF, the other naval – who were standing at a distant desk. After exchanging a word or two, the naval officer came over to the counter where I was standing, saying that I might be the very man they were looking for. Was my name McEwan, and had I a cousin called Thomson, a doctor in Singapore? I said that it was, and I had. He then gave a quick glance at his watch. I might, he said, have about an hour to make it in. Thomson was on the *Empire Star* and she was lying at Tandjeong Priok. She was sailing that afternoon.

A brief word of thanks was offered almost on my way out of the office. Speed now was the essence of my mission, and I needed a good taxi. But I saw my hopes dashed, for at the head of the line was an ancient and dilapidated vehicle, its driver a shrivelled and dusky elder of the tribe, who was lolling half-asleep at the wheel. But my air of urgency galvanised him into surprising animation. 'Tandjeong Priok!' I exclaimed, as I jumped into the cab. '*Empire Star*! *Lekas!*' The Morphean shades that haunted his old mind were banished by instant exorcism. We swung round the corner of the Konigsplein and, crossing over to the Rijswijk, set off on our journey northwards along the Molenvliet. Then a sudden idea struck me. '*Matti, matti!*' I called. 'Go Sourabaya Jalan No.1 – after, go Tandjeong Priok!' He applied his brakes vigorously, bringing his vehicle to a shuddering halt. With fraying patience he sat while I tore a page from my notebook and wrote the address on it, He took one glance at it, then, swinging his taxi round in the road, he set off furiously southwards.

Mevrouw van der Ploeg was naturally startled by the abruptness of my irruption, but a fuller explanation would have to wait till later. Had she, I wondered, a large piece of brown paper and some strong string? I needed it for a parcel. The boy was summoned, and dispatched to the kitchen, whence he soon emerged bringing the things I needed. In my bedroom I spread the paper out on the floor. Then taking my Highland dress from its basket, I folded the garments into a neat pile on top of it. With the string I then secured it into a neat and compact parcel. That done, I wrote on the outside, in large capital letters, my name, and underneath I added these words: TO BE LEFT IN AUSTRALIA TILL CALLED FOR AFTER THE WAR. Then I turned the parcel over and wrote the same inscription on the other side.

Now prepared, I gripped my parcel under my arm and ran back to the waiting taxi. The driver's impatience matched my own. Dizzily we sped northwards: Kramat; Koningsplein; the Molenvliet; the Old City; the cobbled dock-road; in swift and blurred procession they hurried by. But I was looking at them as in a dream, my mind being far away. A respected survivor of the war, I saw myself strolling with just that necessary touch of nonchalance into some shipping office

– it might be in Perth or Fremantle, or even Sydney. 'Have you,' I would ask the wondering clerk, 'by any chance a parcel with a Highland dress in it? I sent it off from Java just before the Japs arrived. The name's McEwan!' Circumstances had denied me the pleasure of wearing my kilt in Malaya, but what did that matter compared to the wild intoxication of an 'Eightsome Reel', or the 'Duke of Perth' in that other Perth in the Antipodes!

Much mischance had fallen upon the docks since last I had seen them – godowns in ruins; others scorched and blackened by fire. The inner basin looked larger, denuded now of its ships, though two still remained over at the far side, both far down on their marks. As we drove along the quay towards them I could make out on the counter of the larger one the words I was looking for: EMPIRE STAR. Paying the taxi-driver his fare, I clambered up the gangway, my parcel tucked protectively under my arm, to find the vessel strangely deserted. In the large and empty lounge a steward at length answered my enquiry: was Dr Thomson on board? The doctor? Yes, he thought he was on board. He would go and look for him. I sat down in one of the chairs, casting my gaze round the modest furnishings of the room. It was now all so unnaturally quiet, though doubtless not so long ago on the way from Singapore the scene here was be one of some animation. So absorbed was I in these reflections that the doctor made his silent entrance quite unobserved, and it was with a start that, raising my eyes, I saw him standing at the doorway.

He seemed a little annoyed, as if my arrival had called him away from urgent professional matters. Singapore, and the voyage to Batavia, had certainly snatched a rose from his chaplet: gone – or at least a little tarnished – were the poise, the aspect debonair that had so characterised his presence in Singapore when I saw him last. True, the dark hair was still gleaming and oiled, the smartly cut white naval uniform just noticeably less well creased, but the brow was furrowed, the cheeks greyer, the pouches under the eyes more marked. In his rather languid voice, he told me something of their adventures on the way from Singapore. They had sailed about 3.30 a.m. on Thursday, 12 February in a convoy of about a dozen vessels escorted by the *Durban* (our companion through the Indian Ocean), the *Kedah* (a Straits Steamship vessel, now taken over by the navy), and a couple of others. Most of the ships had service personnel aboard – they themselves had no fewer than 900. Unfortunately, just south of Singapore the light-buoy that indicated the swept channel through the minefield was missing and they were held up there till daylight. About seven o'clock in the morning the Japanese dive-bomber attack started, and continued off and on throughout the day. The *Durban* was hit forward and had suffered casualties. The *Empire Star* itself had received two direct hits and many on board were killed or wounded. That night they ran into the great flotilla of little boats, all trying to escape south through the Banka Strait, and had difficulty not running some of them down. During the following day, Friday they had, by hugging the Sumatran coast, escaped the attention of the bombers, though the rest of the ships further east had been assailed. They had got into Batavia late that night. They were sailing that afternoon. There was some uncertainty about their destination. The boat lying beside them, the *Plancius* – the Dutch Batavia-Singapore ferry – was to be their companion, rumour having it that the *Durban* would convoy them through the Sunda Strait. After that she would escort the *Plancius* to Colombo while they went on alone to a West Australian port, probably Fremantle.

Then I told him the story of my flight to Batavia in the Catalina, and about the Dutch family with whom I was living. Once my two bomber squadrons were re-formed, I would in all probability be joining them again, though I had no idea where. He would be returning to Edinburgh long before I did. Would he give my best wishes to all in Auld Reekie – to all at home? There was not really much more to say. Unless perhaps . . . The mention of Fremantle had at least provided me with a cue. Taking the parcel from under my arm, where it had remained since my arrival on board, I laid it on my knee. I wondered if he might do me a service? This parcel contained my dress kilt. Did he think he could put it somewhere in his cabin, and leave it in a shipping office in Australia when he got there? It had sentimental associations for me. It would cause him no trouble – I would collect it after the war. If it were lost, I should not mind in the least. The little litany of deprecation froze on my lips; and I saw his mouth harden in a tight line, and his eyes darken. 'Certainly not!' he said unequivocally. He had more important things to think about than a dress kilt. Did I not know the ship was full of pregnant women? If he managed to get all them to Australia safely, he would consider he had done well enough. Of course he was right, and I was crestfallen. There was nothing much more to say. With tepid cordiality I held out my hand, and then, with the incriminating parcel under my arm, I faltered down the gangway. Though I had made no compact with the taxi-driver to wait for me, he was still there, smiling a welcome that he had anticipated. I got in and he drove me back to Sourabaya Jalan.

The kindness of my reception was unction to my wounded spirit; Mevrouw van der Ploeg lent a sympathetic ear while I told my story. Now that it was back might she, she asked, have a look at the kilt? I undid the parcel and showed her the garments one by one, explaining their function. Then she summoned the children so that they, too, might see what a Scotsman wore when he was 'all dressed up'.

Teddy Thomson and his ship full of pregnant women got safely to Fremantle, possibly against the odds, as did the *Plancius* to Colombo. Between them they carried 3,000 refugees. Then Teddy returned to Scotland where he pursued his studies in tropical medicine, taking no further part in active hostilities in the war till he returned with the victorious Allied armies to Singapore after the Japanese surrender.

LORD JIM

The seventeenth of February was a Tuesday, and in the afternoon I had just come out of the office after reporting when I became aware of a strange figure shuffling along the pavement in my direction. He wore an RAF officer's khaki and shorts but every part of his body which normally would be exposed was swathed in bandages: his knees, his arms, his neck and face. A narrow slit had been left uncovered for his eyes, and the cap, which sat precariously on top of the white bandaged ball that was his head, completed the grotesqueness of the figure. As always with mutilation or disfigurement, my first reaction was one of unease. Naturally it was quite impossible to recognise anyone disguised like this, and I was preparing to slip past without greeting when the figure stopped me and said 'Hello!' I asked him who he was, and he gave me his name – an officer I knew well in Singapore. And how, I asked him, had he managed to get into this strange shape. All he said was: 'Shall we go along to the Hotel des Indes and have a drink?'

So we set off, walking very slowly and awkwardly for the tight bandages on his knees made the joints nearly rigid, so that he walked almost as if he had wooden legs. We crossed over from the Koningsplein to the canal and then down the Rijswijk on the far side for about a hundred yards before turning into a side-road, where, in front of us, was the Hotel des Indes.

It was a fine building, full of character. In front was the garden with the traveller's trees, a little less majestic in the towering sweep of their fronds than those of the Raffles. The entrance jutted out, with black pillars curiously veined with white pointing. There were a few steps up to the entrance and these gave my companion great trouble. But, putting a hand on his thigh, he managed to lever up each leg in turn and so reach the top. We went into the lounge and, selecting a table in a corner, ordered a couple of drinks. Then he told me his story.

He had sailed from Singapore shortly after midnight on the morning of Thursday, 12 February on one of the merchant vessels of the convoy in which had also been the *Empire Star*, with my cousin on board. They had embarked as many RAF personnel as the ship would carry, and a cargo of ammunition. When daylight came, the Japanese dive-bombers had set upon them; and attacks continued throughout the day, though they had escaped without serious damage. That night – still the twelfth – they ran into the escaping flotillas of the little ships in the Banka Strait, but got through that too. Next day, the thirteenth, the bomb-attacks began again with daylight, and though several tankers that were with them were set on fire or sunk, they themselves managed to survive. When darkness fell, they thought they had finally won through, for they should be in Batavia by morning. But about nine o'clock that night, when they were no more than fifty miles from Java, there was a muffled but heavy thud up near the bows and the ship shuddered and then stopped. A submarine had been lying in wait and they had been torpedoed. Soon the vessel began to settle by the head.

There was no panic, though all felt natural anxiety, for the boats would never be able to take all the men who were packed on board. For a time they stood around, waiting for orders. Presently the captain and his officers came down from the bridge and were joined by others from the engine room. They came to the after-deck and ordered one of the lifeboats to be swung out on its davits. As this was being done they explained to the waiting men that they were going up to the bows to inspect the damage and decide what was to be done to ensure their safety. Then they climbed into the lifeboat, were lowered to the water, and disappeared from view under the forward bulge of the hull. They seemed to be a long time away; in the meantime the vessel continued to sink rapidly. Then somebody caught sight of a lifeboat pulling away as fast as it could into the darkness. At first the truth was so unthinkable that the men just stared after it in disbelief. But one or two, to make certain, ran along the scuppers right up to the forecastle-head, looking over to see if the captain's boat was still there; but, of course, it was gone. It was the *Lord Jim* situation, fiction being re-enacted as stark reality: the boat, with its officers, had pulled off into the night, abandoning the ship's complement to save themselves. Was it the knowledge of the holds filled with ammunition, liable to go up at any moment, that had prompted this dastardly act?

When the truth became known, a natural howl of indignation rose from the decks, but it died into silence for the RAF were disciplined men. Collecting what life-jackets they could, they formed up on deck, waiting quietly as the ship went down under them. Soon they were struggling in the water, clinging to whatever they could find – planks, rafts. He himself had grasped a plank which was just able to keep him afloat. In this part of the Java Sea the currents run fast, for it is not far from the Sunda Strait; and soon they were scattered over a wide expanse of the dark waters. When dawn at last broke, he could see men everywhere, clinging desperately to little bits of flotsam. Many he saw, too tired to hold on any longer, slip off to their death. He had only his shirt and shorts, and all that day – Saturday the fourteenth – he clung to his plank under the pitiless sun. Burned and blistered, he still held on, though he thought there was little hope of rescue. Then, some time in the afternoon, an Australian destroyer hove in sight. She was on her way from Palembang to Batavia, and fortunately for them had been delayed. Soon she was busy with rescue work. She let down her boats to pick up the stragglers from their planks and spars, while she occupied herself with the bigger rafts. It was a lengthy and difficult task, for the men were by now scattered over a wide area, and it took all afternoon, but they finally succeeded in getting over 200 men aboard. On the verge of collapse, my companion was dragged from his plank to safety. Much of the skin had been burned from his body by the action of sun and salt sea-water; yet he was amazingly cheerful and uncomplaining. What most of all surprised me was the absence of recrimination on his lips. What he preferred to talk about was the courage and kindness of the men of the Australian destroyer, who refused to give up the search till every man afloat was rescued.

Afterwards we walked slowly back to the office in the Koningsplein; and there we parted. I never saw or heard of him again. There was still a chance that he might get on a boat before the Japanese launched their attack on the island, but hope was fading, and I supposed he would have to stay and take his chance with the others. He had been snatched once from the very jaws of death, but in his present condition I think the odds were against its happening again.

By Saturday, 21 February, I had been in Batavia for twelve days and, chafing at my inactivity, I was longing to become involved in things again. Gnawing at my mind was the possibility that, just as at Seletar, I might linger here unnoticed and the squadron complements would be made up without me. But I need not have distressed myself – I had not been forgotten.

When, that morning, I went into the office, I found there was a message for me. I was to rejoin 36 and 100 Squadrons, and was to report in front of the office next morning at ten. Meanwhile would I go round to the Nederlanden Hotel where Squadron Leader Wilkins, who had now been promoted to command the squadrons, wished to see me. His purpose was to send me out that afternoon in a Dutch car to Tjillitan aerodrome to collect some civilian flying charts that were waiting for me there. That was speedily accomplished, and when I got back the Squadron Leader said he would see me next morning before the office at ten.

Next morning, my last in Batavia, I was up betimes and said goodbye to Herr van der Ploeg before he left for his office, which he was still attending normally. Then, a little later, we had breakfast for the last time under the oak-leaved tree in the garden. Seldom have I been more conscious of the poignancy of parting. Thereafter a minute or two sufficed for all the little packing I had to do, and soon I was ready to go. Together we went to the front door, and stood for a little in the lee of that provider of invaluable shade, the *tandjeong* tree, cloaking the turbulence of our emotions beneath a brittle facade of triviality. Then at length Mevrouw van der Ploeg said that they realised that since I was going back to my squadrons I would not be able to carry many extras – nevertheless Tineke and Jan wondered if I would accept a very little present from them. Thereupon the children, in turn, presented me with a photograph of themselves taken in the clothes in which I had first seen them and for which I had expressed some favour. To these photographs I became enormously attached, coming to regard them as a kind of talisman, and through all the vicissitudes that followed they, almost alone of my possessions, survived. Now as I write they are before me still. Then, knowing that it would be a long time before I was likely to see them again, if ever, I shook hands with Tineke and Jan, trying hard to dissemble the emotions that agitated me. Once more Tineke gave her inimitable little curtsey bringing a lump to my throat, and, turning to their mother, I shook hands and walked off down the path. I crossed the road, not turning to look back till I reached the arch of the little bridge. Then a brief glance showed Mevrouw van der Ploeg standing between her children, a hand on each shoulder, while Tineke and Jan waved their hands in farewell. I returned their greeting, then, crossing the bridge, I walked off along Sourabaya Jalan, my basket in my hand, in the direction of the Koningsplein.

When I got there, the truck was waiting in front of the office. I found it piled high with surprising and rather basic things like mattresses and blankets, pots and pans, boxes of food, and – the only indication of our military function – a few rifles. There was another car coming with us and in it were some office staff whose purpose was to see that we had all we needed in our new quarters. But among all those present, there were none from the squadrons I recognised except Wilkins.

Both cars had Dutch drivers. We left the Koningsplein, our way taking us back through Meester Cornelis, and presently we were out in the Javanese country-side which looked extravagantly lush with rice and vegetable fields, roughly screened from the roadway by palms, tamarinds and fruit trees. Here and there were some tumbledown shacks swarming with little brown half-naked children, and now for the first time I saw the mountains whence had come the fierce thunderstorms that had plagued our afternoons. They were strung out along the south-eastern horizon, had edges like a saw, many of them plumed with white vapour, and all were of a deep cobalt blue. Then we came to Tjillitan. It was an immense, sprawling airfield, the colour of a pumpkin, and set down in the midst of a teeming wilderness of paddy fields and jungle. Long tentacles of dispersal-roads ran out from the runways till they lost themselves in the surrounding bush. It seemed to me to be admirably designed for defensive purposes, the numerous hillocks and ridges providing excellent protection for the parking bays against anything but a direct hit. Doubtless heavy pattern-bombing such as the Japanese had carried out against Seletar would reduce its effectiveness, but I could not see it putting the place completely out of action. As we drove round the perimeter, I noticed several Hudsons tucked away from sight, and even a Hurricane or two, but these were further out still and under heavy-leaved trees.

On one runway a great mass of Australian soldiers was milling about rather aimlessly, great husky men with prodigious muscles. We learned later that they were part of the Australian 7th Division who had been fighting the Vichy French in Syria. Pulled hurriedly out of the Middle East, they had been recalled for the defence of the homeland, which was now threatened. But an even greater and more immediate threat had blown up in the East Indies and they had been diverted to Java. Yet, as so often happens in the cross-currents of divided purpose like this, their guns and equipment had not been diverted and were now on their way to Australia without them. The 7th Division were, in effect, virtually weapon-less. That did not end their troubles. They wore sleeveless shirts and brief shorts which had originally been khaki but were now bleached by the Syrian suns and numerous washings to a pale lemon. Against the dark-green of the landscape their bare arms, knees and faces looked either beetroot-red or sallow. Apart altogether from the Japanese, they were easy targets for every kind of mosquito and other pest that the Java jungle spawned.

At last we came to the assembly point. Here we caught up with the adminis-trative and ground staffs of 36 and 100 Squadrons who had all collected here, except for the flying crews who were staying with their machines and would fly them to our new airstrip. I found the reunion greatly exciting, for these were the men I had been with at Seletar, whose companionship I had missed bitterly since they had left Singapore. Sadly, however, not all were here, for the fighting at Palembang and the headlong rush south to the tip of Sumatra, with all the confu-sion and panic that developed there – not, of course, among them – had taken their toll, both of men and machines. But no one could doubt that the two squadrons were still very much a fighting unit. We waited for some time while the checking and marshalling went on; and then I managed to get into a car beside

Trillwood, the Adjutant, and several other officers. At last we moved off, a Dutch car from the Koningsplein leading. Now for the first time I was able to ply my companions with questions about their experiences since they had left Singapore, and by the time we had got to our destination, a pretty clear picture of it had formed in my mind.

Palembang, they said, was the first time they had been given a chance. This came about through a stratagem which, right up to the end, the enemy seemed never to have detected. It came about in this way. About ten miles north of the town of Palembang was the large airfield which was known as P.1, which, since it was also the commercial airport, was also very familiar to the Japanese, and everybody else. Just beside it were the important oil refineries of Pladjoe and Soengi, and the conjunction of airfield and refineries made this a prime target for the Japanese. What the enemy feared was a wholesale demolition which might hold up production even if they succeeded in capturing the oil-fields, and to prevent this they dropped, on 14 February, a large number of paratroops in the jungle surrounding the airfield and the refineries. Confused and bitter hand-to-hand fighting ensued but, at least in the early stages, the defences held firm. There were strong hopes that the counter-attacks which were planned for the fifteenth would clear the enemy out of the area.

About fifty miles south of Palembang was the secret airfield, which was known as P.2. It looked no more than a wide gap in the jungle, and, of course, was clearly visible from the air, but strangely it had not aroused Japanese suspicions, and neither was its purpose suspected nor its surroundings attacked. This was surprising, for throughout the Malay campaign one feature had been the comprehensive and exact nature of the Japanese intelligence and spy system. However, in this case the immunity was crucial for hidden in the surrounding jungle were the Vildebeests and Hurricanes, waiting for the counter-attack. On the morning of 15 February, large numbers of barges and launches were reported in the Moesi River, which leads up to the town, having come from Muntok on Banka Island where the larger transports had anchored. Now the machines from P.2 were unleashed and they kept up their attacks throughout the day. They achieved great success, and with the defenders of P.1 and the refineries still resisting strongly, the Japanese assault looked like it might be repulsed. Then, in a few hours, the situation completely altered, and all because of baseless rumours. Reports of quite fanciful Japanese successes were passed from unit to unit, while all that was certain was that the river forces had succeeded in joining up with the paratroops, who had in fact taken a bad mauling. Inexplicably, the order was given to evacuate Palembang and a confused withdrawal began along the one jungle road that led south to Oosthaven at the south end of the island. At the port even greater confusion developed through the blind determination of a port officer to see carried out an order which he said he had received, that no equipment was to be taken to Java. Eventually the cool-headedness and courage of a few RAF officers restored some kind of order to the situation, and invaluable equipment was shipped over to Java.

We drove along the Bandoeng road and came at length to the small railway junction which is called Tjikampek, where the railway line forks, one branch going on to Bandoeng and the other swinging round north-west towards the coast at Indramajoe, and eventually to Cheribon and the north-coast route to East Java. It was at this point that we turned off the main road into a side way that zig-zagged among the rubber plantations. After about a mile we drew up in front of a row of native huts strung out along the side of the road. The Dutch driver in the leading car got out and, pointing to the huts, told us that they were our new quarters. It would have been surprising had we not experienced some alarm and despondency. By this time, of course, we were not unduly fastidious about living quarters – indeed, all the talk about the need for concealment and remoteness in the choice of our airstrip had steeled us for some measure of austerity. But our anticipation stopped just short of this. Only the stoutest hearts among us did not to some extent quail; the airmen expressed their displeasure in their usual earthy manner; and from a scene so empty of consolation only one crumb of comfort could be extracted: it would be a miracle if some Jap airmen, flying over Tjikampek, ever took this for an RAF Mess.

THE AIRSTRIP AT TJIKAMPEK

Only with difficulty did we stifle our dismay. We looked into the hovels and found them cramped, dirty and without a stick of furniture. Had their erstwhile occupants been dispossessed to make way for us, and then taken to the jungle, they could scarcely have noticed any diminution in their comforts. Naturally, the air was soon vibrant with complaint and lurid imprecation. But it is a typical trait of the British soldier to make his lamentation merely a cloak for doing something about it. So, while the tongues wagged the hands were far from idle, and a mattress being rolled out here and a valise unbundled there showed that they were making a virtue of necessity. The cooks – these resilient lads – were resigned to any makeshift. Contented as long as they had a fire and a pot to hand, they had discovered a kitchen of sorts in a ramshackle shed at the end of the huts, and now were busy. The Adjutant, Flying Officer Trillwood, whose earlier life had been spent with jewellery in the City of London and who was the most patient and conciliatory of men, was going round from room to room smoothing out problems and cooling tempers. 'After all,' he assured the malcontents, 'it's not as if you were to be here *for ever!*'

So we settled in to the best of our abilities. Then came the welcome call from the kitchen: 'Come and get it!' The anodyne that the cooks had prepared against disaffection was, by any strict standard, modest, but it wrought a marked change in our disgruntlement. When at last it was over and we sat propped up and contented against the walls of the hut, we decided it was now time to set off to inspect the airstrip. We crossed over the road from the huts and followed a plantation track which ran at right angles to it into the rubber. After about half a mile, we came to a crossroads. Here, hidden among the trees, was a long, low depression rather like a disused quarry, and in it, stacked in great mounds like potato pits, were gleaming yellow bombs and barrels of aviation spirit.

From this arsenal, the road turned to the east, continuing through the rubber plantation for about another half mile. The south side was lined, right up to the verge, by the rubber trees, while the north side was roughly cleared but unplanted. After leaving the rubber, the road continued briefly across a tract of tall scrub that sloped gently upwards towards a low ridge, from the top of which the airstrip fell away gently to the east. It was a very rough-looking place, covered with short, rank grass, the surface appearing to be very uneven. It was certainly not a place pilots would find it easy to land on, especially in tricky wind conditions or – more seriously still – at night, if our plans for an attack by moonlight still held. The far end of the strip was ringed by an impenetrable palisade of trees and brushwood and there was clearly no way out in that direction. But the whole unkempt place had one advantage over every other airfield I have ever served on: not even Birnam Wood looked less like what it really was.

Along the south – and longer – side of the strip was a thin border of tall dry grass interspersed with thickets of bush and low scrub, behind which was the

rubber plantation with its neat rows of regimented trees. Just about in the middle
of this strip a little oval patch of grass had been cleared, big enough to allow two
short posts to be driven into the earth and a rough deal board nailed on top to
provide a makeshift seat. In all the clearing this was the only visible evidence that
men had ever been here. Behind this seat, and well back among the rubber trees
where it was quite hidden both from the air and the airstrip, was our Ops Room,
though to give it this grandiloquent title is misleading for among all the control
centres ever operated by the RAF, the Ops Room at Tjikampek must occupy a
little niche of insignificance quite on its own. There was hardly anything to it –
a green tent, and inside a rough deal table knocked together from a few boards
which served as our chart table, though the charts matched the table in primi-
tiveness, being the few civil airline sheets I had been given on my visit to
Tjillilitan. At first we could not even sit down to study them, for there was
nothing to sit on, and when someone eventually brought in an old wooden box,
its possession became an object of keen rivalry. There was one other appliance:
an old, battered storm-lamp which hung by a string from the roof of the tent –
and among all my memories of Tjikampek it seems to occupy a very central place.
Even at midday the rubber trees filled the tent with a crepuscular gloom, and the
lamp seemed always to be lit. In its yellow and uncertain glow, flickering in the
wayward draughts, the faces of the flying crews as they pored over the charts,
animated in discussion of some plan or tactic, took on the questing, adventurous
look of Elizabethan sea-dogs.

There was indeed one other item, though we never used it. This was the look-
out post, not very far from the Ops Room, which had been built by natives before
our arrival – obviously skilled tree-climbers. A frail and spidery structure of
bamboos which projected a good way above the tree-line, it was so skilfully
disguised by branches and leaves that it looked at first glance just like an especially tall tree. Right at its top was a small atap-and-bamboo box, accessible only
by rough slats of wood nailed across the bole to form a ladder. But this spindly
eyrie swayed so disconcertingly in the wind that all our efforts to coax an airman
to climb aloft and man it fell upon unresponsive ears. So it swayed there, remote
and tenantless as a winter rookery. For our safety we should have to trust to
concealment or to whatever warning the Dutch would be able to provide for our
benefit.

Next morning we spent on the strip, some of us occupied with our charts and
plans, the engineers and fitters busy with the Vildebeests which, having flown in,
were now hidden in the bush. That filled our time till midday when we collected
near the Ops Room before setting off back to the huts for lunch. It was just then
that I thought I saw something moving among the trees at the far end of the
airstrip, though my companions assured me there could be no one there, for there
was no road to the place except by coming down past us, and we had seen no
one. But I was not convinced and, deciding to investigate, set off for the end of
the strip. I found that the thicket did indeed harbour some visitors: on a bank
under the shade of the thick branches were about half a dozen Dutch soldiers
dressed in green, reclining, and obviously feeling the heat. I approached and
spoke to their leader.

They were much older than normal soldiers, being mostly grey-haired and paunchy, not in good physical condition, and obviously they felt their closely woven cotton uniforms uncomfortable, for the sweat stood out in beads on their brow and down the sides of their necks. They said they were Landstorm (or Homeguards) and had been detailed to patrol the jungle round about the airstrip to prevent any native damaging our aircraft. Not to draw attention to themselves, they were keeping under the trees and out of sight. For a little I sat down beside the Corporal in charge, an elderly man, sallow, with a scrawny neck and intense eyes. At first I thought that he adopted a supercilious attitude, concluding that his interlocutor was a mere airman, but he had some warrant for his presumption for he was a very learned man, and soon began talking with authority about Shakespeare. He said that in his pack he always carried a copy of *Hamlet*, and drew great moral and spiritual sustenance from it, especially in these disturbed days. Vondel too – did I know Vondel? I said my acquaintance extended to no more than having heard his name, though I knew he was a poet. This ignorance seemed still further to fan his condescension. He made no reference to what he did in private life, though I took him for an academic. Meanwhile his companions lay on the bank beside us, listening but not saying a word; whether they understood English I do not know. When at length I rose to leave, they gave a little nod of farewell. I never saw them again and do not know what happened to them.

Arriving back at the other side of the strip I found that my companions had gone, all except Gotto, one of the flying crews, who was sitting on the wooden seat beside the rubber trees. A little apart from him stood a Javanese soldier clad in green, with a long *kris* dangling from his belt. Gotto, having served for some years as a civilian in Malaya, spoke the language, and now he was leaning forward, his elbows on his knees and his hands beneath his chin, talking quietly to the soldier. Malay is a melodious language and their voices, as they talked quietly to each other, had a soft, sleepy note. I sat down beside Gotto, not disturbing their conversation. In the meantime, fitfully over the trees, there drifted from distant jungle villages the rhythmic drumming of tom-toms. Throughout the day this sound was rarely absent; as soon as night fell, it increased markedly; and long into the night these primitive and warning instruments boomed away, calling and answering to each other in their mysterious tongues. After a time the soldier lapsed into silence; then, straightening himself up and taking in the buckle of his belt one hole, he bid a quiet farewell to Gotto and nodded silently to me before wandering off into the jungle in the direction of the Ops Room. I asked Gotto what they had been talking about. 'The war!' he said. 'That soldier was telling me that he is quite certain that a week from now he will be dead!'

For a little we sat on in the hot midday sun, neglecting to return for lunch. Then I saw Gotto lift his head and turn it a little to one side as if listening. For a moment I watched him, thinking that he had heard aircraft engines. Then he gave a little *sh-sh-sh-ing* sound, no more than a whisper.

'Don't move your head,' he said, 'but have a glance along to your right!'

I turned my eyes as directed; there, just at the edge of the strip, was an immense snake, its head lifted right above the grass and its tongue flickering spasmodically in its open mouth. With glassy eyes it watched us intently, while its head swayed ever so gently from side to side. Its incredible size, and the look of cold malevolence in its little beady eyes, froze me into clammy fear. I knew very little about snakes. Indeed, I never imagined that a creature like this existed, let alone knowing what to do when confronted with it at such close quarters beside this remote airstrip.

'What do we do now?' I whispered apprehensively to Gotto.

'Nothing!' he said. 'Don't move!'

'But it'll attack!' I urged.

'It won't attack,' he said, 'if you keep perfectly still and don't meddle with it.'

After a while, it seemed to tire of this distant reconnaissance. Then it lowered its head and the long body, slowly and hypnotically, slithered in sinuous waves out on to the short grass. Now I could see the real size of the creature. Along its back was a series of jade islands, each with a bright golden shore. They were distributed in perfect symmetry against a background of black and russet-brown. A broad yellow band, like a bib, ran down its belly from the head. The creature looked lethal, and yet there was a sinister beauty about it. There was also something more. From the flickering tongue, the beady eyes, and the bejewelled body there seemed to flow out, as in waves, a hypnotic and paralysing power. It was certainly not difficult to imagine an animal or a bird rooted to the spot just as we were and quite helpless to flee.

At length the serpent arrived on the grass just in front of us. There it slowly arranged its endless body into a series of wide, piled coils. When that was done, it slowly began to raise its head till it was up to the level of our own. Then it began a very systematic scrutiny of us, so close that it took all my strength not to move or bolt. First the head swayed to one side, eyeing us carefully from that angle. Then it moved over to the other. Meanwhile its mouth, which was slack and half open, gently panting, revealed an interior which was not red as I expected but intensely white. Still not sure of us, it brought its head round again to the front, and, with infinite caution and alertness, eyed us face to face. Never for a moment faltering, Gotto stared straight ahead into the little glistening black eyes. This was more than I could take. I thought that a sudden thrust of that head, or whip of that great tail, and we should be done for. I whispered that we had got to do something before it was too late, but Gotto sat frozen like stone, staring the creature out. 'Keep absolutely still!' he whispered.

The snake was the first to crack. For a moment or two it waved its head slowly from side to side in a gesture of bafflement that was almost human. Then the tension that had quickened that great body seemed to drain out of it. The head sagged and sank slowly to the ground and the coils unrolled. Then the sinuous dynamics of propulsion swelled beneath the resplendent livery of its skin. Slowly it crossed in front of us, and 'flowed' silently into the rough grass of the bush, vanishing as mysteriously as it had come. I was limp with relief. Then a torrent of questions poured from my tongue. If it had decided to attack us, would it have struck at us with its fangs, or whipped its tail round us and crushed us to death? Gotto said that its sheer size meant it was a constrictor – he thought it was a python – and it lived by crushing its victims. It could swallow things as big as goats, but it would not attack a human being, always provided he sat perfectly still and stared straight at it. I had just seen what happened. It just sat watching us, trying to work up the psychological ascendancy that was necessary before it would attack. But it had not managed it, and so ended up by thinking better of the whole business, and calling it off. Having no desire to invite a second encounter with our sinister visitor, we sat where we were for a time in order to allow it to get well away into the jungle. Then when we thought it was safe enough, we walked up over the ridge to the road and made our way back to the huts and a very late lunch.

Next afternoon I rested, like the others, for a time in the huts, leaving early, though the day was still very hot, to return alone to the airstrip. My purpose was to have the charts to myself for a time so that I might study them more closely, there being little opportunity to do so at any other time. I had got no further than the end of the rubber plantation, where the track crossed the scrub towards the ridge at the end of the airstrip, when I was aware of a strange noise coming from above the trees. It sounded like aero-engines, but its strangeness lay in a mingling of a high-pitched whine, like that of a fighter, and the deep drone which is associated with a bomber. For a little I stood, listening intently, in the shade of the trees; then, just above my head, and almost sweeping the branches, there shot out a Navy O. It was the first time I had seen that formidable aircraft at close range. No sooner had he left the edge of the rubber plantation than the pilot threw his machine into a very steep bank, and, pivoting on a wing-tip, sped along the road in the direction of the bomb dump. I held my breath, fearing discovery, for he could not fail to see the yellow bombs gleaming under the leafage, but blessedly, just short of the fatal spot, he put his machine into another tight turn and vanished over the forest. I sighed with relief, for a bomb dropped on our dump might have caused the greatest havoc and jeopardised our whole venture.

But my anxiety was not to end there for a moment later a second Navy O appeared, this time gliding silently as an owl just above my head. Once clear of the trees its engine gave a great roar as, making an incredibly tight turn, the machine vanished back over the rubber plantation. By this time I had sought the protection of the biggest rubber tree bole I could find, and keeping out of sight as much as possible I waited anxiously to see what would happen. I had not long to wait, for presently an enormous Japanese bomber, the largest military aircraft I had seen of any nationality, followed by four fighters came lumbering almost at tree-top level over the plantation. Painted a deep green, and much splotched over with brown camouflage markings, it blended admirably into its surroundings. It was, however, far from airworthy, the engines making a strange grinding sound and one of its four propellers turning very slowly. It showed all the evidence of having undergone attack, or else some very serious mishap had befallen the engines. I assumed it was flying so very low to escape detection from hostile aircraft; this would also give it greater security if an attack developed. Round it, buzzing solicitously like angered bees round their threatened queen, were its four fighters. Clearly a bomber of this size, and with its escort, was not engaged on any normal reconnaissance. Could it be that some of the Japanese Generals were conducting a survey, in person, of West Java to reconnoitre the land preparatory to invasion? At that time I had no knowledge what their practice was in these matters, but the fate of Admiral Yamamoto at a later date, while engaged on a similar inspection, adds some substance to the speculation.

My first impulse was to get in touch with one of our fighter bases. If a message could have been dispatched immediately to Tjillilitan or Semplak – both near Batavia – or Kalidjati – a little to the east of us, and the main Dutch base – there might just have been time for fighters to scramble and intercept. But, alas, there was no telephone at the airstrip, nor, as far as I knew, anywhere near the huts; and even if there had been, too much time would have been lost in getting there. With this prime target within our grasp, I was powerless to alert the fighter squadrons. I had no idea where the bomber had originally crossed the Java coast, but its nearest base was probably Palembang in Sumatra, or Kendari in the Celebes, and at its present desperately slow speed that was still very far away. Even in an undamaged condition, and with its four fighters, it was still a target well within the compass of a flight of Hurricanes. Had we managed to intercept and shoot it down, this might have had important repercussions on the campaign that was just about to open, though whether it could have delayed, or materially altered, the final outcome is more open to question.

Either by design or accident the aircraft, however, had stumbled upon our hide-out, and though apart from myself there was no one about, the men all being in their quarters, the Japanese could not have failed to detect the purpose of the place. So the surprise that we had counted upon as essential for the success of our enterprise was already lost. Nor was this the only time that Japanese aircraft visited Tjikampek, for a little later a native brought to us, not knowing what it was, a jettisoned aluminium long-range Japanese petrol tank. Offering a small reward for any others like it, we soon had a collection that had been picked up around the airstrip, which testified to the scope of Japanese reconnaissance. Clearly, our position was well known to the enemy and our P.2 stratagem, even if we had had the opportunity of putting it into effect, would in all probability have failed.

Standing behind the rubber-tree, I watched the huge bomber slowly making its way northwards, shepherded by its fighters. Hopefully I waited for an attack by our fighters, but nothing happened. It never rose above the jungle level, and finally faded from sight on the horizon that marked the north Java coast.

Shortly before we began to pack up our charts before returning for dinner, a Dutch green military car arrived from Batavia. The driver was a Dutch subaltern who said he would like to speak to our Commanding Officer privately. We all left the little Ops Room tent immediately so that they could have the privacy he asked for. After a while, I was summoned to attend. I found the CO and this Dutch officer studying a chart, which it seemed he had brought with him, and was now spread out on the table before them. Their faces had highlights and dark shadows, cast by the yellow glow from the oil-lamp, and they looked very grave. I immediately concluded that the officer had brought the operational orders for some strike, and they were discussing some of the details. But I was somewhat surprised when the CO raised his face from the chart and told me that a request had come from Batavia for our 'liaison officer' to return with this officer tonight. General Stilling, at Dutch Headquarters, wanted to have a word with him about the co-ordination of our squadrons in the general pattern of defence. We had no liaison officer, of course, but he had decided to send me.

Almost immediately, we set off on our journey to Batavia. Very soon we were in heavily wooded country and here we left the main road, turning down a side-track that lost itself among the trees. My companion's command of English was no more than rudimentary, but he led me to understand that he had a message to deliver to a military outpost in the forest. Eventually we arrived at a small clearing round about which were a number of green tents, well under the trees and so skilfully camouflaged that at first I did not detect them at all. My guide led me to the largest of these and, taking me inside, introduced me to a group of Dutch officers. They did not speak English, but I gathered he was telling them he had collected me to take back to Batavia for a conference about the use of British aircraft in the ensuing campaign. The face of the man who seemed to be in charge of the proceedings lit up expectantly.

'Hurricanes?' he asked. Seemingly in doubt, my companion turned to me for guidance.

'No,' I said. 'Vildebeests!'

His face fell. Disdainfully he turned round to the rest of the group, and delivered himself of a short, bitter oration, the explosive if incomprehensible Dutch leaving me in little doubt about the low regard in which he held the Vildebeests. Even more painful was the fact that it seemed to be punctuated with oaths, and about one, of a blasphemous nature, I could harbour no doubts at all. This outburst wounded me sharply. I might have swallowed the discourtesy to myself; what I could never forgive was the disrespect shown to the very brave men who flew our machines, and who were here hazarding their lives to protect such as the man who threw the insult. There was nothing further to be gained by staying here. The end of the interview left me with no regrets; crestfallen, but inwardly indignant, I followed my guide out through the encampment towards the car.

Strolling aimlessly about the clearing were some Javanese soldiers. They were dark men with surly, scowling faces, and they had long, bloodthirsty-looking parangs swinging from their belts. My companion told me that they were Madoerese from the island of that name, lying to the north-east of Java, just off Soerabaya. I was to hear a lot about the ferocity and military prowess of these warriors, and their appearance certainly fitted in very well with this reputation. If, my companion assured me, the Japanese landed on Java, the Madoerese would carve them up – and he illustrated his words with gestures of so grisly a nature that, despite the fact these men were our allies, I was momentarily put a little out of sympathy with the Madoerese way of waging war. In the event, I believe that their ferocity waned in face of other opponents no less renowned for that quality.

At length we arrived in Batavia. We motored through a part of the city that was unfamiliar to me, and some of the streets were more dilapidated than I imagined existed in this rich city. Presently we came to a road which was lined on one side by some tall but undistinguished buildings, while on the other was a grove of straggling, down-at-heel-looking trees. Among these I could make out a few rows of wooden army huts. My guide gave a jerk of his thumb towards one of the larger buildings; 'HQ!' he said, using the English abbreviation. We stopped at the opposite side of the road in front of one of the huts, which had a notice above the door and looked like an Adjutant's office. We got out and, taking me into this office, he explained to the clerk on duty the purpose of my visit. The clerk kept nodding his head up and down. Then, with the curtest of leave-takings, my escort walked out of the door, jumped into his car, and was off. Leaving me in the office, the clerk went off to find out what was to be done about me. Then, after a time, he returned, indicating that I was to follow him. He led me out of the hut along a pathway under the trees and into another hut, where he ushered me into a small, plain room. It was sparsely furnished with an iron bed, a chest of drawers, a table and a chair.

'Bed!' he announced, in English.

'But . . .' I stammered, 'General Stilling?'

'Morning!' he said. His rather bleak, monosyllabic utterance dissuaded me from trying to get any further information from him.

Later I had dinner. It was in a large and almost deserted dining-room with merely a handful of airmen and soldiers sitting in scattered groups. The meal was of rice and stewed meat, and was ample. What I found most surprising about the place was the complete absence of any sense of urgency. The soldiers sat about, morose and lethargic, munching away at their meal. My lack of Dutch meant that I could not speak with them, but their possession of it did not seem to encourage them to speak much among themselves.

As darkness was falling, I left the huts and took a desultory stroll along the road. Here, too, the houses seemed unkempt; even in the gardens the weeds appeared to be disputing with the flowers as to which had the mastery, and this seemed a very un-Dutch thing. The road looked as if it led into the city, and I was briefly tempted to make an excursion to the Koningsplein. A half-hour in the Hotel des Indes or the Nederlanden would help to cheer my spirits after the gall I had tasted in the jungle encampment, and the bleak comforts of my barrack room, but a little reflection counselled against this rashness. It was getting dark and I was in a strange city. It was even possible –though unlikely – that General Stilling might want to see me tonight. If he did send for me, and found that I was missing and only turned up later from a hotel in the city centre, that would create a very bad impression. So I retraced my steps to the camp, and went early to my hard bed.

Next morning I was up at first light. Outside, the street seemed deserted though I could hear some men moving about in the huts. When I went for breakfast, I found the dining-room even more deserted and no less silent than on the previous night. Afterwards, I went back to my room, tidied up my few belongings, and then sat for a time at the window looking out at the empty street.

Then, at length, the door of the large building opposite opened. The girl who came out was tall and svelte, with corn-ripe hair, finely cut, sun-tanned features and lithe, brown and not too heavily muscled legs. She wore a military uniform of sky-blue with a short skirt and a slim forage-cap set at a captivating angle on her head. She tripped down the stairs and then came across the road to the Adjutant's office. When her mission was accomplished, she retraced her steps, mounted the stairs, and disappeared behind the closing door. Strangely, I no longer saw the emptiness of the street, the deserted drabness of the place.

Presently a clerk arrived in my small room to say that General Stilling was now ready to see me. Together we crossed the road and climbed up the stairs. At their head I was handed over to the azure-clad loveliness, who led me to a door and knocked gently. From the other side came the sound of a deep voice, reverberant as the ocean itself. She opened the door and ushered me into the portentous presence of the General. Physically he was massive. The main lineaments were distinct enough. His head was closely cropped, with the short grey bristles standing up on end. His eyes sagged slightly, with marked pouches, though their gaze had in it a cold, unremitting quality that was vaguely intimidating. Over his ponderous jowls his heavy moustache drooped as if on the face of Time himself. The breast of his uniform carried the ribbons of many decorations, not one of which I recognised, though they were impressive enough even in anonymity. I had heard the deep notes of his voice from behind the door, but now it surprised me by its musical qualities. It was a Bayreuth voice, and he used it as a trained musician might. His English was fluent.

The room he sat in was small. It was lit from the far side by a window that looked out on a garden. A quick glance showed me the colours of many flowers. The furniture was arranged so that the General's desk was in front of the window, looking inwards, which would cast troublesome shadows on his papers, but it allowed him to see the faces of those he interviewed in full sunshine while his own remained in shadow. He sat in his chair, motionless, the cold eyes gazing straight at me. Then he stood up and offered me his hand. He said he was glad at last to have got in touch with the liaison officer from 36 and 100 Squadrons. He had heard a lot about their exploits in Malaya and Sumatra, and he was sure they had an important part to play in Java. He wanted to keep closely in touch with us, that was why he had sent for me. He wanted to make sure that our flying men would be given every facility they needed. There must be some minor problems, and he would do all in his power to help if only we let him know. Was there anything, perhaps, I might want to ask him now before I took back his respects to the squadrons?

This, then, was the chance I wanted. I found, however, some difficulty in marshalling my thoughts when confronted with this daunting figure. I began rather tentatively. Could he, I asked, give me some idea where the Japanese were likely to attempt their landings? It would help the pilots if they could fly over the beaches where they might have to engage the enemy later, and make themselves familiar with the lie of the land. He never hesitated for a moment. They would try to land, he said, somewhere near Batavia, possibly on the west side. It was also highly likely that at the same time they would attempt a landing at the other end of Java, probably near Sourabaya. He seemed very sure of their plans. Had he got some inside information?

Hanging on the wall, just beside the General's desk, was a large map of Java which would help me with my second question. I said that from our study of the charts at Tjikampek we had learned that the north coast of Java was suitable for the landing of troops almost everywhere. The south coast, however, had only one place, at the small port of Tjilatjap, in the middle. The map here – and I traced out the route with my finger – showed a road running from Tegal on the north coast over the mountains to Tjilatjap. The waist of Java was very narrow at this point. Was there a chance that the Japanese might try to land a force near Tegal and rush them over the mountains to cut the island in two and split the defences?

That would prevent further Allied reinforcements from getting in through Tjilatjap. There was also another possibility about which, of course, I remained discreetly quiet: it would also stop anybody getting out if the worst came to the worst. The General sat impassive. Coolly he eyed me as my finger ran over the thin middle of Java. He listened to my exposition very intently. Then he pushed his chin out a little and said, without giving any reasons, but with an air of finality: 'The Japanese will land near Batavia, and also possibly near Sourabaya.' There was another possibility that we had foreseen when discussing the problem in our tent at Tjikampek. The Japanese might not want to block the road to Tjilatjap. The presence of a large number of Allied troops at Tjilatjap, threatened by Japanese landings in the north, might tempt the British Eastern fleet to try to rescue them. This could be a development that the Japanese naval High Command might have no desire to discourage.

There was one more thing I wanted to ask. Full moon was on 28 February, about the time when the Japanese invasion might be expected. If the moon favoured, would it be possible to launch at least some of our attacks by night? Our machines were very slow. They had attacked at Endau in broad daylight and suffered heavy losses. He said he would do his best to see that our machines operated in conditions which gave them the greatest promise of success. Would we have fighters in support? I asked. It was the Japanese fighters that had caused the disaster at Endau. He said that at the moment he did not have precise figures for the number of fighters that would be available. All he could say, in the meantime, was that they would deploy the fighters in those areas where the need was greatest and where they might have the most success.

While, in the lamp-lit calm of our little Ops Room at Tjikampek, it was easy enough to see our problems in perspective, it was not quite so easy here in the presence of this formidable, critical figure. I hoped I had not omitted any vital point, but this was the end and, rising from his seat, he held out his hand. He asked me to convey to all the airmen of our two squadrons his very best wishes, and said he looked forward to hearing great things about them in the days ahead. He pressed a little bell and the girl opened the door. Her blue eyes, bronze skin and honey hair – set off by the trim, blue uniform – looked enchanting as, with a smile, she led me out of the main door, down the steps, and across the road to the huts where I was to wait for the transport that was to take me back to Tjikampek. There, by the roadside, I stood, slightly forlorn, as I watched her recross the road and climb the stairs to vanish behind the door. I wonder, fairest lady of the honey hair, what happened to you in the end? Were you, like the rest of us, caught up and crushed in the tempest that was so soon to sweep in from the north? I hope against hope that you came to no hurt in it! Memory is jealous of the fleeting glimpses it catches of such beauty as yours. I believe also that it attaches to itself a thin palimpsest of the eternal, and if this belief is true I am sure that your faint but still lovely impress will be traced there.

Soon the car arrived, this time in the charge of a rather impetuous, though taciturn, driver. We drove out fast through the southern suburbs, passing through Meester Cornelis on the way, but I looked for the white walls and the cock-crowned tower of the church in vain. Happily we made no detour to the jungle encampment and soon we were back in front of our huts at Tjikampek. I delivered a report about my visit to General Stilling, first to the CO, and then in more general terms to the flying crews. Now I learned that in my absence the air had become thick with rumour. One report said that a Japanese convoy had been spotted near the Anambas, a group of islands a little to the north-east of Singapore. Another – or possibly the same one – was off Singapore itself, while a later report said that it was even as near as Banka and heading for Java. A further convoy was clearly on the way to East Java, having been sighted, and possibly also attacked, by American Liberators in the Macassar Strait. As yet there had been no general alert, but it could not be delayed much longer now. The Vildebeests had all been serviced and checked and the crews were on immediate stand-by.

Next morning – Friday, 27 February – a dispatch-rider arrived from Headquarters in Batavia with further news: a large Japanese invasion-fleet had been sighted in the lower Macassar Strait, and was now not far from the east end of Java, where Allied ships were waiting to attack it. We might be called upon at any moment to launch a strike in support of our ships. All day we waited for the expected signal – a particularly trying day in any case, being hot and humid. At length a second dispatch-rider arrived from Batavia to confirm the immediate threat to East Java – but, more important for us, with other news. Our two squadrons were now ordered to fly to Madioen aerodrome in East Java where they would operate much closer to their base; and to provide for their reception at their new station, an advance party of about thirty essential ground crew would leave at dawn next morning. Taking with them the necessary equipment, they would travel by road to Madioen.

The dispatch-rider brought another message with him, not of such great importance for the squadrons though with considerable implications for me, for had it been acted upon my subsequent experiences of the Java campaign might have been very different. It is not likely that they would have been any easier, but they might have had a further dimension. In brief, Dutch Headquarters in Batavia had decided they needed a liaison officer from the British forces to be assigned to them. The transmission of orders in this international force would naturally involve some language problems, and in the critical circumstances that might follow a Japanese landing they wanted a native English-speaking officer on hand to deal quickly and accurately with translation. My earlier visit to General Stilling had, it seemed, recommended my secondment for this duty. This was a development which I welcomed. Indeed I was just on the point of expressing my readiness to comply when the Squadron Leader made a sharp interjection. It was, he pronounced, impossible to agree to. As intelligence officer, I could not be spared from the squadrons. The dispatch-rider looked at him in amazement. The request had come from General Stilling, Commanding Officer of all forces in West Java, and here was a mere squadron leader saying that it could not be done! In Headquarters they had emphasised the importance of the matter. But the Squadron Leader was adamant. 'Look here!' he said, rather peremptorily. 'The position is this. I and my officers are flying crew. In a few days there is no saying what will happen to us. When that time comes, I want someone to be here with the men to look after them. That is why I want this officer to stay!' Clearly the dispatch-rider did not consider this justification enough to defy an order from the General, but the Squadron Leader's attitude made compromise unlikely, and he bowed to events. Saying that he would convey the message to General Stilling. he left. Sensing my disappointment, the Squadron Leader looked at me, as if about to express regret for his decision. Then, thinking better of it, he added 'That's all!' and I left the tent too. Squadron Leader Wilkins's outward appearance provided meagre clues to the hard core in his character, for he was a bluff man, extrovert-looking, with the ruddy countenance and thick-set, sturdy frame of the countryman. He had much in common with Rowlands (whom he resembled in appearance) and Markham (whom he did not), especially their courage and professional dedication. What was not so readily detectable was his compassion. Something that had recently befallen him had deepened this. He had a younger brother, the pilot and captain of a flying boat who at the outbreak of the Pacific war was stationed at Gibraltar. At short notice this young man had been ordered to Malaya but he had been only a fortnight there when, on 12 January, he was lost with his Catalina over Singora in the Isthmus of Kra. Since that day, the Squadron Leader seemed to live in the shadow of that disaster, as if convinced that his brother's loss would be followed at no great interval by his own.

About half an hour after the dispatch-rider had gone, Wilkins sent for Pilot Officer Bairstow and myself. He told us that he had decided to send us with the three trucks and the advance party in the morning. Bairstow was to be in charge of billeting and messing, and my job was to navigate the convoy to Madioen and be in general command of the party. We left the tent immediately. Time was short and there was much to be done. Bairstow got the Warrant Officer, and together they sat down to draw up lists of essential tools and equipment, which they handed over to the fitters who were soon busy selecting and packing them. The CO and the Adjutant also had discussions about which thirty men would comprise the party. Meanwhile I was busy collecting whatever maps were available, and studying them closely to see what would be the best route to take.

By the time we had our plans well in hand and the men were putting the finishing touches to the packing and loading, night was almost upon us. An impalpable violet glimmer hung over the rough jungle clearing, softening the edges so that it looked like a large, natural glade, very peaceful. Bairstow and I now left the men and wandered back through the trees to the Ops Room tent, which glowed with a faint green light in the jungle. When we got near to it we found that the flap had been tied back and several very large stag beetles were droning back and forth across the thin slab of light that issued through the slit in the canvas. When we entered, we saw that some of the flying crews had been having a conference and were now folding up the charts, which they had been studying on the table, for the last time. When it was time to go, the Squadron Leader screwed down the wick of the little storm-lamp. Then he lowered his face so that it was caught, dramatically, in the gleam from the diminishing flame. He gave a little puff of his breath and the light went out. The symbolism of the act was too explicit to be lost on any of us though no one said a word. Then we set off along the track beside the rubber trees on our way back to the bomb dump and our jungle billets.

I had not gone far, musing on the extinguishing of the lamp, when I became aware that someone was by my side. It was Wilkins. He asked if we could keep to the track through the rubber for a while: he wanted to have a word with me. So, at first in silence, we walked through the forest. Soon our companions, who had kept to the main track, were out of earshot. Then, almost casually, the Squadron Leader began to unburden his spirit of some of the anxieties that were lying heavy on it. He had, he said, been on many sorties, and so far had always managed to get back safely; but, of course, he never imagined that he could go on like this for ever. On the contrary, he had a premonition, that had now hardened into almost a certainty, that his time was up. He thought that a day or two – possibly a week at the most – would see it through for himself and the rest of the crews. He did not lament it – after all, if you were an airman, that was what you accepted: it came with the job. I had heard, of course, what he had said to the dispatch-rider when he brought the message that I was to be seconded to HQ in Batavia. He was very sorry about that decision, and it had been a terribly hard one to make. He knew I was deeply disappointed: I did not need to tell him; my face said everything. He did it for the best. It was the men he was worried about. They were a genuine lot of lads, and their earlier lives in Britain had given them no training at all for what they might have to face now. When this business was over, perhaps there would be a very few left to lend a hand. At the end of the day, I was as likely as any to be still here. He wanted me to promise him one thing: that I would do all I could for the men. He was sorry that he himself had been able to do so little, but flying took up so much of his time.

What was there I could say – even if I had been able to? It would have been sheer hypocrisy to pretend that what he said was not true, and he would have despised me if I had resorted to facile insincerities now. He held out his hand, and I gripped it firmly. Then having told me some his worries (he never mentioned his brother) he seemed to have shed a little of his burden.

We continued along the path through the rubber and soon struck the main track. Presently we arrived at the corner where, dim in the dusk beneath the trees, lay the stacks of yellow bombs. What would they do with all these bombs and that petrol now? They could not cart all that to Madioen! Down the road towards the huts some of the men were strolling leisurely. The music of their English voices drifted on the night air with never a hint of strain or disquiet. It might well have been an English country lane, with the scent of wild roses in the air, and some cows chewing the cud contentedly in the fields beside the fence.

We were restrained as we ate our evening meal, sitting on the floor of the huts. All around the landscape seemed very peaceful, but our minds did not share in the peacefulness. Before us was a short night, a very early rise, and an unknown journey. Like many others, I slept badly.

TRUCK PARTY FOR MADIOEN

T he bustle and upheaval of departure irrupted unseasonably into that twilight half-consciousness by which, far into the night, and under the leaden weight of exhaustion, sleeplessness had at last been followed. A rough hand, urgent and unceremonious, was at my shoulder, and a brusque voice exhorted me to 'rise and shine'.

A flickering red glow coming from the direction of the kitchen told me that at least the cooks were up and busy over their cauldron, and the Warrant Officer, the gentlest and most painstaking of men, was already in the trucks, assuring himself that all necessary equipment was loaded. A Sergeant, nominal-roll in one hand, was going around the awakened men, ticking off names with a pencil as he made certain that the truck party was accounted for, while the general bustle, and a desire to assist at the send-off, had aroused most of the other men as well.

A perfunctory dash of water to the face answered the demands of cleanliness, but even before that was completed a peremptory summons to 'come and get it' rose on the air. We sat round the room, backs propped against the wall, and dixies in hand, the bully-beef boiled to a watery stew, and the mugs of potent black tea fortifying us against the chills of the pre-dawn. Soon a languor super-vened, offensive to the bustling spirit of the Sergeant, and his earthy Anglo-Saxon reminded us of the need for dispatch. 'OK! OK! Sarge!' called out the men of the truck party appeasingly, as they gave their dixies and mugs a perfunctory swill and prepared for departure. As we gathered round the trucks, a crimson flush crept up the sky, behind the forest, in the east; the last lingering stars were snuffed out; a few hitherto unnoticed clouds in the high zenith glowed with crimson and mackerel; and the white banks of mist, which lay in the hollows beside the rubber plantations, now stirred by a little breeze which had arisen, shook themselves into frail tatters and drifted away. Far to the east, though still obscured from our eyes by the forest, the sun had risen over the Java Sea.

On the road, loaded and ready, stood the three trucks, the Warrant Officer having completed his final check-up and pronounced everything on board. Once again the truck party lined up and was numbered. To provide against dispersal, we carried three nominal-rolls, Bairstow having one in the third vehicle, I one in the leading one, while the Warrant Officer had the third. Each man carried a rifle and ammunition, but apart from the revolvers which Bairstow and I carried, we had no other weapons. On both sides of the trucks we posted sentries with loaded rifles, their job being to keep a sharp look-out, especially for hostile aircraft which, though they would have to come from Borneo or Palembang, might, we felt, be reconnoitring the roadway. The three Bedfords, being new, reduced one cause for concern, for the journey could not be much short of 400 miles; we were heavily loaded and the sun, under which we should have to drive exposed for many hours, would be oppressive. Our maps showed that it would be best to get to the sea at Indramajoe, about 120 miles east of Batavia, and then follow the northern coast by way of Cheribon for about 150 miles to Semarang. After that there remained about 100 miles south-east across the East Java plain to Madioen. The journey would take us two days, and we planned to stop for the night at some town about half way.

After the truck engines were started, and run a little to warm them up, the truck party piled in while the rest of the Squadron stood around on the road, watching curiously. Although the military situation had now become too tense to permit any confident look into the future, we did not anticipate that our separation would be long, and we hoped to have everything ready when our comrades joined us later at Madioen. As we moved off, I looked towards the Squadron Leader who was standing on a little knoll all by himself at the side of the road and holding up one hand. My memory was to hold on to this picture of him, standing a little apart, his hand raised in farewell, for I was never to see him again, though I did not know it at the time. As the gap between us widened, we all gave a loud cheer and waved enthusiastically as long as we could see each other along the road.

Crouching over his wheel, his hands well forward, sat my driver. He was a little stockily knit Scot, swarthy in feature and laconic in speech, one of the dark Celts. He was prickly to the point of uncouthness, and the few breaks which he permitted himself in his long silences tended to be so brusque that increasingly I discouraged them, and was always relieved when they were over. But whatever his shortcomings as a companion there was no denying his virtuosity with a clutch and a gear lever. Under the floorboards the engine purred away with a sleepy murmur like a contented cat, though as the day wore on the heat, welling up from the bonnet, made the air shimmer in front of the windscreen. Before the sun rose overhead, the banyans and the palms which lined the roadway kept off the worst of the heat; without them, the journey would have become well-nigh intolerable.

The early stages of our journey were plagued by uncertainty. The road, which invariably followed the edges of the rectangular rubber plantations, progressed by zig-zags, and in the absence of signposts, which naturally had been removed as a precaution, every crossroads we came to presented us with an enigma. My failure to solve these satisfactorily led us into endless and bewildering diversions, and since I was acting as navigator, with a map spread out on my knees, my capacity was exposed to considerable questioning. Not till, at last, we caught a glimpse of the sea were we assured of extrication; and, a little later, a mirage-glimpse of orange houses in the distance announced the proximity of Indramajoe. But, despite its harmonious name, it proved to be an uninviting township; some bungalows, a few shops, and a hotel did not tempt us to stop. We carried on southwards along the now happily straight and palm-fringed road for Cheribon.

By then the sun's heat was fierce, and a steel army truck without a canopy is not designed for sybaritic travel. Even the palms, as they stood in deferential ranks beside the roadway, now betrayed a flagging droop. I was becoming concerned about how the driver was standing up to the heat for we had no substitute to switch with him and so give him a rest. He still observed the strictest Scottish parsimony in speech, but when I asked him how he was faring he said he was well able to carry on. Shortly, however, we found that the sea was again on our left hand, and right ahead, and quite unmistakable in the distance, was the town! What hospitality Cheribon had in its power to offer we knew not, but even had it been ringed with date-palms and oases, we could not have welcomed it with more expectant – or with more parched – lips. The entrance to the town was dominated by a large ruined pile of mouldering masonry, like an ancient castle. Rounding this, we were confronted by a double row of large banyan trees whose grotesquely arched and stilted roots formed a kind of palisade which screened a *padang*. Through this the road entered by a narrow archway, resembling the drawbridge of a castle; and the impression of fortification was enhanced by several dug-outs and barbed-wire entanglements which were disposed in the vicinity, though we could see no troops.

Driving cautiously through the banyan arch and past the barbed-wire, we skirted the *padang*, continuing on into the town. At the further end of the square, where the road again insinuated itself among the houses, there appeared a big orange building flanked by an extensive rotunda whose high Greek pillars supported a wide dome. It had about it an aura of officialdom – could it be perhaps a governor's residence? – but when we got nearer we saw that it was a hotel, remarkably palatial for a small provincial town like this. The rotunda appeared to be crowded with people and an unexpected air of festivity prevailed. This was no place to cater for our modest needs, but we stopped to ask if they could direct us to some suitable establishment in the town. But no sooner did our arrival become known than there was a general exodus from the hotel and a smiling, milling crowd enveloped us, the warmth of their welcome being quite overwhelming. We were, they assured us, just the people they had been waiting for and we were cordially invited to unexpected hospitality.

But I was greatly perplexed: something, surely, must be wrong! Were we, by any chance, the mistaken beneficiaries of hospitality intended for others? My endeavours to clarify the position were interrupted by the appearance of a large and beaming Dutchman who, approaching our airmen with paternal gesticulations, began to shepherd them away. I was suddenly alarmed: there was something about his roistering conviviality that boded no good for our small party. His legs faltered and swayed, and his slurred speech gave warning that this was no suitable host for our men. Restraining the eager exodus for a moment, I asked him what he had in mind in the way of entertainment once he had taken the airmen away. 'Leave it all to me!' he replied expansively. 'You go and have your lunch and I'll look after the men!' But his casual assurances merely sharpened my determination not to surrender the men to his care without some safeguards. I took him aside to administer a serious word of counsel. The men, I explained, had a long day before them. They were on important duty and much depended on them. They would be very tired before the day was over. Whatever entertainment he was planning for them, he must give me absolute assurance on one point – it would include *no drink*! He listened to my injunctions stolidly, gazing at me with a glassy eye. 'Leave it all to me!' he repeated. 'Besides, would you grudge your men just a *small* glass of beer when all the Japanese fleet is lying at the bottom of the Java Sea? They'll tell you all about it when you're having your lunch. Now leave the men to me!'

The news about the Japanese fleet was certainly startling; but my desire for immediate details could certainly not be met by this unreliable informant. So, abandoning with great reluctance the men to his charge, I accompanied the other guests into the rotunda which, I now found, formed the dining-room of the hotel. We were shown to one of the tables beside a pillar. Over the balustrade, just beside our chairs, lapped the entwining bougainvillaea with a profusion of rich imperial blossoms. At our table I soon became aware of a lean, pale-cheeked, ruddy-haired man somewhat un-Dutch in appearance, who was directing the proceedings with uniform facility in Dutch, Javanese and English.

'Where,' I asked him by way of introduction, 'did you pick up your English?'

'From the very same place that you did!' he replied with a grin; then adding a necessary correction: 'Weel noa!— poassibly a wee bit further sooth!'

His affectation of a music-hall Scots accent was most convincing. Adjusting to life in Cheribon was proving a little traumatic. He was, it transpired, the local manager of the British American Tobacco Co. (or BAT as it was universally known in the Far East) and hailed from Tyneside. Soon, under his direction, there arrived on the table several dishes whose size and succulence even the most rabid urge for activity would be unlikely to survive. I surveyed them with desire, wondering how much indulgence I should permit myself in view of the duties ahead. While we dined I asked anxiously about this rumour I had just heard that the Japanese fleet was at the bottom of the Java Sea. That, explained the BAT manager, was what they were all certain had happened, though they were still waiting for official confirmation of it. A great seabattle had just been fought north of Cheribon. Yesterday they had sat all day and listened to the booming of the heavy guns. It was all very exciting – just like the Spanish Armada! What must have happened was that the Allied fleet had run into the Japanese convoys and was sinking them. That was why all the Dutch people were in the hotel: they were celebrating. We had arrived fortunately just in time for the victory lunch. I said that it might have been wiser to wait for confirmation of the victory before celebrating in a victory lunch, but my faint-heartedness was laughed to scorn. Indeed, the gaiety and assurance of this large assembly was infectious. Gradually my misgivings faded to the accompaniment of their laughter and the tinkle of their wine glasses as they held them aloft to toast their victory.

But time was slipping away in Cheribon, and our destination was Madioen. Dusty and uninviting to the eye of the hedonist imagination the road thither might appear, but that was the road we had to take, and the time was now overdue when we should take it. I called for our bill and got up to go, but the Englishman dismissed the suggestion that we should pay anything with a wave of the hand. It was, he assured us, at any time a pleasure to entertain the RAF – *now* it was an *honour*!

Returning to the trucks we found that the metal, exposed for so long to the sun, was in places too hot to touch. Some of the men had already assembled and were impatient to be on their way, but it was clearly going to be no easy job to round up some of the others. Clearly distressed at what had happened, the Warrant Officer was shepherding the stragglers. Some of these were already belli-cose, some merely silent and sullen. None was likely to take kindly to a grilling and dusty truck for the rest of the long journey to Madioen, but the one that was causing the most concern to me was my driver who was now maudlin as well as truculent; and with him at the wheel I had some fears for our safety. But, as I had no replacement, I could not relieve him of his duties and hoped that the shaking of the truck and the heat would help to throw off his drunkenness.

A Bedford truck, especially after a celebration on a hot Java afternoon, is not a vehicle particularly adapted for any animated contemplation of the surrounding landscape. Comatose from the double assault of the sun and their potions, even the sentries soon subsided from view to a recumbent position on the floors, and for them at least low-flying aircraft ceased to exercise any call upon their attention. This was serious, and might involve us in great danger. In an attempt to counteract it, I called a brief halt and administered a harangue, pointing out that the great naval victory was as yet by no means certain and our duty was to get quickly and safely to Madioen. They listened to me with expressionless faces, and I was doubtful if it did any good. But happily, though he remained as sullen and uncommunicative as ever, and sat with bowed head over his wheel, my driver continued to handle his vehicle with apparently unimpaired skill.

This road beside the Java Sea is quite hauntingly beautiful, and it was galling to have to drive along it beset by the distractions of war. On our left, and approaching at times almost to the roadside, was the sea. It had the clean, washed beauty of an unsullied world: a shimmering commingling of grey and jade-green, and, in the low-lying haze, horizonless where the water and sky became one. Beside each *kampong* jetty were moored a few fishing *prahus*, their nets hung on poles to dry, not a fisherman in sight. Russet and insubstantial, the nets and the furled sails seemed suspended in vacancy. Between the road and the water stretched the beach, broad, coral-white and gently sloping. It was a place apt for the gambolling of nereids, but these, like the fishermen, had gone elsewhere. Alongside the road stood the palms, ranked as they had been all the way from Tjikampek, their bases, at the deeper inlets, almost in the water and magical in the subtlety of their perspective.

Some time round about two or three o'clock, one of the airmen, who had been lying on his back on the bottom of the truck and gazing up into the sky, suddenly gave a great shout. Struggling to his feet and pointing excitedly to the sky he called out '*The Pigs!*' It was a colloquialism which the airmen used to describe the Vildebeests, and it held a fierce endearment. There, flying in formation leisurely above our heads on a north-easterly course that would take them gradually out to sea, were the nine surviving Vildebeests of the two squadrons. But why were they making this sweep out to sea? Could they be searching for any survivors from the Japanese convoy whose reported destruction had set Cheribon *en fête*? Or were they merely looking at the beaches over which they would have to operate? Clearly events had overtaken us, and the machines would be in Madioen before we got there to prepare for them. We stopped the lorries and got out to watch them. Leisurely, like a cluster of migrating geese, they drifted on till they were swallowed up in the blue haze of the sky. We all felt a great stirring of pride in our hearts. It was the last, unexpected glimpse we were destined to have of most of them, and we had already taken our last farewell of most of their crews.

It was shortly after this that we came to Tegal. This was a small town, undistinguished in appearance and offering no temptation to linger, apart from the fact that this was where the vital road left for Tjilatjap. The great mountain range to the south now seemed very close, and from here its walls, though in places fantastically terraced, were sheer and awesome. We now saw how lucky we were in not being called upon to tackle that ascent in this heat. For a little while we stopped at the crossroads to consult my map. The next town was Pekalongan, which was still about fifty miles away, and it was unlikely that we would be able to reach it much before dusk. But the chances were that it might be bigger than Tegal and be more able to put us up. It was worth the risk.

So from Tegal we increased our speed. Soon the water was boiling in the radiator, and a little jet of steam spurted fitfully from the cap. But at least the road was deserted and, now that the sun was declining, travelling conditions were somewhat less oppressive. By the time that coloured walls in the distance announced the presence of Pekalongan, the air held the unmistakable purple of evening in it, transfiguring the wild mountain landscape to something blurred and magical. Around us, on the plain, the countryside was more open, the rubber plantations having given way to sugar cane. At length we reached the town and drove down the main street in search of the mayor's office and a night's lodging.

Happily the office was still open, and happily, too, the festal lamps had not yet been kindled at the feverish flame as in Cheribon. Yet our request for a place where we and our men might rest the night did not meet with any warmth of response. Dolefully the mayor catalogued his difficulties. All the hotels in the town were already filled with refugees or else were empty and locked up, their staffs, now themselves refugees, having taken to more distant parts of the island in search of safety. But at least he said that he would telephone and see what he could do. He might be able to get a room in a hotel for the two of us – but the men! Ah, it would be difficult with the men! It would take much telephoning! It did, indeed, take much telephoning. But, at last he found a hotel that would take two RAF officers. Was it the Java? – the confused happenings of the night have driven some of the details from my mind. For the men, the only thing he could think of was the local barracks. They were very small, at present unoccupied, had no beds and, of course, could provide no food. But at least they were a rough kind of shelter. Perhaps we would like to see the barracks? Accompanied by a clerk, and in no mood of optimism, we set off to inspect them.

Happily our fears proved groundless. They were quite near, small (as the mayor had said) and clean, but they were provided with mattresses and blankets, all neatly stacked, and more important still they had a good kitchen with cooking utensils. We brought the men to inspect them and they pronounced them much to their liking – indeed, much better than Tjikampek. They assured us they would be soon settled in and, given the rice and food that the clerk promised to obtain for us, they would get a meal prepared. Their uncomplaining acceptance of the situation restored our confidence and we left them, promising to come back later to see how they were getting on. Meanwhile, one word of caution! The victory celebrations had concluded for the day when we left Cheribon!

So we set off for the Java Hotel, which we found to be a large, solid building agreeably situated on a low knoll, among gardens round which some huge palms lifted dark crowns into the evening sky. The hotel-keeper, a middle-aged Dutchman, portly and rubicund, gave us a warm welcome. The bedroom he showed us to was large, with two beds, and there was no doubt that we should manage very well here. After we had settled in, the owner, with obvious pride, took us out to the garden to show us the remarkable setting of the hotel. The screen of palm trees which bounded the lawn to the north shut out the view on that side though the owner assured us that the sea was very near, and if the wind was from the north the sound of the waves beating on the beach made a pleasant lullaby which you could listen to in your bedroom before you went to sleep. But on the south side the garden commanded a spectacular view across the town to the mountains.

All day long, as we had driven along the coast from Cheribon, we had watched them. Where the red volcanic mud had poured down, their sides were striated, like Greek columns, with broad, vertical flutes. The rice terraces and patchworks of cultivation, perched high on their threatened slopes, made us wonder that simple farmers should dare to expose their lives to such dangers, and provided a very precarious husbandry. Now the twilight had smudged out details. Stark and magnified by the uncertain light, the peaks towered into the pale sky, most of them active with pencils of smoke trailing lazily from their gigantic cones. There must have been *kampongs* hidden high on the mountainsides, for little points of light began winking out through the dusk, and where the fires had been lit to cook the evening meal, the smoke stood straight up into the still air like white cords.

We stood watching the stupendous ridge in awe while the hotel-keeper volunteered to tell us the names of some of the volcanoes. That one down to the east, he said, near Soerakarta, was Merapi – there was one even higher still behind it, called Semuru, but you could not see it from here. The one nearest to us was Sumbing; that a little to the right was Slamat. Behind Cheribon towered a faultless cone which he said was Chiremai. About half a dozen of the more active ones had watchers at the top, day and night, to give instant warning if an eruption threatened. I said that even the names had a sinister ring to them, but he said that was merely because of the associations I invested them with, for really they were harmonious and he found nothing sinister in them at all. Then I asked him if he was ever frightened, living like this at the foot of active volcanoes – after all, Krakatoa was not very far away! No, he said, he was not frightened. You got accustomed to it. When he was a boy in the Netherlands, his home had been just beside a dyke. On winter nights, when storms were raging in from the North Sea, he used to lie in bed and wonder what would happen if the dykes collapsed and the sea rushed in. But the dykes did not burst, and they got used to it and did not worry. Now, when he looked out of his bedroom each evening and saw the volcanoes smoking, all he thought about was how beautiful they were. Besides, if he stopped to worry he would never be able to get his work done at all. He then told us that Pekalongan had a great reputation for the manufacture of *batik*, its craftsmen being considered the finest in all the East Indies. The rich colours of the designs on the cloth were produced by an elaborate process involving several dippings, during which those parts which were to be protected from the dye were first coated with wax. He then took us into the hotel to show us several examples of this wonderful native fabric.

When we visited the barracks later in the evening, we found the beds neatly made up on the floor, and the men, now restored by a good meal of rice and meat, comfortable and contented. In preparation for the long day ahead they proposed to go to bed early. Cheribon, it seemed, had stimulated no venturesome spirits to renewed carousal.

We had got back to the garden and were just going through the gate when Bairstow stopped for a moment in deep reflection. There was one thing we had forgotten, he said. The petrol tanks of the lorries were not filled and we might waste time in the morning hunting for some garage. I scoffed at his fears. Besides, it was now time for dinner and the other guests, as well as the cooks, would be waiting for us. But Bairstow remained obdurate. It might not be so easy to find a garage open in the morning at the early hour at which we proposed to leave, and this was a risk we should not take. How the event justified his foreboding! So off he went, while I waited in the garden. It was a long wait. When at last he returned he reported that several of the town's garages were already closed, their owners, like the hotel-keepers, having gone inland. Others claimed that they had to reserve their small supplies for their own customers or for an emergency – they had no idea when they were likely to get any more. But in the end he found a garage whose owner declared that, even if all the others had to do without, he would never see the RAF without petrol – not as long as he had a drop in a tank!

We entered the dining-room rather sheepishly because of our delay, and we could see that the other guests had been waiting for us and we could sense their natural resentment. There were not many guests, and the Cheribon variety of celebration was markedly absent. For the most part they looked to be typical Dutch burghers, solid-framed and sober-faced, eager for the companionship of the hotel as well as a meal. They did not speak much, and when they did it was in lowered voices, almost whispers.

The hotel-keeper had earlier told us that they had a radio in the lounge and there was a news bulletin at nine o'clock. We were eager to hear details about the sea battle and, though we did not understand Dutch, we joined the group of listeners round the instrument. The voice of the announcer sounded flat and unemotional, and though I listened for such familiar names as the *Exeter* or the *Emerald* there was nothing I could understand. But as the announcement went on, I could see the faces of those around me taking on a very sober and down-cast look. When it was over, the guests continued to talk quietly among themselves, completely ignoring us. Then the hotel-keeper went off to talk to a man sitting by himself in a corner. We could endure the uncertainty no longer: going over to the hotel-keeper, we insisted that he should tell us something about the announcement. He said that there had been a great sea battle and there had been heavy losses on both sides. The announcer had not specified what these losses were.

Leaving this dejected group, we went out and strolled for a little in the garden. By this time the mountain peaks had become grey shadows silhouetted against a pastel sky. Above them the empty night arched vastly, pricked by a multitude of stars. Everything was very still, and the diminishing lights on the mountainsides told that the tillers at these great heights went early to bed. We, too, had a busy day ahead of us; following their example, we came in from the garden and retired to our bedrooms.

TRAPPED

The night was still and peaceful, and my sleep deep. About four o'clock in the morning I was woken up by my bedside lamp being switched on; a hand, stretched through the flap of my mosquito curtain, seized my shoulder and shook it violently. At its urging I opened my eyes and could dimly make out the figure of the hotel-keeper kneeling on the carpet beside my bed in an attitude of supplication. Even by the uncertain light of the lamp I could make out the broad, fleshy face, haggard and wild-eyed with a wanton despair. 'Hello! Hello!' he was saying. 'Hello! Hello! Are you waking? Do you hear me?' I muttered that I heard him and wanted to know what was the trouble. 'You must get up!' he continued in a voice choking with agitation. 'You must get up *now!*' I asked him why I had to get up now – what was wrong? The answer that he gave swept away all my doubt in a wave of alarm that matched his own. 'The Japanese are landing!' he said. 'Japanese soldiers are landing on the beach!'

My mind was now thoroughly awake and needed no further urging. Pulling the flap of my mosquito curtain roughly aside, I leapt out of my bed in one bound. The hotel-keeper struggled to his feet, his whole body trembling violently. His eyes continued to stare glassily from his face, which was putty-coloured.

'I want to get this very clear!' I said. 'You say that Japanese are landing on the beach? What beach?'

'The beach over there beside the town' he replied, 'over from the garden!' and he extended an arm in the direction of a tall line of palm trees. 'They are landing from boats. Big ships are anchored out in the sea, and the boats are bringing the soldiers to the beach!'

'Now?' I asked, groping for any reason to bolster my unbelief. 'Now – when we are speaking?'

'Yes,' he answered. 'They are landing just now. They have been landing through the night.'

'Who told you all this?' I asked.

'The Politie! The Politie are telephoning all the hotels and the houses telling the people to get up out of bed!'

I went across to Bairstow's bed and lifted up the flap of his mosquito curtain. He was wide awake, resting on one elbow.

'Did you hear all this?' I asked.

'I've been listening to every word!' he said, and with a spring was out of bed beside me.

'I think you would be better to go away now!' said the hotel-keeper, a note of entreaty in his voice. Genuinely concerned for our safety he may well have been; but if he also harboured a thought that the presence of two RAF officers in his hotel would bode no good either for himself or his other guests in the likely event of the Japanese arriving on his doorstep, who is to blame him! Of course, I said, we should have to go. Our men had an important job to do, and our duty was to get them to their destination as soon as possible. Only one thing more: could he possibly give us something to eat before we set off? Anything would do. He said that he had no boys at this time, but he could boil eggs and he could let us have some bread and butter, and tea. We thanked him. That would do fine!

By this time Bairstow was struggling into his clothes and said that he was going straight down to the barracks to warn the men and get them ready as soon as possible. I wanted desperately to look at my maps to make myself familiar with the options open to us if, as seemed most likely, the Japanese had already cut the road to Semarang. So I hurriedly got out a sheet and bent anxiously over it, studying the roads. But the more I examined it the more I was puzzled that the Japanese were landing here at all. This was not the end of the island, as General Stilling had predicted, nor the middle, as I had feared, near to the crucial road junction at Tegal. Had it not been for the fact that the police were getting people out of their beds, I should have been inclined to suspect one of these baseless panics now so familiar. The Japanese purpose, of course, might be to thrust at an unexpected, and thus undefended, part of the coast in an effort to cut the island in two and prevent lateral reinforcement. Whatever its purpose, it was not likely to be a main attack. But that in no way lessened its fatal possibilities for us. A few trees toppled across the road to form the usual roadblock would bring our expedition to Madioen to an untimely, and possibly a bloody, end.

As I saw it, the choice was broadly between east and west. We could go back the fifty or so miles to Tegal and then attempt the crossing of the high ridge, even with our heavily laden Bedfords. But the Vildebeests might be in desperate need of our fitters, and that would add unknown miles to our journey. Besides, we had as yet no firm evidence that the road to Semarang was closed. That clearly must be our first option. If we ran into a roadblock, we should attempt to turn in our tracks; if ambushed and immobilised, take to the jungle. That would be only a last desperate course, and it would hold out very little hope of our eventual arrival at Madioen. One totally disabling handicap we were, happily, spared: Bairstow's foresight had ensured that our tanks were full. And what about the great naval victory that had sent the Japanese fleet to the bottom of the Java Sea and charged the triumphal glasses at Cheribon? Doubtless we had not got the full story about that.

Soon Bairstow was back. He had told the men the position and, good fellows that they were, they seemed in stout heart. They had improvised some kind of breakfast, and when he left them they were packing and would be ready to take to the road by the time we got there. In a little while the hotel-keeper returned, still dressed in his pyjamas, with a pair of trousers drawn over them. He carried a tray with boiled eggs, buttered bread, and a pot of tea. Now that the first shock had subsided a little, I could study more closely his careworn and pathetic face. His eyes were large and desolate, and the jowls sagged down like dewlaps from the grey sunken cheeks. He sat down on a chair, declining to join in our frugal meal, though he poured himself a cup of tea. But he did not drink it, merely holding it between his two hands as if grateful for the warmth.

When we had finished, I asked him if he would let us have his bill. This I did, acting on instructions from Tjikampek, and I gave him a chit in payment made out in the name of the RAF. This seemed a very dubious recompense, and it would certainly compromise him if it fell into the hands of the Japanese, but, while alive to the danger, we had no other way of reimbursing him for his services. Now it was time to go. Getting up, we thanked him for all his help – in particular for waking us up and allowing us a chance to slip through the Japanese net before it closed. He was pale and listless, and seemed not to hear, insulated from understanding as from compassion. There was now nothing left but instinct; under the weight of his own personal crisis, he had reached the point where it was about to sweep over him.

When we reached the door, we held out our hands in farewell. Then suddenly the hotel-keeper seemed to be seized in the grip of powerful convulsions, as though he was struggling to maintain self-control. It took him a little time to speak, but then the words rushed from his lips in a terrible torrent. 'I've got two pistols!' he said. 'They're ready and loaded. One is for my wife . . . and one is for myself!' Startled, I looked at him intently for a moment, wondering whether the crisis had temporarily unseated his reason, or whether he was trying to shore up his dissolving courage by this display of bravado. But this was not play-acting – the febrile glare in his eyes, the comprehensive frenzy that stared out of that demented face, could dispense with facile heroics. I suggested that this might not be a wise thing to do. If he really felt that there was no course open to him but to use the pistols, then it would certainly be better to use them on the Japanese than on his own poor family. But I very much doubted that there would be any need to use them at all. It would be far better to sit down and wait to see what happened. If he started shooting, he would also have to think about his other guests. It would certainly do them no good. Even if the Japanese did come to the hotel, there was no proof that they would hurt them at all. He looked at me blankly like a stone effigy. Certainly he listened to not a word of my advice. 'One is for my wife!' he repeated very deliberately, '. . . and one is for me! We have spent our lives making this hotel. No Japanese is going to come into my hotel and put his hands on my wife. I'll shoot my wife before a Japanese puts his foot in my door. I don't care what you say! I'll shoot her! And then I'll shoot myself!'

His fears took horrible shapes, and were justified; I knew it as well as he. What would happen to the Dutch women and girls if the Japanese took them? The fate of Nanking, not much publicised in Europe but widely known in the Far East, held up a terrible example. There, the women were raped and the whole population of the city, amounting to half a million people, were savagely massacred. What grounds were there to expect that the Japanese would exact from the haughty Westerners a toll less terrible than that they had appointed for the Chinese? But there was now nothing more that we could do, no word of consolation that we could offer that would be likely to allay his fears. So, sadly, we shook hands, and then we walked through the lovely garden that only last night the hotel-keeper had taken such pride in showing us.

The road down to the barracks was quite deserted, and an uncanny stillness hung over the town. When we got there we found that the men were all ready to set off. The trucks were loaded and inside everything was just as we had found it: mattresses stacked; blankets neatly piled; and kitchen utensils cleaned and put back on their shelves, all ready for the Japs! We had a brief conference with the men. I told them what I had heard from the hotel-keeper, and gave them an assessment of the situation. We would try first to get to Semarang. If we ran into an ambush or struck a roadblock, we should turn about and make for Tegal, the third truck now leading. If we were shot up badly or trapped between roadblocks, we should have to take to the jungle, try to reassemble there, and make for Madioen somehow. One vital thing: each man had to stick to his rifle at all costs. We did not know how the natives would react once the Japanese had landed, and there were also wild animals. But things in the meantime seemed quiet and, all well, we might get through unmolested.

We climbed into the trucks and posted a man at each corner with a rifle, loaded; we advised the men to keep down as far as possible out of sight till we were well clear of the town. Then, very warily at first, we set off, slowing down at every corner in case there was something untoward round the bend. The thin mists that collected in the cooler night air drifted from beneath the palms and between the houses like the breath of cattle on a winter morning. We cursed our engines for the whine they made, even though we were running slowly, for it seemed to fill the still air, announcing our presence as unmistakably as a fanfare of trumpets. I kept a sharp eye towards the beach but the palms grew thick on that side and it was too far to see what was happening there. After a time we got out of the suburbs and struck the main road for Semarang. It was clear enough, though un-signposted, being flat and straight and apparently deserted. Like the road from Cheribon, it was lined with palm trees on each side; in the dank air they dropped beads of moisture on to the road, making mottled patches on the surface. The driver turned his head round towards me, looking for instructions. 'All clear!' I said. 'Let her rip!' He put his foot hard down on the throttle, gripped the wheel tightly, and fixed his eyes on the road straight ahead. The truck shot forward. There were some shallow pot-holes in the road, and when we struck one of these the truck bucked alarmingly. I had the map on my knee, trying to iden- tify the features of the landscape as we passed. Still the sea was out of sight, and now on the map I saw that the coast ran out to a blunt headland between Pekalongan and Semarang from the landward side. From time to time I kept an eye on the dark, Italianate face beside me, tense and drawn, but the eyes never for a moment lifted from the road.

By now the dawn was not far off, and a grey glow rested upon the landscape. Glimpsed fugitively out of the corner of my eye, as we rattled along, rose the jagged backbone of Java. Upon the very highest ridges the low rays of the sun were now striking, turning them to a soft cinnamon gold. The grey mist still hung over the plain, but it had a luminous core and vision was clear enough. At last we got past the headland; and we could make out the sea, shouldering its way back towards the road, the long curve of the beaches, white and broad. Here the mountain ridge retreated permitting a broader ribbon of plain. Everything still seemed very peaceful, and it could not be long till we were in Semarang.

My attention must have been distracted for a time, either by the mountains or the sea, for I heard a sharp cry of alarm, and the driver nudged me roughly. 'Look ahead!' he called out. As directed, I gazed along the road towards Semarang and saw the horizon filled with flames, great waving tongues leaping spectacularly into the sky. Above and around them, great banks of smoke were piling up like a dark mountain ridge. Semarang was burning! With a cold stab of despair to the heart, I realised that the Japanese had got there before us. The trap was sprung and we were within the jaws. I called to the driver to stop, and there was a hot screeching of brakes. Then we all piled out and, while the men watched the flames, Bairstow and I got down at the side of the road for a brief council-of-war, the map spread out on the grass. Closely we scanned it, searching for any road that led off to the south and might allow us to bypass the town. But the map showed none. We could not turn back now. There was nothing for it but to edge forward cautiously. Nearer the town there might be some track, too insignificant to put on the map, which might yet allow us to escape.

Fortunately the main road was now flat and straight, and there were no palm trees. That allowed us to see a good way ahead and thus lessen the danger of an ambush. As we approached we could see that just where the town began there was a large iron bridge, painted green, which must span a river which still, however, was out of sight. If we got over that, our chances of finding a side road might be enhanced. On the other side of the bridge we could make out a wide avenue lined by low trees, like tamarinds, which led up a slight incline to the centre of the town where the fires were raging. As we slowed down at the approach, I suggested to the driver that we might charge the bridge, but just in time we saw that it was humpbacked and might break a spring. Out of the corner of my eye I could see our sentries, their rifles at the ready, hanging out over the edge of the truck. Suddenly one of them gave a sharp cry of alarm. 'Look out!' he called. 'Soldiers at the parapet!'

Just as he spoke, a soldier ran out into the middle of the road. He was tall and dressed in green, and waved his rifle above his head. Happily he was Dutch. Another stepped out behind him. With a sigh of relief we drew up just short of the hump of the bridge. How, we asked, could we get to Madioen? Where was the road? The NCO in charge looked at us very coldly. 'There's no road!' he said. 'Every bridge was blown this morning. You're too late. This is as far as you can go! There's no road beyond the bridge.' Desperately we explained our predicament. We could not possibly go back. The Japanese were landing at Pekalongan when we left, and to turn back now would simply be throwing ourselves into their hands. We must get forward, somewhere, somehow to Madioen. The Dutch soldiers looked glum, and had a word with each other. There was just one thin chance, the NCO explained. There was a narrow gravel road running down to the right here which crossed the plains and then climbed up into the mountains on its way to Magelang and Djokjakarta. He could not say whether the bridges on this road were blown as well. Even if they weren't, he was not at all sure if our trucks with their loads would be able to make the mountain road. If the bridges were already down we were, of course, finished. With no option, we were prepared to try. We asked where the Japanese had landed. At Rembang, they said, a little way along the coast. They were not in Semarang yet but they were expected at any moment. The fires raging ahead of us had been started by the Dutch themselves. They had decided to burn down all the main buildings and anything that could be of any possible use to the enemy.

So we set off on our uncertain journey down the side road that ran over the plain in the direction of the mountains. As we left, the Dutch soldiers pulled off their hats, waved them in the air, and called out 'Long live the RAF!' Touched at the leave-taking, and despite whatever doubts we might have harboured about the fate of this little section of the RAF, we responded with: 'Long live Holland! Long live Queen Wilhelmina!' They were hardly out of sight when the crunching of gravel beneath the tyres and the rough jolting of the springs made it clear that, even without the mountains we were not going to have an easy passage to Djokjakarta.

It was not long till we parted from the river. Then, branching across the plain, we came to the shoulder of a flattened ridge. Behind this we came upon the river again, now looking sluggish and deep as it meandered in a long, endless pool across the flat plain. Then ahead we could make out the first of the bridges, and as far as we could see it was still intact. As we got nearer we could see three soldiers standing beside the parapet, but when we slowed down to have a word with them they waved us on frantically. We could now see the reason, for there was a fourth soldier kneeling down beside a hole which had been dug in the road beside the parapet wall. He was fixing an explosive charge in the cavity, and this was why they were so eager to get us across quickly. Sensing danger, my driver set the truck at the bridge like a horse at a jump. The raised arch was higher than he thought, for we lurched abruptly into the air, and came down on the other side with a bump that jarred the chassis violently. Normally, springs would have fractured under an impact like this, but the vehicle was new, or the springs may have been reinforced, for they held. We were sorry at being robbed of our chance to speak to the little, lonely, green-clad company, one of whom was no more than a schoolboy dressed incongruously in a man's uniform, like a child playing a charade. So many of the Dutch soldiers we saw seemed either to be elderly men or mere boys. As we drove on, we turned back from time to time to watch them. At length they dwindled to a little green dot beside the arch of the bridge in the distance.

Before we got to the hills, there was one more bridge to cross. Beside this, too, there was a small company of soldiers, and they had a field telephone which one of them was using. We stopped for a little and they told us that this bridge would not be blown till after the one we had already crossed. The hill bridges further on would be held till they were actually threatened by the Japanese. They were needed to allow refugees from the north to escape, and to get reinforcements up to the front.

Then, at last, we reached the hills. The gradients fully justified the fears that the descriptions of the soldiers at the Semarang bridge had sown in our minds. The road went straight up the mountain side, zig-zagging in fierce S-bends, and almost immediately we were in low gear, crawling noisily upwards. In this we remained for almost the rest of the ascent. The water boiled in the radiators but the engine performed amazingly, never giving the slightest indication of failure. On the way we passed several hill stations. Their chalets were picturesquely tucked away into nooks and folds in the mountains, each with its garden and its beds of glorious flowers. Now, too, we began to encounter the Dutch children. They were flaxen-haired and golden-skinned, seemingly evacuated from Semarang and the other threatened towns on the plain. They were out on the road, standing in little groups, watching the fires raging in Semarang, but when they saw us they forgot Semarang and ran beside the trucks, waving excitedly and calling out greetings and asking questions in Dutch which sadly we could not understand.

The road wound about so much on its upward journey that it was very difficult to make any realistic assessment of the distance we had covered. But after what may have been about ten miles we came to the summit ridge. Beside the road a little belvedere had been built out on a spur which commanded a majestic panorama, stretching from Pekalongan right away round past Semarang to the eastern plains. Just above us was the cone of Merapi, which we had watched the night before from Pekalongan, and which cut off the view to the south-east. Down its sides, from the distant crater, stretched the congealed rivers of red mud, and lower down the wild jungles that clothed its flanks gave it a strangely untamed and forbidding appearance.

Before leaving the belvedere, I took my farewell of the burning Semarang. For me the leave-taking had a bitter savour, for this was not just leaving a burning town. Long ago, as a boy, I had read about Semarang in Conrad's *Lord Jim*, and ever since, in a very special way, it had come to symbolise the romance of the eastern islands. Now it was being consumed by flames, kindled not by the hostile Japanese but by the Dutch themselves.

From the summit ridge, the road ran southwards, though not as steeply as on the northern shoulder. Swiftly we coasted downhill; and about halfway down we passed through the hill station of Magelang. Somewhere near here are the great Hindu temples of Borobadoer, but we did not know about that till later, and to us it seemed just an ordinary hill town with an inordinately long main street. Then, at length, running down an endlessly long hill, and with smoking brakes, we entered Djokjakarta.

The streets had a welcome air of spaciousness, though this may have been heightened by contrast with the narrow hill road by which we had just come. Alongside the road grew enormous banyans, some of the biggest we had seen, and they lent a cool shade. This, in normal circumstances, was clearly a rich and distinguished town. Though out of the shade of the trees it was very hot, there seemed to be a surprising number of people about in the streets, and as we passed they took a very close interest in our trucks. There were as yet no signs of any Japanese about, but already many of those we saw seemed to have a furtive, hostile look.

A bystander directed us to the town hall. My British uniform gained me immediate admittance to the mayor's private office, where a sad scene met my eyes. The mayor himself was busy searching through files and drawers, extracting from them what appeared to be confidential or important documents. These he placed in little bundles on the floor, and a Dutch girl, very young and pretty, was carrying them out into the garden where a great bonfire was blazing fiercely. During all this time tears were pouring uncontrollably down her cheeks. She seemed to be lost and woe-begone beyond all consoling, though never for a moment did she pause from her task. I told the mayor about my need to get the three trucks of airmen to Madioen, and of the difficulty we had run into at Semarang. We had come over the mountains by the Magelang road as the bridges on the main road were down, though we hoped that the road from Djokjakarta to Madioen might still be open. Had he heard any word about the situation in

East Java? He looked at me with cold blue eyes. There was no longer any hope, he said, of getting to Madioen. Japanese parachutists had already landed on the aerodrome and it was in their hands. What, I wondered, had happened to our squadrons? Would he please try to 'phone RAF Headquarters in Bandoeng? We needed new instructions. I would wait till a message came through. When he tried to get through to Bandoeng on the telephone, the line was, as could be expected, heavily jammed with military traffic. But at last he got through to Dutch Headquarters and gave them my message. They promised to get in touch with British Headquarters and then phone him back.

So I went out into the square. Here and there, in this extensive open space, were grassy mounds invitingly shaded by trees and on one of these, sat our airmen, patiently waiting for news. They told me they had been able to buy in a nearby *warung* some biscuits and light mineral water. It was little enough but they seemed to be grateful for it, and even more for the quiet pause after the hot journey in the trucks and the dramatic events of the morning. More important still, Bairstow had succeeded in again getting the tanks filled with petrol. I sat with Bairstow and the men, talking quietly and feeling how remarkable was this quality of ordinary British men to accept crises without fuss or complaint. Then I went back to the office, finding that as yet no word had come through. Still the poor girl carried her bundles of papers out to the fire, and still the tears ran down her cheeks which were now smudged from the smoke and the soot where she had rubbed them, incongruously disfiguring her sad, lovely face. I was sorry that, without Dutch, I could not speak to her, but I sat on a chair, sharing the melancholy of my surroundings, and watching the endless pilgrimage to the fire. Then the telephone bell rang out, harsh and insistent above the crackle of the flames in the garden. The mayor took the call, and as he waited he nodded to me to confirm that it was from Bandoeng. At last the message came and he listened attentively. Then he put the mouthpiece down. 'You are to go back to Bandoeng,' he said. 'You are to take the road along the south coast of Java. You are to come back as soon as possible. That is the end of the message.'

That was all we needed. I thanked him warmly for his help, without which we should indeed have been lost. Then I shook hands with him, and with the poor girl. Her tears stopped just long enough to let the ghost of a smile stray to her wan, stained face, and what a sweetness there was in that pallid smile. How rich must have been its radiance in less desperate days! Then I left the office and stepped out into the blinding light of the square.

The men received the news of our orders to return to Bandoeng with unfeigned relief. But we were by no means out of the woods yet. I explained that the landing at Pekalongan in the morning might have nothing to do with the attack on Semarang but have as its objective the dispatch of a force across the mountains to Tjilatjap to cut the island in two. We could therefore not count ourselves out of danger till we had put the vital southern road junction behind us. It was still more than a hundred miles away, over unknown mountain roads, and our experience at the Magelang crossing had given us some idea of what that might mean. Furthermore, we had only three drivers and they had had a hard enough day of it already. We could make an attempt to get to the crossroads that night if the drivers were prepared to carry on. Alternatively, we could spend the night somewhere along the south coast, and go on to Bandoeng next day, though if we did that, we ran the risk of being cut off. We put it to the men and they were adamant that we should carry on to the crossroads; and the drivers did not seem to be daunted by the many miles still to cover.

So we climbed back into our trucks. A small band of Javanese had gathered round, and they eyed us icily with no friendliness in their faces. As we started to move off we waved our hands to them in a friendly fashion and called out a simple farewell, but they just stood there watching, shifty-eyed and unresponsive. It was an omen which I noted carefully. This was something we should have to take account of in the days ahead.

WE BEAT A RETREAT

Almost immediately after leaving Djokjakarta we plunged into the great tropical rainforest. This was something I had not seen so far, and its fecundity was so overwhelming and its jungle growth so vast, that it filled me with amazement. We drove along a gloomy canyon between the soaring boles of the trees in a grey-purple twilight. Here and there, far above our heads, narrow pencils of light pushed through the leafy canopy, and the effect of these falling obliquely through the grey forest dusk was to create an illusion that we were submerged beneath the waters of the sea, and were driving along beside an aqueous peristyle. Some of the trunks had creepers clinging to them which threw out sinister coils, which in turn leapt the gaps between tree and tree. From the lower branches of these trees which had been invaded by the creepers hung ragged festoons of tangled lianes, while long pale tendrils ran up the bole right to the summit in search of light. It was a cold, pitiless place, and I was anxious to get out of it.

After about an hour's driving from Djokjakarta the road left the worst of the rainforest behind, and shortly afterwards we struck the coast. This was very different from the northern shore of Java, with its wide white beaches. We seemed to be driving along the top of what looked like cliffs, and the shore was beneath us, but it was rocky. The sea was still as a mirror and glowed with a strange blue sheen beneath the hot sun. Strangest of all there was not one ship to be seen – not a junk or a *prahu*, not even the tiniest skiff. It was an empty sea, quite deserted and dead.

It was a little after we had left the coast, issuing on to a rough green grassland, that we stumbled upon a most remarkable relic. Along the north side of the road stretched a terraced slope crowned by a series of pyramid-shaped temples. They were extravagantly ornamented with pinnacles and carved figures, some in bas-relief, and all Indian in character. Though hewn from what looked like the local grey volcanic rock, and exposed to the rains and wild fluctuations of the Java climate, they seemed to be remarkably well-preserved. There was, of course, no one about to ask what they were and we had no means of finding out anything about either the builders or the purpose of the structures. When, at the end of the day, we asked about them we were told that they were probably part of the great temple complex of Borobadoer, and were built by Hindu conquerors of Java about a thousand years ago. This was of course no time for exploration, and we did not stop, but drove on westwards on our way to Tjilatjap.

About mid-afternoon we coasted down a long hill into a small town which may have been Koetaradjoe. It did not look like the kind of place that would be able to supply us with a substantial meal. There was, nonetheless, a large orange-coloured double-storeyed building on the left-hand side of the road which had a single-storeyed wing jutting out from it. It looked like a hotel, with this a kind of dining-room. At any rate, it justified enquiry. So, jumping down from his truck,

Bairstow set off towards it. But just then my driver, who had been peering among the trees that covered the slope on the opposite side of the road, announced that he had just seen a Dutchman standing up there beside a bungalow. When the truck drew up, he had been watching us, but now he had disappeared indoors. I thought this might prove a better source of information and, calling to Bairstow to wait a little, I got down from the truck and set off up the little pathway among the trees. There was a small garden, rather unkempt, with a fence round it and a gate which opened on to the main path. The bungalow itself was small and the paint was peeling. There was a general air of dilapidation about the place. I knocked on the door and waited uncertainly. Then, after a time, a Dutchman came out. He was tall and heavily built with the rugged look of a policeman or a wrestler, and he stood looking at me blankly. I explained to him the purpose of my visit and the plight of our men. Was there, I asked, any hotel nearby where we might get some food? 'Come in!' he said in English, in a flat, somewhat muffled, voice.

I followed him into what I took to be the drawing-room of the house which was plainly, if adequately, furnished in the austere manner appropriate to a planter's house. At the door which led to the back premises stood a woman, youngish, expectant, rather frightened-looking, and presumably his wife. Without speaking the man went over to the little cane table that stood beside the window. Then, coming to a halt, he stood there, gazing stonily out into the garden. There was something disconcerting about his sullen silence. Uneasily I asked again if he could tell me where I might get some food for the men. Rooted to the spot, he just stood gazing out of the window as if in a trance, and said nothing. This behaviour baffled me, and I became alarmed. How was I going to get out of this predicament? Then, without warning, this gigantic man collapsed in a lump into the wicker chair which stood beside the table. He laid his head on his hands and sobbed convulsively; the tears poured down his cheeks and his great frame shivered as if with cold. Silently, and in pain, his wife stood watching him, the only signs of her distress being a slight twitching at the corner of her mouth and the white of her knuckles as she clenched her hands tightly. Strangely, she did not cry.

After a short while, the man lifted his head from his hands and looked imploringly in my direction, making no attempt to staunch or to conceal his tears. To watch a man reduced to the simpering pitifulness of a child is, whatever the circumstances, unnerving. 'What can I do?' he sobbed in fluent English. 'It's my wife. Nobody will help my wife! The Japanese are a kilometre up the road. They will take my wife. They will do something terrible to my wife!' His fears about his wife I shared; his statement about the Japanese being only a kilometre away up the road I was prepared to dispute. Wherever the Japanese were, I assured him, they were not up the road. We had just come over the road from Semarang and there were no Japanese on the road when we came. So how could they be there now? 'It's not that road!' he protested. 'It's another road. A friend 'phoned a little while ago and said that the Japanese were a kilometre up the road. Why would he say that if it was not true?' His eyes gave a flash of triumph as if he had effectively demolished my argument. It was not for me to explain the credulity of his friend; this was the kind of situation that spawned rumours. I asked him if there were no other Dutch in the town with whom he could get together and discuss calmly what they were to do. Then a glint of cunning kindled in his eye, and he looked at me sharply. 'Where are you going with your soldiers?' he asked. It was an odd question, and surely he was not ingenuous enough to expect me to answer it! I told him that we were going to our military post. I could not be any more explicit than that! He paused a moment. 'Could you?' he asked – and then faltered, as if overtaken by shame at the revelation of his plan – 'could you take any people along with you?' I scotched that hope immediately. No, that would be the very worst place for any civilians to be. They were not armed, and would merely get in the way of ourselves who were. In any case it would be a sanguine person who gave them any chance of survival if they fell into Japanese hands when they were with us. His wife stood listening, statuesque, sallow-faced and very still, though obviously in the deepest distress. I did not know if she could understand English sufficiently to follow our conversation, but even without English she could not fail to get the drift of what we were saying. But now, more than ever, I was determined to get out of this house. I made one last effort before I left. Would the large orange building, I asked, perhaps be able to help us? He looked at me blankly. 'I do not know!' he said. 'Perhaps . . .' I bade him a swift and perfunctory goodbye and walked out through the door.

We found, as we expected, that the large orange building was a hotel, the annexe being a dining-room with a bar attached. It was sparsely furnished with a few white-wood tables and chairs. The bar had a long curved front, and round it were gathered a group of Dutch, both men and women, who were talking to each other, quietly and casually, and took not the slightest notice of our entrance. From their appearance of nonchalance one would have thought the Japanese had never been heard of in Java. It may have been courage or bravado; more likely it was just helpless apathy. They were past hope, and now were past caring. They had surrendered to a paralysis of the will. There was little the hotel could do for us. All they had was a little cake – that dry, yellow, tasteless thing they call English cake – but they had plenty of tea and we were thankful for that. So we got the men in from the trucks and we sat round the tables and had our English cake and tea. When it was over we got up to go. The Dutch at the bar showed no interest in us and did not ask where we were going. I paid the bill, as in Pekalongan, with a compromising RAF chit, and then we shepherded the men back into the trucks.

Not long after we left the little town we ran again into the rainforest, not so dense or overpowering as on the way from Djokjakarta. Under the hot noonday sun the stagnant air had lain imprisoned under the trees, and now its breath filled our nostrils with a rank, perfumed foetor as of rotting flowers. It would be about half an hour later that we were startled by a frenzied hooting behind us. Looking back, we could see a large motorcar approaching at great speed. This might spell danger! Was it possible that the large Dutchman's story was true, that the Japanese really were only a kilometre up the road? Quickly we drew into the side and stopped; the men got their rifles to the ready. Then, as the vehicle got nearer, we could see that the driver was a European. As he passed he mounted the opposite verge, bumping along the rough ground at great speed, and now we saw with amazement that he was none other than the man I had just spoken to in the bungalow. His wife was sitting beside him, but we could see no luggage in the car. Where could they be making for now? Might it be Tjilatjap? Did they think they could still get on a boat and get out?

After about half an hour, the car returned, again travelling at great speed. It sounded its horn persistently to drive us off the road, and as before we drew into the side to let it pass. During the rest of the evening – till, indeed, we arrived at our destination – it continued to pass, and re-pass us, always at high speed, and always with the horn blaring. The driver seemed anxious to keep close to us in case he ran into Japanese, but another possibility began to creep into my mind. Could his senses finally have become unhinged under the strain? In the bungalow it seemed that the breaking-point was near. What happened to him in the end I do not know, for we never spoke to him again, and next day he did not appear. After they had got past the first moments of anxiety our men tended to pour scorn upon his panic-stricken driving. But he was essentially a very tragic figure, and in the end I think they all came round to this view for they suppressed their ribaldry.

When we came to the crucial crossroads near Tjilatjap, the evening was almost upon us. It was an insignificant-looking junction of rough dust-roads among the jungle trees. Down to the left lay the port. We should have liked to drive down to see it, but our way lay ahead. Now that we were out of immediate danger we should have been able to relax a little, but the next town, called Tasikmalaja, was another fifty miles further on and we needed to get there to be sure of food and proper rest. My black-avised Scottish driver, sullen and short as ever, had little to say about the prospect but offered no protest when I said that we must drive on.

A few miles further on we fell in with a long column of RAF. After marching all day in the sun they were foot-sore and very weary, but they plodded on doggedly, borne by the thought that they would be at the port in an hour or two, and then they would be getting out. They said they had come 'a long way', though the names of the Javanese places they had come through did not mean much to us. They could not tell us much about the war, though they said that the Japanese had landed in strength at the western tip of the island and were moving on Batavia. They marched away, their boots kicking up the red dust on the road, and we waited for a little and watched them enviously.

What light of day still lingered along the jungle road was by now almost gone, and it was in a soft twilight that we drove at last into Tasikmalaja. The little town nestled picturesquely in a cup of the great mountains. It seemed a quiet and sleepy place with cobbled, uncomplicated streets, and several of the larger houses had courtyards which we looked into, through arches, as we passed. We could see electric lights switched on and people sitting at dinner, as if the Japanese meant nothing to them, and the old way of life would go on for ever. We stopped the first Dutchman we saw and asked where the mayor's office was. He said it was down the first road to the left, then you turned right; and it was the large orange-painted building with the arch above the door. We found it just as he had said, only it looked deserted, though a light was still visible in a window and we hoped somebody was there.

The driver pushed his hands out to the top of his wheel and tensed them rigidly like a sleepy cat. Then he heaved a deep sigh and broke his long silence. At the end of it all, he showed that his dour, dark spirit had been under greater strain than we might have suspected. 'We've made it!' he said. It had, indeed, been one of the finest pieces of driving we would be ever likely to see. Had he faltered in any way, our fate might have been very different.

TROUBLE AT TASIK

The mayor was a tall man, surprisingly youthful-looking, with a shock of blond hair which swept over his tanned brow and temples and above his thin, well-cut features. The assurance and distinction of his presence was matched by a corresponding courtliness of manner, but his suave, cultured voice in no way hid the cutting edge of the displeasure with which he welcomed our arrival. Dutch refugees, he told us, had flooded into the town taxing its resources to the utmost; revelling in self-pity, he chanted to us the litany of his tribulations: there was no room; there was no food; there were so many strangers in the town that he did not know what to do – in any case he had not been told that we were coming. Clearly very near to the end of his tether, he would dearly have loved to see us move on elsewhere. Among all the Dutchmen we had encountered, he was the first whose attitude was studiedly unaccommodating.

But I also was approaching the limit of endurance and, sitting down doggedly on a chair, I cut short his recitation. About one thing he must entertain no doubt whatsoever: we had had as much as we could put up with for one day. Nothing would make us move on from the town that night, and if the worst came to the worst we should sleep in our trucks and eat nothing. Not before morning would we even contemplate moving on towards Bandoeng and, of course, when we got there it would be necessary to submit to Dutch Headquarters a report on the nature of our reception here. But for this night, at least, and in the face of every difficulty and obstruction that might be placed in our way, in Tasikmalaja we were determined to remain. A little daunted by my unexpected intransigence, the mayor took to telephoning. With fading hope I listened as one call followed another, but at last he said that a small hotel – a kind of *pension* nearby – had offered to let him have one room with two beds in it for the officers. For the men he could get nothing, and the only thing he could think of was a school – perhaps we could manage in it since we were staying for *only one* night? Food undoubtedly would be a problem, but he could get some rice, perhaps also a little meat. Did our men know how to make a *nasi-goering*? I said the men knew nothing about a *nasi-goering*, but if we got the rice and the meat we could do something with it. Might we have a look at the school? He said he would get a soldier to show us.

Going out into the ante-room he soon returned with a Dutch soldier, a rough, uncompromising character with lantern jaws and scowling eyes. Even when addressing the mayor his speech sounded abrupt and boorish, though we could not understand his words. For taking British airmen round the town in search of lodgings and food he obviously had little relish, and he took not the slightest pains to conceal the fact. 'Kom!' he said, scowling in my direction. 'We go!' Following him out of the door, I found a Dutch army jeep waiting in the roadway. Standing around in patient groups nearby were Bairstow and some of the men to whom, as I passed, I gave a hurried report on the present troubled state of negotiations. Then we climbed into the jeep and, starting off with a jerk, were soon careering madly along the road, following roughly, but in reverse, the route by which we had come into the town. When we came to the main road we shot across it blindly. Happily there was nothing in the way, or we should have had no chance.

The road on the other side was narrow, and we were bumping madly along it when suddenly, without any warning, we careered with screeching tyres into a narrow lane at the side where four or five native children were playing in the roadway. On seeing us they gave a high-pitched scream and scattered in all directions, but they had been given no chance and one little mite, failing to reach the kerb in time, was struck by the near mudguard and wheel just in front of me and tossed like a sawdust doll into the gutter. He looked badly injured, and I called out to the driver urgently to stop, but he just kept his foot hard down on the throttle and carried on. I turned in anger and shouted at the man. At the end of the lane there was a sharp turn at which he would have to slow down to get round, and I made to jump from the jeep if he did not stop. Goaded into speech, he now exploded in a torrent of abusive Dutch, but I had no trouble with his concluding sentence, which was in English. 'It's only a *wog*!' he shouted at me. 'And this is a *war*!' Although he slackened speed at the corner, it was still too fast to risk jumping off. Once round the corner he shot off again through a baffling labyrinth of lanes and streets till we arrived in front of what looked like a kind of store. Without a word the driver dismounted and entered the building. After a short while, he returned, accompanied by two Javanese who were carrying a bag of rice, which they loaded on to the back of the jeep. Silently, for I was now beyond speech, we set off again and arrived at a white concrete building which looked not long completed. It stood beside a steep bank and had an attractive garden, with some fruit trees at one side. 'School!' said my guide. I went in alone and had a quick look at it. It was unfurnished and austere, but it was roomy, clean and cool and I could see that it had a very modern kitchen. Naturally, there were no blankets or mattresses, but it was far better than Tjikampek and, apart from sleeping facilities, even than Pekalongan. We should manage here tolerably well for the night.

The mayor welcomed me back with an expression of unfeigned relief. I told him the school provided all the basic comforts we needed. We had already collected a bag of rice and looked forward to getting a little meat. There was one thing more: we had knocked a native child into the gutter! I thought he must be seriously injured and would need a doctor immediately. His driver had been driving madly and had refused to stop. Now that he had more time, the soldier would doubtless be giving him all the details. In the meantime, as mayor entrusted with the welfare of the citizens of his town, he would, naturally, be getting immediate help for the child. We took the bag of rice from the jeep and put it into one of our trucks. Then we drove back with the men to the school. They seemed pleased with their new quarters and we left them to settle in. Bairstow and I returned to the mayor's office to see about collecting the ration of meat and to have a look at our own accommodation for the night.

We had barely dismounted from the truck in front of the office when we heard a loud shout, once or twice repeated, and then the excited chatter of Welsh voices.

There, marching through the purple twilight haze along the road from the west, was a long column of khaki-clad British troops, a Colonel and a Major at their head. They were tough-looking men, sun-browned and covered with dust, and obviously weary after a long day. They stood to, and the officers came forward to greet us. They told us they were ack-ack gunners and had been ordered to Tjilatjap to get on to a boat. The men had seen a lot of action and needed a rest. They intended to billet here for the night and go on to Tjilatjap next day. I told them of our experiences and warned them that their reception was not likely to be cordial. But they went into the office, and I followed them, curious. This new demand upon the mayor reduced him simply to despair. There was nothing he could do – just nothing! Our men had taken the last possible accommodation – unless, of course, the soldiers joined the airmen in the school? Perhaps the airmen would help their comrades? So the responsibility was shifted on to our shoulders! He could try to get more rice. The Colonel said they would like to see the school before deciding. So, getting into the truck, we drove off slowly at the head of the column of troops.

We had gone only about a hundred yards along the road and were turning northwards in the direction of the school when suddenly and unexpectedly the air-raid siren began to wail. The sound echoed eerily in the great cup of the hills, and we listened incredulously to its sinister reverberations. We looked to the sky, ears straining for the throb of aero-engines, but we could detect nothing. However, we stood where we were, on the alert, in case an attack developed and we had to take cover quickly. Then someone came running from the mayor's office. He was breathless and said the mayor wanted to see us immediately. So the two officers and I returned, leaving Bairstow with the men, to find the mayor white-faced and shaken. He said a message had just come in by telephone from Dutch Headquarters. The Japanese were coming down the road in tanks and lorries and would be here in half an hour. What could we do to help the people in the town? The Colonel turned to me with thinly veiled exasperation. He said he simply did not believe a word of it. The situation was getting quite out of hand; and the Dutch around here had lost their nerve. He had just come down this road and there was not a Japanese for miles. He was quite certain there was not a single Japanese tank between Bandoeng and Tasikmalaja, and if there were any tanks at all – which he very much doubted – they must be either Dutch or British. Both men explained this to the mayor, but he declined to be convinced. The message had come from Dutch Headquarters, he said, and they knew the situation better than we did. If the British soldiers who were in the town refused to protect them, then what were they to do? After the frostiness of our reception, this sudden throwing of themselves upon our mercy left me unresponsive. But the Colonel said that if he made this all-out appeal, there was nothing they could do but agree. They asked for a plan of the town, and when they got it they studied it carefully, especially the approach roads, and selected likely locations for defence posts. Then they called in their Sergeant-Majors and NCOs and explained the position to them. Thereupon, despite their urgent need for food and rest, the gunners were marched off in their squads to prepare the defence posts. The idea was to hold the airmen at the school as a reserve, and Bairstow drove off in our truck to tell them of this, but they did not take kindly to this order at all, holding that if there was to be any fighting the RAF should have at least some part of it.

After a time I went back and joined the officers, and we went out on a tour of inspection of the defence posts. It was a journey very fortifying to morale. Under hedges or in ditches at strategic points the men crouched with their guns, almost invisible in the twilight, and their coolness and efficiency impressed me. Then we went back to the office where we found that the mood had changed in our absence, the mayor being now embarrassed and a little furtive. No further warning had come and he felt that after all there might have been some confusion – in wartime one had to be prepared for mistakes like this. The officers were not prepared to accept this vacillation quite so lightly, though they listened patiently in silence. Then they decided to recall their men. With no word of recrimination that I could hear, the gunners marched back in their squads to the school where they were given a warm reception by the airmen. From some undisclosed source a small supply of meat had been obtained, and with it a bag of raisins and other dried fruit. More important still, a Javanese cook had been recruited from somewhere, and without a word of English but with great competence and authority this man was presiding over the preparation of a *nasi-goering*!

It was at this point, with the men safely back in school and looking forward to their evening meal, that some new trouble unexpectedly developed. The Warrant Officer took me aside and said he had been asked by the men to approach me about a very special favour. Could they be allowed to go down town for a little after dinner just to stretch their legs? They had been sitting cooped up in the trucks all day and it would do them good. Go down the town at this hour and after such a day! My anger flared up in a bright white flame. Did they not need their beds far more than going down town? Had they any idea what they might meet tomorrow? Was not one lesson at Cheribon enough? At least Tasikmalaja seemed small and remote and would not offer much scope for riotous excesses. If I refused flatly, that might kindle resentments, and I had little need of that at the moment. Perhaps a qualified acquiescence might involve the lesser risk. So I conceded their request on two firm conditions: first, they were to be back in the school within one hour; and second, no one was to touch strong drink.

The small hotel to which we now made our way was simply but not uncomfortably furnished. We were given two small bedrooms with two iron beds in each. Then we went to the dining-room where we found we were alone. Like the men, we had a *nasi-goering*. This most typical of all Dutch-Javanese meals consists of rice, meat and fruit cooked to a brown crispness. In almost any circumstances it is appetising – to us, in our famished state, it was like manna from heaven.

It would be round about nine o'clock, I think, when one of the hotel servants came into the room and told me that a soldier was at the door and wanted to speak to me. When I went out, I found that it was the Warrant Officer, greatly upset. My driver, he said, had gone to a 'drinking den' in a slum quarter of the town, where he had been drinking arrack. This is an insidious native brew which can make men violent. Now he was fighting-mad. He had already knocked down two or three Javanese, and when some of our own men tried to quieten him he threatened to knock them down too. The Warrant Officer thought that only the presence of an officer would have any effect on him, and prevent some serious incident. Would I come to try to quieten him down and persuade him to come home? The presence of an officer in circumstances like this, when he runs the risk of being hit by an airman, is the last thing one wants. The driver had already fallen very seriously from grace at Cheribon. My instructions about the visit to the town had been quite explicit. Besides, we were now in a very serious military situation and any breach of discipline like this was doubly reprehensible. I thought it would be better to have a word with the Colonel before deciding what action to take. When I told him what had happened, he regarded the situation as no less grave than I did and immediately offered the services of a Sergeant-Major and a squad of tough gunners to put the man under arrest. We should lock him up for the night and hold a summary court-martial to deal with him in the morning.

The expedition was brief and effective. When the gunners got to the 'den', they found the driver still standing at bay and threatening to strike down anyone who dared to approach him. Even the sight of the burly squad did not at first quell him, and they thought that he would not be taken without a struggle. But the overwhelming nature of the odds against him at length sank into his befuddled brain, and he submitted to arrest without resistance. Now locked up in a small room in the school, under guard, he could cool his passions there till the morning. We made rough arrangements for the court-martial in the morning, and the Colonel instructed his Sergeant-Major about the procedure. With this last and unnecessary, but troubling, matter out of the way for the moment, it was now time for rest.

Bairstow and I went to our room and, undressing, lay down on our thin pallets on our iron beds. But I could not sleep. Despite the utter weariness of my body, my taut and frayed nerves refused to relax. I could see Bairstow also tossing and turning on his bed, sleepless as I. My mind was filled with anxiety for those we had met recently who had been kind to us, and now were in grave peril. What would happen – what, indeed, might already have happened – to the van der Ploeg family, and little Jan and Tineke, in Batavia? Or the hotel-keeper and his wife in Pekalongan? Or the mayor and the sad-faced girl in Djokjakarta? Or the men of our squadrons in Madioen, where the paratroops had landed?

Some time – when I do not know – sleep at last calmed my troubled brain and brought forgetfulness.

We were wide awake next morning before dawn. Nonetheless, even at this early hour the people of the hotel were already stirring, and some of them were at work. Perhaps they had slept as little as we had. It was not good to let the mind stray too much to what this uncertain day might hold for us, but, mercifully, that was still unknown. What was known was the immediate domestic problem, and that disturbed me greatly for I was not sure how the man would react to a trial, and he was my only driver.

After an early breakfast, while the day was still no more than a grey glimmer over the mountains, we repaired to the school. Like us the men had been up betimes, had had breakfast, and were preparing for an early start. A school-room had been prepared for the court-martial. It had a raised dais at one end with a long table on it, and here the panel sat. It consisted of the two Army officers and myself, the Colonel presiding. When we were ready the accused was led in, flanked by two burly Welsh gunners. He was now sober but looked unkempt, and hung his head in a surly fashion. One or two of the men who had been with him were called to give evidence, and it was utterly damning. After this, the verdict, as the accused must well have known, could have been nothing more than a foregone conclusion. The chairman asked him if he had anything to say in miti-gation but he maintained a sullen silence, and he made a bad impression on his judges. Any sentence, of course, could only be promulgated after the war was over, and the circumstances which had made his crime so very much more serious also saved him from the immediate prospect of its expiation. As he knew, he was the only driver able to get us to Bandoeng, and secure in the knowledge of his indispensability he could afford to indulge his truculence.

With this unpleasant business off our hands, it was now time to be off. The gunners fell in first, brown, hard, seasoned men; after the night's rest they seemed full of vigour and almost debonair. We exchanged farewell greetings hoping, as now seemed very doubtful, that they would get their boat all right, and promising to meet again in various places. The most popular, as far as I could hear, was Tokyo; this distant rendezvous, in circumstances little dreamed of in Tasikmalaja, was destined in some cases to be honoured. Racked by misgivings, I took my seat beside the driver prepared, for the time being, to let bygones be bygones, but he seemed to be in a very different frame of mind, and the knowl-edge of guilt imposed on his shoulders no burden of remorse. He sat hunched and sullen over his wheel and seemed to revel in his role of martyr.

Dawn had now broken, and the light that bathed the little town was bland. How small and puny it seemed when contrasted with the crescent of mighty peaks with which it was ringed! Its few tree-lined streets, with their orderly bungalows set back in their gardens and shaded by trees, were tidy and well cared for. Now, seeing its neat insignificance, I did a thing which I could scarcely have imagined possible last night: I experienced a wave of sympathy for the mayor and his problems. How were hordes of refugees ever to be put up in a glorified village like this? We left the streets behind and drove through the scattered houses of the northern suburb. Soon the mountains seemed almost to overhang us. Right ahead was a green cleft slicing through the mountain wall, and this was where our road ran. Almost immediately we found ourselves on a frightening gradient with the truck lying back on its rear wheels and the engine racing in low gear. I watched the driver nervously to see how he reacted to this situation, but with his arrack he seemed to have shed none of his virtuosity with a clutch and gear lever. Now he was going to need it all. The road seemed to have been gouged out of the almost perpendicular wall of the ravine. It was largely supported on the tangled roots of trees and bushes that lined the precipice, and hung above a sheer drop into the green chasm beneath it. On the upper mountain-side, the boles were in places packed tightly together like organ pipes. This road had never been designed for heavy military traffic, and under its recent pounding the offside verge had frayed and crumbled. Here and there it seemed liable to collapse at any moment, being shakily held together only by a root or two. About halfway up the ascent there was a little lay-by, selected for the view and also to allow cars to stop for a while to cool their engines. It had been formed by levelling off the top of a spur that jutted airily out over the ravine. Far below, the floor of the chasm was carpeted by the glaucous foliage of the distant tree-tops. There were some hidden waterfalls far below us, and their faint, fluting murmur rose pleasantly to our ears. Beyond the ravine the eastern horizon was dominated by several great cones, an ivory-white pennant streaming from the crater of the biggest of them while thin tatters of mist clung to the summits of others.

After a while we set off again. The trees got fewer as we climbed higher, and when at length we climbed out on the high plateau there were no trees at all. Here, despite the height, an intensive husbandry was carried out though we were surprised to find no houses for the labourers among these lonely fields. Rice seemed to be the dominant crop and the harvest now seemed ready for gathering, the wall of golden stalks lining the road like a pigmy palisade.

My driver tensed himself suddenly and jammed on his brakes. He said a Japanese 'kite' was coming down the road just a little ahead. Now we could all see it, flying just above the road and winding in and out as it followed its curves. It was no more than a mile away and could not miss us. So, spilling helter-skelter from the trucks, we scattered into the paddy covering as wide an area as we could in case the pilot should decide to give us a burst or two of machine-gun fire when he arrived. We had no sooner got down among the yellow stalks than a Sergeant leapt up again with an oath and ran back to one of the trucks. He said that we had been running *away* from the Japanese for far too long and from now on he was going to run *at* them. He climbed up into the truck, seized a rifle and then, leaping down, ran for the paddy. We could hear him working the bolt of his weapon as if preparing to fire. Had he lingered a moment or two longer, he might well have paid grievously for his praiseworthy effrontery. The pilot came down the road straight towards us. As he passed he almost skimmed the trucks, and we could see his helmeted head watching the road in front of him. Possibly he thought the trucks were deserted and he never turned his head in our direction, for if he had he could scarcely have failed to see some of us. I heard a click from the Sergeant's rifle and waited apprehensively for the report, but he never fired. He said the machine was past before he could get his sights on him. He protested that if we had all taken a shot at him he could never have escaped. He may have been right, and a fusillade from a dozen rifles at this point-blank range might well have got him. On the other hand, if we had missed he could have turned on us, exposed in the paddy. But the Sergeant's pugnacity had given a welcome boost to our morale, and we climbed back into our trucks for the last long haul to the summit-ridge.

At length we reached the watershed. Before us, basking in the sun, lay the enormous extinct crater in which lay Bandoeng. It was almost entirely overgrown with orderly plantations of trees roughly resembling rubber, but they were cinchona, for this was the place from which before the war almost the entire world's supply of quinine and cocaine was drawn. The town of Bandoeng lay in the very centre, looking like the white button in the heart of a great green chrysanthemum. We sat, letting our gaze wander ruminatively over this great panorama. Then one of our airmen drew our attention to something he had just noticed. Away on the northern rim of the mountains there was a deep notch, and in this an aerial dog-fight was taking place. Each on the tail of the other, two fighters were wheeling in a tight vertical loop. It had all the unreality of two gnats buzzing wantonly on a summer's eve, and seemed far removed from the deadly contention of war. We watched fascinated, unable at this distance to distinguish friend from foe. Then one of the fighters at the very bottom of its dive suddenly broke off and swept out of sight behind the cleft. His antagonist made one leisurely circuit of the ravine and then glided out of sight behind him.

Beside the town of Bandoeng is the airfield of Andir. Just as we were climbing into our trucks again a flight of Hurricanes came in to land. The unexpected sight of the familiar and well-loved shapes in the sky kindled a great warmth of patriotic fervour in all our hearts. For a while the machines circled low over the airfield, waiting instructions to land. Then, as we watched, we saw, under the wing of one of the aircraft the white puff of an exploding shell. Immediately every anti-aircraft gun in Bandoeng seemed to open up on the hapless machines. The Hurricanes took instant action to announce their identity. They fired their recognition cartridges; they dipped their wings; they came down to an even lower altitude where their RAF roundels seemed to protest blankly at the demented gunners. Apart from anything else, the Hurricane was one of the most distinctive aircraft of the war. Had the gunners lost their recognition signals or had Japanese attacks made them jittery? Clearly it was going to be only a matter of seconds till one of the machines was shot down. Spellbound with horror, we sat and watched helplessly. Then one of the Hurricanes –presumably the Squadron commander – peeled out of the circuit and streaked away northwards from the town, immediately followed by the others. We had seen no machines actually shot down, but some must have been peppered by shrapnel, and their escape from Bandoeng did not end their troubles for where were they now to go, the northern Javanese airfields being probably in Japanese hands and their fuel supply running low. Perhaps the best they could hope for was a speedy return to sanity on the part of the Bandoeng gunners, which would allow them to return and land.

Dispirited and embittered by this failure in co-operation, we continued down into the town which we found to be a pleasant garden city, designed on spacious lines. We had little difficulty in locating RAF Headquarters and, pulling up in front of the main entrance, I went in to report and hand over the men to their charge. There was an air of general tension and indignation in the building, the shooting-up of the Hurricanes having unleashed some tongues, usually very temperate, to a more forthright expression of their feelings. But round the imperturbable figure of our Adjutant, Trillwood, all this tide flowed unnoticed – or ignored. Quietly he took us into his office where I gave him the rough details of our journey round the island. When I had finished my report, I turned anxiously to enquire about the Vildebeests.

As I had feared, the news was grave, though still confusing. The squadrons had gone into action at Rembang, bombing the Japanese transports, but with what success was still unknown, though in the process some of the machines had been shot down. The reports that had come in about the Squadron Leader left much still in doubt. It was he who had led the machines in to the attack; but beyond that they had few firm facts to go on. An indirect report had come through Dutch sources that a damaged Vildebeest had struggled back to within sight of Madioen before crashing into a paddy-field, with the death of both the pilot and the navigator, though the air gunner had been taken to hospital in a serious condition. The name he had given was Booker, and we did have an air gunner of that name, though he did not fly in the Squadron Leader's plane. Later enquiry, however, established that on the fatal night, Wilkins's own air gunner having been taken ill, Booker had volunteered to take his place. So the evidence seemed to point to the loss of both Wilkins and of Chisholm, his navigator, who was considered one of the ablest officers of the squadrons. Trillwood said that as far as he knew no British personnel had been able to reach the crashed Vildebeest. The Dutch sources, however, had reported that a Dutch woman and a Dutch Catholic priest had made arrangements for the burial of the two dead officers. I later learned that after the war both this woman and the priest had been imprisoned by the Indonesians, but whether it was on account of the part they played in this act of humanity, I do not know.

Now the fighting capability of the Vildebeests was clearly very near its end. I asked what we were going to do now. Trillwood replied that we were clearing out of there in the morning.

'Where to?' I asked.

'Tasik!' he said.

'We've just come from there.'

'I know,' he replied.

CRASH IN THE HIGH PEAKS

Bandoeng was the administrative capital of Java, as well as of the whole Dutch East Indies: all the government offices were here, and also the Headquarters of the military, naval and air forces. RAF Headquarters were to remain here too so that they could keep in close contact with their allies, and the Hurricanes, with their pilots and ground staff would stay on at Andir to provide air cover. All other RAF personnel were to move to Tasikmalaja. I now, to my great surprise, learned something about Tasikmalaja that I had not suspected before: it had an airfield of sorts. It was strange that no one mentioned it to us when we were there. Perhaps they were too busy with other things; perhaps they thought it better not to mention anything that might tempt us to delay our departure.

In the morning a long line of trucks assembled in front of our quarters, brown-and-green mottled like an enormous caterpillar. Preparations for departure went ahead very methodically, as if the Japanese were not on the island, or did not matter. But at length we lined up, numbered and were checked, and we climbed into our trucks. As we slowly drove off, I thought we might make a tempting target for any fighter that might be patrolling the road as the one yesterday. Now I had no responsibility for organising the expedition. Now, also, I was not sitting in the front seat of the leading vehicle beside the driver, and seeing the nature of the road we had to travel over. But he who was there was clearly taking his responsibilities very seriously, for when we entered the ravine our measured progress diminished to a crawl. With the weight of the heavy loads behind them, the braking engines gave out a protesting, high-pitched whine which never relented during the long descent. I could now see that further long slabs of the verge had collapsed since we had come up, leaving raw, jagged cavities that bit into the road ominously. When we came to the worst of the subsidences, we hugged the mountainside tightly and moved forward at a snail's pace till we were past. But nothing untoward happened, and at last the long descent was over and we came to the great trees of the valley floor. The little town lay just ahead of us, peaceful as when we had left it.

We made our way to the mayor's office and drew up in a long line on the roadway in front of it. Inside, the negotiations for our reception and billeting seemed to be fraught with as many difficulties as when we had first arrived. At least on this occasion the mayor could hardly object that our arrival had been unannounced. Eventually, a school on the northern perimeter of the town, but not the one our men had earlier lived in, was allocated to the officers of our squadrons, and to this we made our way. It proved to be a white, open and airy building in an orchard, nestling under the last outcrop of the mountain spur. Grey-tiled and spacious, its floors were cool, and on these we staked our claim for sleeping space. There was no kitchen but this was a trifling inconvenience, for we were informed that a small *pension* nearby had agreed to provide us with food.

The setting was quite superb: above, the great mountain overhang, and around, the scattered fruit trees, all bathed in the cupped sunshine. Those who esteemed the pastoral life could not have wished for a better retreat, and even upon the more practical airmen, who were now about to occupy it, I think its bucolic appeal was not exerted in vain. Jarring slightly upon the eye were a few innovations consequent upon the current disturbances, most prominent among these being a brown gash which defaced the green sward of the orchard where some coolies were digging a trench under the trees. The purpose of this was to provide a refuge against any wanton disruption of our peace by the Japanese. Above it two workmen were busy rigging an *atap* canopy to keep out the sun and prying eyes.

Having roughly settled in, we went off to inspect the airstrip, its nearness to the town surprising us with our failure even to suspect its existence on our first visit. On the town's south-east side an approach road led through some pleasant orchards, from the edge of which the airstrip stretched downwards – a rough clearing with an uneven surface, and covered with a spiky grass resembling stubble. It ended in a low, circular basin which, as the focal point of local drainage, was waterlogged. Along the southern side of the strip, extending round this extremity, grew dense thickets of trees and brushwood admirably suited for the concealment of aircraft. Of our Vildebeests only three, I now learned, had survived, and these, having flown in, were secreted somewhere in the bush.

That first night we spent in the school was peaceful, but soon we were to discover that this was deceptive, for that very afternoon we were roughly shaken from our complacency by the sudden sounding of the air-raid siren. At the time most of us were stretched out on our valises enjoying the siesta, and I for one found no reason to believe it any more than the false alarm which had troubled us on our first night here. But, dubious, Trillwood got up and, going over to the window, gazed at the sky. Suddenly he called out that he could see Jap fighters, down at rooftop, shooting-up the town. No further prompting was needed and, rising as one man from the floor, we made for the trench under the trees, diving into it and crouching low while pulling down the edges of the *atap* to conceal our position. A gap, however, remained at the lower end and through this we watched one of the fighters flying up the street straight towards the school, its machine-guns crackling. Hitting the roof tiles, or the cobbles, some of the bullets ricocheted off with high, singing sounds. Then a hail of bullets rattled menacingly across the tiles of the school, to be followed a moment later by a burst which whipped through the *atap* above our heads and thumped, like a row of stitching, along the wall of the trench at our side. It was a close shave, though none of us, incredibly, was hit. The pilot pulled his machine up sharply to avoid the trees and then, swinging round, proceeded to come back at us. We waited for another burst; but this time he passed over our heads without firing; reaching the bottom of the street, he was joined by his companions who in the meantime had been machine-gunning the southern suburbs of the town. Then, breaking off the bombardment, they flew off in a westerly direction.

The presence of enemy fighters above our last operational airstrip was a very disturbing development, introducing new problems, for with fighters they would also have reconnaissance machines, and our every movement would be under surveillance. In addition, where were they coming from? The Japanese could surely not already have taken Andir? And if they were based on Kalidjati, they would have the high mountain wall to negotiate. One problem admitted no solution: before any night attack could be mounted the Vildebeests had to be taken from the concealing jungle out on to the airstrip in daylight, a proceeding made necessary by the fact that a twig, overlooked near a vital part of the engine – but especially the propeller – might strike the rapidly revolving blade causing in the laminated wood a small indentation, yet able to set up vibrations strong enough to wreck the machine. This half-hour, then, just before dusk, when we were removing the branches, was a highly critical time. Nonetheless, on the nights of Wednesday and Thursday, 4 and 5 March, our three Vildebeests were able to deliver successful attacks on Kalidjati, causing damage to aircraft parked beside the runway. The following night, we planned to launch a third attack.

That Friday evening, as twilight was thickening the shadows in the lee of the mountains, we made our way leisurely down to the airstrip. It was a night far removed from the things we had in mind, the woodlands haloed in a purple glory, and the air under the orchard trees cool almost as in an English autumn. Then, getting out on to the runway, our shoes scraped against the dry bents with the susurrating music an autumn scythe makes in the meadow hay. Just ahead of me strode one of the pilots, a tall youth with a robust frame, heavily boned, especially in the legs. Yellow as corn, his hair was closely cropped and curly. His dress was the conventional flying uniform of the airman, apart from his stockings which, unorthodoxly, had black and white stripes. These intrigued me, stockings like these being worn by Royal High School-boys in Edinburgh; suspecting a connection, I asked him if he had been educated in Scotland. No, he said, he came from Timaru in New Zealand – and these were the colours of his school rugby team; but the bonds of kinship may have been closer than he imagined, for Timaru is not far from Dunedin which is a daughter city of · Edinburgh. He assured me that he never flew without them, now regarding them as an indispensable talisman for success. Bruce Appleby was his name, and with him were his navigator, a taciturn and inscrutable Australian called Atherton, and his air gunner, John Blunt, a genial Australian, anything but taciturn. Walking down the airstrip, we talked about the uncomplicated, open-air life which they had led in the Antipodes, and listening to them I was transported in spirit far from our immediate concerns in Tasikmalaja.

We had left our visit a little late, for by the time we reached the end of the airstrip the dusk already lay thick in the shadow of the jungle trees. But we set to with a will, pulling the branches from the fuselage of Appleby's aircraft in preparation for hauling it out on to the runway. Only about half of our task was done when, eerily, the siren began to wail. For a moment we hesitated, uncertain whether to replace the branches or to run for cover. But our doubt was speedily resolved for, just above the tree-tops, there was a swooshing sound as if a flock of owls was approaching, and a Japanese fighter grazed the branches above our heads. As it passed it let fly a hail of bullets, some of which split the branches or spattered the leaves, while others hit the soggy ground with a dull plop. At the heels of its leader there followed a second fighter, which renewed the fusillade. Scampering into the bush, we looked round frantically for anything that could provide shelter. No trenches had been dug, of course, in anticipation of such an eventuality, for they would have filled with water as soon as completed. Through the jungle, however, there ran several deep, wide ditches designed to drain off some of the stagnant water, and earth from these had been piled up at the sides to form a rough rampart. In the lee of one of these we crouched down, hoping to escape the ricocheting bullets that sang among the trees as several other fighters continued the attack. Then, abandoning the jungle, the fighters turned their attention to the airstrip, flying up and down the field and liberally peppering the unoffending earth with their bullets. This was a development we viewed with no misgivings, and it brought forth a vivid brand of comment from my companions. When the pilots were satisfied that the field had had enough, they flew off westwards.

The raid now seemed over, and none of us had been hit. Back then we went to our machine, hoping that it had been blessed with the same good fortune. But we had got no more than a few yards when a heavier droning sound fell upon our ears, and about a hundred yards away there was a great roar. As one man we plunged into the red slime-filled ditch at our side, having no idea how deep it was and clinging to each other in case we went right under. It proved, however, to be no more than about five feet deep, though both the bottom and the sides were sheathed in a glutinous red mud that provided no grip for hands or feet. Standing there for a moment or two in silence, we listened, and then another bomber glided low over the trees and a heavy bomb crashed through the branches, exploding with a great roar in the next ditch. Instinctively we ducked till the water came up to our very mouths, while the branches of the trees, sheared off by the bomb splinters, crashed round about us. Two other bombers followed, dropping their loads a little further up the side of the runway, near where we thought the other two Vildebeests were hidden in the bush. For a time we remained in the ditch, uncertain whether we were to be subjected to a third visitation. But all seeming quiet, we now turned to the problem of getting out of the ditch. It was no easy task; scrambling on each other's shoulders, we managed to reach the bank. Filthy though we were, we yet experienced a deep feeling of relief, for had one of the bombs landed in the water of our trench, or detonated on impact with a tree anywhere near us, we should have had little chance of survival.

Covered in mud, we made our way out of the jungle to the airstrip where we saw other groups emerging like ourselves, equally filthy. Anxiously we examined our Vildebeest to see if it had been hit by splinters, but we could detect no damage and it seemed to have escaped. Being in too filthy a state even to contemplate preparing the machine for the night's sortie, we set off for the school in search of a shower. Appleby's stockings were now caked with shining red mud so that they looked like bronze greaves. Clearly they would not be accompanying him on this night's flight, which seemed to vex him greatly, and he took it as a very bad omen. He also seemed to find the whole experience particularly humiliating – rather than go through this kind of thing again, he said he would face Navy Os any day in the air. There, at least, you could *do* something; but sitting up to the neck in a dirty ditch seemed to him to demean the status of a pilot.

On reaching the end of the strip, just where the road went off through the orchard, we were unexpectedly met by a strange Wing Commander who said he had come down to see how we were; having had a look at us, he now knew. He asked us if we had been practising with our revolvers recently for we might have to use them very soon, indeed, it would be as well to have some practice himself. So, taking from his pocket a cigarette tin, he removed the few remaining cigarettes and then propped it up on a tuft of grass at the side of the strip. Then he paced out twenty yards, I think, turned around, pulled out his revolver, took aim, and fired. He was clearly a marksman for there was a sharp *ping* as the bullet hit the tin. Grinning with satisfaction, he then asked if any of us would like a shot, but, not surprisingly, there were no volunteers.

That shower in the school was one of the most delectable I can recollect, and in its cleansing flood the greasy slime melted from our bodies. Afterwards we swilled our soiled clothes in a tub till they were reasonably clean, and hung them out to dry. We had little to change into but at least it was good to feel dry and clean again. The dinner that followed was simple but appetising.

We waited till the moon rose before returning to the airstrip. Being now in its last quarter, it flooded the valley with a ghostly half-light and under its cold gleam the mountains took on a greyer, vaster shape than in day time. Night had also brought a new hazard for up on the high ridges lay white banks of fog which in places spilled over the rim of the precipices like huge cornices. The aircrews did not like this at all, fearing fog in these high and inhospitable places. Though naturally shaken by the bomb attack, the flying crews betrayed no signs of it. The fitters, having inspected all three flying machines most carefully, pronounced them to be without damage. So, one by one, the three Vildebeests taxied out from the shadow of the bush and made their way to the top of the runway, where they turned for the take-off. Then the whine of the run, and they were airborne, making for the mountain ridge and climbing slowly under the weight of their bombs. I stood watching them till, like ghostly dragonflies, they faded in the shadowy glimmer.

The estimated time of return saw us back at the airfield, and we had not long to wait for out of the night sky glided down an almost silent Vildebeest, followed shortly by a second. The crews reported that, the mist having lifted from the high ridges, they had a surprisingly good crossing and found Kalidjati clearly visible in the moonlight. They had attacked aircraft parked round the perimeter and thought they had destroyed, or at least damaged, some of them. Before they had cleared the aerodrome, however, the Japanese had got to their guns and some brisk firing ensued. Though they themselves had not been hit, Appleby, who came in last, got the worst of it, but they had seen him flying out of the bursts and they felt sure that another half-hour would see him home. But that half-hour extended to the full hour, and was succeeded by another, and we waited for Appleby's return in vain.

Next morning, at about ten o'clock – all my companions being away, some at the airstrip, some on other duties – I was sitting by myself in what we called the dining-room in the school. Spread out on the table before me was a map of the south-west of Java, the only one I had, but very inadequate with – as on the other Dutch maps I had seen – the mountain masses indicated by a type of hachuring so heavy that it looked like a goat's pelt, and was well nigh unintelligible. What

I was searching for was some road or path which led into the mountains by which we could send in a search-party with a truck to see if they could find out anything about the missing Vildebeest. With my head lowered, closely scanning the map, I gradually sensed that there was some one near me; raising my eyes, I saw before me the very substantial figure of John Blunt, the air gunner of the missing machine. Smiling broadly, and obviously savouring the effect that his unexpected arrival was having upon me, he beckoned to me to come out with him for a moment or two.

When I got out to the front of the building, I found a car standing in the road, the driver being a Javanese soldier in the green uniform of the Dutch army; beside him sat a second soldier. In the back, unperturbed as ever, was Atherton, the navigator, who then got out of the car and, with Blunt, went up to the driver and his companion. With earnest expressions of gratitude for all their help they shook the two men warmly by the hand, after which the soldiers turned the car and, with beaming smiles, drove off, while the two airmen came into the school to tell me about their adventures. They reported that, the mist having lifted by the time they got to the upper ridges, their crossing of the mountains had been uneventful. They were the last of the three machines to arrive at Kalidjati, and by the time they were ready to make their run-in the AA guns were already alerted, the earlier attackers having stirred up the nest. However, they took their time and dropped their bombs on some Jap machines parked in a corner of the airfield, but just when they were pulling out, the fuselage was raked by a burst of fire. Fearing for the engine, the pilot turned immediately southwards, making for the mountain crossing. Their fears were justified, though it was not till they began to climb steeply and a heavier strain was thrown upon the engine that the damage manifested itself. Soon there were loud splutterings and back-firings which grew so ominous that Appleby decided that his crew must bale out. While they were preparing to do so the engine picked up again and they managed, with great difficulty, to scrape over the coll. The worst now past, they hoped, the rest being descent, to make their base. But something further failing in the engine, accompanied by grating noises, Appleby re-issued his orders to abandon the craft. By this time they were above a yawning ravine and, banking his machine, Appleby called to Blunt to jump, which he did, drifting down safely to land in thick bush. Atherton followed but his parachute failed to open properly and he plummeted into the summit of a tall tree which cushioned his fall, saving him from serious injury. The pilot had now no chance to save himself and as Atherton fell he caught a swift glance of the Vildebeest diving into the mountain side.

Buried in the jungle, Blunt now looked around for some means of escape, deciding that a faint clearing high up on the side of the ravine, held out the best promise. His struggle to reach it proved exhausting, but he succeeded, finding there a small native hut, untenanted. After he got down from his tree Atherton found a vague track through the bush which led him, after about a couple of hours, to the little hut in which Blunt was sitting, dejectedly pondering his destiny. Together again, they now made their way across the ravine, heading for the lower ground. At length, having reached the opposite side, they fell in with a group of natives who led them to a tea factory where they found a telephone, with which they were able to get in touch with the manager, whose home was further down the valley. At this point another group of natives arrived with the news, which they conveyed in signs, that they had found the crashed plane. Leaving Atherton to man the telephone, Blunt then returned with the group to the scene of the crash, but all they could at first find was one wing of the Vildebeest, which was lying on a steep bank. Then, wandering further into the jungle, they found the air heavy with gasoline fumes and presently they came upon the point of impact. So violent had been the shock that of the aircraft nothing remained but scattered fragments, strewn widely on the mountain-side. About twenty feet below his shattered machine, they found Appleby. He was sitting on the slope and gazing out across the valley as if searching for his lost comrades. His knees were bent as if he was still at the controls, and he looked so life-like that, at first, Blunt found it hard to believe he was not still alive and unhurt. But then he saw the crushed skull and he knew there was no hope.

They then returned to the factory. By this time the manager himself had arrived on the scene and he immediately sent off a group of natives to bring back the body of the dead pilot. He said he would see it was given a proper burial. When that was done, they accompanied him to his home where his wife had breakfast awaiting them. Afterwards two soldiers brought an estate car from the plantation, and in it they drove the two airmen back to the school in Tasikmalaja.

CALLICK'S PLAN

The news that came to us during the first week of the Japanese landings on Java was scanty and often conflicting, but in one respect it was consistent: it was always bad. Not even the most optimistic imagined that the island could hold out long. Of course, the mountains and the jungle were excellent terrain for a skilfully conducted guerrilla war, but we had not the equipment or the trained men – in particular, we had not the aeroplanes – with which to wage this.

An officer who had given the matter deep thought was one of our pilots, a lean, swarthy, resourceful Londoner called Callick. He had closely cropped jet-black hair which stood straight up on end. Callick was a man with a great reserve of character, and he had the power to look far ahead and size things up. Now he approached me with a project that had been simmering in his mind for some time. In short, would I, after 'this show has packed it in', care to join him, and a third who had not yet been selected in getting a boat and sailing it to Australia? The project was the kind of thing that appealed to me, but I emphasised the need for very careful planning. The risks of an adventure of this kind in a strange country, especially if impetuously embarked upon or haphazardly provisioned, could very well be fatal. In view of the vast distances to be covered and the treacherous nature of some of the waters to be crossed, in particular the Timor Sea, I thought it essential that the third member of the crew should have some practical experience of sailing and navigation. I also mentioned some of the essentials that came immediately to my mind, things like charts, navigational instruments, medicines, fishing tackle, and, of course, food and water-collecting and storing devices, though we should be able to pick up basic food on the way. I had none of these of course, and in some cases, knew little about them or how to get them. But I did possess one faculty which, conceivably, might be put to some use on a voyage such as this, and which indeed, for I think I had mentioned it to him earlier, may have prompted Callick to approach me in the first place: I could speak Chinese Mandarin.

I had acquired this during an earlier three-year stay in China. I had spent three months in Nanking studying the spoken language. In addition, I was familiar with Asiatic people, their outlook and ways of thought and life. We had seen enough to realise that, if the island surrendered, we might expect little help from the Javanese. Not one of us, however, anticipated the rabid xenophobia which the end of the war was to unleash upon prisoners-of-war, internees, their British rescuers, and the returning Dutch. But one thing we could be certain of: no Chinese, in any conceivable circumstances, would regard the Japanese as anything but inveterate enemies. So the help of the Chinese would be an important factor in our plans. We might even go to the lengths of enlisting a Chinese member of our crew who would be useful in making first contacts ashore, and if we were surprised and boarded he might ward off too close an inspection of our craft. One difficulty was that the Java Chinese were likely to speak Cantonese or some other southern dialect equally unfamiliar to me. Yet my possession of the northern, and generally respected, form of the language should dispose local Chinese, if not actively to help, at least not to obstruct or, worst of all, betray our venture.

To a very clear grasp of the technical implications of our project and the things we should be likely to need on our voyage, Callick allied a skill in their acquisition that bordered on the uncanny. He would sit by himself, hunched up in a corner of the school, withdrawn and conspiratorial, with a little notebook in his hand in which he drew up lists of the things we needed. Then he would sally out into the little town. He possessed scarcely a word of Javanese and, since I did not accompany him, I never knew how he conducted his purchases. But it was not long till he was back, laden with his spoils. In this way he laid in a large stock of things that were virtually unobtainable at the time. Among them were numbered yellow quinine tablets; water-purifiers; a small medicine chest and a few rolls of bandages; iodine; sunburn lotion; disinfectant; needles and thread; fish-hooks. After that came a small but efficient stove; some tinned food, especially condensed milk; a compass; a few charts – not good but the best available; and, more ingeniously, some native garments, and coffee to rub into our skin if it became necessary to resort to disguise. To this kind of masquerade Callick's dark features would lend themselves, and I later regretted that I never saw it put into effect. With my red hair and fair skin I could never see my own attempts along this line carrying any conviction. All this hoard he revealed to me surreptitiously, with the stealthy glee of a schoolboy, bit by bit as it was acquired. Then it was secreted in obscure caches in the school, whose location I never sought to know. Though it was fundamental to our plan, the boat had to come last. But Tasik was far from the sea and we could not possibly have foreseen that, on the capitulation of the island, the Javanese would burn every boat that could be of any use to us. Possibly they had been hostile to us all the time; perhaps they wanted to curry favour with their new masters. Surprisingly, Callick never confided to me the identity of the third member of the party, and I am not even sure that he was ever approached or enlisted.

Then, when the time was at hand when we should embark on our project, events took a totally unexpected turn, throwing it into disarray by the removal of its chief architect and agent.

THE FINAL SORTIE

After the death of Squadron Leader Wilkins, command of the two squadrons fell to the senior surviving officer, Flight Lieutenant Hutchison. Early in the afternoon of Saturday, 7 March, he returned from his daily visit to Headquarters clearly upset. A signal, he said, had just come through that we were to burn the two surviving Vildebeests before taking to the jungle as guerrillas. This announcement was met by a wave of incredulity and resentment, which was particularly evident among the flying crews. All the way from North Malaya right down to here in Tasik they had flown the Vildebeests and never once during all that time had they turned a cockpit from the Japanese. Was it fitting, then, that they should now consign the last two survivors to the flames? Could not some more useful – even, indeed, something more in line with their record, more typical and, if you like, heroic – be devised for them to end their days?

Once the idea had been broached, it immediately took wing, gaining instant and enthusiastic support. But having claimed a role, it was not so easy to envisage just what form this role might take. Presently Hutchison suggested that we should all mull over the problem for an hour or so and, meeting later on in the afternoon, pool our ideas. So we dispersed, and the afternoon saw small groups of men huddled in animated conversation in the school, the orchard, down the street to the town, proposing, modifying, rejecting and again proposing various schemes. When the meeting was again convened, a proposal was submitted right away by, I think, Flt Lt Allanson of 36 Squadron. Its novelty and boldness commanded instant and enthusiastic approval, and afterwards I heard no other scheme mentioned. Briefly, instead of burning the Vildebeests, the plan proposed that they should each be manned by a crew of four (the normal complement being three) who would be selected by ballot and flown out of Java by night. The time of departure should be fixed so that their fuel would be exhausted about dawn. They would try to find a junk or some other small craft and ditch alongside it. Then they would seize it, holding the crew to man it and allay suspicion if approached, and then sail it to India, Burma or Australia, as the case might be. Failing this, they would land near a beach and try to find a boat there. As a last resort, they would take to the bush. The chances of success might in the long run hinge upon their choice of direction.

Thereupon I was instructed to get out the biggest map I had and spread it out on the table. It was one of the obsolete Dutch ones I had been given at Tjillilitan, and would not be of much use for navigation, but at least it would give us a fairly good idea of the distances and the dangers involved. The range of the Vildebeest when fully loaded was about 500 miles. With a pair of compasses, and with this radius, I drew a circle with its centre at Tasik. In the east it passed through Bali, and in the west near Padang on the west coast of Sumatra. But we had heard rumours that in an effort to isolate Java the Japanese had landed troops on Bali, and there were even reports that they had seized Timor. Besides, the monsoon had already broken and, flying east, they could expect to encounter headwinds all the way to Australia. Padang, on the other hand, being the only effective port on the Sumatran west coast, had this in its favour: there would be a greater likelihood of shipping in the vicinity. Flying west, they would also have the monsoon behind them. So a decision was taken to make for Padang.

This proposal required, of course, official sanction for its adoption, but that was expected to be no more than a formality. So, in high spirits, Hutchison set off for Headquarters, little expecting the response that his plan was to receive. Permission for the fly-out would be granted only on condition that bombs were carried, and that some target was attacked on the way. With an extra man on board, and with full tanks, their take-off would be difficult. Add to that two 250-pound bombs and it would become hazardous. Even if they accomplished this safely, their range might be cut down, placing Padang beyond their reach. In a situation like this an outburst might be expected, but tongues that were normally ready enough for imprecation remained strangely silent. Perhaps the moment was too tense, if not for anger, at least for its expression. So we proceeded to ballot for places in the aircraft. Few ballots could match the dramatic expectancy of this, conducted on that sultry Java night, a tense silence lying over the land. We each wrote our name on a piece of paper and put it into an RAF cap. The names that were drawn from the cap were these. They deserve to be recorded in full:

From 36 Squadron: Flt Lt Allanson; FO Callick; and WO Peck
From 100 Squadron FO Reginald Lamb; FO Thomas Lamb; FO Taylor; FO Gotto (my companion of the python encounter, and fluent in Malay) and Flt Sgt Melville.

Those, like myself, who were overlooked in the lottery tended to bemoan their ill fortune. Hindsight later revealed they were luckier than they knew.

Midnight was decided upon as the time for departure. Almost every RAF man in Tasik assembled on the airfield to watch the Vildebeests take off. Taxying to the lower end of the field, the first machine paused for a little, its engines purring expectantly. Then the pilot opened up the throttle and there was a great roar. The take-off being to windward, the aircraft had to climb the long slope before becoming airborne; burdened by its excessive load it appeared very sluggish on leaving the ground. There followed a sickening moment when it seemed impossible that it could clear the trees at the upper end of the field. We held our breath in fear. But, almost it seemed by will-power, the pilot heaved up the cockpit before contact, the undercarriage grazing the branches and leaving them tossing and dishevelled as the grey shape was swallowed up in the night. A similar narrow brush with destruction attended the second machine. Flying even lower than its companion it ploughed into the topmost branches, which whipped wildly against the night sky to conceal its passage from our view.

A darkness no less profound than that of that dramatic Java night descended to shroud the fate of the last of the Vildebeests. Whatever the circumstances, the bold adventure ended in failure. The information that filtered through to us subsequently was of a tantalisingly fragmentary nature. Not till the war was over did we receive the first reliable report when one of our Warrant Officers, who had been left behind wounded in Java and was later reunited with the survivors of the squadrons, brought news which he had picked up in Singapore that five members of the crews had at one time been in a prison camp in Palembang, which is on the other side of Sumatra from Padang. Another report was current that Callick and Peck had last been seen in the sea off Padang, and must now be presumed drowned. Neither machine, possibly because of its load, succeeded in reaching Padang. Just short of Bencoolen, some way south, Allanson ditched his machine in the sea and not far off land. All the crew survived the ditching and managed to swim ashore. Expecting Bencoolen to be in enemy hands, they gave it a wide berth and headed north, keeping to jungle tracks. They still clung to the hope that, once out of Java, they had put the worst behind them. But Sumatra offered no more secure a sanctuary than Java. Inevitably, they fell into enemy hands and were confined in Palembang. All four of them survived the war. For some obscure reason Reg Lamb, the pilot of the second aircraft, ditched in the sea some miles from the shore. All the members of the crew survived the ditching, but only one of them succeeded in making it to land. Drifting for long hours, at times semi-conscious, at others unconscious, Flt Sgt Melville was kept afloat only by his Mae West. But in the end he got ashore, and eventually was reunited with his comrades in the prison camp at Palembang. For a time his survival was despaired of, but he rallied and pulled through. He survived both captivity and the war.

The brief reference to this daring exploit which appears in the official *History of the Royal Air Force* is strangely at odds with the facts. Probably it was written before these were known. It reads as follows: 'On the morning of the 6 March, they [i.e. the two surviving Vildebeests] were ordered to seek the dubious safety of Burma, but both crashed in Sumatra and were lost.' Thus, for the last time, Vildebeest torpedo-bombers took to the air on active service. But, as it turned out, they had had their day. In the minds of High Command they had become too inescapably identified with defeat and were never again assigned a fighting role.

Next morning – Sunday, 8 March 1942 – we were due to move out of Tasikmalaja. Our first objective was Garoet, a small town, then famous as a health-resort, which lay cupped in the mountains further west. From Garoet, a narrow road led south into a wild, largely unexplored region known as Preanger, where the Dutch were reported to have secret caches of arms and food, to which we should be given access. More practical plans for the conduct of operations had still to be formulated, but the general idea was clear enough: we should just vanish into this trackless fastness where it would be fruitless for the Japanese to try to find us. From time to time, as opportunity offered, we should issue to harry isolated groups of the enemy. Alternatively, we should provoke them to pursue us into the jungle, where there would be good opportunities for ambushes. The actual damage we might be able to inflict was not likely to be very extensive, but our capacity for spreading alarm and despondency would be considerable and was calculated to justify the risks involved.

No one could dispute that these risks were formidable. A guerrilla campaign of this nature, conducted by Europeans against Asiatic troops in tropical jungles, had never, as far as we knew, been attempted before. We had thus no precedent to go on. The jungle's neutrality extends no further than combatants from the same part of the globe – and even, indeed, of the same, or similar, race. As Europeans, we suffered from the handicaps peculiar to our stature and pigmentation. With us, the ability to melt unobtrusively into the native background did not exist. The Java jungle, especially in the wet monsoon season, is one of the most hostile environments known to the European. It is a hotbed of unfamiliar and deadly diseases such as malaria, dysentery, typhoid and cholera. To add to the dangers there are venomous reptiles, scorpions and tarantulas, and some so insignificant-looking that the unsuspecting European would never know of their danger till too late. Training, of course, would help men to take the precautions necessary for survival. But we had no training and now time was too short to obtain it.

Another necessity would be adequate medical supplies, and, even more important, people trained to use them – in a word, medical officers with a knowledge of tropical medicine. In the present instance this meant the Dutch, and if the Dutch were forced into surrender, or for any reason became unsympathetic to our aims and efforts, we should be forced to rely upon our own resources. That would mean that no matter what local and short-time successes we might be able to achieve, the outcome would never be in any doubt – it would be disastrous. Equally essential would be the co-operation of the Javanese. Without the co-operation of the native population a campaign of this kind is probably always doomed to failure. In Malaya the natives were at worst indifferent, but throughout the peninsula there existed a vigorous Chinese element, fired by what had taken place in their homeland with an undying hatred of the Japanese. It was not so in Java. The Javanese had always resented, and at times openly resisted, Dutch domination. Moreover they tended to be a volatile people, ready to throw in their lot with whatever side seemed to be in the ascendant. If this meant the Japanese, and the end of Dutch rule, so much the better.

About our jungle adventure there was a romantic ring which commended it to some of the more swashbuckling spirits among us. But as a practical exercise in the mechanics of war it was more difficult to defend it wholeheartedly. Nevertheless, on the afternoon and evening of Saturday, while the crews of the two Vildebeests were getting ready for their own venture, our preparations went on apace. With only a pack on our back we had to concentrate on bare essentials. To allow for fast and unrestricted movement through the jungle, our clothing had to be light and serviceable. Unfortunately we had only khaki shorts and this gave no protection at all against mosquitoes, leeches, and the poisonous thorns whose wounds festered into tropical ulcers. What we needed was green Dutch uniforms, but we had none.

Now we discovered another vital deficiency: our ammunition would never meet the needs of any lengthy campaign. A particular shortage was revolver ammunition, which was very serious as the revolver promised to be a most practical weapon in close jungle combat. While we were discussing what we were going to do about this, one of the officers slipped quietly out of the school. Soon he was back with a heavy sack slung over his shoulder. He heaved this on to the table saying that it was his personal contribution to our armoury. We looked into the sack and found it half-full of cartridges. Some of us tried them in the breech of our revolvers, and they fitted perfectly. One of the officers, who knew more about firearms than the rest of us, seemed to be fussing over the cartridges. He took out a penknife and started scraping the bullet of one of them. Then he announced that this was dum-dum ammunition. It was designed for use against wild animals, and was outlawed in war. If one of us happened to be caught with some of this ammunition on him it was not difficult to imagine what would happen to the rest of us if we fell into Japanese hands. He advised us to take it back to where it came from. The trouble was that we had nothing else, and we finally decided to take it with us. We hoped that no occasion should arise for us to use it against the enemy. It might be useful for shooting animals for food.

Next morning we were up at the crack of dawn. We each had a bath in cool, comforting water, knowing that it might be the last we should have for a long time. We put on the best and cleanest of the clothes we had. Then we again checked our equipment, stowing what we should need in the jungle carefully into the pack for our backs and leaving the rest in our valises, which we should have to dump somewhere on the way. Now at last I had to make up my mind about what I was going to do with my Highland dress. In the event, and much to my surprise, the decision, once it was forced upon me, caused me much less distress than I had thought possible. For some days I had thought that fire would provide the only appropriate end, but the bold decision to spare the Vildebeests a similar fate must have worked upon my imagination. In the end, I decided to spare it too. Underneath the window-sill in the school-room where I slept were two shelves designed, I suppose, to hold books, though now empty. Waiting till my companions had taken all their belongings from the room so that I remained in it alone, I took from the basket in which they had reposed all the way from Lorne Road in Singapore my kilt, coatee, the stockings and the silver sporran. Folding them carefully, I laid them on the two shelves. Then, leaving the basket in a corner and shouldering my pack, I left the room. But at that moment I probably suffered more deeply than I was prepared to admit to myself, or was even aware, for there was a symbolism – an ominous foreshadowing – in the renunciation that seemed destined to be fulfilled.

Despite the fact that the men were soon ready and fallen-in beside their trucks, some delay developed which rumour attributed to Dutch obstinacy. Indeed they were said to regard the whole adventure with ill-concealed disapproval as little likely to make any useful contribution to the war. With their practical knowledge it was not surprising they tended to dwell upon the hazards that we should be exposed to in Preanger, and if to those they added others that Dutch women and children evacuated to this part of the island might, through our activities, have to undergo, who could question their logic? Impressions of the intensity of the opposition we encountered have been put on record – a British officer, for instance, who claimed to be in charge of the convoy is reported as writing that 'we had practically to fight our way through the mess to prevent our lorries being forcibly stopped'. To frustration, as to metaphor, some latitude must be allowed, but I must record that, being myself in one of the leading lorries in the convoy, I failed to observe this.

At last we set off along the forty switch-backed miles to Garoet, finding the southern aspect of the mountains no less spectacular than on the north, and, in a grandiose kind of way, beautiful. From the road right to the base of the steep slopes the jungle rolled up in waves, above which were the terraces, elaborately constructed and cultivated. Towering over everything were the peaks, possibly about 10,000 feet though, hanging above us, they appeared to be higher still. From the cone summits descended the rivers of brown volcanic mud, now congealed and sculptured by the fierce rains and winds of the monsoons into fantastic intaglios.

Nearing Garoet, we found that the valley opened out into a kind of hollow or saucer ringed by five magnificent peaks, the floor of this plain being studded with clusters of low hillocks, the débris of volcanic or flood action. These hillocks being mostly of stone, there was little evidence of cultivation, though the short scrub with which they were overgrown made them ideal for the concealment of troops. We never actually entered Garoet, taking the road which led south to Preanger, leaving the main road at a T-junction just short of the town. A little before this crossing, the convoy drew up while some palaver went on up at the front. At first the reason for this was obscure until, about a hundred yards from the road, a head crowned by a British military cap, cautiously raised itself from behind one of the hillocks and eyed us critically. Then, getting to its feet, the figure established itself as belonging to an incredibly youthful-looking subaltern of the British army. With a lordly swagger this young man strode over to the head of the convoy. Tall, spare and ramrod-straight, he carried himself as if he were on the parade ground at Sandhurst. A little way from the leading truck he halted, and there followed an exchange between him and the commanders of the convoy.

Towards his military superiors the young man seemed to adopt an unexpect-edly imperious and uncompromising attitude, permitting himself, in the heat of the moment, some excesses in curtness. The burden of his argument seemed to be that, the Japanese having been reported as about ten miles up the road, he had been ordered to hold this crossroads at all costs and with his men already deployed in defensive positions it was clear that he could not carry out his duties satisfactorily as long as our lorries were where they were, blocking the way and interfering with his lines of fire. He was sorry, but he would have to insist on our moving on. Then, summarily breaking off the parley, he stalked back to his hillock where he continued to eye us, a typical Kiplingesque figure, admirable in his way, the embodiment of a legend which had contrived to survive into an age which had lost the taste for formal heroics. For a moment or two I felt that the convoy commanders, wounded in their pride, were about to dispute the sover-eignty the young man claimed over the crossroads. But, wiser counsels prevailing, they gave orders that we should move on.

Turning into the side-road that led south to Preanger, we immediately found it to be narrow, rough-surfaced, and clearly never designed for convoys such as ours. Presently we arrived at a very narrow humpbacked bridge that spanned a deep drainage-creek, and we were almost upon it before we realised it was defended by a small detachment of British troops who were concealed about the parapet and had a gun, which looked like a Bofors, covering the approaches from Garoet. They looked grim and determined men, and watched our trucks intently as we passed by. Surprisingly in this chance meeting, so far from home and in such critical circumstances, there was no exchange of greetings – no word of Godspeed from us to this forlorn hope. I wonder what, in the end, became of them and their resolute young commander?

From the little bridge the road led southwards across open undulating country, around us lying the paddy-fields with their intensive tillage, their crops now yellow with the fullness of harvest. Far ahead, and ringing the southern horizon, arose a tangle of wild mountains tinted to a faint eau-de-Nil and shimmering distantly in the hot moist air. Seen now in more just perspective as we receded from them, the five peaks we had left behind at Garoet seemed to crouch protectively, as if with linked hands, round their little town.

A hot and trying journey brought us, at length, to the Preanger mountains where the road wormed itself into a long valley which led southwards. High on the slopes that rose on both sides were little plateaux, each claiming its tea-planter's house, most of them looking picturesque, a few precarious. To the cultivation of the tea-leaf every available part of the mountains had been devoted. The further south we drove, the closer approached the mountain walls till they assumed the aspect of ramparts, standing straight up above us; while away to the south, and glimpsed fitfully through a narrow cleft, was a magical blue mist which must have been the Indian Ocean. In the steepest parts the road clung to the flanks of the gorge, winding in tight zig-zags round the outcropping precipices beneath which, lost in the bottom of the ravine, flowed the river. When, from time to time, we stopped for a break, the music of its waterfalls rose soothingly to our ears.

At last we came to a fork where an even narrower road led off to the east. Following this, we soon entered a deep and even narrower gorge where the trees were more numerous and attained gigantic proportions. Perched on the very summits of blue-rock pinnacles, some of them displayed a lonely splendour, very dramatic, prompting us to speculate about how they managed to survive the monsoon gales exposed in such exalted positions, or escape the thunderbolts during the many tropical storms. How, for that matter, did they obtain any nourishment perched on these bare, lofty crags? At length the road escaped from the defile into a small cup in the mountains, in the middle of which was a huddle of buildings with corrugated-iron roofs and a gaunt metal chimney sticking up from one corner into the sky. Driving up to the front of this building, we got out and now learned that it was a tea plantation with the melodious name of Parmegatan, which seemed much in keeping with the romantic beauty of the mountains around. Somewhere nearby was a mysterious retreat known as 'The Valley' where Blackforce, a combined corps of British and Australian troops who had won some conspicuous successes against the Japanese west of Batavia, had already taken up its position. The general plan, it seemed, was that we should collaborate with this body in a concerted guerrilla campaign.

The factory being still in production, its buildings were naturally not available to us for billets and we could see some of the workers going about their tasks. They were timid, willowy young girls with large, lustrous squirrel eyes, and bare to the waist. Upon this unexpected and arresting scene our airmen tended to cast too curious a gaze which spread such alarm and dismay that the manager promptly urged upon us the need to head somewhere further up the valley where our presence would be fraught with less menace. A narrow road strewn with boulders wound steeply from the factory into the gorge, and up this, leaving our heavier luggage in one of the sheds to lighten our vehicles, we set off. After a time it levelled out into a field planted with pineapples, all set out in neat rows. Leaving this, we climbed still further through a dense plantation of enormous steel-blue trees till at last we reached a perfect little amphitheatre, enclosed by the trees and the mountains. In the centre were a few simple huts with, beside them, some concrete tables which obviously served some purpose in the preparation of the tea-leaf. But they lent themselves with equal propriety to what we had in mind, for in a shed nearby were several boilers, and round these presently clustered our cooks. Soon they had the fires going, the blue wood-smoke rising into the breathless air like fakir's ropes, and in a surprisingly short time we sat down at the concrete tables to our first simple meal in the Preanger mountains.

Had we immediately committed our fortunes to the jungle we should have had to live and sleep rough, but we needed a little time to collect and prepare our equipment. Even more important was our need to discuss plans for operations in the jungle so that each man knew exactly what was required of him. In addition we had to get in touch with Blackforce to learn what schemes they had in mind, which meant that, unless molested, we should spend a day or two here, and that also demanded, if possible, the procurement of a roof over our heads. The likeliest place to provide this – the factory – was clearly out of bounds, but there must be some native quarters about, though to dispossess the occupants would incur the risk of losing their support at this very critical stage in our operations. We sent out a few airmen as scouts to explore the valley and the surrounding hills and they brought us back news that, in a dell among the great trees on top of some spectacular cliffs was a long line of huts apparently empty. Climbing up the mountain to inspect them we found them to be very primitive, being built largely of bamboo with the fronts plastered over with a kind of white adobe. Small and dirty, the rooms looked bug-ridden as well, and though empty their condition suggested they had been recently lived in. We sent a man to the manager to see if we might be allowed to occupy them temporarily, and I think the message he brought back was that they had been vacated specially on our behalf. At first the prospect of sleeping in these insalubrious quarters did not find much favour with the men, but their reluctance waned when they learned that in the vicinity there was a rough kind of football pitch.

Down in the floor of the valley, not far from the huts where we had dined at the concrete tables, was a bungalow with a fine garden in front and, behind it, a horseshoe of magnificent trees which gave it shade. Its front verandah provided a spectacular view of the southern ridge. Someone said that this was the home of the assistant manager, but since he was away we took possession of it. There on the floor, sleeping on our valises, we spent the first night.

Next day, however, our explorations revealed a more remote and even more spectacular, retreat, a small bungalow apparently not occupied for some time and in consequence a little decrepit, but possessing the most dramatic and splendid site I have ever seen. Perched right on the top of a tremendous precipice, from the edge of which it was separated by a lawn of fine grass, this bungalow almost cowered in the shade of a gigantic tree which was supported on a great plinth of coiled roots, some of which curled from sight over the lip. Beyond the valley arose a jagged line of blue peaks, while to the south-west, over by the factory, was a distant notch in the mountains through which, the natives later told us, one could in good weather see the Indian Ocean. This may very well have been true, but we were never to know for a haze hung over the notch all the time we were there.

On the second day, most of us lugged our valises up to this high bungalow and slept the night there, again on the floor. The following morning, as the first light of dawn was streaming through the eastern windows, I was woken by a noise coming from the lawn outside. Crawling from my valise and stepping warily over my sleeping companions towards the window, I now, for the first time, witnessed a ritual whose daily repetition later secured for it a place in the established pattern of our lives. Just beside the great tree, and close to the lip of the precipice, lay a supine figure clad in nothing but a scanty and tattered pair of underpants, his feet pedalling vigorously in the air. At a distance stood a native, lost in wonder, his whole being absorbed in the performance. The object of the native's curiosity was one of our officers who was engaging in his morning exercises. As a child he was reputed to have been delicate, and his appearance lent some substance to the rumour for he wore white army metal spectacles through which his dreamy, other-world blue eyes gazed with an absentmindedness that suggested the don with vaguely metaphysical or mystical leanings. But nothing could have been further from the truth, for any interval in the day's proceedings would find him seated, hands on knees like a guru, gazing into vacancy and – *breathing*! In a society as aggressively masculine as ours such eccentricity inevitably drew down upon his head the fiercest ridicule. But to all disapproval he was impervious, even when, at a later date, his activities were used as a lever to demand labour from British officers who were obviously possessed of such a superflux of energy. To this extent, then, his antics were a costly frivolity. Later, through constant exposure to the sun, his skin acquired a light walnut colour, suggesting a vigorous health; but in the enchanting half-light of this second dawn in the Preanger mountains, the peaks beyond the valley tinted with the palest rose and every dewdrop on the grass blades lit with diamond flames, this pallid and almost naked satyr, pedalling away and blind to it all, appeared to me not so much an irrelevance as an impiety.

Far below, at the foot of the precipice, was a gentle glade which ran up into the mountains. I never got to its head but it seemed to lose itself among the high peaks. It was a quiet, sequestered spot with soft, short grass and scattered spinneys whose trees were much smaller than the giants further down the valley. All that was needed to complete the impression of an Alpine scene was a dappled cow or two with bells tinkling at their necks and a peasant with green feathered hat and lederhosen, returning from a day's hay-making on some high alp.

On the northern and sun-facing slope of this glade was a clump of trees in front of which was a walled enclosure with a wrought-iron railing and a gate in front. It proved to be a family cemetery with a double line of graves, each marked by a small marble headstone, most of them in memory of children of very tender years. It almost seemed that this idyllic valley harboured something inimical to their nurture. This unexpected discovery shocked me, this not being a place appropriate for the tears of bereavement. Never, I felt, had these sunlit and lonely crags been designed to throw back the echo of voices raised in lamentation, and the bright sunlight that each morning poured into this lovely hollow was tempered to the living and not to an eternal repose. But the little graveyard harboured a poignancy deeper still, for the simple memorials to the dead children now lay shattered and defaced. Most of the small brick vaults had been forced open, exposing to the eye of day the rotted and decayed coffins, the mouldering cerements, and the dust of mortality. What, I wondered, did those who had wrought this outrage hope to achieve by their senseless and vile act? This, at least, was one crime that could not be laid at the door of the Japanese invaders. It was the saddest thing in Parmegatan, and it was, I think, one of the saddest things I saw in all of Java. Even in a spot as lovely and remote as this, war had spawned a barbarism which sought no justification beyond its own fulfilment.

To the airmen, resigned to the grim privations of the native huts, the football pitch promised some atonement, but at the same time it haunted them with visions of fulfilment beyond their reach. What, above all, they wanted was to feel on their bodies the manly caress of striped shirts and cotton shorts; what they needed was the chance once again to assert their ascendancy. Their souls panted for that mystical communion between toe and leather ball which transcends mere dexterity, and shares with inspiration its elemental core. For them imagination summoned up the intoxication of a cup final at Wembley – or, at a lower level, the homely thrill of their local derby when they pitted their skills against the elect of the neighbouring town. But all this was no more than a pipe-dream, for where were they likely to find anyone able to appreciate, far less match, their skills? Where – to come down to more mundane matters still – could they even find a ball?

A ball, surprisingly, was produced from somewhere, a relic of multitudinous encounters bearing the scars of hectic embroilment, but a genuine football nonetheless. Elated with their discovery, they spent some exhilarating hours dribbling it up and down the field, passing and shooting for goal, heading audaciously. If only there had been a team to give them a game! Some scouts, dispatched for the purpose, brought back the gratifying news that a team of sorts might be enlisted from among the workers on the tea estate, though it would need diplomacy to persuade them to take on the RAF. After all, they played in *bare feet*! To the suggestion of a football match the CO did not take kindly at all, being concerned about how this might affect our relationship with the natives generally. What, for instance, might happen if, in the heat of the moment, bare feet were wantonly hacked or – even worse – a leg was broken! In what light might the flighty and touchy Javanese regard too resounding a defeat? Too much was at stake, he thought, to risk any affront to national pride at this stage. But, the captain giving a solemn assurance that they would take the greatest care to keep their boots from bare ankles, and that they would stop scoring goals after a modest victory was assured, he finally relented. How groundless were his fears – and their confidence!

At the end of a bright tropic day, with the mountains bathed in the luminous blue glow of twilight, all the population of Parmegatan, from tottering babes to gibbering patriarchs, congregated on the football field to witness the encounter. Silent, but expectant, they watched as the RAF team trooped out on to the pitch, brimful of confidence and prancing about the field as they juggled with the ball in a deft mastery of foot and head that was designed to impress the spectators, as much as the opposing players, with the traditional skills of English football. It also liberated in their hearts a genuine exhilaration. Then a hush fell over the field, and even the surrounding peaks seemed to watch with interest as the whistle blew.

Rout is an ugly word, and one not to be used lightly, especially when, as in this instance, it refers to a casual encounter between friendly teams. But to use another is to palter with the truth; however much we try to disguise it, a rout it inescapably was. What in the face of all expectation – even on the part of the spectators – was harder to bear was that it was a British rout! That whistle unleashed a pack of brown demons who wove the ball in deft flicks that mystified the opposition. How these caloused Javanese feet side-slipped and feinted, accelerated with the speed of panthers, poised suddenly on distended toes, and drove the ball into the back of the net with the speed of a javelin. Great now was our dismay that the CO had omitted to have a word with the Javanese captain about keeping the score within acceptable limits! Not only were we out-played – after all, some crumbs of comfort may be salvaged from an honourable defeat – but we were humiliated, ground into the dust, degraded. Wearying, in time, of doing what they found gave them so little trouble, the Javanese relented in their attack, diverting their efforts to individual displays of showmanship. In the end it was a hang-dog and incredulous RAF team that dragged its exhausted bodies from the field that had witnessed its disgrace.

The wound of the Parmegatan defeat rankled deeply, and never afterwards did I speak to one of the team who had suffered the humiliation but he still felt the shame of it. An immediate admission of inferiority, in a jovial, friendly way, might have cleared the air, but this painful therapy they could not face. To the English goalkeeper, whose position gave him an unrivalled vantage-point from which to assess the Javanese attack, it was all a question of the light; a forward put it down to the hardness of the ground; another held it was the altitude and the climate. In each there was perhaps a grain of truth, but there was a more comprehensive reason still, too wounding for admission.

LASSIE WI' THE YELLOW COATIE

On the second day after our arrival in Preanger, the manager of the tea plantation invited the officers to come and inspect his factory with him. Perhaps he thought that we, as representatives of a notable tea-drinking nation, would welcome an opportunity of studying the sources of their beverage, perhaps also, in view of the vulnerability of his employees, he detected some advantage in having any inspection of his factory by our men conducted under his protective eye.

Great was my surprise then, on arriving at the appointed time in front of the factory, to find that I was alone – not one of all the officers in the valley evinced the slightest interest in tea beyond its appearance in a porcelain cup. Embarrassed by the affront, I thanked the manager for his courtesy and endeavoured to excuse myself on the grounds that duty permitted few excursions, even those as pleasant as that he now offered. But undismayed by the slight, or cloaking his disappointment with great civility, he insisted on taking me on a tour of the building. He explained the processes the tea went through from the time the leaves were gathered on the mountains till they were dispatched in boxes from the factory. When the panniers were brought back by the pickers, they were emptied out on to concrete floors where the leaves were then graded into different categories, this work being done by girls who sat on the floors in rows with baskets in front of them into which they put the different kinds of leaf. The deftness and speed of their agile fingers was quite amazing. No less alluring to me was their youthful and captivating beauty which, like that of the Chinese, had a singularly transparent and fragile quality about it. Their faces, however, were a little rounder and broader than those of the Chinese, and their skin had a different texture, being darker and having a curious dusted effect which may, however, have been due simply to the application of powder. Brown and lustrous, their eyes spoke of a gentleness of disposition, while their breasts, which were uncovered, were firm and well-shaped.

Once their baskets were filled, the girls rose and carried them to another part of the factory where they fed the contents into the drying and processing machines. Carrying their baskets, they walked with a curiously undulating and rhythmical motion which seemed to me to be the very epitome of grace. From under their heavy eyelashes they glanced with a curiously ambiguous half-smile, expressing at once a natural timidity or shyness, and also a native, or racial, pride. Even among the jangling and discordant machinery of the factory they carried about with them, as a garment, a kind of haughty apartness which was possibly a legacy of their jungle nurture. Seated on the floor at the end of one of the groups was a very remarkable girl, possibly a little older than most of her fellows, and occupying some higher office or rank. With a face that was at once serene and radiant she – unlike her companions who were naked to the waist, their sole decoration being in some cases a string of beads round the neck – wore a tight-fitting and quite captivating little saffron bodice, which served to enhance her superb figure. Standing up round her slender neck was an embroidered silk collar, which emphasised its poise; and this, allied to the bodice-girt, delicate frame gave her a singular statuesque quality. From beneath her silken eyelashes flashed a dark, winsome, and at times almost coquettish glance.

As I watched this enchanting creature grading her leaves, recollection, in the felicitous way that is often its prerogative, called back to my mind the lilting strains of an old Scottish ballad about a lover's longing for his 'lassie wi' the yellow coatie'. No maiden in a Java tea factory had inspired that melody, but the tributes which adoration pays to beauty wherever it is found have much in common. My utter vanquishment was obviously betrayed by my fascinated eyes, and the manager was not blind to the power of the spell. Taking my arm sympathetically, he remarked on another part of the factory that would repay a visit, and my feet, leaden in their reluctance, were coaxed away. But the lineaments of that lovely face have stayed with me. No power that the manager – or any other – ever wielded would be able to erase it from my memory. Even to this day, some quirk of the passing hour will summon back from the shades that frail beauty. The moment of its happening is quite unpredictable, sometimes asking for catalyst nothing more romantic than a commonplace restaurant. There, at a table, I shall be sitting, Java and all its happenings quite forgotten. But before me, on the table, is a cup, and on its side some Chinese or Japanese craftsman's hand has traced a figure. Then the strange alchemy takes over. Slowly the figure dissolves, and in its place, crystal-clear as when I last saw it, is the image of that delectable creature. There she sits, yellow-coated and quite untouched by Time, busy with her basket of leaves on the floor of the tea factory among the mountains in Parmegatan.

Taken by the Insolent Foe

A couple of days, I imagined, at the most would see us deep in the jungle, as we had to weigh up the lie of the land, reconnoitre possible camp sites, and find out where the Dutch caches were and what stores we might be able to get from them. Most urgently, we needed to sense the pulse of this unfamiliar, hostile and lonely existence before tackling the Japanese. But, surprisingly, we lingered in inactivity. Like the others, I harboured suspicions about the cause of our delay, but only later did I learn what held us up. On that same Sunday that we drove in our trucks from Tasikmalaja, a dispatch-rider had arrived in Parmegatan from Bandoeng bringing the news that the Dutch forces in Java had unconditionally surrendered, which meant that we should have to face the future alone. No longer could we look to the outside for any help – by the terms of the surrender even the caches of food and equipment in the mountains might be denied us.

On the second day after our arrival, going into one of the bedrooms in the lower bungalow, I found piled up on a table a considerable collection of art books, sumptuously illustrated with fine plates. This surprising library, which was to come to my notice on many occasions long after this, belonged, I learned, to Squadron Leader Barnley, one of the Blenheim pilots who earlier in the war had operated out of Sembawang aerodrome in Singapore. Now attached to Blackforce in the 'Valley', he, along with some others, had come over to Parmegatan to strengthen the links between us. Presently we were summoned to a conference where, as senior officer present, Barnley read out a letter which had just arrived from Headquarters in Bandoeng with instructions that its contents were to be communicated immediately to all ranks. It dealt with the question of just how much information we were at liberty to divulge under interrogation. 'So that's that!' concluded the Squadron Leader in a flat, incredulous voice as he laid down the letter on the table.

That same evening the CO delivered a brief address to the men assembled for their evening meal. Never in so many words did he say that surrender had been decided upon, or even contemplated; but he went on to explain that if any man now considered his fortunes might be enhanced by entrusting his person, on his own responsibility, to the jungle, military considerations would no longer offer any opposition to his departure.

Later in the evening I had an unexpected visit from a man I had not met before, a New Zealander with a gangling but muscular frame and a modesty that in a grown man was quite extraordinary, though engaging. The problem that was on his mind admitted, at first, no more than the most oblique approach, though after a little conversation he became a little more forthcoming. He said that back home in New Zealand he had been a farmer and had learned to 'muck round a bit'. He had been thinking over what the CO had said about drifting off into the ulu and, if anyone could make a go of it, he reckoned that his chances were as good as any. He really had not wished to come and trouble me like this – only he had been told that I knew something about mountaineering. Deprecatingly, I confessed to an amateur acquaintance with the craft, acquired in the Cuillins in Skye and elsewhere in Scotland, though that did not make me a real climber of the Alpine breed. That did not trouble him, he said, for it was not really climbing that he was after; but could I perhaps give him some idea of how to make a 'ruckbag'? The principles are simple, and I set them out in as uncomplicated terms as I could – the simple metal frame with a webbing strap at the bottom to keep it off the back, and the canvas haversack sewn on at the three corners. Designed to throw the load on to the hips, thereby keeping the back well ventilated, it enabled much heavier loads to be carried for far greater distances, with greater freedom and less fatigue. To what I had to say he listened with the closest attention, and when I had done he asked if I would listen while he went over the details again. Without distortion or misunderstanding he rehearsed the steps in the construction of a rucksack, showing that behind the casual, country manner there was a sharp intelligence at work.

Next morning, even before breakfast, my visitor was back, a piece of soap in one hand and a large towel draped rather ostentatiously over an arm. Profuse with apology for having to 'pester me again', he wondered if I would mind coming with him, just for a minute, into the bush? Once concealed by the trees, he now unrolled the towel, revealing beneath its folds a rucksack which only the expert would have detected as not professionally made. In amazement I studied the skill of its workmanship while he watched diffidently. Would it, he asked shyly, get by? His doubts on that score were easily allayed – but how, I asked him, had he acquired the materials for the work? He had just scrounged them, he said; the tubing he had picked up from an old 'plane some time ago, thinking that it might come in useful sometime, while the rivets and leather straps he had 'salvaged' from an abandoned car down at the factory. The canvas he had got from an officer's valise, also down at the factory – the green colour he thought might be useful for camouflage in the jungle. It hadn't taken him so very long to make, really, since he was a pretty handy man with tools and could 'bash things together', having learned it all on the farm.

Then, deciding to take a risk and venture upon private matters where he might not be so forthcoming, I asked him what were his plans. Franker than I expected, he confessed that he was going off into the ulu, possibly that night. Remembering Callick's cache, so assiduously acquired, I then ran over as many of the essentials for jungle survival as I could remember: quinine, certainly, and water purifiers; iodine for leech-bites and scratches; bandages; a bit of mosquito netting; a burning glass for lighting a fire; and some kind of native disguise. He listened thoughtfully to all I had to say, adding that though he had not got everything he needed yet, he would forage around during the day and hoped that by night-time he would have most of the essentials. Then I hazarded my last question – was he going alone? 'No,' he said. 'Jock from Glasgow's coming with me!' The information was of so unexpected a nature that with difficulty I concealed my surprise. Jock from Glasgow I knew fairly well – at least from appearance. A dark-skinned and somewhat Italianate-looking young man with sleek, oiled hair, he wore a distinctive peaked cap, very jauntily tilted, the rim broken so that it stuck up in front with the swashbuckling look of a Death's Head Hussar. His appearance pointed to Jock's distinction lying rather in the ambit of a Glasgow dance-floor than the lonely hazards of the bush. But that flamboyant exterior must have concealed depths of character I never suspected. He certainly had courage or he would never have faced the risks of the jungle, and the New Zealander certainly reposed great faith in him.

Next morning at roll-call, alone among all the airmen the New Zealander and Jock from Glasgow did not answer to their names. Their planning had been conducted with great secrecy, for I met no one who as much as suspected their intentions. That their bold example should not have been followed by others was, in the circumstances, not surprising: the intimidating distances to be covered for escape, the unknown and hostile jungle, the lack of equipment and time for preparation, all eroded whatever chances there might have been for success.

How the bid to escape fared in the end I never heard, the nearest I got to first-hand information being some years afterwards when I met a prisoner-of-war who perhaps was able to throw some light upon it. For three or four months, this man said, after the surrender of Java he had been held a prisoner in Tasikmalaja where one day, towards the end of his stay there, a New Zealander crawled into their camp ravaged by malaria and other diseases, and clearly at death's door. He said he had had a friend in the jungle, but the man had fallen ill and, though he had nursed him as best he could, he had eventually died. After burying his friend in a jungle grave he had tried to carry on alone, but the odds were too much for him and, realising there was no hope, he had at last, at the end of his tether, thrown in the towel. The details were close enough to point to the New Zealander and Jock from Glasgow. If this indeed was how it all ended, it was a melancholy conclusion to an enterprise embarked upon in boldness and hope. The prisoner-of-war did not even know whether the New Zealander survived, though it is my earnest hope that he did, and I am sad that Jock from Glasgow with his dark handsome face and jaunty cap did not make it.

On Wednesday, 11th March, we were told to pack up in readiness to leave early next morning, still in ignorance as to our destination and the general situation of the war in Java, though only to the blindly optimistic could the signs be anything but unequivocal. With the meagre kit we had packing was not a matter of difficulty, though at the last moment, as memory or rumour insisted upon the indispensability of certain items, there were sundry scurryings to and fro, aimed to restore the deficiencies. For us the future was dark, and fraught with real but undefined fears, though one thing was clear enough: for whatever lay ahead we were lamentably unprepared.

Next morning we assembled before the factory where our trucks were drawn up and waiting for us. Surprisingly, and sadly, out of all the Javanese in the factory area not one turned up to say goodbye or wish us Godspeed, the victorious football team being busy with their tasks on the plantation while the goddess with the 'yellow coatie' would be assorting her leaves on the factory floor. Even for the manager I looked in vain. Uninvited we had come and unwanted we were to go, painfully aware of how swift can be the flight of fair-weather friends when Fortune frowns. Yet desertion could not rob me of the deep regret with which I left the place. We had, it is true, been here no more than four short days, and yet in that interval the wonder and the beauty of the valley had passed into our lives, becoming part of us. Now that others did not wish to befriend us, it bestowed a comfort and a consolation that were the more welcome, and nowhere, apart from a great cathedral, have I been so conscious that peace and loveliness are to be contemplated only fittingly upon the knees.

Climbing into our trucks, we cast our eyes for the last time round the empty hills of Parmegatan and the deserted road before setting off into the narrow defile that led out to the Garoet road. From the junction extended the long, steep, tortuous ascent up the side of the ravine, and, climbing, we were alone, all else – both man and beast – resting from the sun. The arduous nature of the ascent made the engines boil and on several occasions we had to stop in order to let them cool. During these welcome interludes we got down and, sitting on the verge of the road, gazed down into the deep ravine where, far below, the waterfalls, hidden under the dense leaves, maintained their endless murmuring descants. Drifting from the abyss the thin, fluctuating waves of sound fell soothingly upon our ears. Fed by the tropic rains, they never wearied, and every scene in Java seems linked in my memory with this dulcet and bewitching harmony.

About half of the ascent had been completed when we were met by a dispatch-rider from Bandoeng who delivered a message to the CO in the leading truck. A long conference followed, during which news began to filter back along the convoy that, their position irrevocably compromised by the capitulation of their allies, the British had decided to follow them into surrender. What, it seemed, had been the factor finally influencing the decision was the threat to hold Dutch women and children hostages, answerable for our behaviour. With him the dispatch-rider had brought from Bandoeng an order, issued by the British Commanding Officer, General Sitwell, that we should lay down our arms. To most of the RAF round me this was a name unknown and, in understandable confusion, we assumed that the temperamental American General, Stilwell, who had been operating with the Chinese in north Burma, had been seconded at the last moment to conduct our irregular operations in the jungle.

For a time, we strolled aimlessly and bewildered around our trucks, each turning over in his mind the reflections that the crisis occasioned. That this was a national disaster, by no means ended, with incalculable ramifications not one of us doubted, and most, I think, experienced some degree of relief. But of that feeling of degradation and shame which is supposed to overwhelm the soldier when he relinquishes his freedom I was, surprisingly, at that moment unaware, being shielded from it by my knowledge of the gallantry and steadfastness with which the crews of the Vildebeests had, during their long campaign, unflinchingly faced impossible odds. Having known these men, and the comprehensive nature of their sacrifice, what feelings could I entertain then – as I do now – but unquenchable pride?

After a time a Sergeant came down the convoy, a brisk and curt man who said he was an armourer and had instructions to inspect all our ammunition. Being handed some of our dubious Tasikmalaja cartridges, which he submitted to a close inspection, he pronounced them categorically to be dum-dum, outlawed by the conventions of war, and a most hazardous possession if we fell into the hands of the enemy. We should go, he advised us, through every piece of kit we possessed with the greatest thoroughness and dispose of every cartridge we found. So, carrying our packs over to the verge of the road, we went through their contents meticulously, doing the same with our pockets, and heaping the incriminating cartridges into little piles on the roadway. Then, quite satisfied that no more remained concealed, we began, with the glee of schoolboys, to toss them into the ravine, the little yellow tubes soaring in the air and, when they caught the sun, throwing off flashes of golden light like firecrackers. Our cartridges disposed of, we then took our rifles and dispatched them likewise. Only the firmest of pressure restrained those of us who possessed them from divesting ourselves of our revolvers in the same way. But the instrument of surrender, we were informed, included a clause stipulating the handing over intact of all weapons, and while we might protest to the Japanese that we carried nothing more than a revolver, it might be less convincing to maintain that we carried nothing at all.

This unhappy task over, we resumed our journey up the long, steep climb towards Garoet, and reached at length the water-shed from where the road wound for some time along the flat bottom of the ravine till it came to a little village at the end of a small landlocked basin planted with paddy. At the side of the road, just before we entered the village, was a larger building which looked like a headman's or official's house, and was agreeably shaded by a cluster of tall trees. In front of the entrance was an open gravel courtyard, and on this stood a small group of RAF officers, the rings on their epaulettes too inconspicuous to permit any reliable conclusions as to their rank, though clearly they were of high seniority. Someone gave it as his opinion that one of them was an Air Commodore, and if this were indeed the case it might very well have been Maltby, who was the officer commanding all RAF forces in Java. On the other hand Maltby would most likely be in Bandoeng, involved in the negotiations for surrender. Someone also produced the information that the British commander was, indeed, called Sitwell, which removed the confusion with the gifted but idiosyncratic American who had been operating with Chinese forces on the Sino-Burmese border.

But our speculations on these and other matters were suddenly interrupted by a loud exclamation from someone at the front of the column. 'Target for Tonight!' he called out as a tall, smiling and debonair officer emerged from the door of the house. His was a face familiar to thousands for his having played the role of Station Commander in the film of that name which had won considerable acclaim in Britain at the beginning of the war. Clean-cut and tanned, his features were remarkably handsome; and his bearing displayed that dashing quality, fed by a natural assumption of authority, which seems to be a distinguishing mark of all true leaders. We had been unaware of his presence in Java – indeed a rumour presently ran along the convoy that he arrived on the island only a day or two before, in time to share our captivity. What, inwardly, Group Captain Staton felt about the new role he had been called upon to play we did not know, and his demeanour was too distinguished and disciplined to provide a clue. In front of the group of officers lay a pile of weapons, distressingly large; and upon this, advancing one at a time, we laid our revolvers. As with my comrades, this renunciation caused me deep pain, for all the way from West Kirby I had carried mine and had never had the opportunity to use it against the enemy. This done, we stood around for a little, ill at ease, and impatient to be into our trucks and on our way.

It was at this moment that a lorry filled with Australians and going in the opposite direction drew up beside us. At its front was Ted Eckersley, the navigator of one of the Vildebeests shot down at Rembang; it had returned, I know not how. He held aloft a bamboo pole from the top of which fluttered, in place of a pennant of submission, a dirty white rag. His eyes aflame, and with this pole in his hand, he looked the very picture of an ensign of cavalry about to lead a charge. Ignoring the romantic undertones in the venture, one of the Australians on the ground, with a little kindly banter in his voice, laced perhaps with envy, enquired of Ted where they were off to in their truck. Melbourne perhaps? But for cynicism, Ted had as little time as for faint-heartedness. 'True bloody true!' he called back defiantly. 'Do you think that I'm going to be a ricksha-coolie for Tojo?' Brave words! So we wished them well, and they set off. For a time we watched the lonely lorry as it wound its way down the ravine that led to the Indian Ocean, till it was out of sight. It is sad to have to relate that within a couple of days Ted and his gallant band were back with us, having searched the coast in vain for a boat, and having lost Atherton, one of the two survivors from the high-mountain crash, who now, in an accident, was shot through the chest, the bullet narrowly missing the heart and lodging under the skin on the other side, whence it was removed by a native with a razor blade. Nursed by a planter's wife, he was later removed to a Bandoeng hospital, defying all the odds of probability by surviving not only the accident but the war.

Leaving the weapons dump with its handsome guardian, we made our way across the little valley, arriving after a time at a small river which flowed into the ravine up which we had just climbed. Over this stream the road was carried by a very primitive, stone-built, humpbacked bridge. Beside it stood a solitary Japanese soldier, an utterly diminutive and wizened little man, grasping a rifle with a bayonet which was much too big for him. His round, flat face, split across by a mouthful of gold teeth and set in a permanent grin, was fixed in vacancy, and on his head a gigantic topee descended to his eyes. Doltish and droll, he surveyed us with stealthy eyes as we drove slowly past. The spectacle of this specimen of our enemies filled to overflowing the cup of our humiliation. Was this manikin the best that the Japanese armies, which had surged invincibly over south-east Asia striking terror wherever they went, could produce as a foil for the dashing British officer we had just left? Strange, indeed, had been the disruption in nature that we had lived to see! To compensate for our common shame, which had been exacerbated by the sight of this little soldier, some of the men permitted themselves a few barbed sallies which would have done little to bolster his self-esteem had he been able to comprehend them; happily, comprehension seemed to be beyond him. At last, one of the airmen, hoping to goad him into some kind of response, called out in a very loud voice: 'Hello Tojo!' The remark had no malice in it and the little fellow maintained, unmoving, his metallic, expressionless grin, though I could have sworn that in those topee-shaded eyes I could detect a glint of understanding, deeper than we suspected. Happily, however, the encounter was not to be prolonged and, crossing over the bridge, we soon left him behind.

Driving over to the other side of the valley, we found that the road climbed up a gentle slope before coming to a cluster of houses which marked the end of the village. Here was a market-place, a square compound surrounded by a high wire-netting fence designed to keep out wandering predators. Its furnishings extended to nothing more than a few bleak stalls with some bare deal tables, surmounted by mouldering *atap* canopies to keep out the sun. In front of this compound we drew up; and to our alarm it was announced that this was to be our prison camp. Incredulously we looked at the comfortless cage, and turning to a little Javanese boy who was standing at the side of the road, I asked him what the place was called. 'Wanaradja!' he said. Like Calais, the name was to be inscribed on our hearts.

Dismounting from our trucks, we unloaded what luggage we had. Clearly unconvinced that we could be confined in a place like this, some of the airmen shouldered their packs and, gathering their small parcels, waited for instructions to move off. But presently confirmation came that here, indeed, we were to stay. For as long as we could, we lingered outside the fence, putting off the inexorable moment and not saying much to each other as we waited. Irked by the prevailing uncertainty, one or two of the airmen finally ventured inside to report to those on the outside what they had found. Presently we heard a dismayed voice raised loudly from the passageway that led through the stalls to the back of the compound: 'There's no lats! There's not a bloody lat in the whole place!' With commendable aplomb, a Sergeant, who had been conducting his own investigations, sought to pacify the malcontents. 'Don't get het up about it!' he assured them. 'We'll soon dig some when we get hold of spades!' But this discovery merely deepened the gloom, paving the way for the endless line of others that were to follow. For the beasts of the field civilised men endorsed their humanity by making suitable provision. This foretaste of captivity starkly revealed to us the contempt with which our uncouth and savage conquerors regarded us.

From contemplation of the prison-cage, I turned my eyes to gaze, with relief, south to the fastnesses of Preanger, that wild, romantic and incredibly lovely place in which we had planned to fight our guerrilla campaign – and in the end never did. Blue and mistily insubstantial, the peaks stood out, delicately etched against the pearl-grey sky. What perfect symmetry was displayed in their towering cones! To them the gossamer haze lent a strange quality of unreality as if it was no more than the figment of a dream which would dissolve and fade on waking. Yet about these faery summits blew winds that were fierce in their independence and submitted to no Japanese yoke. On the threshold of captivity they spoke to us of something whose relinquishment could cause us infinite pain, as also of a tenuous hope that even the most barbarous of the days ahead were never quite able to extinguish, though the margin by which they failed to do so was often slender.

A sharp order put a term to my daydreaming, as to our liberty; sullen and dejected, we slouched through the wire into the compound. Thereupon a Japanese soldier appeared outside the gate. Taller and more robust than his comrade beside the bridge, he was nonetheless, no remarkable specimen of manhood. Leaning his rifle with fixed bayonet against the wire, he fumbled in his pocket for a key with which he locked the padlock on the gate. That accomplished, he retrieved his rifle and, clicking his rubber-booted heels together, stood to attention, gazing outwards. Eventually, the rigidity of his posture proving irksome, he thrust his left foot out to the side and stood at ease.

On the left, Ted Eckersley. It was he who held aloft the bamboo pole with the white rag when the truck left Wanaradja for the coast. In the middle is Charlie MacDonald, the navigator of Jock Forbes' Vildebeest at Endau. He escaped to Australia.

Basil Gotto, companion of James McEwan during the encounter with the serpent at Tjikampek. He flew out on the last sortie. Gotto survived and took up farming near Cork in Eire.

The officers at the coal-mine in Ohama. *Front row, left to right:* Captain Hands (Australian Army), Major Newton (Australian Army), Squadron Leader Wyrill (RAF) and Captain Millin (RAOC). *Back row:* Pilot Officer Green (RAF), the author, Pilot Officer Jukes (RAF), Dr René Ploegman (NEI Army Medical Corps) and Dr Perilman (US Army Medical Corps).

PART THREE

THE COAL-MINE AT OHAMA

O, alas, the byrnied warriors!
O, alas, the people's pride!
Ah! how perished is that time,
Veiled beneath Night's helm it lies,
As if it ne'er had been!

The Wanderer
from *The Exeter Book*

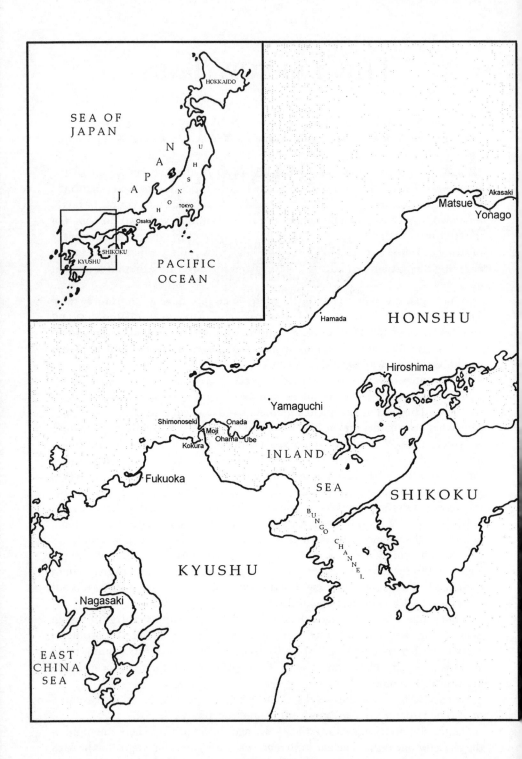

Map of Japan

THE YELLOW TABS

Hugging the north coast of Kyushu, the *Singapore Maru* came, as evening fell, into the roads at Moji where she dropped anchor.

Next morning I was Orderly Officer of the Day and went to the Adjutant to learn what my duties were. He had no office as such, but functioned in a corner of one of the holds where he had a small table and a couple of boxes up-ended to serve as chairs. I found him in consultation with two doctors. On the table in front of them were several piles of small yellow tabs, each with a piece of string attached to it, just like a luggage label. It was these which seemed to be engaging their attention. Lifting his eyes from the tabs, the Adjutant looked at me.

'You're just the man we're after!' he said. 'The Japs have given us these tabs. They say that each tab will entitle one sick man to be taken off the ship and admitted to hospital. The trouble is that there are not nearly enough tabs to go round. That's what we've been discussing. We've been trying to figure out what would be the best way to allocate them.'

'What duties have you got for me?' I asked.

'That's just where you come in!' he said. 'We've got thirty men down in one of the forward bilges. I've never had a moment to go down and see them myself, but from what I can gather they're in a pretty bad way. The most we can let them have is eighteen tabs. We want you to go down with the Orderly Sergeant to the bilges and select the eighteen men you think'll be most likely to benefit from getting a tab. Of course you'll have to use your judgement. If you give a tab to a man who's able to walk off the ship under his own steam, then obviously you're just throwing it away. On the other hand if you give a tab to a man who's clearly beyond hope, then you're wasting it just the same. Your job is to allocate these tabs in a way that will keep most of these men in the bilges alive. Now it's up to you!'

'You can't surely ask me to do a thing like this!' I protested. 'If you give me eighteen tabs for thirty men, then you're simply asking me to send twelve men to their death. That's no job for me! I'm no doctor! Get one of the doctors to do it – it's his job! Why not send one of them?'

'That's just the point!' said the Adjutant. 'We've simply not got enough doctors to go round. Every doctor on this ship has his hands full with problems every bit as bad as this. You'll just have to make the best of it. If you slip up in some of your judgements, no one's going to haul you over the coals for it. There are your eighteen tabs!'

He handed me the eighteen tabs and a sheet of paper which had thirty names on it. The Orderly Sergeant was waiting, and together we set off.

'Things are pretty grim down there!' warned the Sergeant. 'There's no light in the place for one thing. The one bulb there was fused some days ago and the Japs refused to give us another one. But I've managed to get hold of a torch. Maybe it'll give us enough light to get by.'

Climbing down the narrow companion-way to the bilges we were met by a heavy, sickening stench which was drifting upwards. When we got to the door the Sergeant clicked forward the button on his torch and thrust it into my hand.

'Have a good look round first,' he warned, 'before you go in!'

I moved the probing yellow beam across the floor of the low-roofed bilges, trying to make out what was there. As I did so I became aware of a soft, swilling sound which made me stop. Across the stationary beam of the torch there passed a low but very definite brown wave which was urged on by the gentle rocking of the vessel on its keel.

'Its *benjo* [night-soil]!' explained the Sergeant, seeing my bewilderment. 'The volunteers used to come down and empty the *benjo* buckets. But now they're all flat on their backs themselves and there's nobody to come. Not that it would matter much anyway for the buckets were too full and capsized. That's what's on the floor.'

Slowly I moved the beam across the floor, looking along the narrow wedge of light. From side to side, in time with the ship's motion, swilled a shallow surge of ordure. A few wooden buckets were at the back, all lying on their side. Between them and me lay the men, their clothing, the blanket which one or two of them possessed, everything about them saturated with the vile sludge. Some had a shirt and shorts; some had only a pair of shorts. A few were naked, apart from a singlet. Most likely they had fallen from a bucket when the ship rolled, and being too weak to pull up their shorts had let them slip off. The faces of most were blotched and polluted where soiled hands had touched them. Swallowing my horror, I turned the beam of the torch on the sheet of paper in my hand and ran my eyes down the names. A...B...C... Chatfield! *Chatfield?* That was a name that rang a bell! At Seletar aerodrome in Singapore our Warrant Officer had been called Chatfield, and no more efficient and spruce airman ever stepped on to the tarmac of an airfield. Surely the brisk and debonair Chatfield was not among the human wreckage stretched out on this festering floor.

'Is Warrant Officer Chatfield here?' I asked. 'Chatfield of 36 and 100 Squadrons? He was at Seletar?'

Rising from the floor, a skeletal hand pointed to a figure lying motionless in the middle of the floor.

'That's him!' said its owner. The voice was husky with weakness. 'That's him there.'

I took a couple of steps through the swill and shone the torch down on the man's face. Two large and vacant eyeballs stared up into the beam. The face that framed them was fleshless.

'Are you Chatfield?' I asked. 'Chatfield? Warrant Officer of 36 and 100 Squadrons?'

The wasted lips moved wearily, and from them issued a confused mumbling which may or may not have been assent. I could not be sure. Bending down, I shone the torch more closely, but in that foul and shrunken face there was no feature I could seize upon and say, without a shadow of doubt, 'Yes, that's Chatfield!' Taking from my bundle one of the yellow tabs I thrust it into his wasted hand, and the fingers closed round it gratefully.

With the Sergeant at my side, I went round the bilges, flashing the torch into

the upturned faces, trying to connect them with the names on my sheet. From a
mumbled phrase or a raised arm, a liveliness in the eye or an animation in the
flesh, I tried to gauge a man's chances. Even in a place as bereft of hope as this,
the hands clutched hungrily at the proffered tabs, seeming to regard them as
passports to continuing life. Others there were who merely lay in the filth making
no effort to claim a tab, watching in resignation as it went to a comrade, in their
eyes no trace of resentment or rancour.

At last the hateful task was at an end and it was time to go. What should we
say – indeed what *could* we say – to men who had been so shamefully abandoned
and betrayed? Muttering our incoherent and embarrassed farewells, we climbed
up the companion-way. At the top, the wind that blew in from the Sea of Japan
smote our faces like a whiplash. I went straight to the Adjutant and told him what
I had found, and had done.

'Good show!' he said. Then he added: 'Have you heard that Frow and Barnley
are down? Stoke-on-Trent's down too. He's not critical yet, but he's causing the
doctors some worry.

Frow and Barnley? Frow was our CO in our first camp at Kalidjati in Java,
and Barnley was one of the Blenheim pilots who had operated out of Sembawang
aerodrome in Singapore. Both were robust men. Indeed two nights before, when
I had stood with Barnley watching the sun go down in flaming pomp over the
China Sea, I would have sworn he was one of the fittest men on board. And
Stoke-on-Trent? He got this name from the American sailor's hat which he habit-
ually wore, and across the front of which he had printed this, the name of his
home town. He had been one of the first volunteers to go down to the lowest
holds where dysentery was rampant and carry the *benjo* buckets up to the deck
and empty them over the side. He was a frail lad, cut out, one would have said,
as a victim. But he survived and worked tirelessly at his task till the doctors came
round to the conclusion that he must enjoy some personal immunity beyond
medical explanation.

I went immediately to see Frow and Barnley and found them on a shelf in a
dark corner of the hold. Both looked very sick men, with faces haggard and
sunken. They said they had contracted a very virulent form of dysentery which
had allowed them no sleep. I asked them if they had been given yellow tabs.

'They did offer them to us,' said Barnley, 'but we were having none of them.
We're going off this ship on our own two feet. Anyone who stays on board here
is just signing his own death warrant!'

The Japanese had issued orders that all fit men were to parade on deck, ready
for immediate disembarkation. When the muster was complete, the Adjutant
appeared, bringing his book to record the roll-call. These are the figures he jotted
down:

Prisoners on board when leaving Singapore:	1,080
Discharged sick at Takao:	29
Died on board and buried at sea:	62
Left sick on the vessel:	280
Paraded on deck:	709
Total	1,080

Six weeks later, of the 280 men left on board, 127 were dead.

Once the roll-call was over the men stood in their ranks, waiting in the bitter cold. Then one of the men broke ranks. Laying his pack down on the deck before him, he walked very slowly and deliberately over to the ship's rail, where he stood for a while with his head bowed, gazing down at the sea. Some thought it was in prayer. Then he climbed up on top of the rail, hesitated for a moment; and jumped into the sea. There were Japanese guards near him who were watching what he was doing, but none of them raised a hand to stop him. Near where he fell into the water a few sampans were moored, and their occupants also saw what was happening, but not one of them made any effort to save the man. He sank swiftly in the icy water, having chosen his own fate. A man ran below to summon the Adjutant, who had gone away on some other business. When he appeared he was told what had happened. Taking out his book again, he made the necessary correction in his figures:

Died on board and buried at sea:　　　　　　　　　63
Paraded on deck:　　　　　　　　　　　　　　　　708

Presently the *Singapore Maru* came alongside and tied up.

LEFT TO DIE

About the docks at Moji there was nothing that was peculiarly Japanese. In a dozen European ports one could have found their fellows. Beyond the wharf was a godown, its gable-ends facing us, with a large door in the middle. To the left of it was an inner harbour, much smaller than ours, which looked as if it catered for coastal traffic, probably from the Inland Sea. Beyond that again were other godowns. Their tiles were grey; their walls were grey; the sky above them was grey – all functional and bleak and grey as the spirit of the land itself. The wind that blew over the docks was pitiless. That was not surprising since it was winter, and it came from the frozen plains of Manchuria and the Mongolian deserts beyond them. From its bite every living thing had fled the docks – that is, apart from a few Japanese soldiers who, in little groups of two or three, paced aimlessly back and forth, the hoods of their duffle-coats pulled right up over their heads leaving little more than their eyes and noses uncovered, and making them look like trolls.

From dawn the prisoners had been lined up on deck waiting for disembarkation to begin. But nothing happened, nor looked as if it was likely to happen for some time. Round about noon the cooks brought up on deck several coppers filled with boiled rice. This warmed the men up for a while, but under the blast of that Manchurian wind they were soon cold again. Then at about two o'clock some activity became apparent in the godown facing us. From the door there issued two Japanese who wore white coats like medical orderlies. They took up station at the foot of the gangway, then disembarkation began. Each orderly had a large syringe in his hand, something like a garden greenfly-spray, and with this he squirted a little cloud of white powder over the shoulders of each man as he passed. If it was intended to serve some prophylactic purpose it obviously was a complete failure. Possibly it was no more than a piece of eyewash. Once on the wharf the men were ordered to fall-in in their units, lay their packs down on the granite setts before them, and await instructions.

Against that implacable wind nothing short of long woollen underwear and a heavy greatcoat would have offered any real protection, and most of the men had nothing but the tropical shirt and pair of drill shorts they stood up in, these being in many cases in tatters. A few had wisely retained the woollen undervest which had been part of their home issue. Before leaving Parmegatan in the Java mountains where we had been planning our guerrilla campaign, I had salvaged from a pile of discarded baggage a greatcoat that had belonged to Squadron Leader Wilkins, who had been killed during the attack on the Japanese vessels at Rembang. Its weight had almost deterred me from taking it in the first place, and had almost persuaded me to abandon it on the way to Japan. Now it had come into its own.

Working on their starved and disease-stricken bodies as they stood endlessly waiting on the quay, the intense cold brought on the gripes of dysentery. It seemed unthinkable that men in this state should be denied all access to toilets. Retching soon became widespread, and in many cases was followed by vomiting. Gripped by a particularly bad spasm, men would double up and groan.

But still nothing happened.

At length a Japanese issued from the door in the godown carrying a box which he placed in front of the muster. Then, climbing up on it, he cast his eyes contemptuously round the ranks of the prisoners before he began to address them in a very hectoring manner. '*Speck-shon!*' he shouted. '*Cus-tom speck-shon!*' The whole situation had so much of the ludicrous about it – this preposterous announcement and the outlandish accent in which it was delivered – that a faint titter could be heard from the ranks. Sniffing contumacy, the Japanese raised himself on his toes. '*Speck-shon!*' he shouted at the top of his voice. '*Speck-shon! Speck-shon! Speck-shon!*' Then, stepping down from his box, he swaggered back to the godown. This was the sign for a gang of soldiers to issue from the godown and descend upon the men. Every pack, every haversack, every pocketbook, every purse – even a matchbox – was seized and their contents tumbled out on to the granite setts, there to be thumbed, taken apart and scrutinised. Everything that was tied had to be opened. But to fingers blue and numbed with cold so that they had lost all sensation, this was a task that was beyond their execution. For some, even to undo a buckle proved too much, while to untie knots in the string that secured their packages was beyond even trying. I saw one of the gunners who was standing near me looking down in bemused helplessness at the package at his feet. Wrapped in a large blue handkerchief, it had been secured at the top with a knot that defied all his efforts to undo it. Observing his bafflement, a Japanese soldier approached.

'*Kurrah!*' he barked out, giving the package a kick.

'Cold!' explained the gunner, holding out his blue, frozen fingers for the guard to see. 'Cold!'

'*Kurrah!*' bellowed the guard with mounting menace. Kneeling by his side, a comrade wrestled with the obdurate knot.

On the dockside now lay the men's trivial possessions, scattered in rank confusion. Probed, opened, pawed, pulled apart and examined, they were then tossed aside. Not till every item had been submitted to the most rigorous scrutiny did the pitiless charade relax. Then the spokesman issued again from the godown and, climbing on his box, announced: '*Speck-shon ovah!*' Getting their packs and parcels undone had taxed, and in some cases defeated, the men's frozen and numbed fingers. To put their contents back again in any semblance of order was a task no less difficult. Most merely shovelled the things back haphazardly into their packs, making no attempt to stow or tie them up. What was the use? It was all a mummery that had degenerated into a nightmare.

Again time slowly dragged on. Then the Japanese appeared once more and climbed up on his box. '*Im-mi-gray-shon speck-shon!*' he shouted. Too numbed to disbelieve, too cold to care, the men waited dejectedly while the pack of soldiers issued once more from the godown and descended upon them. With assiduity unslaked, they tumbled out and rifled every package that not long before they had examined with vindictive zeal. Any tardiness on the part of a prisoner was met with a snarling '*Kurrah!*' If persisted in, it was reinforced by a kick on the shins. At last, jumbled and confounded beyond all redress, the things were raked back and the string looped over the top of the pack to a tentative knot.

Again time passed on leaden feet, and no whit did that icy wind relent. Once more the Japanese emerged from the godown, and climbed on his box. By this time the men had surrendered the will to listen to him. This explains why I am not in a position to say with any assurance what he did announce. I have been told that it was: '*Me-di-cal speck-shon!*' Not that it mattered! It was the same painful and rancorous routine all over again. By this time we would have watched the Japanese toss all our possessions into the dock without compunction. Even in human malevolence there comes a point of diminishing returns.

Some time after this visitation had been endured to its tedious end, a newcomer arrived on the scene. He was tall for a Japanese, and gross, with a puckered face and eyes that were half lost in his puffed-out cheeks. He must have lived for some time in America for his command of vernacular US speech was too convincing for it to have been acquired in Japan, whose citizens are not conspicuously proficient at mastering European languages. Ponderously he mounted the box. 'Scott!' he shouted out. 'Scott, I want you! Come here immediately! *Scott!*' His summons meeting with a stony silence, his indignation mounted. Slowly he gazed round the ranks of the prisoners, seeking his man. 'Scott!' he shouted again, raising his voice to a shrill pitch. 'Come here now!' The person addressed in these uncompromising terms was none other than Colonel Scott, who was CO of the British troops in the *Singapore Maru*. Working himself up to a frenzy of petulance at the non-appearance of the man he wanted, the Japanese turned to one of the officers who was standing in front of the men. 'You, officer,' he shouted. 'You go and tell Scott come here *immediately* I call. I want him *now!*' From some pestilent hold, where he had been trying to make arrangements for the care of the men who were imprisoned there, Colonel Scott was retrieved and brought back to face his inquisitor.

The contrast the two men presented was striking: the reserved, quietly spoken and disciplined British officer on the one hand, and this posturing buffoon on his box on the other. Confronted with a deportment and presence which he could neither understand nor match, the Japanese resorted to bluster to cover his inadequacy. What the issue was it was impossible for those a little further back in the ranks to know, though it probably had something to do with some protest which the Colonel may have lodged about the condition of his men on the ship.

So long had been the ordeal both on the ship and on the docks that by now many of the men, with no access to a toilet, were on the verge of collapse. Even those who had imagined themselves to be fit were surprised to find themselves attacked by fits of vomiting. For the less robust, and those most desperately in the grip of disease, the body's resistance finally collapsed, and to their suffering was added their shame. Driven to desperation, one of the men finally broke ranks. Going over to one of the guards, he pleaded with him for permission to go over to the edge of the inner dock to relieve himself. The Japanese grunted a sullen refusal and turned his back on the man. Both Frow and Barnley had stuck to their resolve to leave the ship, come what may, and now they were in a very bad way. They had taken a keen interest in the sick man's approach to the guard and his rebuff by him. Now Frow decided that the time had at last come for him to take the matter into his own hands. He walked up to the Japanese who had refused the sick man and in pantomime, asked to be allowed to go over to the dockside to relieve himself. '*Nai!*' said the guard. Very slowly and methodically, Frow went through the charade once more. '*Nai!*' repeated the guard, this time more emphatically. Frow decided that the time had come to replace pleading with action. Squaring his shoulders and thrusting out his jaw in a way that was very typical of him, he strode defiantly over to the edge of the dock and, before the guards had time to stop him, he dropped his shorts and squatted down over the edge. Following his example, Barnley strode over and squatted down beside him.

Being terribly weakened by disease, both men had the greatest difficulty in maintaining their balance, and for a time it looked as if one – or both – of them might topple into the dock. But by thrusting out one hand and gripping a cobble, they managed to steady themselves and remain on the wharf. Clearly their sudden action had caught the guards unprepared, and those nearest to the two men quickly got into a huddle to discuss whether to seize them and drag them back to their place in the ranks, or let them stay where they were until they had finished. Finally, but reluctantly, they seemed to have concluded that it would cause least trouble to allow them to stay where they were. The example set, others attempted to follow, but they were met by a fence of lowered bayonets. This narrow breach in Japanese discipline was not to admit any further widening. Pulling up their shorts, Frow and Barnley came back from the dockside, but such was the imperious nature of their disease that no sooner were they back than renewed spasms sent them again in search of relief, the guards making no effort to impede them. Meanwhile, denied this easement, others endured desperately till the flesh could sustain the effort no longer.

At last a rumour, which originated somewhere at the front, was passed swiftly back through the ranks: we were bound for Hokkaido to work in coal-mines there. If it was like this in Moji, which after all is in the south of Japan, what would it be like in northern Hokkaido, which is next door to Siberia? Those who realised where Hokkaido was now felt hope slipping away from them. But even upon minds as resistant to change as the Japanese, it must by now have dawned that the whole project was futile. Most of us would be dead long before we got to Hokkaido, and the exercise would defeat its own ends. Were there not some coal-mines nearer to hand to which we might be sent? Certainly there was nothing big enough to accommodate all of us as one unit, but in the region were various camps in the course of construction; if we were broken up into smaller units, it might be possible to fit us in there. Some solution along these lines was, it appeared, being thrashed out.

Then an order was made. From the end file of the muster 170 men were commanded to fall out. These included both Frow and Barnley, as well as myself. Having been counted, we were painstakingly counted again to ensure the accuracy of the computation. A detail of guards was summoned to take charge of us. They looked like raw recruits, all very young and almost engulfed in their hooded duffle-coats. Being new to the job, they were ill at ease and fussy. Kicking their heels in the air in a kind of goose-step, they marched us off.

After a time we came to a long wharf that ran alongside the biggest dock we had seen. Here, to our astonishment, we found men lying on the granite setts, having been abandoned by their captors. Their long-sleeved shirts, and slacks in place of shorts, identified them as Americans. One or two of them possessed a blanket which they had wrapped round their bodies, but most of them had nothing beyond their thin drill. The first we encountered were lying in twos and threes, but soon this mounted to groups of about ten or so. They must have come from one of the other ships in our convoy. Probably having been kept standing in the cold as we had, they were now too weak and numbed to march; having collapsed on the way, they had been left to lie where they fell. Now, ill-clad and helplessly frozen, they were waiting to die. As we marched by them, some of our men made determined efforts to have a word with them. But the guards were very vigilant, rushing up and down our column and threatening with their bayonets any man who opened his mouth. As we passed them, they gazed up at us with empty, curious eyes, their faces grey with the pallor of approaching death. Exposed to that wind, no less merciless than their captors, and lying on the frozen granite, their period of waiting would be brief. At most, a few hours would see it through for them. In all probability those responsible for this heinous act would never be called to judgement before a tribunal on earth.

Leaving the hapless Americans to their fate, we trudged on, our ill-shod feet cruelly bruised by the uneven cobbles. Eventually we came to a large dock which, apart from a couple of hulks which were moored to an inner wall, was empty of shipping. They looked as if they had once been junks, the decks and masts having been ripped out to convert them into barges. We were called to a halt just along-side them. Lashed to rings on the quayside, and hanging over the wall, were a couple of makeshift ladders, their ends stopping a good couple of feet short of the gunwale of the hulks whose interiors glistened as if they had recently been given a fresh coat of tar. Pointing to the ladders, one of the guards said 'OK!!!' Especially in our weakened condition, embarkation without injury was going to present problems. Throwing his pack down into a hulk, one of the fittest of our men volunteered to make the first exploratory descent. Arrived at the foot, he began groping for the gunwale, but the edge was slippery, denying him footing, and in a wild skid he shot to the bottom. Struggling to regain his footing, he began to scrape from the back of his clothes the thick deposit of black sludge which now adhered to them. 'It's coal muck!' he called out in dismay to those above. 'It's a coal-barge!' We had been spared the coal mines of Hokkaido only to be consigned to others nearer home.

The general embarkation which followed involved some of the weaker men in falls, but happily none received more than bruises and no bones were broken. With their last reserves of energy drained from them, the men dumped their much-examined packs down in the sludge and sat disconsolately upon them. Soon the pangs of dysentery demanded relief. But in this coal barge no provision had been made for men in our condition. At the edge of the wharf above us stood two coolies, their vacuous faces gazing down on us. The men made a desperate effort to enlist their help.

'*Benjo! Benjo takusan* [toilet plenty]!' they called desperately.

The coolies seemed not to understand what was required of them.

'*Benjo? Ah so ka?*' they reflected, puzzled.

From beneath, the chorus was renewed. Still the coolies failed to grasp our need, until at last, in the murky caverns of their understanding, a spark kindled and they were off.

'*Benjo? Ah so!*'

The fruit of their expedition was a large empty kerosene-tin, from which the top had been roughly hacked with an axe – most inimical to bare buttocks.

'*Benjo takusan!*' The men kept up the clamour. A second expedition produced another tin. From a third they returned with empty hands.

By now it was late and night was closing in fast around us. From dawn, with no respite, the ordeal had lasted, and now the men's strength had finally deserted them. In silence and dejection they sat on their packs, only reviving when, the spasms of dysentery becoming insistent, they clamoured for the *benjo* tin. Beside me sat Frow and Barnley, both looking spent and slumped in weakness. Barnley sat on one of the two cases he had lugged all the way from Java. They contained the heavy art books which he hoped to study in preparation for his intended enrolment in the Slade School in London after the war.

Hidden from us by the hull, a tug puffed in front of the first barge, announcing its presence by the noise of its engine and a whorled ribbon of smoke which drifted above us. From it a rope was thrown over to us and one of the men lashed it to a cleat. On the wharf the two coolies untied the mooring ropes from the bollards and, with a measured cradle-rocking, we edged out of the dock into the open waters of the Inland Sea.

Being high, the side of the barge shielded us from the sharpest edge of the wind, yet down in the bottom it was still bitterly cold and the men huddled together for warmth. For a time I sat on the bamboo-covered wooden suitcase which served me as a pack and watched the night sky drift back and forth drowsily, keeping time with the slow rocking of the boat in the swell, its swinging constellations tracing out their thin arcs. How immeasurably distant they seemed, eternally cut off from our petty plight down here on this little earth. But at length utter weariness overcame me and, closing my eyes, I fell asleep and forgot our miseries.

Some time around midnight the steady, soporific throb of the tug's engines spluttered for a moment and then dwindled to a murmur. Shaken from sleep, I opened my eyes and could make out the tall legs of a gantry stalking by, looking spectral and gigantic against the night sky. In their wake was a high jetty made of tree trunks, and on its top was a row of little men jabbering and gesticulating wildly in an effort to direct our attention to some ropes which they were throwing down to us. They all wore the same kind of black, hessian *happi*-coats, and when the wind caught them they flapped open to reveal their naked torsos. Catching the ropes, our men belayed them to the cleats in the barge's hull and we were slowly pulled alongside and secured. The swell was considerable, making our hulk heave sullenly. Meanwhile the jostling faces craned over the top edge of the jetty to have a closer look at the strange white men who had just arrived. Then one or two of the little men got down on their knees and held out their hands, inviting us to make an attempt to get up on the jetty. The ascent did not look particularly easy but, heaved up by some of his friends, one of the tallest and fittest of our men did make the attempt and managed to grasp one of the outstretched hands. For a moment he swung there and it looked as though he might pull his helper into the barge, before his numbed fingers lost their grip and he skidded to the bottom. But, undismayed, and with more men pushing from below, he renewed his efforts and succeeded in reaching the jetty. His success encouraged others, and after a time the disembarkation was safely completed, the little men keeping up a chorus of '*Dammée desu!*' when a man fell, and '*Euroshi!*" when he succeeded.

From the jetty a rutted and boulder-strewn path led up a very steep hillside to be lost in the darkness. Up this we climbed, lugging our packs. Barnley, who was beside me, was finding his load almost too much for him and paused repeatedly to regain his breath. My own load being much less than his, I offered him a hand. But he declined this wearily, saying that he had carried the cases all the way from Java and he thought it would be a shame were he to give in when the end was so near. Presently we arrived at a terrace, which was about the size of a basketball pitch and had been dug out of the hillside. At each end was a pole from which was suspended a single electric bulb, and in the dim illumination which these cast we found our reception committee waiting to meet us. This consisted of the *shoko*, or Japanese camp commandant, and some guards. At a distance – and deferentially as the strict caste system in Japan prescribed – was a group of mine officials.

Counting men was always, as we found, a laborious and repetitive business, and this one conformed to custom. But eventually, to the satisfaction of the *shoko* and his tellers, it was established that we numbered 170 men. That problem resolved, we set off, led by the *shoko* and his party, for our new home and presently came to a gate which provided entrance to a compound which was surrounded by a wooden fence with three strands of barbed wire along the top. Just inside the gate was the guard-house, from which a dirt road descended sharply to a little ravine beyond. In this were two long wooden buildings, both two-storeyed, which were linked by a smaller one-storeyed building. Into this we were ushered and found it to be the dining-room, with the kitchen attached to it. The dining-room had three long deal tables, scrubbed till the white wood gleamed, and alongside them were benches. On the tables the cooks had prepared bowls of steaming rice, boiled cabbage, and *daikon*, which is a kind of coarse radish, much used in the country. Our men were invited to take their seats at the tables and partake of the meal, but at the sight of any kind of food our stomachs, after the day we had just gone through, would have rebelled. One or two of the men, trying to avoid the total rejection which would have hurt those who had gone to such trouble to provide for our needs, did nibble at a spoonful of rice, but soon they had to desist.

Leaving the cooks perplexed by our failure to eat the meal, we were then shepherded from the dining-room to the lower of the two big buildings which we found to be the dormitory that had been prepared for our occupation. Each storey consisted of a long row of bedrooms giving on to a corridor which ran the length of the building. Each room contained ten *tatamis*, the standard-sized rice-straw mats designed to accommodate a man. We were now divided into tens, according to rank, and allocated to our rooms. At the head of each mat we found a neatly folded pile of bedclothes, consisting of a flock mattress, a blanket, and a quilt with a gay floral-patterned cover. In addition there was a block of wood with a hollow at the top which was intended as a pillow, and which, of course, is standard in Japanese bedrooms. But this we speedily consigned to a corner of the room for later use by Oriental heads, which were obviously much less tender than ours. Before entering our rooms we took off our footwear, stowing it under a shelf in the corridor which was designed for its reception. The rest of our possessions we placed on a high shelf which was fixed on the wall above the head of our beds. Strictly speaking, all this, in the way of luxury, did not amount to very much. But to our weary and disease-infected bodies no bed majestical could have offered such promise of bliss. In utter thankfulness we crawled under our flower-bedecked quilts and blessed the coal-mine owners of Ohama.

On the mat next to mine lay a very young and boyish-looking Welsh Second Lieutenant whom I had not so far met. He said his name was Johnnie Probert, and that he came from Barry in South Wales. He will appear later in these pages. For a time he lay wide-eyed, still, it seemed, wrestling with some problems. At last he heaved a deep sigh.

'Roll on that boat!' he said wearily as he pulled his quilt up to his eyes.

We slept like the dead – whom some of us were presently to join.

FOR A CHARNEL DUNGEON FITTER

Dawn stalked silently over Ohama, almost afraid, it seemed, lest its foot-falls disturb the sleepers below. Nothing stirred till, clutching a blanket round his nakedness, a scarecrow figure, the spasms of dysentery urgent in his belly, would crawl from beneath his quilt and stagger along the corridor to the *benjos*, which were at the end. Over the camp there hung the air of a morgue, from which, in fact, it differed but little.

As the morning progressed it was clear that among the worst of the sick was Barnley. He was young and robust but the events of the preceding day had taken it out of him, and now he lay listless on his mat, his face sunken and grey, his dark eyes tranquil, his heavy black beard accentuating his pallor. He had grown it in Java and had vowed never to shave it off till we were once again free men. A message being sent for medical help, a Japanese doctor came to see him. A frail old man, he had a wizened face which was brown as a nutmeg, and which looked incongruous under his thick thatch of snow-white hair. Helpless to do anything for his patient, he looked at him for a while, then muttered a baffled '*So desuka!*' On sturdy legs a little nurse trotted behind him, with almond eyes and eyebrows arched in unconscious coquetry, her white *kimono*-style uniform belted round her little barrel-body, chastely. With her breath indrawn in a polite hiss, like a faint echo, she repeated her master's '*So desuka!*' Then, on their double-ribbed *geta*, or wooden clogs, they both clip-clopped rhythmically along the corridor and were gone. Presently a brown powder, which looked like pepper and was wrapped in a rough paper spill, arrived for Barnley. It was administered to him but had no apparent effect.

The thirtieth of November was the third day since we had arrived in Ohama. By that evening it was evident that Barnley's illness had reached a crisis. The last reserves of his strength had drained from him, leaving him with no resources to fight his disease. Some of his friends undertook to sit by his mat during the night, but, a little before dawn came, he died. We held the funeral service for him the same day. The Japanese provided a coffin, crudely knocked together from pine-wood boards. On the lid we laid the dead officer's service cap along with his flying wings, which we had cut from his tunic. His closest friends gathered round the coffin in his room, while all the men who were able to get up from their mats lined the path outside, or stood on the opposite bank. Frow being too ill to rise, the service was conducted by Wing Commander Matthew, who had had some expe-rience of broadcasting in Singapore and had a good voice. He used the Burial Service as instituted by the Anglican Church and contained in its *Prayer Book*. In the alien surroundings of the Japanese prison camp the noble cadences provided comfort and consolation to those among us who now also lay under threat. A funeral party was provided from among the fittest of the men. Slipping rope slings beneath the coffin, they threaded through them two bamboo poles which they then hoisted on their shoulders. They were followed by the fuel party carrying logs for the furnace. Their climb was arduous, the crematorium being very near the top of the hill. From the camp we could detect its location by the tall cedars which grew around it. Like the rest of us, Barnley had few possessions apart from the heavy art books, whose carriage had undoubtedly played some part in the swift course of his illness. But in addition to these he did have one possession whose survival every effort should have been made to secure. While in Kalidjati, in Java, he had worked hard on a novel he was writing. He had shown it to no one though he did admit he was 'pretty far on with it'. It dealt, he said, with a 'modern theme'. Paul Wyrill, a Squadron Leader, being the senior officer who still remained fit in Barnley's room, took charge of the manuscript. Despite some earnest pleading from his colleagues he decided, no doubt misguidedly, to hand it over to the Japanese, seeing in this course the best hope for its survival. Nothing more is known about the document's fate. It would, no doubt, fall into the hands of censors, a sceptical tribe who would regard anything written by a Briton as suspect, and, after scrutiny, consign it to the flames. A happier fate befell Barnley's art books which, though much less important, got in some cases as far as the United States, and probably back to England.

The day Barnley's coffin was carried up the hillside to the crematorium also saw a marked turn for the worse in Frow's condition. Adding to his distress was the appearance of a disfiguring symptom which also greatly increased the difficulties of his nursing. Frow naturally had a very large head, which now swelled alarmingly, the swelling almost closing his eyes and his tongue becoming so bloated that it was next to impossible to force any food between his lips to provide nourishment. Summoned once again, and this time with some urgency, the little doctor gazed at his patient with the same helpless benevolence. But at his disposal was no medication other than the brown powder he had prescribed for Barnley, and of which another dose presently arrived in its paper spill. Faced now with a crisis, Frow rose to the challenge, displaying a fierce tenacity to live. By dint of a painful struggle, and helped by Wyrill, he did succeed in forcing the doctor's brown powder between his lips, though nourishment was still out of the question. Having undertaken the nursing single-handed, Wyrill now realised the time had come to spread the load and a roster of officers was drawn up to watch by the sick man's bedside. Monday, 7 December was the first anniversary of the opening of the Pacific war; it also saw a marked deterioration in Frow's condition. As darkness fell he was much troubled; after midnight the pain subsided but, drifting into a deep and peaceful sleep, he breathed his last. As with Barnley, we held the funeral service in the same room where he died, but the service was not for Frow alone, but for three other men as well, including one of the Sergeants.

Frow's death was a heavy blow to us, for no other among us possessed so unmistakably the qualities of leadership, which even the Japanese acknowledged by displaying unwonted deference in his presence. Had he lived they would, no doubt, have made strenuous efforts to tame him, but they would never have succeeded. With him gone there was no one left to whom we could look with the same assurance for leadership. Wing Commander Matthew, who took over, possessed a native pugnacity without that diplomacy which should sustain it. To him, the only way to deal with the Japanese was to oppose them on every issue; Frow knew better, realising that it often paid to be concessionary over trivialities, while remaining inflexible when it came to fundamentals. When it was a question of brutality to his men or demands that impinged upon his loyalty to his country, no man could have been more fearless and unflinching.

There now followed an event which was to shake the confidence even of the fittest among us. One of the officers was a New Zealander, called Hunt, who hailed from Otago where his powerful physique had ensured his automatic inclusion in the university rugby squad. He had obtained a degree in mining-engineering and now, with almost a mischievous desire to observe their response, he conveyed this information to the Japanese. Their reaction came as a surprise, not only to Hunt. A small group of prisoners, including Hunt and Wyrill, was presently directed to attend the mining office where they were given instructions to trace underground maps of the mine. Naturally, the project was soon discontinued, and the most likely purpose behind it was to uncover any talents which some of us might possess and which might later be put to undesirable use. One day Hunt came back from his work in the mine office complaining of feeling ill. He said there were severe pains in his chest and he felt great difficulty in breathing. Indeed, before the evening was out he had an attack that looked for a time as if it might choke him. Next morning the doctor was summoned and found his patient on the verge of collapse. To the crisis he reacted with unexpected urgency. On the mat beside the sick man he rigged up an apparatus which consisted of a tripod, a spirit-lamp, and a flask containing a colourless liquid. From its top he led a rubber tube into the patient's nostril. But all efforts proved unavailing and during the following night Hunt died. When news of his death was broken, a kind of panic seized the camp. If a man of Hunt's physique was vulnerable, what chance had some of the rest of us – even the fittest? If any man fell sick, he had to face the likelihood that he might not recover from it.

But though we were not to know it at the time, the worst of the crisis had already passed. Deaths were still to occur, but not with such chilling inevitability. By the end of January 1943 the sick bay held only two patients. Though both of them were seriously ill, no immediate fears were entertained about their survival. The first of these was a very remarkable Air Force Corporal called Gittins, who suffered from an accumulation of illnesses among which were pellagra and beri-beri, both, of course, on top of the endemic dysentery. So much flesh had he lost that he looked like an Egyptian mummy, his thighs no thicker than a normal man's wrist, and the withered skin which covered his rib cage sinking into the furrows between the bones. His tongue was swollen and protruded from his mouth. Being able at best to mumble, he could express neither wish nor need. The Japanese brought a coffin and put it in the next room to be ready for him. One of the men had brought from Java a tin of condensed milk which he intended to use if he became sick. With noble generosity he surrendered this for Gittins's use. Sweetening a little pap-rice with this, some of his friends forced it between the patient's lips. What alone kept the Corporal alive was his indomitable will.

Before leaving England he had become engaged to an English girl. Let illness, starvation, and every privation the Japanese could devise be loosed upon him, that was one pledge he was determined to honour.

The other patient in the sick bay was a Corporal in the gunners called Davey. He was a gangling lad with a face that was naturally cadaverous, this impression reinforced by his large and melancholy eyes. He was a lonely man, isolated from most of his comrades by a retiring disposition. Like Gittins, he was a victim of beri-beri, one of the symptoms of which disease is a swelling of the legs. But, that apart, he did not look very seriously ill. Then, for no obvious reason, he suddenly took a turn for the worse. His friends did all they could for him but he did not respond to any treatment. He continued to sink, and at last drifted into a coma from which he never emerged. Davey left a small haversack, but apart from that he had no possessions. As part of my duties as Officer of the Day on which he died – 28 January 1943 – I examined this haversack after his death. In it I found a diary which he had scribbled in pencil in a large school notebook. It contained a record of his experiences from the time his battery arrived in Java up to the time when, with his comrades, he was confined in Glodock Gaol, a penitentiary for convicts in Batavia. While in the gaol he had become sick, and this had forced the discontinuance of the diary. He had never been able to resume it. It thus contained nothing about his experiences on the *Singapore Maru*. If we may judge from the rest, his views on these might have been valuable. The appeal of the document lay in the freshness and frankness with which he recorded quite abnormal circumstances. Davey possessed a very sharp eye, and with it a gift for putting into simple, vivid prose what it saw. From his friends he kept all knowledge of the existence of this diary, and none I spoke to as much as suspected this side of his nature.

With the probable fate of Barnley's novel still painfully in mind, I now urged upon Wyrill the advisability of keeping Davey's diary out of the hands of the Japanese. At least, if he was still bent upon handing it over, might he not first give me the opportunity of making a copy of it? Not only did he readily agree to this proposition, grave doubts had now invaded his mind about the wisdom of handing over Barnley's novel and, smitten by remorse, he undertook to secrete Davey's diary somewhere in his dormitory. But, sadly, concealment did not guarantee survival and, not surprisingly, it fell victim to one of the searches of the *kempetai*. A happier fate attended the copy I had made: it survived the searches and outlived the war. On my return to Scotland I made a further copy, which I posted to Davey's next-of-kin, whose address, in Morley near Leeds, I had got from his paybook. But to my regret my letter failed to obtain acknowledgement. What happened to this interesting document in the end I do not know.

THE CAMP

About fifteen miles east of Moji a small diamond-shaped peninsula juts out from the southern shore of the main island of Honshu into the Inland Sea. On the west side of this peninsula is a picturesque fishing village called Neshi Ohama, and on its east side the mining village of Ohama. Further to the east is another mining village called Motoyama, clearly visible from miles away by reason of its huge heap of coal waste just near the water's edge. This peninsula is joined to the mainland of Honshu by a broad neck of flat land, on the east side of which is a fair-sized town called Ube, and on the west a much larger town called Onada. The chief industry of both towns being the manufacture of cement, their tall chimneys belched forth a constant cloud of white smoke which deposited a fine dust on the rooftops, making them white.

In 1942, the village of Ohama was a mean and dilapidated place boasting several rows of low wooden hovels, all grossly insanitary. Their floors were *tatami*-covered, but on them stood little in the way of furniture. With the miners returning daily from the mine in their filthy clothing, it can readily be imagined that the efforts of their womenfolk to keep their homes clean could not meet with much success, *tatamis* and pit clothes not being a happy combination. In the village a communal bath was provided for the men, and to this, having left their clothing in their homes, they made their way, clad, summer and winter, in nothing more than their loincloths and returning red as boiled lobsters. Just below the village were the twin entrances to the mine, which ran under the sea, and towering above them was the loading gantry which was the first thing I had seen on our arrival. From the water's edge the hillside rose sharply. On the slope was the lamp-room, staffed by young girls uniformly clad in *mompis*, or rompers, who tended to giggle a lot, especially in the presence of prisoners. Near to it was the mining office.

A little to the east of the village was a narrow, steep-sided ravine that ran up into the hillside which for the most part was heavily wooded with small pine trees. At the lower end of this ravine was the camp where the prisoners were confined. Before their arrival, it had been used by migrant mine workers, mostly Korean. In the village one still saw several children with very Korean-looking faces, but whether they were the offspring of Koreans still living there or of mixed marriages it was difficult to say. The walls of the dormitories were wooden-framed and faced with untreated shingles, their cavities packed with clay to provide insulation. The rooms were separated from the corridor by sliding doors which were panelled with oiled paper, and were called *shojis*. On the opposite (or weather) side were also sliding windows whose glass panes were loose and unputtied, and through which, especially in winter, blew – or more often whistled – chilling draughts. Naturally a gimcrack building of this nature offered very little protection against the cold, and in Japan the winters can be exceptionally severe.

Against fire, the building offered no protection whatsoever. Schooled by a long and terrifying catalogue of holocausts which had devastated their cities the Japanese cultivated a healthy fear of fire, but this was not shared by the often nonchalant, and at times simply irresponsible, British soldier. A cigarette butt tossed (as it often was) thoughtlessly aside, or smoking in bed, might well have set the building up like a torch, with consequent heavy loss of life – a grim prospect which left many relatively unmoved. 'What if we do burn down the place,' they would observe, 'what then? The Japs'll just have to give us another one!' Far-flung are the fields where ignorance is bliss! But the Japanese did make some attempt to provide fire-fighting equipment, however ineffectual this might have proved even to arrest, far less extinguish, a fire had one broken out. Round the building several large concrete troughs had been built and were kept constantly filled with water. At each end of the corridors stood a couple of barrels half-filled with water, and a few buckets of sand. Beside several of the upper windows were coils of rope which could be tossed out to act as life-lines. But their purpose may have been to inculcate in the prisoners a realisation of the dangers rather than to cope with what might have been the disastrous consequences of their carelessness.

During our first weeks in Ohama the sky had been cloudless, and the light had a strange purple core to it which was almost Athenian. Then one morning a dark cloud settled on the hilltop, blotting out the cedars. By mid-afternoon the first snowflakes were falling, thronging in the little ravine. As evening approached, and with it a freshening of the wind, they whirled about in the enveloping darkness like gesticulating ghosts. Next morning the lower hollows were piled high with drifts, and on the hillside a rare sorcery had been at work transforming the landscape, bowing the fir trees with glistening coats of ermine and deeply arching the resplendent fronds of the bamboo groves with the fragile grace of ostrich-feathers. But a thaw soon followed, and the silver glory departed. During the rest of that first winter in Ohama the wind that blew across the Sea of Japan from the Manchurian plains was for the most part dry; well-clad and well-fed men might have found it invigorating, though it had a cutting edge to it. But the nights, especially, were often savage with frost. In Ohama the cold on occasion reached a severity few of the men had experienced at home, and after all they were ill-clad, ill-fed, and had just come straight from the tropics.

When sickness was at its height, the Japanese provided a brazier for each room. A wooden box, lined with tin, it was filled with earth on which reposed never more than two dying sticks of charcoal. These did virtually nothing to raise the temperature of the room while markedly increasing the risk of fire, for was not a faintly glowing charcoal stick an open invitation to a man to light a cigarette, if he had one, and smoke it while he was sitting on the *tatami*? It did not take very long for the Japanese to realise the hostage they had placed in fortune's hands, and the braziers were promptly removed. After the withdrawal of the braziers no other form of heating was provided for the dormitories till the following winter, that of 1943–44, when the Japanese devised a very safe and practical system of heating. From the main boiler, which heated the water for the miners' bath, they led a single steam-pipe under the floorboards of the dormitories, and though the steam proved to be erratic, as long as it was maintained the worst of the winter cold was kept at bay. During the winter of 1944–45, however, though the pipes still functioned perfectly and a plentiful supply of old logs was available from the mine – and had that failed, the hillside plantations offered an inexhaustible source to supplement it – the system was discontinued. The only feasible explanation was the Japanese had concluded that deprivation should be endured by all in their islands, and whom better to start with than the prisoners?

Linking the dining-room with the lower dormitory was a covered pathway at whose lower end were a couple of cold-water taps that discharged into an iron trough. But in the summer the little dams on the hillside which supplied the water often dried up, and in the winter they froze so that for long periods the supply was often interrupted. It was here, in the early mornings, that the men queued up to wash. The intermittent resources of the cold-water taps could not, of course, have met the needs of the miners, returning filthy each day from the mine. For them a bath-house, basic but thoroughly practical, had been devised. A concrete tank, about ten feet by fifteen feet, had been sunk into the earth, leaving a high rim above the ground. The water in it was heated by a steam-pipe led from the main boiler. On their return from work the men, using wooden ladles, douched themselves and scrubbed their bodies rigorously clean. Not till this was done were they admitted to the bath, in which they sat immersed to the neck, luxuriating in the warmth. In their bitter lives this represented a rare indulgence, though the practice drew from Dr Ploegman strong disapproval. To this practice he traced most of the skin diseases that were endemic in the camp. But, when icicles hung by the dormitory walls, the doctor's humanity submerged his medical conscience and he allowed the men their fragile bliss.

The cold was seasonal; some other afflictions were not. Among the most unremitting of these vexations were the vermin. For those pests the two-and-a-half-inch-thick mats of rice-straw, and the open wooden structure of the building itself, provided an ideal breeding ground and lodgings. These pests appeared to observe mutually exclusive zones of operation within the camp. Bugs and fleas, for instance, confined their depredations to the persons of the officers, while some of the men's quarters were the exclusive haunts of lice. Of the two the fleas were the more detestable since, once they had gorged themselves, they did not invariably withdraw to their haunts but remained in the men's clothing where they laid their nits in the seams and almost defied eradication. The numbers of these parasites almost beggar belief, Paul Wyrill, for instance, claiming in one night to have accounted for eighty-four bugs, though even this claim paled in comparison with that of a gunner who declared that, again in one night, five hundred of the pests had fallen to his hand.

Japan enjoys a continental type of climate, and in summer the heat, like the winter cold, can be extreme. Once they had had their bath and their meal the miners, wearing only their *fandushi*, or loincloth, would throw their weary bodies on the mats and promptly fall asleep. Undeterred by the bright sunlight which streamed on to them, the fleas, issuing in swarms from their lairs, would fasten on their bodies. So stippled with flea bites did some of the men become that they came to look like the victims of a loathsome medieval pestilence. The summer plague of fleas was swelled by the mosquitoes, to curtail whose ravages the Japanese provided mosquito nets. Unlike the form these take in the tropics, where each bed has its individual net, the Japanese variety enclosed a whole room. In addition to providing a defence against mosquitoes the nets also served as a trap for the bugs. Each morning would discover a cluster of these parasites who, having mistaken their road home in the darkness, were now lodged in an upper corner of the net like a cluster of hiving bees. Their disposal was effective but messy. By grasping the net in one hand a little distance from the corner, one cut off their escape. Their bloated bodies could then be squashed with the other hand, the released blood giving off a very characteristic but offensive odour. To arrest, or even to curb, the attacks of those pests no remedy proved effective. From time to time the Japanese provided a powder which resembled, and indeed smelt like, Keating's Powder, but its only observable result was to inflame its intended victims to renewed rapacity. Sunshine being advocated, we dragged our *tatamis* out from the rooms and exposed them to its noontide fervency, but all to no avail. One thing alone would have put an end to their depredations – a match applied to a *tatami*. But, devoutly as this consummation might be wished, the cure might prove worse than the canker.

Up to a point these torments, odious as they were, could be endured: others admitted no such redress. Among the most conspicuous of these was hunger. During our first weeks at Ohama the staple of our diet, which was (and continued to be) rice, was supplemented by a ration of potatoes (mostly of the sweet variety) and a small allocation of meat, which never amounted to more than forty-five pounds to be distributed among 151 men, nineteen of our earlier number having died. On a few occasions tins of fish were added, this being a dubious increment which we regarded with the gravest suspicion, the tins being invariably rusty and leaking and obviously rejected as unfit for Japanese consumption. Only starvation prevailed upon us to add them to our diet; and the consequences were predictable and only, in some cases, just stopped short of being fatal. Presently the danger was removed by the departure from our diet of both fish and potatoes. When the men began shift work at the coal face, which was strenuous and protracted, their ration was, for some reason known only to the Japanese, cut. In consequence they lost weight dramatically, the loss accompanied by a corresponding surge in the incidence of those diseases such as beri-beri which are associated with starvation.

In September 1944 the arrival in camp of the Australian contingent from Siam threw an additional load on the messing which it was quite unable to meet. Rations were now cut dramatically and a scale, drawn up by the Japanese, was immediately put into operation. A worker below ground was allowed 860 grams of boiled rice; a surface worker, 720 grams; camp workers and officers, 520 grams; and the sick, 420 grams. At the cook-house counter a pair of scales was installed where the prisoner watched his ration being carefully weighed out. The American blockade, which at first threatened and finally severed Japan's life-line with the Asiatic mainland, rendered the position desperate. Crowded on their mountainous island, Japan's vast population could never hope to subsist on the produce of its paddy-fields. Now the ration for prisoners was reduced to one cup of boiled rice and a small bowl of brown water, in which floated two or three cabbage leaves, three times a day. Amazingly, on this diet men continued to work fourteen hours a day, twelve of them at the coal face. But the end was not in doubt. They wasted visibly away.

On what form the end might take, speculation ranged widely. The general consensus saw it as inevitably violent and bloody. From Ohama no prisoner was destined to emerge alive. On the other hand, a resort to violence might never be needed. Even had they been spared the bullet or the bayonet, a further year at most might have witnessed a few cadaverous scarecrows still tottering aimlessly about the camp, so long closeted with Death that they had come to regard him as a friend, as they would soon welcome him as a deliverer. But one thing was certain: not one of them would be down the mine, pick in hand, digging coal.

The general policy governing the treatment of prisoners-of-war was laid down in Tokyo, but at Ohama the implementation of that policy bore so unmistakably the stamp of the *shoko*, or camp commandant, that one cannot escape the conclusion that much was left to the discretion of the man on the spot.

From February 1943 till 15 July 1944, the *shoko* at Ohama was Lt Fukuhara. He was so small a man that he was virtually a dwarf, though his frame displayed none of those deformities which are often associated with arrested growth. He made a fetish of physical fitness, and to show his athletic prowess he would often swing – especially when prisoners were watching – on a crude high-bar which he had erected at the back of the camp. About his dress and appearance he was fastidious, always appearing in a neat, trim uniform which was carefully pressed and in jack-boots that were polished till they shone. They were, at the same time, several sizes too big for him and had probably been chosen in the belief that they would add a few inches to his stature. But their main effect was merely to add to his gait a characteristic waddle. Seeing him for the first time, one was struck not so much by his lack of size – though that was remarkable enough – but by his face. It was an evil and vindictive face with a pursed-up mouth and sloe-black eyes, in which, especially when he was enraged (as he often was), there lurked the gleam of fanaticism. Curiously pointed at the top, his ears stuck upwards and outwards rather like a bat's – or an elf's. The purpose that directed Fukuhara's waking hours was to make the life of each prisoner as miserable as he could, and it is a tribute to his capacity that in this lamentable pursuit he achieved marked success. Very few among the prisoners could claim never to have felt the edge of his abusive tongue, or the even more painful impact of his flailing fists or the heavy split-bamboo sword which he frequently carried.

On 15 July 1944, he made a tawdry departure from Ohama standing on a ramshackle farm-cart while his bowing and fawning guards lined the roadway. The whole performance was a farcical mummery, which even a child would have laughed to scorn. But perhaps the most remarkable thing about it was that those who participated in it seemed to regard it with unquestioning solemnity. Fukuhara left us for another camp. For the acts which he was later to carry out there he was to be arraigned before a war crimes tribunal in Tokyo, where he was convicted and sent to the gallows. Since the crimes he committed in his second camp must have been considered to be more serious than those in Ohama, they must have been of a heinous nature. None of the men who suffered under his infamous regime could doubt that he got his deserts, and few could have woven more assiduously the hempen noose which finally put an end to his evil life.

Of Fukuhara's will the immediate instruments were the guards Yamamoto and Ueda. In stature Yamamoto was somewhat above the Japanese norm. He had a fleshy, vapid face, and he certainly was of low intelligence, though he did possess a low animal cunning which was more sinister. Like most of the guards he had seen active service, in his case in China, though unlike them he showed no sign of having suffered a war wound. Like his master Fukuhara, upon whom he diligently modelled his behaviour, Yamamoto had a nature that was volatile and quite unpredictable. The moment he displayed his affability was that when the prisoner had most cause to be on his guard. If he responded by being familiar, or took the slightest liberties in speech, Yamamoto went into a towering rage and the victim had cause to regret his indiscretion. Scarcely a day passed without some prisoner being in the guard-house on a trumped-up charge. Mostly the administering of punishment was something which he took upon himself, though on occasion he would hand the victim over to one of his minions while he stood by and watched. Essentially there was a sadistic streak in his nature. Yamamoto spent the first weeks of his stay in camp scouring the place for any prisoner who had inadvertently left a button undone. It was from this activity that he came to be known in camp as Buttons.

A miscreant of an altogether subtler grain was Ueda, whose badge of office was a sinister, watery smile. He had a war wound in one heel which left a disfiguring scar and added to his gait a characteristic lope. He was thin and rather good-looking, in a European way, and he had a pale cast of countenance. Unlike Buttons, his smile never tempted the unwary to take liberties with him. In camp he was known as The Snake, and the name gives a fairly reliable clue to his character. While in the presence of officers, even British ones, Ueda tended to be sycophantic, but towards other ranks he displayed an unflagging ruthlessness. His role was that of the spy rather than the agent, and to others he preferred to leave the dirty work. For the crimes which he claimed to have detected there were plenty of other guards only too willing to exact the penalties. The true extent of his machinations it is difficult to assess, so clandestine was his method of operation. Towards the sick, in particular, he conducted an implacable vendetta. In the eyes of Ueda every man claiming to be sick was a potential malingerer, his task being to sniff him out. It was on his instructions that, time and again, men who were manifestly sick were hounded out to work. If Ueda happened to come along a corridor when an officer was engaged in reading a book or in some other perfectly legitimate activity, it was not long till Buttons, or the *shoko*, would put in an appearance, shouting '*Damme!*' (bad), or brandishing their wooden swords.

Among the other guards pride of place must go to Fuji, whose chief distinguishing mark was a constant grin, which uncovered a mouthful of gold teeth, and a peculiarly mirthless laugh which, like an adder's hiss, was a warning of danger. A congenital underling, Fuji was consistently affable to British officers (he was never anything but polite to me), but from the men he kept this side of his nature diligently concealed. By general consent he was held to be among the most brutal of the guards, and on their release from the guard-room his victims would reveal evidence to support this belief.

To the relief of all, Button's malign reign came to an end late in 1944 when he was posted to another camp. But to the dismay of those who had rejoiced at his departure, his replacement displayed all the worst of his predecessor's vices. The name of this man was Kotakihara, and in camp he was known as The Panther.

His favourite stratagem was to creep up stealthily behind an unsuspecting prisoner and, for no reason at all, hit him hard on the neck or shoulder with his
wooden sword, those best qualified to judge declaring that in the manipulation
of this painful weapon he displayed conspicuous skill. Against the Australian
newcomers to Ohama he conducted an unremitting vendetta. After the war it was
rumoured that his Australian victims had decided not to let the infidel escape the
consequences of his crimes and, dragging him before a drum-head court-martial,
proceeded to administer summary justice. But this being a matter of whispered
report, I cannot vouch for its accuracy.

Moving in a sinister twilight of his own was an auxiliary who, in the sum total
of the suffering he was indirectly responsible for, possibly exceeded the contribution of any of the others with the necessary exception of Fukuhara himself.
This was Tanaka, whose nominal employment as camp dentist and general interpreter provided a secure cover for his real function as an auxiliary of the secret
police. Tanaka had been educated, and for some time domiciled, in California
which had enabled him to pick up a convincing competence in the American
vernacular. He gave it out that he was secretly an American sympathiser; only
the outbreak of the war, overtaking him when he was on holiday in the land of
his ancestors, had marooned him here. But this fact was not to be taken as in any
way diluting his loyalty to the Allied cause: he had just to act with discretion. So
smooth an operator did Tanaka prove to be that many of the men were taken in
with this tale, and refused to believe that he was anything but an honest and
truthful friend of theirs. Upon Tanaka the dual role of dentist and interpreter
conferred a franchise to move about the camp at all times of the day and night
without arousing suspicion. But when Tanaka was within earshot, it behoved
every man to be wary of what he said. Issuing silently from his room at night on
the way to the *benjo*, an unsuspecting prisoner would sometimes catch a glimpse
of a ghostly eavesdropper retreating incontinently into the shadows. When there
was any major development in the war situation, there was sure to be the dentist,
buttonholing the unwary, alert to catch the slip of the tongue that would betray
the presence of the radio which the Japanese were always convinced we had
hidden in camp. But this also operated in the opposite way: when Tanaka was
most active we could be assured that Japanese fortunes had taken a turn for the
worse. In the end even the least security-conscious among the men came round
to the view that Tanaka was a man who was best avoided. But he remained with
us to the end, fawning and reptilian, moving about the camp like a man who,
having lost his allegiance, had also lost his way.

To enforce camp discipline the Japanese drew up a code of regulations, many
of them petty but all enforced with Draconian severity. A button inadvertently
left undone was regarded as a crime. A trace of dirt under a fingernail – a regu-
lation which was particularly vexatious for miners constantly exposed to coal
down the mine – had its appropriate punishment. Hair had to be kept closely
cropped – *atarashi* (manly) they claimed. A *tenken*, or name-tally, left unturned
on the movements board that hung outside of each room involved the delinquent
in appropriate chastisement. Any alleged failure, even by the most senior British
officer, to salute the lowest order of Japanese soldiery was looked upon as a
major crime which could be expiated only by the summoning of the whole camp

to the parade ground and their submission to saluting practice for an hour, or longer. For any major offence, such as being outside the camp without permission, in any circumstances, or striking or being grossly insubordinate to a guard, the punishment was summary execution, the victim in many cases (as we had found in Java) being compelled to dig his own grave.

The beginning of 1944 saw a marked intensifying of discipline. Slapping of the face – in other words, a *karate* chop, which could fell a man – which earlier had been sporadic, now became a feature of daily life. During what came to be known as 'hate campaigns', the incidence of these attacks rose conspicuously. They observed a certain pattern which must have been instigated from above, and which, we later discovered, operated concurrently in other camps. During the winter of 1944–45 when the possibility of invasion became imminent, the persecution rose in a crescendo, the guard-house rarely without its victim. The systematic brutality which the Japanese practised upon their prisoners-of-war was a natural result of the light in which they regarded them. To them, the inmates of their camps – as to the Germans those of their concentration camps (but not their PoW camps) – were men who, the one by their behaviour and the other by their race, belonged to a lower order of humanity to whom civilised 'rights' did not apply. Thus in their treatment of prisoners the Japanese were never troubled by what may loosely be described as 'conscience'. Had not these wretched men by the very act of surrender achieved the ultimate debasement of the profession of arms? In a similar situation, every Japanese would honourably have destroyed himself – as, in all the fields where Japanese armies fought, they had conspicuously shown. To them the very idea of a Japanese prisoner was abhorrent – a man who had forfeited his manhood and who, if he ever returned to his homeland, would be shunned as a pariah. That their lives had for the time being been spared should, on the part of the prisoners, be no ground either for gratitude or gratification. To the Japanese mind, men who had basely purchased their lives with their honour possessed no 'rights', their sole justification for existing expiring with their ability to work for their captors. From Ohama no prisoners were destined ever to depart. For them awaited only the crematorium on the hill and the final oblivion which would be their kindest memorial.

With this assessment of their prospects, it must be admitted (though they might not be prepared to confess it openly) that the bulk of the prisoners were in broad agreement. Right up to the sudden and unforeseen end of the war, most of them could not conceive of any set of circumstances in which they were likely to emerge alive from Ohama. The most probable scenario would involve a general slaughter of prisoners, which would start as soon as an American soldier set foot on the sacred soil of Japan. If the war went badly, the women and children would perish. Finally the men would fight to a finish till, with the end in sight, the survivors would commit *hara-kiri*, by which grisly ritual the Japanese people would purge the shame of defeat by the redemption of self-destruction. To those ordained to be the first victims, the reflection that their captors would be overtaken by a fate no less terrible and on a far greater scale than that which they had appointed for themselves afforded a slender – and indeed the only – consolation.

Senior NCOs at Ohama. In the front row fourth from the left is Warrant Officer Root (RAF) and seventh from the left Staff Sergeant Westripp (77th Heavy Anti-Aircraft Regiment).

NCOs of the 77th Heavy Anti-Aircraft Regiment (Welsh) with Second Lieutenant John Probert standing on the right.

The path to the Hill. This photograph was taken on the occasion of the visit to Ohama of Dr Paravicini, the Red Cross representative, on 16 March, 1943. It was distributed abroad, the intention being to convey an impression of the liberal régime under which the camp was operated. The names of the first five officers, counting from the head of the file are Wing Commander Mathews, Squadron Leader Wyrill, Flight Lieutenant Frankie Knight, Captain Millin and Pilot Officer McEwan – the author.

This photograph of the entrance to the mine was taken by Reg Newton on his return to Ohama in 1970.

THE COAL-MINE

The vertical shaft and winding-cage type of mine, which is more suited to the working of seams at a great depth, is that most commonly found in Britain. The mine at Ohama was, however, of the drift variety, which is usually preferred when the coal seams lie close to the surface and can be reached by a downward-sloping tunnel or drift. Since the Ohama mine was worked under the sea the vertical shaft was, in any case, out of the question.

Since the ground rose very steeply from sea level, the entrance to the Ohama mine had to be placed dangerously close to the water. In a gradient of about one in three, a tunnel descended through a brick archway to pierce the stratum of sandstone which overlay the coal, the latter being about seventy to eighty feet below the bed of the sea. The tunnel enclosed a steep stairway, the steps of which were constructed of old pit-props laid transversely and supported by a wooden peg driven into the ground at each end. So thin in places was the roof that it was not uncommon for miners working at the face about two miles from the entrance to hear the thrash of ships' propellers as they passed overhead. When one remembers that Japan lies in an earthquake-prone zone, and that the engineering of the mine was not above suspicion, it is not difficult to realise that working in this sub-aqueous mine was a highly dangerous occupation. A consequence of the mine's being under the sea was that the roof constantly dripped, and in places poured water, and each step cradled a puddle of mud which was treacherous for rubber boots, especially when (as was usually the case) the tread was worn off them or they were falling apart and tied with rope. Slips or falls were a daily occurrence, most often when the men were on their way back from a shift, with limbs too exhausted to make sure of their footing.

Parallel to the main tunnel by which the men entered and left the mine, and very close to it, was the auxiliary tunnel. This served as an escape route in the event of flooding or a roof-fall blocking the main tunnel though its main function was to provide a route for the *hakkos*, or coal-hutches, which were hauled to the surface by a wire rope connected to a large *maki*, or engine, which was situated in a hut just below the lamp-room. These *hakkos*, on their way up and down this steep gradient, were assembled in batches and piloted by boys who were charioteers of very tender years, great courage, and phenomenal lung power. As they rattled on their hair-raising journeys, the roofs of the tunnels and galleries echoed eerily to their cries of '*Hakko! Hakko! Hakko!*' At the foot of the long descent, both tunnels opened into a long gallery which ran out under the sea. Its floor was occupied by a deep and treacherous sump into which was pumped the water from the various workings before the main pump carried it to the surface. On occasion when a brake failed, a convoy of runaway *hakkos* would come charging down the slope, swiftly gathering speed while its *Jehu* bawled at the pitch of his voice till it was quenched in a watery gurgle as he sank in the sump. Surprisingly, on the occasions when I was a witness, he always seemed to surface, silent and sodden – but still alive. Considering the frequency of these accidents, it is inconceivable that none of the *hakko*-boys was ever injured, though I never heard of one of them losing his life. The crossing of the sump always involved danger. The only practical way was to shuffle along one of the rails, which were always submerged, while maintaining one's balance by holding on with one hand to the roof timbers. But here lurked another peril, for a *hakko* with sharp pieces of coal on top was likely to strip them of insulation, or at times sever them. One day I was edging along the rail in the wake of my ganger when a blue glow appeared at his head; there was a crack and he was thrown violently into the sump. I thought he was electrocuted but he struggled from the water back on to the rail, shaken but still alive. Such is the indestructibility of the race that several similar skirmishes with death that were reported all ended happily.

At its seaward end the main gallery forked into two secondary drifts, or *codas*. *San Coda*, or No. 3 Drift, turned sharply to the right and continued parallel to the coast for about a mile till it ended in what was the wettest group of headings in the whole mine. It was here that the sound of the ships' propellers overhead could be heard at their loudest. Being very close to the sea-bed, the roof was very friable and unstable and in places water poured down as if a pipe had burst. For this reason the *coda* was permanently awash, and to reach the headings the men had to wade through a lake of stagnant water which was never less than a mile long and about a foot and a half deep. Had the sea burst into the mine this was the point at which it was most likely to happen. *Ni Coda*, or No. 2 Drift, continued from the main sump out under the sea. But having immediately encountered very contorted strata, it plunged down in a very steep descent to a sump, on the far side of which it rose in a correspondingly steep gradient. This sump was a critical point in the drainage system of the whole mine, for once the main pump broke down it was the first to flood, thereby cutting off all the men who were working on the far side of it.

On our arrival in Ohama, the coal was extracted using two systems: the conveyor belt or the stall. In constructing a conveyor, a heading was driven for about fifty yards immediately under the seam to be worked, and from its far end a vertical shaft was then driven up through the coal seam. From the top of this shaft, and at right angles to the first heading, a second was driven for the full length of the conveyor belt. One side of this now formed the coal face to be worked. Hewn from the face, usually by means of pneumatic jack-picks, the coal was shovelled on to the conveyor belt which carried it along to the top of the vertical shaft, down which it was tipped into a *hakko* waiting beneath. As the coal was dug out, so the face receded, and the conveyor belt was moved forward correspondingly. The Japanese made no attempt to underpin the roof, which gradually settled as the face advanced, its pressure helping to dislodge the coal at the face. This, they claimed, was standard German practice. But the roof was criss-crossed with fissures, and in addition was always saturated. It was thus almost impossible to control sinkage or anticipate a fall. If this occurred near to the mouth of the vertical shaft, it was likely to cut off a gang's only means of escape.

This was what, in effect, happened. In July 1943, with no warning, the roof of a conveyor belt caved in trapping six prisoners who were working there. But the

A/A Regiment, which had been raised in Cardiff, numbered in its ranks many men who had been miners in the Welsh valleys. From this number we contrived to have a Welsh miner in each gang down the mine, their earlier training and traditions being a protection to other prisoners whose ignorance of danger might expose them to it. As the roof was collapsing around them, this man ordered his companions to collect as many big stones as they could, and with these he hurriedly built a pillar about a couple of feet from the face. As it settled, the roof crushed the whole heading out of existence, apart from a small cavity between the face and the pillar, in which six men huddled. Luckily the air-pipe for the jack-picks had not been severed in the fall, and this provided them with a supply of air without which they would have quickly died. To the camp came a call for volunteers to form a rescue team, and true to the traditions of the Welsh valleys every man who had been a miner stepped forward. From these a team of the most experienced miners was selected and dispatched down the mine. But when they reached the scene of the accident they found a Japanese rescue team vigorously at work. Being smaller men, they could operate in more restricted conditions than Europeans. Digging with great skill and vigour, they succeeded in driving a tunnel through to the entombed men only to find that the Welshman and his trapped miners could not escape by it, their frames too big for the aperture. The escape tunnel had then to be enlarged. But in the end all were got out safely. The rescued men were loud in their praise of the professional expertise and energy of the Japanese team. After the accident the Japanese were prevailed upon to provide some pit-props for roof-pinning in conveyor belt workings, but this only diminished, and did not remove, the dangers, which continued to be excessive. It was remarkable that during the years they worked in the Ohama mine no prisoner lost his life in a conveyor belt working.

The other main method of coal extraction, the stall, was that which is traditional in primitive mines. This involved running a heading along a coal face from which the coal was picked out, usually by hand-pick, and loaded into *hakkos*. But here the roof was always unstable, and the seams thin. With the heavy seepage of water, the roof often sank unpredictably. But rarely was a stall abandoned because there was too little room to work it. Lying on their side, in the most cramped and exhausting conditions, the men continued to pick out the coal till the seam petered out or they were unable to reach it.

As the American blockade tightened its grip, so the clamour for coal became more insistent. The manner of its procurement seemed of little consequence to the Japanese. It was then that they introduced at Ohama a system which came to be known as 'ballrooms', and was indeed murderous. A heading being driven into a seam, its far end was then enlarged, no attempt being made to underpin the roof, till it eventually collapsed, crushing the ballroom out of existence in a moment or two. The instant of collapse often came with little or no warning. It was now that the training of the Welsh miners stood our men in good stead, for their ears could pick up the first, faint warnings of danger long before the others were aware of it. Without them, many would certainly have died. During one shift, on my round of the headings, I stopped in a ballroom to have my *meshi*, or rice, with a gang which was working there. Suddenly, as we were eating without a thought of danger, the Welsh miner gave a shout of alarm: 'Get out! For God's

sake get out!' sending a mad scramble for the narrow exit from the heading. As
we did so the roof groaned, writhed, and crashed down upon us, great slabs of
rock, many tons in weight, peeling from the roof as the earth heaved around us.
Shoving each man in turn violently into the narrow tunnel, the Welsh miner came
last, just managing to get through the opening in the nick of time before the whole
ballroom vanished under the rending rocks. It was a system which would have
been resorted to only by men for whom human life had ceased to have any value.

From each gang the shift assignment varied, according to the difficulty of the
strata, from twenty-five to forty *hakkos*, each *hakko* containing fifteen cwt of
coal. The job of the Jap ganger, who was one of the regular miners in the mine,
was to see that this target was met; apart from this, he usually did not harass the
men. Failure to meet the target had, however, to be reported to the guard-house,
whose task it was to reform the defaulters. To boost output, bribery in all its
forms – such as soap, tea, cigarettes, and (shamefully) British Red Cross parcels
– was constantly employed. But those who were foolish enough to succumb to
these blandishments were soon to find they had merely compounded their hard-
ships since the new production level was now taken as the basis for fresh
demands. Learning from bitter experience, most of the gangs kept output just
above the threshold that would escape reprisals.

Almost from the outset sabotage down the mine became a fact of life. The
commonest trick was to ballast *hakkos* with substances other than coal, those
most ready to hand being stones and bits of pit-props. In this field perhaps the
most ardent and successful operator was an Australian called Joe Demery. For
a saboteur Joe possessed several impressive qualifications, among them being a
slow drawl and a quite misleading impression of slow-wittedness, which led the
Japanese to conclude he was not quite of miner material. They therefore relegated him to a post at a *coda* junction where *hakkos* were coupled up into batches
for dispatch to the surface. This proved to be an ideal stage for Joe's numerous
ploys. When he was not engaged in ballasting *hakkos* with stones, he was refining
schemes for their 'accidental' derailment. But he had his moments of misfortune.
One day, on approaching Joe's place of operation when he was patently engaged
on his nefarious activities, I saw a Japanese overseer lurking in the shadows and
keeping an eye on the busy saboteur. Going up to Joe, he politely borrowed his
shovel and removed from the *hakko* that with which the prisoner was 'doctoring'
the thin layer of coal. Evidence could scarcely have been more irrefutable.
Producing his little pocket-book, the Japanese jotted down Joe's number and,
without a word, went on his way. Arrived back in camp, a tap on the shoulder
heralded Joe's removal from the companionship of his friends for remedial treatment. But in Joe's make-up one emotion that had been overlooked was the
penitential. When, at length, he was released, the Japanese, with incredible short-
sightedness, restored him to the old junction from which his removal had seen a
sudden diminution in mishaps. It took no more than a day or two before he was
picking up the threads of sabotage exactly where he had left off. The end of the
war found him just as enthusiastically thwarting the Japanese war effort as on
the day when he had first gone down the mine.

Joe was the kind of man who could well dispense with collaborators. But had
he looked for one, he need have sought no further than Staff Sergeant Westripp,

one of the Welsh gunners. As driver of the *maki* for the main pump, he was at the very centre of the web of sabotage in the mine. Whenever Westripp thought fit to 'fix the *maki*', the main pump stopped and the sump in *Ni Coda* filled immediately. The Japanese employed a junior clerk whose duty it was to keep an eye on the sump and report any sudden rise in the water level, but sometimes he failed to give adequate warning and the men in the further workings were trapped. When this happened a bell was rung, on hearing which they rushed back to the sump. Provided there still remained a few inches between water and roof, they would strip to their loincloths and, carrying their clothes and lamp-battery on their head, wade through to safety. But Westripp had an uncanny knack of getting the *maki* back into operation before any real danger threatened them. His engineering skill defeated every effort of the Japanese to catch him out in crime, though they obviously had grave suspicions. The amount of disruption and consequent loss of production he was responsible for in this way must have been considerable.

With the war situation fast approaching a crisis, desperate efforts were now made to boost output at any price. To exhort miners to an all-out effort, teams of higher officials were now dispatched down the mine. Before going below these men would remove their trousers, socks and shoes but retain their jackets, waistcoats, shirts and ties. Then, having put on split-toed rubber boots, they would, in this grotesque attire, set out on their mission of patriotic exhortation. In some lonely, dripping heading, a gang of our men would see approaching a swaying line of lamps looking like aqueous fireflies, and underneath them shadowy figures with bleached and bandy legs, lurching towards them through the mud and water. To these visitors the Japanese gangers showed reverential respect which, naturally, our men found some difficulty in simulating. Nevertheless, they dutifully went through the appointed ritual of *kirei*-ing (or saluting) and bowing.

The rigours and perils of the coal mine at Ohama our men endured, and cursed the Japs – but never their fate. As the days passed, the flesh fell from their bodies, leaving skeletons in a wrinkled carapace of skin. But nothing the Japs could do could break their spirit. For what they did and for what they endured in those dripping midnight tunnels no medals were struck or tribute paid. But beneath those filthy hessian *happi*-coats beat hearts as steadfast as under braided tunics proudly displaying the ribbons of valour. The difference was that what they achieved, and what they suffered, took place in a remote coal-mine under the Inland Sea of Japan on the other side of the earth, too far away for those at home to know – or in time to care.

A CHRONICLE OF WASTED TIME

Long before the *Singapore Maru* arrived at Moji, it was abundantly clear that some effort must be made to compile a dossier on the appalling things that were happening on board. Upon the minds of those who had suffered and survived, or even of those who had been no more than witnesses, the more tragic and sordid events would leave an impression that nothing would ever efface. But with the passing years images inevitably blur, and to the impact and reliability of a contemporary written record even the most retentive memory must yield. For what was happening on board, eternal justice demanded that somebody, somewhere, would (unless retribution was to be left to Heaven) have to be called to account, and when that solemn day arrived documents would be needed.

The sad thing was that those in closest contact with the events were not best placed to compile these documents. Upon the CO and the doctors the burden of work was overwhelming; besides, they were under the constant eyes of the Japanese and were exposed to sudden searches. Weighing up the situation I concluded that, being relatively inconspicuous and thus not subject to the same suspicion, I might be as able as any to keep a tally of what was going on without running too great a risk of being caught. So, in an effort to compile this dossier, I went about the ship industriously and unobtrusively collecting and collating all the information I could. I recorded the names of those who died, giving the time and the circumstances of their death. I wrote down details about the conditions in the holds; the lack of medical supplies; the lack of food; the appallingly insanitary conditions; the general indifference of the Japanese to it all; and their deafness to all appeals for help.

From Java, with nothing more than a general feeling that it might some time come in handy, I had brought with me a notebook. In appearance it recalled the school-room rather than the court, but for the purpose now in hand it possessed some undeniable advantages. Its pages were of thin India paper which, if fingered while secreted in clothing, gave out no tell-tale crinkling. A curious glance from an inquisitor might not at once reveal to him its nature. In this I recorded the harvest of my researches. By the time we got to Moji my record had swelled to fifty closely-written pages. When the day of reckoning at last arrived it would have its part to play, supplementing any records which the doctors might have been able to compile, and which managed to survive. By the same token, its uncovering by some curious Japanese hand would have rendered my fate somewhat more precarious. To ensure that it got safely off the ship, and to disguise as far as possible its true nature were it to be discovered, I went to considerable pains. First, across the top of each page I wrote a heading, its intention being to suggest that what followed was no more than a quotation from some book I had read which was merely waiting transference to a more permanent commonplace book. The page numbers I introduced at odd places in the text, using Arabic and Roman numerals as well as French, German, and especially Lallans words, to thicken the web of deceit. I then shuffled the pages. A Japanese investigator from the lower echelons of cryptography would, I imagined, undoubtedly succeed in restoring the pages to their correct order, but the task would involve some juggling. Finally I divided the manuscript into three sections, one of which I sewed into the crown of my cap and the other two in the padding under the epaulettes of Wilkins's greatcoat. Any systematic search could not, of course, have failed to uncover the deception, but with some luck I survived the far from perfunctory searches on the dockside at Moji, and got safely into the camp at Ohama. There my dossier would have to find a more secure and permanent home.

In the ramshackle construction of the dormitories almost every board or shingle could, with little difficulty, be dismantled and later replaced without leaving tell-tale signs that it had been tampered with. In their multitudinous crannies the opportunities for concealment were unlimited, but they had one great disadvantage: their possibilities for secreting things were much more likely to be known to the Japanese, who had constructed the buildings, than to the prisoners who had just arrived in them. This consideration persuaded me to abandon the idea of concealing the manuscript in the buildings; instead, I turned my attention to the cheap suitcase which contained the few possessions I had brought from Java. A stout wooden box, about twenty-four inches by fifteen, it had a thick red wallpaper lining and was bound outside with woven cane. To procure a false bottom for it I enlisted the services of Johnnie, who contacted his versatile ally in the mine, Westripp, who made it on his *maki*, his isolation shielding him from discovery. When completed it was smuggled back into camp, piece by piece, and with agreeable irony concealed in the 'false bottoms' of the miners' *fandushis*, or jockstraps, the miners (as always) readily co-operating though the purpose of the enterprise was, naturally, kept from them.

In its final stages the work was much hampered by the unrelenting attentions of Buttons, who harboured a suspicion that something mischievous was afoot. But I told him that, the case being bug-infested, the paper lining had to be removed and disinfected by exposure to sunlight. Soaking the lining in water till the gum was dissolved, I managed to slip the paper out without damage and exposed it in the sun till it dried. Naturally, Buttons's presence was dispensed with when it came to the crucial operation of placing my manuscript in the bottom of the case, securely fixing the false bottom on top of it, smearing the lining with rice-paste and then replacing it, and finally trimming down the protruding edges. Filled with my clothing and other odds and ends, the case was then restored to its place on the shelf, where I fondly imagined it would see out the war in unmolested peace.

In the cook-house worked Cpl Smith, who had been a barber in Luton before joining the RAF as an air mechanic. No more wily and discreet a man existed in camp; keeping a vigilant ear to the ground, he was to prove an invaluable agent in tipping us off about Japanese intentions. When, therefore, one afternoon in

April 1943, Cpl Smith casually sauntered past the officers' quarters, no one was misguided into thinking he was merely taking exercise. The *kempetai* (or Japanese secret police) were, he confided, planning a swoop on the camp next day. His prophecy and warning were menacingly fulfilled when, at dawn next morning, a gang of villainous-looking men swept through the dormitories like a tornado. It was clear that anyone falling foul of this ruffian pack would not have his sorrows to seek. All prisoners were immediately lined up in the middle of their rooms and forbidden to move while, from room to room, they systematically ransacked the buildings. They hauled up the *tatamis* and prodded the earth beneath with iron spikes, searching for the buried radios they were convinced we operated. Out went the contents of every cupboard and every receptacle, to be gone through meticulously. They kicked, they shook, they probed, they hauled things apart.

It would have been surprising if, in their search for contraband, my fatal box had escaped scrutiny. Barrel-chested, long-armed, short of stature, and bandy-legged, one of the most villainous-looking among them reached for my case and unceremoniously tossed its contents out on to the *tatamis*. Kicking the case, he put it to his ear to see if he could detect the hollow sound that would have betrayed its secret cavity. But for a man of his profession and undoubted dedication, he signally failed to apply the simple test that would have blown my ruse, and sealed my fate. Applied to the outside, and then to the inside, a foot-rule would have laid bare the damning discrepancy. As the examination relentlessly proceeded, my knees turned to water; in even more desperate straits was Johnnie, who was in on the secret and standing next to me. Turning ashen grey, he began to sway gently from side to side; clearly he was on the point of falling down in a faint. It was odd that our inquisitors did not notice it, for only by a supreme effort of will did he manage to stay on his feet. Had the ordeal gone on a little longer, I have little doubt he would have collapsed. But before that fatal crisis arrived the *kempetai* admitted defeat and, smouldering with frustration, went on to the next room. But the experience had taught me a lesson: my papers would have to find a home elsewhere. Through Johnnie I made contact with the resourceful Westripp. With admirable ingenuity he acquired two identically shaped tins and, soldering a thin strip of metal round the open end of one of them, he fitted the other into it to form a box. Retrieving my dossier from the false bottom of my case, I put it into the tin box, sealing the joint with a slip of paper which had been saturated with lubricating oil from the *maki*, thus making a watertight joint. The next steps in the operation needed the cover of darkness. With my room-mates posted as spies, I slid aside the *tatami* which had been used by the dead New Zealander, and had since been left vacant. It was my hope that, if discovered, I could disclaim all knowledge of the tin, attributing its presence to the dead officer. I dug a hole under one of the floor beams, where it would be less likely to be detected by a metal probe, and in it I buried the tin, strewing some cobwebs on top of the replaced earth to make it look undisturbed. In this new resting place the papers remained for the best part of a year.

It was the ever vigilant Cpl Smith who once again sounded the faint tocsin of alarm. From some tattling Japanese miner he had picked up a rumour that the *kempetai* had been making enquiries about spades down the mine, and had ordered that some should be kept for their use. This pointed only to one thing: they were going to dig up the earth under the floors of our quarters. Where probes had failed, spades would be certain to uncover my secret. With the news of the threat, Cpl Smith also offered an ingenious stratagem for its defeat. Just that day, he said, Japanese workmen had been repairing broken patches in the cement floor of the cook-house; having filled in the holes with rubble, they were returning next morning to cement them over. If, said Cpl Smith, we had any valuables that we wanted safely hidden, he would undertake their secret transfer to the bottom of the rubble in one of those holes, where they would be sealed away beyond all possibility of discovery till the war was over. A proposition so tempting almost demanded acceptance. There was no doubting the reliability and resourcefulness of Cpl Smith, but this was an undertaking he could not carry out purely on his own – at the very least, one or two cooks would have to be let into the secret in order that they might be posted as look-outs while the operation was carried out. Could we rely on their discretion, or their courage and sharpness of invention if caught in the act? Long reflection convinced me that the risks were too great; I had to seek a solution elsewhere.

What softened the renunciation of Cpl Smith's scheme was the unexpected opening up of an alternative possibility. The *shoko* had appointed me to what had become the sinecure post of officer-in-charge of the hen-house. Having long lost its tenantry, the shed was a ramshackle structure on the point of falling down. To allay Buttons's insatiable curiosity, I thought it expedient to enlist his services; telling him that I intended to repair the hut, I asked him if he could procure some timber for me for the job. Not only did he provide boards, nails, hammer and saw, he also gave generously of his assistance in the carpentry. Where I failed to enlist his help was in the operation that lay at the heart of the stratagem. When my secret manuscript was slipped into the cavity that now existed between the old wall and the new, and the boards were nailed on to conceal the cache, Button's curious eye was engaged elsewhere. There, in its final resting place, my manuscript safely reposed till the atom bombs on Hiroshima and Nagasaki announced the time had arrived for its retrieval. Now, of course, Buttons was no longer in Ohama, either to help or to hinder operations. Getting an axe, I prised off the boards that guarded my secret. Then, to my dismay, I found not the papers I expected but a curious slab of a white substance that had the consistency of rubber. Between the mandibles of a colony of termites, or white ants, my record of the voyage of the infamous *Singapore Maru* had perished, the facts it recorded lost for ever. Dismayed, but not yet defeated, I tried to repair the loss. Enlisting the aid of friends I went about compiling a second dossier. But since these eventful days on the China seas years had passed, while subsequent sufferings had blunted the memory of these earlier ones. Gone beyond all recall was the immediacy of that first, and first-hand, record.

In due course, the captain of the *Singapore Maru*, along with the officer-in-charge of the draft of prisoners and two conductors, were arraigned before a war crimes tribunal. But Fate, in the shape of a colony of industrious and rapacious ants, had removed from their scrutiny a document which might have proved of some assistance to the judges in arriving at their verdict.

Preparations for the first (and only) visit from a representative of the Red

Cross to Ohama, which took place on 16 March 1943, became apparent on the day before his arrival. The initial announcement that something unusual was afoot was the arrival of a lorry, from which a small sectional hut was unloaded and set up just to one side of the entrance to the dining-room. Its glass front admitted examination of its shelves on which appeared such unheard-of things as tins of red salmon, tins of meat, tins of fruit, and bottles of sweets. But the prisoners' enjoyment of these delicacies was never to advance beyond the visual, nothing on these shelves ever leaving them. Apart from the time when the visit was underway, the door of that hut was secured by a stout padlock whose wards no key disturbed till, in the fullness of time, both hut and contents were loaded on to the same lorry which had brought them there to be transported (so we presumed) to repeat their tantalising unfulfilment at another camp. On the heels of this first lorry came a second, its load consisting of *bonsais*, these stunted but quaintly picturesque conifers which the Japanese grow in tubs, to which they attribute great age and which they treat with notable veneration. Of this load the choicest specimens were reserved for the dining-room, while the less picturesque found their way into odd corners of the compound, there to waste their fragrance on the desert air while adding a transient greenery to their barren surroundings.

At the same time, the Japanese let it be known that as a signal instance of Japanese benevolence a small deputation of prisoners would be permitted to lay before the visitors any useful proposals they might care to make for their betterment. Among the prisoners speculation ranged widely over what matters it might be considered fruitful – or, for that matter, prudent – to bring to the notice of the delegation. Certain things, of course, selected themselves and occasioned no debate. Among these were medical and surgical facilities (if a need for them should arise), food, clothing, heating, soap (this, in a mining community, being a basic necessity). Inspired by the arrival of the hut and its mouth-watering contents, it was decided (not without malice) to introduce some query about tins of fruit and meat, and also bottles of sweets, these being things *we never saw in camp*. On one very arbitrary but very vital matter, opinion was divided: would it serve any useful purpose even to make oblique reference to the outbreaks of brutality to which we were exposed, or might it be more prudent to restrict ourselves to the suggestion that, purely on grounds of incompatibility of temperament, Buttons might be translated to another camp?

The Red Cross representative turned out to be a Dr Paravicini. A Swiss national, he had long been domiciled and practised in Japan, acquiring over the years an easy familiarity both with the Japanese language and traditions. A tall man, and very spare, he had a bearing that was unmistakably patrician. Cropped like that of an American GI, his sandy hair stood up *en brosse*, while his eyes were set in a deeply tanned face of a reflective and melancholy cast. Somewhat at odds with the Calvinistic *gravitas* of his demeanour was the floppy American-style suit which he wore, and even more so the Bohemian bow-tie which drooped at his throat. In his wake stomped a troop of Japanese military dignitaries, their gait distorted by the outsize jack-boots they wore. Bringing up the rear were the *shoko* and the elect of his underlings, all unnaturally reverential.

The inspection began with a general tour of the compound; once ended, the visitors retired to the sick-bay, which had been prepared as an interview room.

Down the middle stretched a deal table, at one side of which sat the Swiss flanked by a couple of whey-faced Japanese officers. The three-man deputation from the prisoners (the present writer being one) was shown in and given seats at the opposite side. From the outset it was made clear that the proceedings were to be conducted in terms which never strayed far from the brusque and the uncompromising. Even to the most reasonable and bland of requests the Japanese response was curt and hostile. For the most part the Swiss screened his feelings by a veil of impregnable detachment. Once or twice, when some question seemed to raise a doubt in his mind, he did consult with his Japanese colleagues, the exchanges revealing his easy mastery of the Japanese language. Only on two points was any useful information provided: our next-of-kin had already been (or else would shortly be) advised that we were alive and in Japan; and the question of letters both to and from home was a matter that would be dealt with by the Protecting Power. All other questions were met with a stock reply: 'That is difficult!' So darkly hostile was the reception given to our mischievous question about tins of salmon, meat and sweets that instinct forbade any suggestion that Buttons might find more appropriate scope for his activities in another camp. In view of what had gone before that, undoubtedly, would have provoked a convulsion. Only our eagerness to detect some understanding of our plight, especially on the part of the only visitor from outside Japan we were ever likely to see, can explain our failure immediately to realise that Dr Paravicini's apparent cold detachment was a condition of his being allowed to see us in the first place. Any display on his part of partiality towards prisoners would have seen a speedy termination to his mission, endangering further contact between the Red Cross and PoW camps in Japan. What he was to achieve behind the scenes in the brief months vouchsafed to him we were never to know.

When the interview was over, Dr Paravicini was taken to the office and had explained to him the formalities that were observed when one of the prisoners died. For his inspection a funerary urn was produced, the simple, untooled, white-wooden box which was in standard use in the Japanese armed forces. The remarkable thing about this casket, however, was that one side of it bore a legend, seeing which the Swiss got out his notebook and pencil and copied it down. What later use he was to make of it is unknown, but for some obscure reason the name and details thereon recorded were those of Johnnie Probert, officer of artillery, whose state of health at that moment did not make the disposal of his ashes a matter of extreme urgency. Attention was next directed to the kitchen and dining-room which, from an early hour, had been the scene of feverish activity. Our cooks having been banished to their quarters, their duties were taken over by a squad of immigrant Japanese, who prepared lunch. When all was ready the men were summoned and, being stationed in their places, were drawn up stiffly at attention. On the tables before them was displayed a meal, lavish beyond all Ohama standards, consisting as it did of a bowl of soup in which floated pieces of real meat, a bowl of rice, a piece of bread, and an orange. Then, with notable ceremony, the Swiss was ushered in. An inspection of the tables led to the inescapable conclusion that, if this represented their customary diet, it could be regarded as meeting basic requirements. Meanwhile, assiduous behind their lenses, the press photographers compiled their record. When the inspection was over, the Swiss and the Japanese officers, climbing into their waiting cars, were driven off, presumably to repeat the performance at another camp. With no long interval the lorry returned and, the hut and its contents of meat, fruit and sweets being loaded on to it, took its departure. Shortly afterwards we said farewell to the *bonsais*, less lamented transients. Of this whole canting performance perhaps the most nauseating aspect was the blindness of the Japanese to its hypocrisy and their total failure to be disturbed by it.

On the morning following the Red Cross visit the whole camp, with the exception of the sick and a few cooks with a guard or two to supervise, was paraded for a *sampo*, or organised walk. Pointing to the importance the Japanese attached to the occasion was the presence of the *shoko* himself and the rest of the guards. Prominent in the procession, lynx-eyed for the revealing snap, were the photographers who had covered the events of the preceding day. Setting off in a ragged crocodile, the column made its way along the road that skirts the Inland Sea and leads in time to the neighbouring village of Motoyama. Its objective was a picturesque little headland, its top crowned by a cluster of venerable cedars, its shore girdled by a selvage of the whitest sand on which rested several huge boulders. Here the column halted, and the order being given – 'All men merry!' – the prisoners fell-out. In the camp at Ohama merriness was not an emotion that was much in evidence and the men responded by a show of simulated gaiety for their own entertainment and the satisfaction of the cameramen.

The beach charade successfully completed, the men were recalled; formed again into their column they set off once more, now deserting the sea and following a path that wound steeply up the hill. So densely overgrown was it in places with thickets that they had to force a way through, exposing in the process their bare legs to thorns which were at times as long and sharp as scalpels, which lacerated them and left them streaming with blood. But at length they reached the plateau with its grove of majestic cedars, finding it a place of sylvan charm which provided some consolation for the pain which had attended its achievement. In the middle of the plateau stood a little shrine. Built modestly of wood, it rested on a solid granite plinth. In front was an open door, indifferently daubed with red and blue paint. The shrine housed an image whose face bore a lively if enigmatic smile, and before which some tokens of piety in the shape of a couple of empty jam-jars holding the charred stumps of joss-sticks testified to the persistence of its religious function. Before the shrine couched a pair of granite lions, their faces distorted with intimidating grimaces to scare away hostile spirits, their sightless eyes gazing in eternal fixation out towards the placid waters of the Inland Sea. Quite incidental to its function was the shrine's most remarkable feature: a roof of dazzling green tiles whose horned eaves, in enchanting curves, swept outwards to hang suspended in vacancy. In groups the men sat under the cedars, or strolled hither and thither over the dried bents, identifying features in the landscape below, never far from the ardent cameramen, haunting as shadows. In agreeable but imperceptible procession the hours slipped past as the bright day waned till presently in their ears echoed the sharp summons to fall-in for the march back to the camp. Not till the war was over did any foot of theirs again tread the soft turf of the plateau in the cedar shade, nor did any eye survey the panorama which it subtended.

Linked inescapably with the visit of the Red Cross representative to Ohama was the arrival of the first Red Cross parcels. These had been brought by the Swedish vessel the *Gripsholm* which, in July 1942, had gone to Lourenço Marques in Mozambique to effect an exchange of stranded diplomats and others whom the outbreak of the war had left marooned on foreign shores. Trans-shipped to the *Asama Maru*, the consignment was brought back to Japan, some subsequent exchanges arranged in a similar manner. In view of the distances they had to cover and the obstacles that were placed in their way, surprise should not be expressed at the relatively modest nature of the operations, but that they should have taken place at all. On average, during the whole period of his Japanese captivity, each prisoner received the equivalent of one parcel a year. But to reckon the value of this in material terms would be to miss its point, representing as it did the sole link visible to him with a remembered past and a dubious future. As long as a parcel succeeded in reaching Ohama, so long persisted evidence that he was neither abandoned nor forgotten.

The lofty ideals which had animated the institution of the Red Cross, and had sustained its operations, found no echo in the minds of those Japanese into whose hands was entrusted the distribution of its parcels. This, they realised, was a weapon they could deploy to boost coal production, and callously and consistently they exploited it. A graduated scale of allocation allowed face workers to have one parcel among four men; other miners one among six; officers one among seven; and those they consigned to a special category of odium – a class which embraced all detected in trying to thwart the Japanese war effort – one parcel to ten. No parcel was ever issued to prisoners unopened. Before it was ever seen by them it had been opened, submitted to rigorous scrutiny, and rifled, its contents redistributed to defeat any attempt by comparison to detect theft. Among the things especially susceptible to pillage were butter, chocolate, raisins, but above all cigarettes. Following each issue, guards made no effort to conceal the fact that the cigarettes they were smoking were American, some, indeed, brazen enough to make a joke of it. Whole parcels, especially under cover of dusk, were seen to make their way under the perimeter fence into the hands of accomplices – mostly relatives of the guards – on the outside. Evidence indicated that parcels had originally contained vitamin tablets, but invariably these were abstracted in advance. The time selected for an issue of parcels was determined with the aim of causing maximum confusion among the prisoners and thus defeating any attempt to uncover theft. On the point of departure for the mine, or return from it, a shift would suddenly be summoned to the dining-room to collect its allocation of parcels. No provision existing in the dormitories for the storage of food, everything had to be consumed on the spot; thus jam, butter, cheese and corned beef would be haphazardly divided, incongruously deposited in dixies, and eaten when received. Inevitably an issue of parcels was followed by the onset of diarrhoea, this, with cynical logic, being used by the Japanese as an argument against further issues.

Included in the first batch of Red Cross supplies to arrive in Ohama were several pairs of excellent South African field boots. Despite muted protest, these were issued by the Japanese to miners who lacked footwear for the mine. In a matter of days the salt water, in which they were constantly immersed, rotted the stitching and they fell apart. Accompanying the boots from South Africa was a consignment of warm clothing. On first arrival in Japan most of the men possessed only the tropical kit in which they stood up, and in the bitter conditions to which they were immediately exposed this clothing would have been a boon. But, locked in a store-room, the clothing was never issued. For a time the rigours of the weather were mitigated by an issue of Japanese Army uniforms. Padded with cotton-wool, these garments proved to be reasonably warm. But, the Japanese physique being on average smaller than the European, the bigger prisoners could not be catered for. In any case their deprivation was to be short-lived for presently all uniforms were withdrawn, presumably to clothe the expanding Japanese Army, and in their place denims were issued. But, having been stored in a damp place, these garments disintegrated. To succour the unclad, recourse was thereupon had to ingenuity and a spare blanket, cut up and stitched together to form a rough jerkin, proved surprisingly efficacious.

The dispatch of letters home had briefly preceded the arrival of Dr Paravicini in Ohama: as early as 31 January 1943 prisoners signed the first of several stereo-typed postcards, the last being on 28 December 1944. Taking, on average, about three months for the journey, most of those appear to have reached their destination, a remarkable achievement in view of the tortuous route they followed: first to Shanghai and thence over the Trans-Siberian railway to Switzerland, whence they were forwarded to Lisbon for the last lap to home. Roughly a similar number of letters made the journey in the opposite direction, the average time in this case being twelve months, the delay explained, presumably, by the vigilance of the Japanese censors. With few exceptions letters were exchanged and read by friends, a practice not immune from drawbacks and embarrassments, especially when a letter contained matter of an intimate nature whose revelation, even to a friend, discretion should forbid. On the other hand, if a prisoner kept a letter to himself it was immediately interpreted as a bringer of bad tidings which he was too embarrassed to disclose. In the case of a few letters, the recipient would have fared better had it never been penned, conveying as it did veiled hints of vows betrayed or marriages dishonoured. Throughout captivity some of the men received no letter at all, and were unable to account for the neglect. In a sad little niche of deprivation all on their own were those few who confessed that, in all the wide world, they had not a soul to write a letter to them.

JOHNNIE

In December 1941 John Probert, then a Sergeant, arrived in Java with his regiment, the 77th Heavy A/A, which had been raised in Cardiff. From Batavia, where it disembarked, the regiment was posted to Malang in East Java. But, at a place called Singa Sari, which is not far from its destination, their troop train rammed the back of a goods train which was loaded with bombs and fuel, the first four carriages being badly damaged and three others plunging into a ravine which they were crossing at the time. Circumstances, of course, pointed to sabotage, but in view of the ambiguous attitude of the Javanese both to the British and the Dutch it was considered at the time advisable to describe what happened as an accident. In the disaster five officers and sixteen other ranks lost their lives, and nearly a hundred were injured.

Commissioned on the field, 2nd Lieutenant John Probert soon proved his mettle in action in the Batavia area, to which his regiment had been withdrawn. But soon Allied resistance in the island collapsed and he, along with the rest of the regiment, passed into the hands of the Japanese. For a time they were confined in Boi Glodock Gaol, which had earlier housed convicts. Later, this short and unhappy incarceration was highlighted in his memory not by the actions of the Japanese, which indeed were not easily forgotten, but by some courageous gestures on the part of the Dutch. Coming up to the gaol gates, Dutch children would push small parcels through the bars, saying to the guards, 'For the British soldiers!' They contained food, often no more than a couple of sandwiches, but as long as spontaneous kindness like that existed in the world – especially since the Dutch families might soon themselves be facing starvation – there was no need, despite the evidence around them to the contrary, to take a gloomy view of mankind.

Johnnie, as he was universally known, had spent his youth in Barry in South Wales. From school he had gone straight into the employment of a large provisions company. He had thus been denied a university education and, quite illogically, tended to regard those who had been more privileged academically as the possessors of greater abilities and accomplishments than, indeed, were theirs. It was thus left to the Army to reveal, and in great measure to fulfil, his potential. As an officer on the parade ground drilling a large number of men, Johnnie had, at least in his regiment, no peer. The unusual conjunction of a ringing and imperious word of command and an engaging, very boyish face, with large blue eyes and an infectious smile, won for him the respect and indeed the affection of his men. In the matter of honour and friendship, both of which were often tested to the limits in the harsh conditions of a PoW camp, Johnnie was 'steel-true and blade-straight'.

In the field in which, at a later stage, he was to display such flair and achieve such success – i.e. the collection of news – Johnnie at first exhibited little evidence either of interest or aptitude. But for the task Nature could not have fashioned

a more effective instrument. Who, on seeing that disarming smile and that bland
and frank brow, would ever have suspected that behind them there lurked a
subtle and wily brain? For their total failure even to suspect, far less uncover, the
plots he hatched, no blame is to be laid at a Japanese door. But when, at last,
Johnnie turned his mind to the business of collecting news, it was clear he had
found his métier. Once engaged, he bent all his energies to scheming, to bluffing,
to intriguing, and in the process he often took fearful risks which amazingly
always seemed to come off. Watching Johnnie at work one always had the
impression his guardian angels were never far away. Not only was he never
caught – and the consequences of *that* would have been calamitous – but, as far
as I am aware, suspicion never fell on him. One of the reasons why, at the outset,
Johnnie's talents were never called into play was that they were not needed. From
25 January 1943 a propaganda sheet, which was printed in English and called
The Nippon Times, was circulated in camp. It was produced, of course, with the
large English-speaking populations of East Asia in mind. Its purpose was to extol
the achievements of the Imperial Japanese Army, while at the same time belit-
tling those of its enemies. This policy was continued by the *Mai Nichi*, which was
later to supplant it. To the sustained campaign of denigration of the Allies which
these two newspapers mounted must be conceded a degree of skill. Subjects
which received repeated emphasis included the alleged exploitation by the British
of the native races of Malaya and elsewhere in Asia, and their blatant cowardice
in face of the hardy sons of Nippon. Also attracting repeated attention was the
corrosive influence upon native cultures and customs exercised by the materi-
alism of the West, in particular British and American – a theme, incidentally,
which did not die with the defeat of Japan. Frequently ridiculed were the
pampered and degenerate lives allegedly lived by the imperialist officials and
soldiers in the colonies they had conquered and subsequently subjugated and
controlled.

In March 1943, almost a year to the day after the fall of Singapore – there
appeared a disturbing article which purported to come from the pen of General
Heath, then a prisoner but earlier holding a command in the Malayan campaign.
Its mastery of detail was too convincing to admit forgery. Was this a report which
General Heath had written prior to capture by the Japanese, when it was intercepted? Or had it been extracted from him under duress? Or had he merely,
fearing the unlikelihood of surviving the war (he had, in fact, been severely
wounded in an earlier campaign) wished to put on paper a record of the events
as he saw them, which would otherwise remain unknown? In any case, the
appearance in an enemy propaganda journal of military matters of this intimate
nature was disturbing to men who had been ordered to reveal to the enemy
nothing beyond their name and regimental number.

As long as the victorious progress of Japanese or Nazi arms maintained its
momentum – that is, up to June 1943 – copies of the *Mai Nichi* continued to arrive
in camp. But the Allied landings on Sicily cast (it would seem) a changed light
on enemy fortunes. While the last issue we saw confidently predicted that Sicily
was 'too tough to take', the ruins of that prophecy demanded an eating of words
which was not consistent with the continuing issue of the paper. An order went
out that any prisoner found to be in possession of a newspaper, or even a frag-

ment of a newspaper, would meet with the punishment that such an offence prescribed. For as long as these news-sheets were issued to us, we had submitted them to the closest scrutiny, but we gleaned more from what was between rather than on the lines. Any clues we gathered we collated with the information we got from other sources, of which the mine was the most prolific. The Japanese gangers usually wrapped their *meshi-hakko* in a sheet of Japanese newspaper, and it aroused no suspicion in their minds when our men borrowed this for 'other purposes'. Fragments of these newspapers were siphoned back through various channels to Johnnie, who passed them on to me. Recurring attacks of 'dysentery' provided me with an excuse to linger in the *benjo*, which was the only place in camp that was relatively safe from surveillance. There I examined them before tearing them up and consigning the fragments to the cesspool beneath. From Java I had brought with me to Ohama a large volume of *Langer's Encyclopaedia of World History*. It was an admirable volume, not the least of whose virtues was the provision of several maps which helped me in my interpretation of the information I collected from the Japanese newspapers, though problems did arise. I remember a long and fruitless search through all Langer's Pacific maps in an effort to find 'Ray-tay', having overlooked the Japanese tendency to confuse 'R' with 'L'. The object of my search was, I later found, Leyte.

In the country districts of Japan, at least at the time we were there, sanitation as it is known in the West simply did not exist. Lavatories consisted of one or more wooden cubicles built over a concrete cesspool. From these cesspools, night-soil was periodically collected in large wooden buckets which were slung on a bamboo pole and carried on the shoulders of two men, walking in file, to the fields or gardens where it was poured on the soil as manure. In consequence, and especially in summer, most cultivated land stank, and low-lying fields tended to become awash. Though Ohama lay beside the Inland Sea, no sewage was discharged directly into it. From time to time a squad of our men, declared unfit for the mine, would be taken to work on these Japanese gardens on the hillside. On one of those occasions Johnnie's sharp eye detected a scrap of *Mai Nichi* which had come from some *benjo* sump. Examining it furtively, he discovered that it had not been too offensively tainted by previous use to obliterate the date, which was *later* than the capture of Sicily by the Allies. Though the news-sheet was no longer being issued to prisoners it appeared from this that copies were still arriving in camp. Discreetly concealing the scrap of newspaper in a cabbage leaf, Johnnie transferred it to his pocket and in due course it was delivered to me. A quick examination in the camp *benjo* confirmed that, though heavily stained, the date was unmistakably subsequent to the Sicilian campaign. Careful enquiries now led Johnnie to suspect the guards' *benjo* as the source of the news-paper, and to no one familiar with his craft would it come as any surprise when presently he had himself appointed officer-in-charge of the party that was detailed to empty it. From these expeditions there soon began to flow back to me in camp a prolific stream of newspaper fragments. Though it would be misleading to attribute to these malodorous palimpsests any sudden enlargement of our knowledge of the progress of the war, they did provide a useful supplement to those sheets we managed to procure from the mine. In particular, during the relatively barren middle period of our captivity they helped us to gain a general, and in the event fairly reliable, picture of how in the military field things were shaping.

Captaincy of the *benjo* detail never quite satisfied Johnnie's thirst for news, and in the search for other avenues to explore he turned his attention to the wood-pile. At the back of the cook-house was a vacant piece of ground where heavy logs of wood, having served their purpose in the mine, were sawn up and split into firewood for use in the kitchen fires. A detail of our men was regularly engaged in this work, and to the captaincy of this party Johnnie presently engi-neered his translation. One day Kusimoto, who was Fukuhara's successor and an altogether more humane and reasonable man, approached to observe the men at work, and Johnnie took the opportunity to engage him in conversation, suggesting that while they were at it, it would cause the men no trouble to split a few logs for the *shoko*'s own house. To this generous suggestion Kusimoto offered immediate and grateful agreement. That evening saw two men carrying an improvised litter piled high with sawn logs, and with Johnnie at their head, leave the camp and make their way to the *shoko*'s house, which was down in the village. There they were welcomed with formal Japanese courtesy by the lady of the house. If on going next morning to light her stove she failed to find the copy of the *Mai Nichi* which she had laid out for that purpose, it is little likely she would direct her suspicions towards the smiling young prisoner in whose stocking, which was concealed by the pair of baggy slacks which on this occa-sion had replaced his usual shorts, it had departed. Consistent pilfering of this kind would inevitably have led to discovery, though Johnnie's mind was fertile with variations. The door to the *shoko*'s house being very narrow, it was difficult to get the litter in without some spillage, and while the lady and the other two men were engaged in retrieving the errant logs, Johnnie was allowed some scope for the exploration of the house. Topics of common interest could also provide a useful diversion, and the lady could not fail to be surprised at times by the numerous progeny claimed by the prisoners and the lengthy explanations of their nomenclature, sex, age, nurture and genealogy. Upon a conscience as sensitive as Johnnie's, this betrayal of a trust inflicted a wound, and he confided to me that only the need for the men to be furnished with news of the war's progress over-rode his scruples. One small consolation was that it was almost certain the victim of the deception remained in total ignorance that it was being practised upon her.

Johnnie's culminating coup was the most daringly conceived and executed, as well as being the most successful, of all. At the same time it came within an ace of total disaster. At one end of the lower corridor was a mysterious compartment which was just the width of the door that provided access to it. What preserved the mystery was a heavy padlock by which it was secured, but which, as far as we could observe, was never opened. What lay behind that door excited our curiosity while defeating all our efforts to find an explanation. Then one day, sitting in his room, Johnnie saw a couple of the guards come down from the office carrying a heavy parcel which, having opened the padlock and the door, they deposited inside. That subtle brain had seized a clue to the mystery of the missing *Mai Nichi*s. On the wall of the Japanese office, and just behind the *shoko*'s desk, was a key-rack on which hung every key that was used in the camp. The security which governed the issue of these keys was very strict and no prisoner was ever allowed to have a key except for the briefest periods and then only under the constant supervision of a guard. By a process of discreet enquiry among the cooks and others who were given access to the key-rack, Johnnie established both the shape of the key he wanted and its precise location on the rack. To the elaboration and refinement of his plan he directed all his energies of research and observation, but after a week or so he felt that the time had come for putting it into execution.

Choosing the afternoon of the day on which he was Duty Officer, he went to the office to report some discrepancy which he alleged to have found in the roster for that evening's shift for the mine. On the desk he laid the sheet with its list of names which both the *shoko* and *gunzo* (Sergeant) who was with him began to study, following Johnnie's finger as it pointed to the problem. What was less open to observation was his other hand whose nimble fingers, with notable sleight-of-hand, removed the key from the rack. At this juncture Johnnie paused as an idea had just come to him. Why not enlist the help of *Gunzo* Westripp, the versatile director of the *maki* at the mine? If anyone knew about rosters and shifts it was he. A word with him might well solve the difficulty – might, indeed, hold the key to Johnnie's stratagem. Going out into the corridor, Johnnie called loudly for Westripp; after some searching the Sergeant was run to earth and summoned to the corridor, where Johnnie was waiting for him. Their brief consultation provided an opportunity for their hands to come into unseen but firm contact and for the piece of soft soap in Westripp's hand to acquire a clear impression of the key in Johnnie's. Returning to the office, Johnnie smilingly laid Westripp's solution to the shift problem before the *shoko*. Meanwhile an unobserved flick of Johnnie's wrist returned the 'borrowed' key to its place on the rack. The duplicate key which Westripp was presently to make on his *maki* must, in the circumstances, be regarded as a triumph of the amateur locksmith's craft. When tried in the padlock, it worked as if it had been the original.

Up to this point, and apart from Westripp, Johnnie had operated on his own, having, as he later told me, serious doubts about whether his office stratagem would ever succeed and being unwilling to implicate any accomplice in the event of a likely failure. But from now on he needed a collaborator and enlisted my services. The assault on the office key-rack having, against the odds, succeeded, no less formidable hazards attended the attack upon the padlock and all that it concealed. At first we favoured the interval between evening *tenko* (roll-call) and lights-out, when we should then have the protection of darkness. But soon realising that it offered the same advantages for detection to the guards as concealment to us, we soon abandoned it. Besides, there would be too many men about at the time and they would get in our way and question what we were doing. Then we directed our attention to the afternoon changing of the guard, when there was usually a brief gap between the departure of the old guard and the assumption of duty by the new, in which surveillance slackened. Buttons, the Argus-eyes, was our main concern here, though it was his usual custom to call in at the cook-house for an exchange of civilities and a cup of tea. We also considered, and in turn dismissed, various schemes for a diversion such as letting out from their pen a couple of our starving and featherless hens and organising a general hunt for their recapture. Or one of the men could go into the *benjo* and groan with simulated pain till the guard arrived to investigate the trouble. The common disadvantage was that all these involved the widening of the circle of our accomplices, and the risk of a discovery – a risk we could not take.

A couple of days later, at the time of the afternoon changing of the guard, Johnnie and I sat idly chatting on the steps of our room. The dormitory was deserted, apart from a couple of gunners halfway along the corridor similarly engaged, though quite unaware of what was about to take place. The old guard was dismissed; with mounting tension we saw the new guards, with Buttons at its head, take over and then march down the hill towards the cook-house. Getting languidly to his feet and sidling along to the door, Johnnie leant his back against it while, unseen, his fingers were busy with the key and the padlock. A scarcely audible 'click' signalled his success and in one deft movement he was through the slit of the partly opened door which then, with the padlock swinging on its hasp, was pulled to from within. There followed a pregnant moment of suspense which was presently shattered by a resounding crash and an oath indifferently smothered, which signalled Johnnie's encounter with some unseen obstacle in the dark. Then another brief interval of silence, followed by some groping noises, and ending in a dull thud as a very heavy object was overturned and struck wood. Unnerved by these unexpected events, I looked along the corridor to see if anyone was within earshot of the noises, and my heart sank as, striding along the corridor towards me, was the baleful figure of Buttons. He had, on some fatal whim, denied himself the cup of tea and the causerie in the cook-house. Nemesis was on our doorstep! Johnnie's stealthy infiltration of the door must not have gone unobserved by the two gunners sitting along the corridor, and while they were quite unaware of what was afoot, they sensed that Buttons's approach signalled danger. With great presence of mind they came to our rescue. Grabbing a blanket they stepped into the corridor, obstructing the passage of the threatening presence, while they began an animated search for fleas. But Buttons was never an easy one to hoodwink, and his suspicions were aroused.

'*Frea nai!*' he said dismissively.

'*Frea nai?*' the gunners responded vociferously, pushing the blanket under his nose for him to see for himself. '*Frea takusan!*'

The wrangling had consumed no more than a few moments, but it sufficed for me to slip the hook of the padlock back into its socket – I could not lock it as Johnnie still had the key. A whisper conveyed to the noisy pioneer in the cellar that his life hung by a thread. Breaking off his conversation abruptly, and brushing aside the blanket, Buttons left the men to pursue their hunt for imaginary fleas and strode on towards me. With disastrous affability he opened the colloquy.

'*Konnichi wa, Rokuban!*' (Good day, No. 6) he said as, sitting down on the ledge beside me, he stretched out his legs.

'*Konnichi wa!*' I responded apprehensively, hoping he could not hear the pounding metronome of my heart. The conversation thus courteously begun showed no sign of terminating, though I made desperate efforts to staunch his eloquence. But once again the two gunners came to my rescue. Sensing the malignity that was in the air, they set upon their flea-infested blanket with a fury that could not be ignored. Getting to my feet, I set off to investigate, whether Buttons wished to accompany me or not. With obvious reluctance he got up and followed me.

'*Frea takusan!*' insisted the men.

'*Frea nai!*' said Buttons, not even bothering to look. Clearly he felt that knavery was afoot though he had not the means to uncover it. Affecting indifference, and with a wicked twinkle in his eyes as if to say 'You can't fool me! You just think you can!', he sauntered off in the direction of the cook-house. But the man who trusted Buttons was the man who lived to regret it. Too much was at stake to risk a false step. I dispatched one of the men to keep an eye on him and ensure he was not plotting a sudden return, and after a time he came back to report that Buttons was in the cook-house, his feet up on a chair and a cup of tea in his hand. A message whispered through the door brought from the vaults beneath a dusty and cobweb-draped figure whose bulging sweater concealed his haul of *Mai Nichi*s. He seemed totally undismayed by the close brush he had just had with consequences too awesome to contemplate.

After this hair-raising experience, no one in his senses would have dared a repetition. But the stakes were high, and on one or two subsequent occasions we did make raids into the underworld. In each case the haul was respectable though one aspect of the operation continued to baffle us: how was it that the disarray in which Johnnie had left its contents never seemed to alert the Japanese to the fact that their sanctum was being violated? In making known the news we had collected by this and other means, we observed precautions no less strict than those that had marked its acquisition. Apart from Johnnie and myself, no one ever saw or handled the newspapers. After reading each sheet in the *benjo*, I tore it up and consigned it to the cesspool beneath. We decided that the safest time to tell the officers was during lunch in the little annexe where we dined, and where we were relatively free from interruption. Here I gave them a résumé of what I had discovered, and they, in their turn, passed it on as casually as possible to the men, always fostering the impression that it came from sources in the mine. Neither Johnnie nor I ever started a false rumour deliberately, though that is not to say we discouraged those which were started, often quite innocently, by others, realising that in their number and diversity rested our surest guarantee of immunity from discovery.

So complete, in the event, was the success of our operations that even so perceptive and generally reliable a witness as Ray Parkin, whose book *The Sword and the Blossom* deals in part with the camp at Ohama, failed entirely to discover where the news came from, and the explanation he gives is false. None of the Japanese, and no more than a handful of British and Australian officers – as well as Sgt Westripp – ever suspected the central role that Johnnie played in all this, and in the end most of them came away from Ohama quite unaware of the immense debt they owed to him.

At Ohama the core of what we euphemistically called our 'Library' remained the shrunken windfall which had unexpectedly fallen into our lap at Kalidjati, in Java, and which we had brought with us. Salvaged from a bungalow abandoned by an Englishman in the small town of Soebang, it reflected the scholarly tastes of its erstwhile owner. It had been eked out by some less learned accretions, in particular the contents of a box which arrived each month and was provided by the YMCA of Geneva. In Switzerland, it seemed, the literary tastes of British PoWs in Japan were not rated highly. Into this latter had incongruously strayed a two-volume abridgement of Gibbon's *Decline and Fall*. The Roman, obviously, presented some parallels with the British destiny. To those volumes I, for a time, devoted every hour that could be gleaned from mine shifts and camp routine.

One evening, my companions being in the dining-room, I found myself alone in my room. Folding up my blanket, I placed it in the middle of the floor. I pulled down the electric bulb which was suspended by a flex from the ceiling. Seated on my improvised chair I sought, in the majestic narrative, brief escape from the squalid circumstances of captivity. So totally absorbed did I become that I relaxed the vigilance I carried about with me almost as a buckler against unexpected assault. Suddenly the volume was snatched from my hand and tossed up on the main shelf. A knee in my ribs sent me sprawling on the mats. The bulb was jerked back to its former place. Looking up I gazed, eyeball to eyeball, into the leering face of Buttons. Guilty of any conceivable offence I palpably was not. I was engaged in reading a book at a time when it was perfectly legitimate to be reading a book. But in the eyes of the vicious guard to be engaged on *anything* that seemed to give pleasure to a prisoner was *ipso facto* a crime. Not only must prisoners be made to suffer, they must also look as if they were suffering. Muttering curses, Buttons strode off along the corridor. Prudence advised against too speedy a resumption of my activity, but, allowing a modest interval to elapse, I collected and replaced my blanket, pulled down the light again and, retrieving the book from the shelf, straightened its crumpled pages and resumed my reading. As a man less rash would have foreseen, Buttons had not departed; he was merely lurking in the shadows and waiting to pounce. So silent and stealthy was his second approach that I failed even to suspect it till his wooden sword struck me a violent blow at the point where the neck meets the shoulder, sending a jab of exquisite pain down the side of my chest wall. Looking up, I saw Buttons gloating over me, his sword poised for a second blow. Goaded by the pain and the sheer iniquity of the attack, I cast discretion to the winds and rounded on my tormentor.

Four months after our arrival in Ohama, the Japanese, as a signal expression of their desire to bring us within the orbit of their language and thence their culture, had allowed us to purchase from our 'wages' several volumes containing the fruits of Japanese civilisation. Not unexpectedly, these amounted to little more than blatant propaganda. Among them, however, was a primer entitled *Japanese in Thirty Hours*, which offered possibilities for exploitation in ways which the Japanese might not have entirely approved of. Attached to the primer was an appendix which included a list of phrases which were declared to be 'Useful in Everyday Life in Japan'. One of these was 'Hark a fire!' which, in a land so combustible as Japan, might not be out of place. Also interesting, if not so immediately useful, was 'You are a rude, uncultured fellow!' Obviously the time was not yet ripe when one might direct this remark at a son of Nippon with impunity. But there was no saying what the future might bring forth, and the foolhardy trait in my character persuaded me to commit it to memory. Now, unexpectedly, the moment for its use had arrived. With all the pent-up venom in my body, I snapped in Buttons's teeth: 'You are a rude, uncultured fellow!'

The result could not have been entirely unforeseen, but had I anticipated the dramatic effect the words were likely to produce there is little doubt I would have strangled the invective in my throat. The sword, uplifted in menace, dropped to his flank. The face that was naturally sallow seemed, even in the dim light, to assume a deeper grey. Shouldering his wooden sword like a rifle, and in a loud barking voice, he ordered me to attention (*Kiotsuke!*) and, with my fearful presence wallowing along in his wake, he set off along the corridor to the seat of judgement. At its end was the stairway that led to the second floor. As Fate would have it, just as we reached its foot Fukuhara appeared at its top. Seeing him, Buttons came to a halt abruptly. Then, in an explosive rant, he announced my offence, to which narration Fukuhara listened with rapt attention. *Japanese in Thirty Hours* had not, of course, provided me with the competence to understand what he said – that is, apart from the concluding words. With literal accuracy he repeated the damning sentence: 'You are a rude, uncultured fellow!' That changed the scene dramatically. His jack-boots seeming to disdain converse with the steps, Fukuhara descended the stair like the wolf on the fold. Reaching the corridor, he drew himself up to his dwarfish height, looked straight in my eyes, and in vengeful outrage he unleashed his fist in my face. Again he struck – and yet again. Nothing, it seemed, could assuage his lust for vengeance. To flailing fists were presently added flying jack-boots, and I went down. After he had finished his deadly work, friendly hands carried me to my mat and, bathing my bruised and bleeding face and body, covered me with my quilt.

Naturally for a transgression so obscurely offensive as mine retribution could not be expected to stop here. Some message would be dispatched to the *kempetai*, who would soon arrive to deliver the *coup de grâce*. The hour just after breakfast would be the fatal time. A tap on the shoulder, or a call of *Rokuban!*, would announce my fate. When at last I came round, my mind was haunted by visions of renewed violence. What clouded the issue was my ignorance of what grossness insult was concealed in what, in English, seems to be not so heinous an insult. My companions advised me to fear the worst. Next morning came – and went without incident. So did lunch. The excessive brutality of Fukuhara's reaction may have done me a good turn in that it preserved me from something even worse. Had he not been so intemperate, he might have thought that duty demanded his summoning of the *kempetai*. Of that step imagination readily pictured the consequences. But from that painful fate I was happily spared. But many months were to pass before I was to learn the true degree of offence of which the words were capable.

O, There be Players

When, in December 1943, it was mooted in camp that Cpls Smith and Kelly, both of whom worked in the cook-house, were thinking of putting on a pantomime at Christmas, it was regarded as a joke. The very idea was out of the question; perhaps the fact that both had good singing voices and lost no opportunity of using them had gone to their head. When, later, it came to our ears that they had dared to go to the *shoko* and lay their proposal before him – and, more amazing still, that the grim Fukuhara had agreed – we laughed the news to scorn. Yet, in the face of all probability it proved to be true. What in that dark and demonic soul had kindled this spark of human charity who can even begin to conjecture?

This first, and most formidable, hurdle having been cleared, some almost as daunting lay ahead. Of the basic props essential for a pantomime Ohama possessed scarcely any at all. The dining-room, for instance, which was the only possible venue for the show, had no stage – it had not even lighting, that is if we are to except the single bulb which hung from a flex at each end. Where, in a place like Ohama, was one going to find costumes, or musical instruments,– or even for that matter a cast? Was it likely that rough airmen and gunners, returning dirty and exhausted from the mine, would take kindly to the demanding routine of rehearsals? Not all were fired with the histrionic enthusiasms of Cpls Smith and Kelly! Yet all these obstacles were faced boldly, and somehow in the end overcome. A producer was enlisted, a cast was recruited (or probably, with greater accuracy, *impressed*), and a script was concocted – all under an impenetrable secrecy. The less that came to Fukuhara's ears the better! Let him have no excuse or sudden whim to nip the project in the bud!

Both Christmas Day and Boxing Day, 1943 were declared a holiday. For two consecutive days (an unheard-of thing!) no shift would be called upon to go down the mine. Equally acceptable was the promise of a special Christmas dinner. By the standards of the West it might be regarded as falling somewhat short of the sumptuous; by those of the Ohama prisoners it was remarkable enough. Each man was given soya-bean sauce to pour over his usual rice. In addition he had five persimmons strung out on straws like the onions the Bretons used to sell, five cigarettes, half a small towel, and (a special present from the mining company) a bottle of beer between each two men. It was a welcome feast, and when it was over the men were shepherded back to their quarters to await the revels to come.

Expectation mounted with the passing hours. At last came the summons for a return to the dining-room. There they found the tables had been pushed to one end and made a tolerable stage. Above this was strung a broad paper banner which acted as a proscenium arch, and on which, in somewhat amateurish lettering, a hand had inscribed the legend: OHAMA PRESENTS SNOW WHITE. Only one factor marred the festive air of the place: in the first two rows of seats sat

Fukuhara and his guards along with some dignitaries from the mine. Obviously any excesses the prisoners might be disposed to indulge in would be undertaken at their peril!

The first item was a dance ensemble performed by a chorus of dwarfs. Issuing from behind a curtain in one of the wings, they shot across the stage in an uncontrolled glissade, followed by a quaint pirouette enacted with such *élan* that it almost deposited one or two of them in the lap of the guests in the front row. From somewhere or other they had managed to assemble a surprising variety of costume. From a nigger-minstrel face, whose acquisition in Ohama presented no great problem, Bashful smiled broadly, though his gaudily striped shirt was not the kind of thing for which Ohama made much provision. Dopey had a straw hat, spectacles, and a smock of many colours – provenance obscure. So vigorously did Sneezy enact his role that his countenance writhed in perpetual contortion. The ditty which they sang did (if the truth must be told) lean rather heavily on the licentious, though this in no way impaired its appeal. For its lustiest sallies the loudest guffaws were reserved. Happily these passed harmlessly over the heads of our guests. Had it been otherwise, I hesitate to speculate what might have happened.

The dwarfs having departed, there now strode on to the stage the prince, resplendent in a blue velvet jerkin and white smock, a silver-pommelled sword dangling from his belt, and the swaggering virility of his carriage setting off to perfection the mincing daintiness of Snow White at his side. On her long flaxen hair was poised a crown of gold, while her white gown, slashed with a fetching band of blue, swept the ground with regal amplitude. For this exacting role nothing could have been more eminently suited than the wide-eyed look of innocence and the girlish smile of Johnnie Probert. But for a triumph of characterisation in a situation like this, the embellishments of art were not enough; they had to be underpinned by very substantial natural accomplishments.

To Cpls Smith and Kelly, the true begetters of the pantomime, was rightly entrusted its musical core. Wandering on to the stage in the guise of Provençal troubadours, they sang the old, well-loved songs such as *Roses of Picardy* and *The Rose of Tralee*, each charged with remembered sentimentalities personal to its hearer. Whether they sang solo, or joined in harmony, they displayed equal mastery. Drawing generously upon their extensive repertoire they were brought back again and again to enraptured shouts of: 'Encore! 'core!' Hearts so long denied sentimentality knew no satiety.

The act which followed was quite unexpected and turned out to be a *tour-de-force*. On to the stage strode a Cockney who, in response to the most persistent enquiry, never offered any satisfactory explanation of how he came to be associated with a regiment of Welsh gunners recruited in Cardiff. Despite the frailest of bodies and spidery legs, he was a remarkably spry and wiry man. His face was pale, the cheeks sunken, but his eyes danced mischievously and his wit was nimble. Now his dress consisted of a miner's *happi*-coat and hessian pants so wide and floppy they made his legs look more sparrow-like than ever. Over his shoulder was slung a miner's *tourabashi,* or pick, while his face, blackened with coal-dust, was puckered with devilry. From the moment he opened his mouth to sing it was abundantly clear his earlier career had embraced some acquaintance with the professional stage. The song he sang he must have made up himself though the tune he must have known earlier. So happily were they welded that they appeared to have sprung from the same brain in an inspired moment of composition. His accent was the broadest of East London Cockney which, in the circumstances, was just as well. The words went something like this:

> O, my little *tourabashi*!
> My little *tourabashi*, wacky woo!
> O, my little *tourabashi*,
> You're the best of *tomodachis* [friends]
> Me an' yew!
> Fo' Ah tykes yew dahn the mine,
> An' then Ah fills the 'akkos up
> Wiv stones an' slag, an' so Ah sells
> Our pals a propah pup!
> O, my little *tourabashi*,
> My little *tourabashi*, wacky woo!

As he reached the end the applause broke out in a full-throated roar that made the welkin ring. Sniffing offence, the Japanese in the two front rows glanced anxiously at one another. The singer's accent, of course, baffled them, though not its satirical purpose. After an ominous moment or two of silence they added a mirthless cackle to the general acclaim to conceal their embarrassment.

In the summer of that same year, 1943, a Japanese clerk, having visited Shimonoseki on the south-west tip of Honshu, opposite Moji, returned with a catalogue of gramophone records. The connection of this with its outcome was never made clear, though there are grounds for suspecting Cpls Smith and Kelly to have had a hand in it. Certainly the *shoko* was approached and gave his approval to a plan whereby each prisoner could make use of and even buy one of these records, at a cost to be defrayed from his 'wages'. But, as in the case of so many other promising schemes, it came as no surprise when this one ended in failure. 'All *rekordu* sold!' reported the clerk, and the explanation scarcely raised an eyebrow. Yet the Japanese had gone at least some way towards redeeming their pledge, though the details were shrouded in secrecy. At last it came to the ears of the inquisitorial Corporals that two records had, indeed, been acquired in Shimonoseki, and would be played for the first time at the pantomime. As to their nature the sole disclosure was that one of them was the *No. 1 Chrisamasu Rekordu*, while, even more cryptically, the other was referred to as *No. 1 Nippon Rekordu*. This second, it was generally concluded, would be the *Kimigayo*, the solemn and somewhat lugubrious national anthem of Japan.

The pantomime arrived at its end and the cast lined up on stage for the curtain-call. From their seats, the first two rows of Japanese struggled to their feet, the prisoners behind them following suit. From the office came the first wheezing sounds of the gramophone being started up. Then, on this alien air, there floated a melody poignant with memories of happier days and places: *Stille Nacht, heilige Nacht* . . . From the quietude of spirit which the Christian festival solemnises nothing could have been more alien than the unholy hunger and heartache of Ohama – nowhere else on earth was one less likely to find the *himmlischer Ru'*! With full hearts we waited for the reverse side of the record to be played. To this the general reaction was less dramatic because the carol was less well-known, but for me it was charged with very personal and poignant memories for I had often sung it as a boy in the parish church of the village of Saline in West Fife. In the light of later experience how prophetic now seemed the well-known words:

> Childhood years are passing o'er us;
> Soon our schooldays will be done.
> Cares and sorrows lie before us,
> Hidden dangers, snares unknown.

Never in those carefree Fife boyhood days could imagination have conceived the shape these 'hidden dangers' were to assume. The air is, of course, one long since sung by Sicilian mariners, though nowadays it is more generally known by its German title of *O Du Froliche*.

Now arrived the moment for the secret of the second record to be revealed. Not the *Kimagayo*! Not the *East Asia Co-Prosperity* tune, or some other rousing air designed to inflame patriotic fervour! What fell upon our astonished and incredulous ears was the notes of *Auld Lang Syne*. What was more, the Japanese, to a man, burst out into full-throated song – and the words they were singing were *Japanese*! Long have the Scots held to the belief that *Auld Lang Syne* is native to their land and indigenous to their culture. Was it not obviously written by Burns, that most Scots (if also universal) of poets? Yet the scholarly point to an earlier ballad upon which Burns based his version, and other research has traced its origins to some Alpine valley. But that does not hinder the Japanese from claiming it to be theirs, nor the aboriginal tribes in Taiwan from making a similar claim. What has never been in dispute is the universal brotherhood of mankind of which it is so uniquely an expression. If proof were needed could not this scene in distant Ohama have convinced the sceptic? Here were British prisoners-of-war and their Japanese captors, between whom normally little love was lost, singing their hearts out in the fellowship which music has it in its power to cement.

When Christmas 1944 came round, an attempt was made to revive the pantomime. But by this time circumstances had altered. For one thing, the complement of the camp had been swollen by the arrival from Siam of 250 Australians, from whom it was hoped to enlist new talent and new ideas. But these hopes were soon to be dashed, the Australians showing little interest in, and few any aptitude for, theatricals, tending to regard such fopperies as somewhat beneath the notice of the no-nonsense men they prided themselves on being. After their first experience, the Japanese, suspecting what they could not understand, seemed also to have lost interest. Nonetheless, the British, in the face of discouragement, persevered, and *Snow White* had a second showing, relying for the most part on the same cast and props as a year before. But the life seemed to have gone out of it. Gone beyond recall was that first rapture, and even its most enthusiastic supporters could not claim it was a success. The Australians came and watched, but they were not so much unresponsive as simply uninterested. In ears nurtured in another culture, and attuned to a different brand of humour, *Roses of Picardy* and *The Rose of Tralee* – even indeed the effervescent *Tourabashi* song – evoked a subdued response. In their hearts the British knew that the Spirit of Christmas Present had departed from Ohama for ever; even had they lived to see another Christmas there, the pantomime would never have been revived.

GIVE THEIR CITIES TO THE FLAMES!

In the spring of 1944 Guam, Saipan and Tinian, islands in the Marianne Archipelago, fell into American hands. With phenomenal speed vast airfields were built on them from which long-range B-29 bombers could operate. The way was now open for an assault on the Philippines. Next in line for attack was Okinawa. The home islands of Japan could be devastated from the air. For the warlike islanders, no longer could the Pacific Ocean serve as a moat defensive to their house.

From earliest times Japanese cities had been built largely of wood and bamboo, which flimsy architecture would, it was believed, save lives in the recurring earthquakes to which the islands are prone. But in a new age in which warfare had taken to the skies, and against an enemy possessing all the technical skill and materials to wage it, this turned out to be a terrible hostage to hand to fortune. Scattered indiscriminately over a city, a rain of incendiary bombs could send through its streets a tornado of fire whose passage would leave in its wake little but a blackened desolation. The risks being what they were, why did Japan's military junta expose themselves to them in the first place? Was it through hubris, the fatal flaw in the temper of the race which promised to be its undoing? Throughout a history stretching back some 2,000 years, Japan had preserved an immunity from foreign invasion. Against the Japanese nation in arms not even the greatest empires – among them the Mongol, the Chinese and (more recently) the Russian – had prevailed. Could they be blamed for thinking that, alone among the nations of the earth, the sacred soil of Japan had been decreed by Heaven to be inviolate?

To every Japanese his duty was appointed: to obey his Emperor and to fight to the death in defence of His sacred person and soil. The struggle might well last a hundred years (it had every appearance of doing so), the present being nothing more than the opening campaigns. Reverses were inevitable, but would not affect the outcome, which was never in doubt. Among all nations, Japan had been assigned a unique and heaven-decreed destiny of invincibility in war. Faced then with a future as bleak as any ever encountered by a nation at war, the Japanese (though they refused to regard it in this light) reacted with a resolution that matched the hour. To the threat of invasion their response was characteristic and vigorous; and all classes and all ages were inspired by a warlike spirit. Evidence of this was daily before our eyes. Drawn from the village school, bands of children clad in their ugly *mompis*, with many of the girls in their even uglier gym-slips, their ages ranging from mere infants to puberty, paraded through Ohama chanting in their shrill, falsetto voices the *Co-Prosperity March*. From time to time they would brandish the wooden swords which they carried and pipe in

imitation of their elders '*Banzai! Banzai! Banzai!*' Meanwhile on narrow, unde-
veloped shoulders their older brothers and sisters would lug from the hillside
pit-props for the mine. All toiled in the futile race against time. From the hillside
jungle above the village, mothers and aunts hacked little garden plots in which
they planted sweet potatoes and brinjals, otherwise known as aubergines or egg-
plants, in preparation for a long siege. Equally zealous, their men-folk divided
their time between furiously digging coal in the mine and driving air-raid tunnels
into the lower escarpments on the hill.

   Goaded into emulation, our men in camp set about constructing their own air-
raid shelter. They tunnelled into the bank beside the guard-house, working as
they did in the mine, and shoring the sides and roof with heavy sections of pine
trees. The shelter was shaped like a boomerang, with two entrances (or exits), in
front of which they built earthworks, faced with boards to act as baffles against
bomb blast. At the sides narrow passages were left by which the prisoners could
get in and out. Above both openings they hung a black curtain to prevent the
escape of the (admittedly dim) light within, and higher still they raised a curved
tree-trunk on two heavy supports to look like a *torii,* the idea being that, seeing
it, an American airman would mistake it for a temple and thus spare it from
bombing. At a pinch the shelter could hold all the British contingent, but only at
the expense of overcrowding and discomfort if they were to be kept in it for any
length of time. The Japanese laid down very specific instructions for the conduct
of each prisoner in the event of an air-raid. If he happened to be away from his
quarters at the time, he was to rush back and seize *all* his clothing, and *one*
blanket before making his way to the shelter with all possible dispatch. Once the
men were inside, all conversation was forbidden – as Buttons quaintly put it,
'Men speako, Americano pirot rissen!' Surprisingly, and to the relief of addicts,
smoking escaped the interdict. It was also about this time that the *kashira naka*
made its appearance. Built of bamboo canes, it was a high outlook tower with
an open platform at the top. A couple of guards were posted to this platform,
their job being to give early warning of any enemy aircraft that approached the
camp.

   The arrival of the Australian contingent in September 1944 brought with it
new problems. Our shelter could never accommodate them, and a new shelter
had to be built. This was constructed on principles very similar to the first but in
a bank at the opposite side of the camp. Rather proud of their tunnelling achievements, the Japanese now insisted on building a third tunnel which would be much
nearer to the lower dormitory and provide shelter in the event of a late warning.
But in this area there were no natural banks, and in their absence they foolishly
decided to tunnel into the ridge which carried the road from the main gate to the
village, and which, having been constructed from rubble excavated during the
making of the parade ground, had never settled and was in a very unstable condition. The tunnel had been driven into the bank no more than about twelve feet
when, at the end of a three-day deluge of torrential rain during which, despite the
danger, the men had been compelled to continue their excavation, the roof
suddenly caved in. One of the three men who were working in it at the time tried
to run out but, being caught by the avalanche, was crushed and killed. The other
two, following the instructions they had received from the Welsh miners down

the mine, flattened themselves against the wall at the tunnel-head. The earth slid over and around them, but they escaped with nothing more serious than bruising.

Early in 1945 the systematic assault from the air on the Japanese cities was gathering momentum. Among its early victims were Ube and Onada, both not far from where we were at Ohama. Set on fire by incendiaries during a night attack their buildings burned fiercely, the flames throwing a great red corona into the sky where it hung all night, clearly visible for miles around. To supplement the air attack upon Japanese cities, the Americans now began to deploy another weapon, equally deadly in its effect though perhaps not so spectacular. Presently this exerted a stranglehold upon Japan's precarious and vulnerable life-lines, and hence her capacity to wage war. Operating on its own, and in no great time, it is reasonable to assume it would have brought the island-empire to its knees, if not to surrender.

To this novel form of warfare the geography of Japan lent itself with fatal aptitude. Leaving out for the moment the great plain that surrounds Tokyo and some outlying centres of industry in the northern island of Hokkaido, the major Japanese industrial plants were strung along the north coast of Kyushu and round the shores, and especially the northern shore, of the Inland Sea. At its western end, this picturesque and busy water-way has two entrances. Towards the south is the Bungo Strait, which leads into the Pacific Ocean and could readily be blockaded by submarines. In the north-west is the Shimonoseki Strait, which is even narrower, and provides access to the Sea of Japan and the China Sea. Through this latter strait ran Japan's main shipping link with the Asiatic mainland, and in particular Manchuria which – apart from Indonesia, which was her main source of oil – provided most of her war materials. Like the Bungo Strait, this was very vulnerable to submarine blockade though the vessels would have a longer and more dangerous voyage before they arrived at the scene of their operations. Nightly above these restricted waters there now prowled squadrons of American bombers. In their bomb-bays they carried deadly magnetic mines which they released, slung from parachutes, to drift down into the sea and block the shipping-lanes. So successful were these operations that soon all shipping in the Inland Sea was brought to a standstill. The channel which ran in front of Ohama, narrowing as it approached the two vital straits, had now become one of the decisive theatres of the war, and almost every day we heard the dull thud of exploding mines. We never saw any large vessels fall victim to this deadly weapon, for the simple reason that large vessels no longer sailed these dangerous waters. But one day a shift returning from the mine witnessed a large launch being hurled skywards in a gigantic waterspout, and a string of barges it had been towing sink drunkenly in a boiling whirlpool.

The great wave of aerial assaults that finally laid waste the industrial heart of Japan and its pullulating cities was launched on 19 June 1945. One of the first to catch its blast was Fukuoka, the capital of the Prefecture in which Ohama lies, about fifteen miles west of Moji. Then, on 28 June, Moji itself fell victim. But for us at Ohama the most spectacular of all the conflagrations was reserved for 1 July, on which night both Shimonoseki, and Ube for the second time, were laid waste. On this occasion we were for some unexplained reason allowed to remain in our quarters where we watched the bright aurora that all night long lit the sky.

To home in on their targets the bombers seemed to use the coastline of the Inland Sea as a navigational aid. This naturally involved risks since, once the practice was established and detected, the Japanese could take steps to interfere with it. This they did at Ohama by installing two heavy A/A guns on the ridge above the village. Beside them they fixed a searchlight. On the night of this double attack one of the bombers flew past Ohama, apparently unaware of the danger. Suddenly the searchlight was switched on and caught the aircraft in its beam. The guns opened fire. The bomber was hit and plunged into the sea. From the village, the guard-house, the mining office, from every spot where there was a Japanese watching, rose peal after peal of quite delirious cheering. But as far as we knew this was the only success they had.

When, on 21 June, Japanese resistance on Okinawa finally collapsed, there was unleashed upon the south-western islands of the archipelago a concentrated attack by fighters, which the capture of Okinawa had brought within range. Japanese airfields now came under more or less continual attack, and soon most were rendered unserviceable. This allowed Allied aircraft carriers, which had been waiting further out at sea, to approach close in to the coast. Their fighters now swelled the attack. One day a force of between twenty and thirty stub-nosed fighters appeared over Ohama. For about half an hour they reconnoitred the area, no opposition being offered, before they flew towards Motoyama and were soon lost in the mist. Later a sortie of large fighters repeatedly attacked Motoyama. These were twin-fuselaged machines of a design we had not seen before and which we learned later were Lockheed Lightnings. Leaving Motoyama, they came along the coast towards Ohama, attacking every target they saw on the way. Flying very low, when their American markings and even the pilots' helmeted heads were clearly visible, they vectored over the camp several times, but they must have sensed there was something unusual about it for, among all the large buildings in the area, it alone escaped attack. Just when they were on the point of flying off, a small steamer appeared round the point between Ohama and Neshi Ohama. Coming from Moji it was hugging the coast in an effort to escape the mines but trying to escape from one danger it had run into another. Swooping down on it, the fighters peppered it with machine-gun fire. We imagined it would take more than this bombardment of low-calibre cannon to sink the vessel, but it was remarkable how quickly it slid beneath the water. With this final success, the fighters departed.

IF YOU WRONG US, SHALL WE NOT REVENGE?

Upon a people as fanatically patriotic, and at the same time as volatile, as the Japanese the immediate effect of the systematic fire-bombing of their cities was entirely predictable. In their hands they held hostages, the visible symbols of the desecrators of their sacred homeland, and upon them they could now vent some of their anger and anguish – both immeasurable.

During that first air attack on Ube and Onada, when incendiaries started a great conflagration in both cities, our men spent the whole night in the shelter. Not till dawn broke were they allowed to leave. The exit being narrow, the men fell in in single file to negotiate the space between door and baffle. Finding myself towards the end of the file, I hung back a little to ensure the departure was orderly before tagging on at the end, being followed by the last man to leave, a gunner called Sullivan. I had gone no more than a few paces down the road towards the kitchen and dormitories when I heard a scuffle break out behind me; turning round, I saw Sullivan being set upon by Buttons, who was screaming like a madman. The uproar brought a crowd of guards rushing down from the guard-room to join in the attack on the hapless gunner. Kicked and beaten into near insensibility, he was then pinioned with his hands behind his back and dragged down the road towards the kitchen. Fukuhara must have been there at the time and, hearing the commotion, came out to see what was happening. They met just short of the kitchen entrance. Buttons stammered out some kind of explanation, whereupon Fukuhara ordered the guards to force Sullivan to his knees and hold him there, still with his arms pinioned, facing up the slope towards the guard-house. Very deliberately Fukuhara then stepped out about seven paces up the road, turned round, steadied himself for a moment, and then launched himself upon his victim. With all the strength in his small, taut, but muscular body, he drove his jack-boot into Sullivan's face. There was a sickening thud as boot met bone. Very coolly he went back up the hill, turned round, and repeated the attack. If that were not more than enough, he went through the sickening ritual for a third time. So engrossed did he appear to be in his vile act that he seemed to be quite oblivious of everything else around him. Certainly he did not at first see me though I was standing no more than a yard or two away from him. When at last he realised another of the prisoners had been a witness to what he had just done, his anger and annoyance knew no bounds. Turning savagely upon me, he screamed in my face, '*Kurrah! Kurrah! KURRAH!*', his teeth bared like an animal's at bay. For a moment or two I imagined he was about to order the guards to seize me so that he could mete out to me the same treatment he had given to Sullivan. My instinct told me to get out of his sight as quickly as I could and, retreating precipitately, I escaped his fury.

For three days Sullivan was held in the punishment hut at the guard-room. Every hour and upon the hour he was beaten. Periodically he was brought out and made to kneel on a pile of ashes on the roadway. From time to time, to exacerbate his suffering, a guard would leap upon his back. The men going on shift, who were counted before the guard-room, were sometimes able to catch a glimpse of his grossly contused and lacerated face, still blood-smeared from the kicking. But by this time he seemed not to be fully aware of what was happening to him. Had he tried, he might well have been harder put to it to understand why this was happening to him at all. Had the Japanese thirst for vengeance been so inflated that it regarded being last out of the shelter as a crime to be expiated only through this barbaric punishment? After several days a notice was posted in the dining-room which stated that Sullivan, being last out of the shelter, had subsequently resisted a guard. The penalty for this crime was death. But on this occasion the *shoko* had decided to exercise his prerogative of clemency and commuted the sentence to imprisonment. At the foot was Fukuhara's chop, or signature. This was to be regarded as a stern warning to others.

Craig was one of the Australian soldiers who had arrived from Siam. On top of general debility he, like many of his comrades, suffered from acute malaria, which he had contracted in the south. Despite his very obvious incapacity for work, he was hounded out after a particularly severe malarial bout to join a party that had been detailed to carry logs from the mine for use in the cook-house. The log he was given to carry was far beyond his strength but, making no protest, he shouldered it and somehow managed to carry it back to the guard-house. But by this time his strength had deserted him. While attempting to salute the sentry he lost his balance and the log slid from his shoulder and fell to the ground. He was immediately seized and, on the ridiculous charge of maliciously attempting to wound a guard, he was lodged in the punishment-cell. Like Sullivan (and many others) he was from time to time brought out and made to kneel for long periods on the pile of ashes on the road. But his case was exceptional to the extent that his knees were covered with boils, a symptom of his malarial condition, and this kneeling on ashes involved excruciating pain. Fearing for his health – and, indeed, for his survival – Dr Ploegman went to the *shoko* and lodged a plea for Craig's release on medical grounds. Kusimoto's response was that he was well aware of the condition of Craig's knees, and the pain from the infected wounds was to be understood as an integral part of the punishment.

With exemplary courage, and with no complaint, Craig endured his sufferings till presently he collapsed. He was then taken from his cell to the sick-bay. But by this time it was too late to do anything for him. Sinking rapidly, he developed malarial meningitis and died. The progress of Craig's sufferings had been monitored very carefully by some of his Australian comrades, who compiled a dossier on the most savage of his persecutors. Nothing, of course, could be done about it till the war was over. But when the time came it was strongly rumoured in camp that they had rounded up these criminals. After a brief drum-head tribunal they pronounced sentence upon them, its dark nature vaguely hinted at but never acknowledged.

SAGIO NAI – MESHI NAI!

Almost from the first days of our arrival in Ohama a bitter struggle was waged over the vexed and hotly contested question whether officers were to be called upon to perform manual work. More volubly at first, more circumspectly later, the British prisoners invoked the Geneva Convention which absolved officers from work, but which the Japanese had not signed and cared nothing about in any case. To reinforce their arguments they resorted to every form of obstruction they could think of, though few went to the lengths of Captain Millin, the oldest prisoner in camp, who made it perfectly clear from the outset that in no circumstances whatever was he prepared to do manual labour – let them do what they liked! What they liked turned out to be a shameful campaign of persecution, which Millin endured with exemplary fortitude, his gentle smile and utter detachment often driving his tormentors to fury.

The opposing view was expressed by the Japanese with at least unequivocal clarity. *Sagio nai – meshi nai*! was their slogan. No work – no food! Incessantly was the slogan drummed into our ears, vigorously reinforced by harassment and starvation, both effective arguments. After a long and bitter struggle a compromise was arrived at which seemed to show that any advantage there was lay on the British side. It was agreed that one officer should accompany each shift down the mine, though he would not be called upon to dig coal, his duties being merely of a supervisory nature and to smooth out any misunderstandings in communication that might arise between gangers and gangs. The other officers undertook to perform duties about the camp, none of which was of an onerous nature. But there was one proposition the Japanese made that was not met with the customary hostility. For two hours each day, and then only when weather conditions were favourable, the officers would clear away the jungle growth from selected areas of the hillside above the camp and make gardens. In these they could grow vegetables and fruit which would be reserved solely for their own use, the needs of the sick men being firmly kept in mind. So small parties of officers, reinforced by sick men who were not fit for underground work, hacked at the bush to reveal the red and fertile earth beneath. Most recalcitrant to their efforts were the clumps of bamboo, a plant which as well as being the most versatile in its uses for mankind is at the same time one of the most intractable. But having, with blunt machetes and blistered hands, finally mastered and uprooted it, they shovelled the earth into terraces which they shored up with low stone walls. On the terraces they planted sweet potatoes which for some obscure reason never prospered, and brinjals, which did, though their food value was practically negligible. Much more important were tomatoes, which Dr Ploegman assured us had a higher content of valuable vitamins than almost any other vegetable. Like the brinjals, the tomatoes flourished, but not for our benefit for under cover of darkness and when we were safely back in camp the Japanese guards, or else the villagers, raided the terraces and plundered the fruit.

So the revolving years brought round the spring of 1945 which, in its turn, gave way to the usually hot and humid summer. The three officers who had volunteered to accompany the shifts down the mine were Jack Hands, an Australian from Perth in Western Australia, Bertie Green, from Sussex, and myself. The reasoning behind our decision was simply that if anyone had to go then it was only sensible that these should be the fittest, and we seemed to meet that condition. But we had not reckoned with the rough conditions underground with the very long hours, but especially with an officer's diet which was less than that of the miners who accompanied us. From the time we first went down, our health showed a marked decline; by April 1945 it had become clear that our continuing with this work would presently result in a total breakdown. Faced with this prospect, we decided to go to the *shoko* in his office and put our case for release from the mine on medical grounds. He gave us an unexpectedly sympathetic hearing and, much to our surprise, and our relief, he agree to release us. It was this decision that explains how it came about that when, on the morning of 9 August 1945, the sick party set off for its day's work on the hillside gardens, Jack Hands and I went with them.

The men who made up the garden party for the hill were mine rejects. One glance at their starved, scrawny, bleached bodies was enough to convince even the Japanese that they could never stand up to the long, exacting shifts at the coal face. Their arms and legs carried the tell-tale tattoos of rough laceration by sharp coal edges, and some of their wounds, having become infected, refused to heal and were tied up with stained strips of rag that had been boiled again and again for use as bandages. They were for the most part sullen and dogged men, rendered stubborn by the treatment they had received. Never did they do a stroke of work beyond the bare minimum demanded. The tool they used was a *chunkal*, the heavy adze-like and very practical instrument which the Japanese and many other Asiatic peasants use instead of spades, and often instead of ploughs. In charge of the party was Kotakihara, alias The Panther, he of the volcanic temper, implacably at odds with Australians. Having set the men to their tasks he squatted Japanese-fashion on his haunches, his back against a terrace, contemplating the Inland Sea.

The north-east corner of the garden was the French-beans patch. Here parallel rows of bamboo stakes had been pulled in at the top and tied so that they formed a kind of pastoral mansard roof. On these grew the French beans, clothing them with their rich canopy of leaves. Collecting a skep, or shallow basket, I crawled out of sight into the tunnel, pretending to weed. What I had in mind, of course, was a transient vision of *dolce far niente*, unmolested, out of sight of the meditative one on the terrace. I had not been long in my retreat when, lifting my eyes to the opening at the end, I saw Jack Hands, obviously agitated and trying to attract my attention. He was a very big man, and since his vast frame could never adequately subsist on the food he got, he suffered more than most from starvation. Now he took to waving his arm to get some response from me. But, imagining that some unfortunate had provoked the Panther and was paying the penalty, I thought it wise to stay where I was for the time being, out of sight – and out of danger. Losing patience, Jack hissed out a summons that had me clambering incontinently from my hide-out: 'For God's sake, Jock, get out and *look!*'

All work had come to a standstill. The men leaned on their *chunkals*. Even The Panther had broken off his meditation and got to his feet. Every eye was fixed on *something* that had just made its appearance in the sky. From behind a notch in the Kyushu Hills, a little south of Moji, a gigantic column of smoke was rising swiftly into the high heavens, its outer skin glowing with a nacreous iridescence, within it something writhing as if alive and struggling to get out. Its head bulged out, spreading like a vast mushroom in the sky. Fascinated and awestruck, each man continued to gaze, saying nothing. At length Jack Hands turned to the men to ask if any had heard an explosion – any noise? No one had heard a thing. One of the men, who claimed to have been among the first to see it, declared that when it first appeared it was red – or at least redder than it appeared now. Jack Hands said he was sure it was the Yawata Steel Works at Kokura. It was in the right direction. The B-29s must have got them. They must have dropped a bomb on a huge ammunition dump and this was what had gone up.

For more than a week now the B-29s had been very active, mostly during the mornings. Flying one or two at a time, and at a very great height, they first appeared over the Inland Sea to the east and making for Moji. After a time they would re-trace their course, leaving in the clear bright air thin vapour trails at whose heads the aircraft looked no bigger than silver beetles. No Japanese fighters put in an appearance to try to intercept them, and no A/A guns were fired at them – probably they were flying too high for both.

In normal circumstances a sight like this in the sky would have been calculated to rouse the volcanic temper of The Panther to convulsion. But, like the men hypnotised into silence by the sight, he continued to stand on the terrace and gaze at it. At length, shaking his head, he announced, '*Yasume!*' (Stand at ease – in other words, 'Take a rest!'). So unheard of was such a command in the middle of a morning that the men looked at him in unbelief, seeing which he added, '*Sukoshi yasume!*' (a small rest). But the small rest presently became a big rest, and lasted till lunchtime when The Panther announced: '*Sagio oware!*' (Work is over!). We threaded our way down the steep winding path under the fir trees and among the bamboo clumps to the camp.

We arrived there to find the greatest excitement prevailing. Tucked in between its ridges, the camp had not enjoyed the grandstand view that had been ours on the hillside, but the vast pillar in the sky had not gone unnoticed and they had followed its progress as it began its slow drift eastwards. It had thinned out a little, and in time the middle was to sag, though its head, after a struggle to disengage itself, still clung tenaciously to the body. They had watched it lean over the Inland Sea, roughly in the direction of Ohama, though it never quite reached it. Every channel through which, in the past, news had filtered back to camp was now vigorously explored: the mine, where a garrulous miner might let something slip; the *hackensha*, or village store, where the men went to collect the rice, and where an odd civilian might be less tight-lipped than the military; any of the various hangers-on who might in the course of their duties visit the camp – with each of them the indefatigable inquisition went on. Never in the past had it drawn a complete blank. But now, for some inexplicable reason, it did. Either the Japanese were unaware of the nature of what had happened or else they had been cowed into silence by threats of the most blood-curdling punishments on anyone who blabbed. Every question was met with the stock response: '*Wakarimasen!*' (Don't know!)

Yet in the hitherto immutable Japanese mind a slow change was working its way. What had yesterday been impossible, or unthinkable, was at least being considered. Their hitherto unquestioning trust in the Imperial Army was showing a hairline crack here and there. Even (one or two were heard to confess) the glorious *kamikazes* could not be expected to keep the detested Americans for ever from the sacred soil of Japan. Into their cryptic remarks was creeping a faint but unmistakable note of pessimism. The first American soldier to set foot on Japanese soil would give the signal for the immediate execution of every prisoner of war. To the slaughter would then be added all the wives and children. Finally the men would fight to a finish, and when the end was in sight the few survivors would commit *hara-kiri*. Thus would Japan's national honour be redeemed and sanctified.

The five days that followed the appearance of the strange portent in the sky were sunny, unclouded, and uneventful, but that did not prevent the suspense from mounting. On the sixth day, having come back from our morning's work on the hillside garden, we were having our lunch in the little annexe in the dining-room hut when suddenly the loose glass pane in the window was slid back and Sgt Maxwell thrust his head in. Sgt Maxwell was the Australian who assisted Mr Root, the British Warrant Officer in the PoW Administration Office, whose window faced the Japanese office and let them see what was going on there. He announced that some very important broadcast was taking place in the Jap office, every Jap in camp – soldiers, guards, civilians alike – having been ordered to attend and listen to the radio. They were all standing with heads bowed and looking very solemn. He had no idea what it was all about, but he would let us know if he heard anything.

Lunch over, and back once again on the hillside, The Panther sat slumped on the edge of the terrace with his head in his hands. One of the men, curious if not compassionate, asked him if he was sick. '*Bioki nai!*' (Not sick!) he replied list-lessly. From time to time, raising his head from his hands, he gazed longingly at the scene before him, almost as if he feared it might be snatched away for ever from him.

Right at the top of the garden, and above the French beans, grew an isolated pair of sorghums. These are tall, millet-like plants which have a thick stalk, rather like sugar-cane, and just strong enough to support a man's back provided he does not lean too heavily against it. Propped up against the sorghum stems, Jack Hands and I sat watching the Inland Sea while the men stood about, doing no work, some of them leaning on their *chunkals* talking casually among themselves. An uncanny stillness had fallen on the land. In the paddies not a coolie was to be seen. Even the interminable clatter of the *hakkos* on the loading gantry had stopped. Such a thing had never happened before in our experience. Beneath us lay Ohama, basking in the sun. We were just far enough away from it to be spared the sight of its squalid shacks. Thrusting itself out over the water was the jetty where, three years before, we had first landed on that unforgettable night. To one side of it, the two eyeless sockets of the mine entrance gazed up at us. The sea was so still that the reflections of the Kyushu hills in its waters were as real as the hills themselves. Not a ship was to be seen anywhere. 'I would not be at all surprised,' said Jack Hands at length, 'if this whole show were to pack in tomorrow!'

About four o'clock we set off down the path to the camp. About halfway down, we met Shigenaya on his way up. One of the shift bosses, he was a man who revealed his insecurity by always standing very much on his dignity. Now he appeared strangely affable and, turning round, he accompanied us back to the guard-house where, having been numbered, we were dismissed in a spirit of unwonted geniality. Back in camp we were now to learn that the rice party, after only one trip to the *hackensha*, were told at 2.30 p.m. that they need not come back. During the afternoon, no prior notice being given, there had been a Red Cross issue: one box between four men, irrespective of rank or occupation. At five p.m. a group of surface workers returned to the camp. After being dismissed at the guard-house, they uncharacteristically broke ranks and stampeded down the road to the office, the Sergeant-in-charge of them not stopping there but continuing through to the washing taps, beside which some of the officers were sitting, discussing the day's events.

'Have you heard the news?' asked the Sergeant, almost breathless with excitement. 'It's over!'

'What's over?' asked Wyrill.

'The war!' said the Sergeant.

'How do you know?' asked Wyrill, schooled by earlier disillusionment to scepticism.

'I'll tell you how I know. When we were coming across the road we saw three women in a huddle. They had a couple of kids with them. As soon as they saw us, one of the kids belted across the road to speak to us. It shouted out, *"Sensu oware! Sensu oware!"* The war's over! That's how I know!'

Even as late as nine p.m. doubts still lingered among the sceptics. At that time Mr Root, being sent for by the office, was told that the morning shift would not go out. No sooner had he got back than he was sent for again to be told this time that there would be no further mine work till instructed by the *shoko*. To put this to the test the night shift, despite instructions, fell in as usual at the guard-house, but they were told they were not wanted and sent back to billets.

All this was unheard of. Whatever had been said in that radio broadcast, it had certainly brought about a remarkable change in the Japs. Along with Sgt Maxwell, Mr Root had watched the proceedings in the Jap office. When they came out, he said, the tears were pouring down their faces. They made no attempt either to staunch or conceal them. They were just broken men, or, as he put it in his Cockney, 'Blubbing like bybies'.

THE COMING OF THE B-29s

Next morning some of our men climbed on to the roof of the dormitory and rigged up a makeshift flag-pole. It was a long bamboo rod which they secured with ropes and nails at the point where the roof ridge met the gable-end. Through its top they had bored a hole into which they inserted a rope, with which they hoisted a Union Jack. How this flag had appeared just when it was needed remained a matter of doubt. According to one report, it had been hurriedly stitched together during the night from remnants of red, white and blue cloth which had been left over from the pantomime and had been hidden away for some future use. Another had it that it was one of several such flags which had been smuggled all the way from Java. However it had been acquired, it fluttered bravely in the gentle breeze, an inspiring sight to all the prisoners beneath. Having succeeded in hoisting the flag, the men then turned their attention to announcing our presence to any enquirers who might approach us from the air. From the mine they now acquired a large brush and a pail of whitewash and with these they painted on the dormitory roof P O W in letters large enough to catch the eye of any American aviator who approached the Ohama area.

About all this there were those who had grave misgivings. Were we not rushing to anticipate events too rashly? After all, the black-out was still being enforced. Much more disturbing still was an event which had taken place at six a.m. on Friday, 17 August. Just in the middle of *tenko* the air-raid siren had sounded, causing widespread consternation among the guards. There could be little doubt that an armistice of a kind had been arrived at, but who was to say that all elements in the army would obey it? Were there not hot-heads who, unable to accept the fact of their nation's defeat, might take the law into their own hands, in which case the prisoners would be the first to suffer. In the very delicate situation in which we found ourselves, prudence counselled against any affront that might provoke the desperate and undisciplined to a massacre. But soon we were provided with evidence strong enough to dispel the last, lingering doubts. Overhead flew several Japanese aircraft, the rising sun on their wings now surrounded by painted white circles. Later, two cruisers appeared on the Inland Sea, approaching from the direction of Moji, sailing very slowly eastwards and tailed by a couple of destroyers. They were followed after an interval by a heavy cruiser, escorted by five very large destroyers. Last of this strange cavalcade was an aircraft carrier. A vast and awesome vessel, it rode very high out of the water, its flimsy-looking superstructure perched right on the edge of its huge flight deck. On board we could detect no sign of life at all. Silently, and almost eerily, it drifted past our small coal-mining village, eastward-bound, a moribund kraken, its fighting days over.

A week before, as all the world (except ourselves) had by now learned, the Emperor had addressed the Japanese people over the radio, ordering them to lay down their arms. But, relegated to a limbo, we were cut off from events, hearing nothing. Then, unable to endure the uncertainty any longer, Reg Newton, the CO of the Australian contingent, and Paul Wyrill, senior officer of the British, decided to bring the matter to a head by a daring and admittedly very risky piece of bluff. Marching boldly together to the *shoko*'s office, they demanded an interview, during which they informed him that by means of the secret radio which we had been operating in camp they had just received instructions from General MacArthur's Headquarters in Manila. These stated that *all* weapons in Japanese hands, be they military or civilian, had to be collected and surrendered to the nearest PoW camp in the area. The final date for the completion of this surrender of weapons was twelve noon on Friday, 22 August. Any failure on the part of the Japanese to comply promptly and effectively with this order would be regarded as a breach of the terms of the general surrender, and would be reported through our secret radio to US headquarters, who would take the appropriate action.

On the face of it the statement was preposterous. A telephone call to the nearest army post would have exposed its falsity, and it is scarcely conceivable that the *shoko* did not later take this corroborative step. Nonetheless doubts about the existence of a secret radio in camp must have troubled the Japanese – was not the purpose behind the periodic *kempetai* searches its uncovering? However, bowing respectfully, the *shoko* listened to the British officers with formal earnestness and inscrutability. But whether he had any intention to comply with the order was a matter which he kept to himself.

No sooner were the two officers back in camp than they began to have doubts about the wisdom of their stratagem. Had they not overplayed their hand? What would happen if the Japanese simply decided to call their bluff and ignore the order? As the deadline approached, so their confidence ebbed. With their watches pointing to five minutes to noon, they finally conceded that their plan had misfired. Then, precisely on the stroke of twelve, the guards swung open the main gate and there trooped into the camp a motley cavalcade carrying an armoury of perplexing diversity. There were rifles and other firearms. There were one or two machine-guns, all clearly obsolete. There were several modern hand grenades. There was an array of swords of imposing antiquity. Bearing their weapons, the bearers lined up before the guard-house looking rather forlorn and expecting the worst. As soon as they saw them enter, Newton and Wyrill, their morale completely restored, marched up to the gate and took charge of the proceedings and possession of the heterogeneous arsenal. They gave instructions that the weapons should be deposited in heaps according to their nature. When this had been done, they proceeded to inspect them with mock solemnity. Finally they declared that, the terms of the American order from Manila having been observed to their satisfaction, the mob was now at liberty to disperse. Meekly they slouched out of the gate, looking like murderers who had been granted a last-minute reprieve from the gallows.

Two squads of our men, who had earlier been detailed for this purpose, were now summoned to remove the arms to a place of greater safety. There they were classified, catalogued, cleaned, and an inventory compiled. The more serviceable of the rifles were then issued to a guard platoon who thereupon took over the policing of the camp-compound. The first mounting of the new guard proved to be a memorable occasion. Though not the first contingent to arrive in Ohama, the Australians were the larger, and to them was accorded the honour of the day. From every corner of the camp items of uniform were collected so that in the end the guard was tolerably well turned out. Every officer and man in camp was present, the sole and sad exception being myself whom a sudden return of scorbutic symptoms, which were accompanied by a disfiguring and painful swelling of the face (rather like Frow's), had stretched on a sick-bay mat. Standing on the spot beside the guard-room, where the grey stain of ashes on the road reminded those present of grimmer proceedings in the past, the new guard presented arms. On the flag-staff another of the hoarded Union Jacks was broken, replacing the rising sun of Japan, now in decline. It was a moment charged with emotion, its poignancy deepened by thoughts of the many who had not lived to share it.

On Friday, 24 August a Japanese officer, accompanied by an interpreter who was also a Japanese, arrived in camp. Their purpose, they said, was to bring us official confirmation of the Japanese surrender. They also informed us that all prisoners would be under their own jurisdiction soon. Our food rations would be increased to the extent of availability of supplies. Sadly, however, nothing was available from Red Cross sources since all their stocks had been destroyed in the very heavy air-raids that had been carried out against all the large Japanese cities. In the meantime we were at liberty to augment our rations from any sources that were available. Among these they suggested any livestock that might have survived. But they had not seen them: two pigs, a few hens, and one or two rabbits, all in such a pitiful state as to suggest the ossuary rather than the pot as a suitable vehicle for their disposal. On 7 September our interpreter was back, this time accompanied by a Swiss who was called Wiedman and a Swede called Walden. They gave us what little news was available, of which the main item was that we should be out of Ohama within a week. They also said they were prepared to collect from prisoners any evidence of brutal treatment by their captors.

Now at long last Dr Ploegman was given access to Red Cross medical supplies so long denied him. From one of the boxes he extracted some sulfaguanadine and multivitamin tablets, which he administered to me. The transformation in my condition which they effected was quite remarkable. Indeed, so rapid was my recovery that I was able to get up from my sick-bed and make my way to the office to catch a glimpse of our visitors. As he emerged from the door of the office, the interpreter passed sufficiently close to me to allow me to detain him for a moment in search of enlightenment on a semantic problem that had been troubling me for some time. He was a slender man for a Japanese, who on the whole tend to be a stocky race. In contrast with those with whom it had been our misfortune to be closely associated over the preceding three-and-a-half years, he was urbane. His spoken English was of a kind we had not so far encountered on Japanese lips. His grammar was precise, and he handled English idiom as if to the manner born. Spoken Japanese is an explosive language, but his English was soft and cultured. As well as the accents, he displayed the mannerisms of an educated gentleman. This, as I was later to learn, was not at all surprising, considering that he was an alumnus of Cambridge University. To what I had to say he lent an earnest ear. I saw his brow noticeably furrow as I explained to him how, on the spur of the moment, I had addressed to Buttons the phrase I had picked up from the *Primer*. Had, I asked him, the words any connotation beyond what was apparent from their English equivalent? The word, he explained, which in the *Primer* had been rendered by 'rude' was not one which one was likely to find on the lips of an educated Japanese, being confined to the general vocabulary only of the lower classes. But on the tongue of a foreigner, who in any case would be innocent of the niceties of Japanese speech, it was little likely to cause offence. 'Uncultured' would fall broadly into the same category. But *ya tze*, which the *Primer* had rendered by the innocuous 'fellow', was a very different matter, being a word which polite society would banish from its vocabulary. Clearly the thirty-hour road to spoken Japanese was beset by pitfalls, perilous to the unwary!

On Saturday, 25 August Komo, one of the guards, brought news that American aircraft had, on the previous day, flown over some camps in north Japan and dropped supplies to them. They were expected to repeat the process over Ohama at six p.m. that very day. Komo was not a gentleman on whom we built an absolute trust, but, to take a bond even against the improbable, some of the men climbed up on to the roofs of both dormitories and the cook-house and painted additional P O Ws there. The failure of Komo's prophecy did not disturb us unduly, and a continuous deluge of rain on the following day denied its fulfilment then. But the day after that about a dozen American fighter 'planes flew over Ohama, obviously reconnoitring the area. Three hours later three very large 'planes arrived, being clearly B-29s and having POW SUPPLIES painted under their wings. They made several trial runs over the camp, but what they saw seemed to convince them this was not a suitable terrain for dropping supplies. They then flew along the coast to Motoyama. From their bomb-bays there then issued a shower of large containers which, suspended on billowing parachutes of many-coloured silk, drifted slowly to earth. But we had no cause for anxiety. In the days that followed returning B-29s did not all find the Ohama camp inaccessible. From the skies there now descended a bounty so varied and so large that it tempted us to dangerous over-eating, and taxed our store cupboards to their limits.

Not all the containers, however, managed to land in the target area. In those cases where the parachutes failed to open, they often fell wide and came bounding down the hill in terrifying leaps and bounds, uprooting trees in their mad career. One of the most spectacular of these descents occurred when a container plunged through the lamp-room, churning it into matchwood. A horde of very young girls worked here, and they owed their survival to their curiosity about the *Ni-Chu-Kus*, which had earlier persuaded them to abandon their work and go outside to watch the huge machines. But most dramatic of all was the career of one of the drums which landed far up the hill, and by the time it reached the camp area was travelling at high speed. With the velocity of a cannonball it crashed into the *kashira naka*. At the moment of impact the platform at the top was occupied by a couple of guards, who were directing their attention rather to the B-29 than to what it dropped. In the twinkling of an eye all that stood between them and the distant earth was a whirling cloud of dust and splintered bamboo. To the astonishment of everyone, their swift and involuntary descent from this high perch was accomplished without irreparable damage to their persons. This merely reinforced the belief which had been inspired by the many encounters of miners with uninsulated electric cable down the mine that the Japanese are, as a race, remarkably durable.

In addition to the food, clothing and medicines which the B-29s dropped, one of the early drums contained a copy of a newspaper which had been published in Honolulu on 17 August, just a week after we had seen the cloud rising in the sky, and which indeed had come from Nagasaki. From this we learned for the first time the true nature of the bombs that had devastated the two Japanese cities. We also learned that the Russians had now entered the war against Japan and were rapidly advancing through Manchuria.

One of the pilots mistaking, it seemed, the neighbouring village for ours discharged his load above Neshi Ohama and the containers were scattered over a wide area of distant mountainside. Their retrieval would need the dispatch of several search parties, of one of which I was put in charge.

I had not gone with my party very far beyond the main gate when I met Frankie Knight on his way back to camp. He was among the officers who had originally come to Ohama but who had later been taken away along with some others to the new camp which had been set up for senior officers at Zentsuji, on the island of Shikoku, which encloses the Inland Sea on the south side. After the Japanese surrender he had made his way back somehow to rejoin his old comrades at Ohama. Now he was leading one of the *hakko*-boys, that innocent but trumpet-tongued fellowship of charioteers down the mine, whom he claimed to have caught in some felony. So improbable seemed the charge that I asked Frankie what the boy's crime had been. His answer was so curt that it obviously covered something he thought better not to reveal. 'He insulted me,' he said. 'That's enough!' For a *hakko*-boy to insult anyone, far less a British officer, smacked so much of the improbable that I declined to believe him. Taking the boy back to the guard-house, Frankie Knight handed him over to the guard, giving, I suppose, some account of his offence. Thereupon the boy was clapped in a cell. I re-joined my search party, and had just breasted the ridge above the village when I was met by a couple of Japanese guards who told me that they had just caught some thieves red-handed stealing food. Presently the two alleged culprits were dragged before me. They were mere boys, their rags barely covering their nakedness, and clearly in an advanced state of poverty and starvation. Expecting no mercy from me, they hung their heads and remained silent when the guards ordered them to make an open confession of their crimes. It was not made clear to me what exactly they had been stealing, and when I asked for enlightenment on the point the guards invited me to accompany them to the village where they would show me the evidence so that I could judge for myself. Skirting the upper rows of huts, we soon arrived in front of a miserable hovel which stood somewhat apart from the general housing. It had no windows and a dirty sack, suspended over the entrance, took the place of a door. 'Bad man house!' said one of the guards as, pulling the sack aside, he invited me to enter.

The lintel was very low, and to get under it I had to lower my head. Once inside, I found myself in total darkness and at first could not see a thing. But after a time sight gradually returned, and in the gloom I could see there was no stick of furniture in the place, not even the usual *tatami* to cover the earthen floor. There was, indeed, nothing at all apart from a heap of rags which was propped up against a wall at the far corner. I was nonplussed, and called to the guard to come in. My voice stirred the heap of rags to movement, which coalesced to assume a shape vaguely human. I looked at it intently and then I realised it was a crone. Stricken by years and poverty, she looked witch-like in her squalor. From her withered features her sunken eyes gazed out blankly. Her wasted body lacked even a decent covering. On the earthen floor beside her I now discovered the evidence I had come to look for – two small tins of Campbell's soup! Whoever had been guilty of this petty theft, it clearly was not this old woman. Were the two ragged youths perhaps relations of hers and had they stolen the tins on her behalf? Or, having been detected in theft, had they slipped their spoils in here to escape arrest?

If ever a moment called for understanding and mercy, this was it. From our bulging cupboards would the departure of two small tins of soup constitute a loss we could not afford? To this pitiful creature, whose existence of grinding poverty was obviously guttering to its close, would it have been too much to ask of me to present the tins to her, and even half a dozen more, with my blessing? That was what my better judgement told me I should do. But at that moment I was not master of my better judgement, nor subject to its counsels. I had been given a role to play. Against those who had treated us shamefully, we had in turn to act shamefully. Putting on a hollow show of indignation, I ordered the guard to tell the old woman that she was a thief – and the destination of all thieves was the gaol. With sagging mouth, she listened as the guard translated my words. Then, when he had finished, she emitted a low strangled sob. Then from her lips issued a shrill cry of despair, like that of an animal caught in a trap. Clearly she thought she was about to be seized and dragged off to custody. But I spared her that injustice, and myself the shame of perpetrating it. Lowering my head, I left the hovel. Then, with the two guards in tow, each grasping a tin of soup in one hand and clutching an alleged malefactor by the other, I returned to the guard-house. I handed the two youths over to the guard, who promptly clapped them in the cell beside the *hakko*-boy. Later the police arrived to take them away for correction. They were anxious to take the *hakko*-boy as well, but for some reason he was not surrendered to them. Possibly the evidence of his crime was too flimsy even to justify this step.

Next day, out on the hillside, I was approached by an old and kind-hearted miner whom our men knew as Pop. His grotesquely twisted body testified to long years of crouching at the coal-face. He had come, he said, to make a personal appeal to me: could nothing be done to save the *hakko*-boy from his fate? His parents were now convinced he would be beheaded. Such a thing, I assured him, was quite out of the question. I did not know what crime the *hakko*-boy was alleged to have committed, but I was certain that whatever it was it could be no more than trifling. A day or two would see the boy released from the cell and restored to his family. But nothing I said would convince the old man that the *hakko*-boy would ever come out of that cell alive. The following day, however, the *hakko*-boy was given his freedom and, to the unspeakable joy of his parents, was reunited with them. Like the old woman in the hovel, the *hakko*-boy, I was firmly convinced, was guilty of no crime. Like myself, Frankie Knight was no longer the prisoner of the Japanese but of destiny.

NEWS OF HIROSHIMA

For three years our world had been the prison camp, its horizon the perimeter fence. But, the gates now thrown open, distant places beckoned. Presently the camp was in the grip of a wanderlust. Paul Wyrill declared his intention to set out, along with a few others, for Onada. If their luck held they hoped to get to Yamaguchi, the capital of its prefecture lying about thirty miles north of Ohama. The attraction of Yamaguchi was that they had been told there were fine kimonos to be had there at quite modest cost. Their luck did hold, at least as far as travel is concerned, for they did manage to get to Yamaguchi. But there it appeared to have deserted them, and the tawdry and over-priced kimonos they brought back with them did little credit either to their business acumen or their aesthetic taste. Undismayed by their dubious success, I determined to set off on my own. Following the path that crossed over the hill above Neshi Ohama, I was soon on the main road for Onada. But presently I heard the hooting of a motor-horn behind me and a heavy truck drew up at my side. Its genial driver asked me where I was going and, with no definite destination in mind, I said on the spur of the moment, 'Yamaguchi!' As chance would have it that was his destination too; and, being invited to join him in his cabin, I shared his sprightly company all the way to Yamaguchi.

The town enjoys an enviable setting and a mild climate. From the cold winter winds which blow in from the Sea of Japan it is sheltered by a ring of hills. In addition to its prefectural status, it enjoyed at the time a double reputation as a spa and an educational centre, and it possessed a rich variety of baths, schools and colleges. My driver took me to the prefectural building, which is in the centre of the town, where he proposed to drop me. But, learning from some casual conversation with a group of bystanders that there was another party of prisoners already in town, he generously volunteered to drive me round in search of them. Such a haphazard quest was little likely to discover our quarry, but much to my surprise, and after further questioning of citizens, he ran them to earth in a hotel on the outskirts of the town. There we parted, with heartfelt thanks on my part to my courier and guide.

I found the party in a special guest-room at the back of the hotel and engaged in some kind of celebration. They were seated on the *tatamis* in a ring round a low table on which stood a few bowls of food and glasses of what I took to be *saki*. My unannounced entry seemed to cause them some confusion. Raising two very unwelcoming eyes to me, one of them said very brusquely, 'This is a Motoyama party! *Go away!*' Such a greeting I was not likely to disregard. Silently I withdrew, and found a smaller and less pretentious room at the front of the building where I had a frugal meal of rice and vegetables. Then, wishing to distance myself from the unfriendly group, I left the hotel, directing my steps aimlessly through the streets till I came to a long avenue which was shaded by huge trees through which, from time to time, I caught arresting vistas of the surrounding hills.

I had been walking slowly along this for some time when I became aware of eager steps behind me; turning round, I saw a Japanese who was endeavouring to overtake me. In appearance he was undistinguished, being slight of build and wearing a dark, tight business suit which gave the impression of a minor clerk. His manner was taut and nervous. When he began to speak he showed he had a fairly competent command of English. He asked me if I was English.

'Yes! I said, stretching the term a little.

'Are you prisoner?'

I said I had been, but was one no longer. He then went on to say how deeply shocked he had been by the stories that were now being published in the newspapers about the ill-treatment of prisoners by the Japanese. This, he declared, had come as a total surprise and revelation to all Japanese, who were very proud of their army and its achievements. They could not conceive how this kind of thing could ever happen. To treat defeated and helpless enemies badly was a barbarous thing. It would besmirch the good name of the Japanese army. Indirectly, it would besmirch the good name of the Japanese people as a whole. Would I (and here he made the most formal and humble of obeisances) accept on his behalf, and on that of all the Japanese people, his profound apologies for all the bad treatment that I and my comrades might have received at Japanese hands. From that he went on to speak of a frightful thing which, he said, had just taken place at Hiroshima. He had met, personally, one or two people who had been there at the time, and had got the story from them at first-hand. I could rest assured, therefore, that what he was about to tell me was true.

Shortly after eight, he said, on the morning of Sunday, 6 August, a B-29 had flown over Hiroshima at a great height. There was nothing very remarkable in that for during the past week or two they had been frequently flying over, reconnoitring the city. But since they did not drop bombs the people were becoming accustomed to them and lost some of their fear. However, on this occasion the siren did sound and they responded to its warning by going dutifully to their shelters. For a short while the B-29 circled the city before departing. Thinking that it had been merely taking photographs, the people emerged from their shelters again. But some minutes later it was back. Once more it made a run over the city, but this time the people did not return to their shelters but stood in the open watching it. This run, however, was different, for the next thing they were aware of was something dangling from a parachute and drifting down towards them. When it got to a certain height (from indications I estimated this to be about 200 feet) it exploded, and this was a kind of explosion they had never experienced before. There was a flash, and a blinding light seemed to engulf the city. Up into the sky rose a great pillar of smoke. So great was the shock that the ground beneath their feet rocked and trembled as if in the midst of an earthquake. The destruction was on a scale that defied description. The dead, he said, were to be numbered in thousands upon thousands. But the fate of those who were not yet dead was more pitiable still. Their wounds were quite different from those that doctors had hitherto been asked to deal with. When a syringe was pushed into a victim's arm to give him a pain-killing injection, the skin and flesh simply came away on the needle. In Hiroshima people were still dying in their hundreds. The newspapers said that the same thing had just happened in Nagasaki, though he had not met anyone from that city and so could not speak with authority about it. Had the Emperor not addressed the nation on the radio, telling the fighting men to lay down their arms, he was sure that other Japanese cities would have shared the same fate – Tokyo (certainly) then Kobe, Osaka, even the sacred Kyoto might have been devastated. All the people of Japan were thankful that this terrible war had now come to an end.

With this litany of the incredible my mind found it hard to come to terms. Indeed there was something quite unreal and nightmarish about the whole experience – the quiet stroll under the outstretched arms of the great trees; the town asleep in the cradle of the hills; this little Japanese beside me chronicling horror on a scale that defied comprehension. The Japanese glad that peace had come! Atrocity committed *upon* the Japanese rather than *by* them! How could one reconcile this with the grim reality of our own experiences in Ohama, on the *Singapore Maru*, in Singapore and Java? My shock and horror were momentarily dispelled by the hooting of a horn and a screech of brakes as a heavy truck drew up alongside me. In it was the Motoyama party on its way home. Possibly feeling a little guilty about their churlishness towards me in the hotel, they resorted to flippancy and sarcasm to cover their unease. Would I care for a lift? they asked, unless I was enjoying my walk so much that I preferred to carry on with my Japanese till I got to Ohama.

It would be idle to pretend that I found this return in the truck to Motoyama anything but distasteful. In the resonant box of the truck the cackling of their forced laughter oppressed my ears as their choicest sallies were flicked back and forth like verbal shuttlecocks. They were still hard at it as we passed the whitened skeletons of Ube and Onada. In these hilarious heads no thought, or knowledge, of what had happened at Hiroshima, at Nagasaki! It was with undisguised relief that I climbed down at last from the vehicle in the camp at Motoyama. There I found some difficulty in disengaging myself from several who offered their companionship on the walk back to Ohama. Among them were a British officer, an Australian who claimed to have been the scene-writer for Gordon Harker, the actor, and the local chief of police. Making a fourth, and in a niche of uncongeniality of his own, was the ineffable Tanaka. But I managed to give the slip to them all, and, still haunted by what I heard about the people of Hiroshima with the skin and flesh peeling from their arms, I walked the sea road back to Ohama and the camp.

I had a story, of course, and was eager to tell it. But to my dismay no one seemed to want to listen to me. Shortly I was to learn the reason. In my absence other reporters had been on the scene, and this time they were not a clerk in Yamaguchi but officers from our camp. That very morning a couple of them had gone to Onada and boarded the first train that came into the station. It was going eastwards. They had no destination in mind, but at length descended at a station on the outskirts of Hiroshima. They had, of course, no inkling whatsoever of what they were about to find there. But their story confirmed, in broad detail, what I had heard in Yamaguchi. Hiroshima, they reported, lay in a bowl ringed on all sides by mountains, except to the south where it looked out over the Inland Sea. Within this area, practically nothing had escaped destruction. Even the mountains had been seared by the blast and now showed horizontal ribs of incineration, rather like a zebra's hide. In the gutters were small streams, but when one trod on them one found that they were glass which had melted and then congealed. The whole city was, in fact, a grotesque, calcined bowl littered with débris. There was no sign of life anywhere. They had explored at will. There was nobody about to say 'Don't go there!' or 'Keep out of that!' Exhausted at length by their explorations, they returned to the station where they had alighted from the train and where they now saw their first Japanese. Stunned men and women, they seemed, who were walking about as in a trance. They seemed to take little notice of the two foreigners, and certainly displayed no resentment or hostility towards them. Whatever had happened to Hiroshima was something that, up to that hour, had been unknown and unsuspected by mankind. But against weapons of this kind, directed against its major cities, no country on earth could hold out for more than a day or two at the most.

On one other aspect of their eventful journey they failed to make comment, being, of course, entirely unaware of its existence or nature. But from these polluted ruins what seeds of future corruption did they carry away in their flesh and bones? Were they also destined at some future date to share, in some measure, the fate of the citizens of Hiroshima? I was never to know.

WE REVISIT MOJI

From that unhallowed day when we had first set foot on the soil of Japan, the docks at Moji held a macabre fascination for us. Now that travel was unfettered, might it be possible to go back and see them? Now to us as free men, would the quayside where in those freezing hours we had submitted to the searches, the dock where we had come upon the Americans abandoned and dying, the place where we embarked on the coal-barges, look the same as they did then? To get to Moji we had first to cross the straits, and that might prove to be an insuperable difficulty. But it might be worthwhile to make the attempt.

Accompanied by one or two of the Sergeants, Johnnie and I set off for Onada. Arriving at the station, we found it swarming with intending passengers. To avoid them for a little we strolled to the end of the platform. In a nearby siding stood a large steel wagon, loaded with coal-dross. In its bottom was a narrow sliding door which an old and dwarfish woman was operating to release the dross. Once a pile had accumulated, she loaded it with a shovel that was too big and heavy into a *hakko* that was too high for her feeble strength. From head to toe she was covered deep in coal dust – face, arms, clothing, everything about her – a pitiful sight! She waved her arm in friendly greeting as we watched her. Presently a train pulled in to the platform, westward-bound. Every one of its coaches was already bulging with passengers, but this in no way dismayed those who were waiting on the platform and who, in an irresistible avalanche, launched themselves upon it. They mounted every footplate; they sat on every coupling-chain; they clung to every bar that would accommodate a fist. One thing they did not do: on the train was one first-class carriage, and with the deference which is innate in the lower orders of the Japanese nation they left it inviolate. Promptly, having neither tickets nor authority, we took possession of it.

From Onada to Shimonoseki the track keeps very close to the shore. As our journey progressed, little scalloped bay followed little scalloped bay, each one dotted with the inevitable rocky islets, each with its coif of stunted *bonsai* pines. All were trimmed with thin beaches of the whitest sand, which contrasted sharply with the fir-forested hills that rose sharply almost from the water's edge. It was all very picturesque, indeed romantic, in a typically Japanese way. Almost without exception the stations were situated at the head of the bays. As soon as we arrived at each of them a fresh avalanche of humanity descended upon us. To secure, or even to retain, their hold on the swaying train would have demanded powerful hands on the part of the more daring of the outriders. At none of the stations where we stopped did I see a single passenger get off the train, nor, happily, between them did I see one *fall* off. At length, puffing stertorously as if exhausted with its load, the train pulled into the station at Shimonoseki, or rather what would have been the station had it still been there.

In the history of Japan, and indeed of the world, Shimonoseki deserves a minor, though significant, footnote. It was in this hitherto unheard-of place that, in 1895, Japan imposed a merciless treaty upon China whom she had humiliatingly defeated in war. This granted to Korea, which traditionally had admitted its suzerainty to China, what the Japanese were pleased to call 'independence' but what in reality was Japanese hegemony. Japan also took possession of the Island of Formosa, later to be known as Taiwan, which was later to prove an essential stepping-stone to more grandiose ambitions (and conquests) in the south. To these was added, almost as a matter of course, an astronomical indemnity. But now, from the victors in that distant conflict had been exacted an awesome penalty. Into the rubble of the town which had witnessed its signing, and given it its name, the B-29s had ground both the treaty and all it stood for.

One justifiable source of pride Shimonoseki had – its tunnel, which ran under the strait to link the islands of Honshu and Kyushu, and which had been completed not long before. Leaving the station we went in search of it, hoping that it might provide us with the means of getting across to Moji. But to our dismay it had suffered irreparable damage. Large slabs of concrete and piles of glazed tiles which the bombs had ripped from its walls blocked its entrance. Our only hope now lay in getting a boat. On arriving at the ferry we discovered to our relief that a boat was still plying. In our new role of superior guests we embarked without tickets or question, and presently found ourselves on the other side of the strait.

It did not take us long to realise that in the desolation that here met our eyes it would be manifestly impossible to find the docks we had come to seek. Even had we managed to find the place we could not, in their dereliction, have recognised them. We appealed for help to one or two of the passers-by, but our questions were met by puzzled faces, language defeating them. With no hope of ever finding the docks we had come to see, we turned our attention to the hospital to which the sick prisoners had been taken from the *Singapore Maru*. If any of them had survived, this was as likely a place as any to find them. After much fruitless questioning, we at length found a Japanese who seemed to get the drift of our intention. Leading us along some battered and faceless streets, he brought us at length to a high wall which had several strands of barbed wire strung along the top. This did not look at all like a hospital, but it did look very much like a camp. Going up to the heavy door we knocked, and it was opened by a British soldier, who looked ill. Presently we were reunited with the few survivors from among the sick men who on that grim day had been taken from our ship. There was a brief exchange of news, little of it that was not depressing. In this camp the death toll had been exceedingly heavy. The survivors whom we saw looked, many of them, as if they had not yet emerged safely from its sentence, and on their persons they carried the scars of long illness. A few of them gave us the impression that their struggle to keep alive had now gone on so long that it had begun to lose its point. Colonel Petrie, their CO, was out of camp at the moment, having gone to try to contact the Americans and arrange for the worst medical cases to be flown out. With those we met we tried to pick up the broken threads of friendship, and we expressed our sorrow at these other friendships which had been dissolved for ever. So demoralising did the experience prove to be that some of us began to wonder whether it might not have been better had we not found the place at all. Certainly in Ohama we had not had our sorrows to seek, but they had never drained us of hope to the extent that we saw here. When the time came for us to leave, we set off almost with relief.

For our return journey to the ferry we were without the services of a guide. Through the rubble we tried to re-trace our steps, looking for any feature that we might recognise from our earlier passage. But to tentative navigation luck lent its aid, and we reached the ferry without serious deviation. Once again our luck held, for there was a boat on the point of sailing. Soon we were in Shimonoseki, and thereafter in the station where, scarcely believable, was a train standing about to leave for the east and Onada. Along the sculptured coast, in an evening of saffron and gold, the train made its leisurely way, now less burdened with frenzied humanity. As we progressed, twilight thickened in the bays, and by the time we reached our destination night was upon us. We had been to Moji, and we had tasted defeat. The infamous docks no longer existed for us – for anyone – to visit. We had learned a lesson which, had we known of it earlier, might have spared us the visit in the first place: scenes of former suffering are far better left unvisited.

A Green Hill Far Away

The crematorium was at the top of the hill. Despite its high and exposed position, the huge cedars by which it was ringed sheltered it from the fiercest of the sun's rays. In the shade of the cedars grew some scattered cypresses. In Japan as in Europe they are regarded as emblems of death. The reliquaries, containing the ashes of the dead, were arranged in neat rows along the terraces. Between them grew tall grasses, their rank condition showing that they had not been cut and were wild. Here and there a cluster of wild flowers put up a brave struggle for survival against the more vigorous grasses. Round the borders mourners had planted garden flowers. They, however, looked to be well tended, and it was they which gave to the air its characteristic fragrance. At a little distance from the reliquaries stood the furnace. A thoroughly practical structure, its recurring heatings and subsequent exposure to the rains had left it red with rust. It consisted of two low brick walls, parallel to each other and about a yard apart. These supported a long iron tube which formed the oven. Inside the tube was a hollow iron tray which could be slid out and in on runners, and on which the corpse was laid for insertion into the furnace. The doors at one end being open, we could see inside several stumps of charred bones which had survived the flames. Beneath the tray was a long ridge of silver-coloured ashes which had dropped on to the embers of the faggots.

For a while Johnnie and I strolled curiously round the furnace and among the reliquaries. None of them contained the ashes of our dead comrades. At length we made our way over to the lip of the steep escarpment below which, in the distance, lay Neshi Omaha. At this point the cedars were very big and, choosing the biggest we could see, we sat down at its base, propping our backs against the bole. Though we were very high up, there was scarcely a breath of wind. Yet the topmost branches kept up a soft, elegiac murmuring as if for the dead. Now that the rain had stopped, the sun had come out again and its rays were fierce. Far beneath us, silent and very peaceful, Neshi Ohama basked. Round its jetty some fishing boats were moored, though there was not a fisherman in sight. For centuries, we reflected, boats just like these had gone out to their fishing grounds and returned with their catches. In the lives of their crews, as of so many millions of others, war had wrought great havoc, but when it was over the tasks of the fishermen would be resumed as before. Once their time was up, they would themselves be carried up to this lofty plateau, where a reliquary or two might keep alive their memory. But, coming to Ohama, a stranger would find nothing to remind him that we had ever been there. Despite the obvious danger from mines, a couple of tugs were puffing away stertorously as they towed five barges westwards. In the hope of escaping the danger, they were keeping tightly in towards the shore. For a time we watched them, expecting at any moment to see them hurled skywards. But nothing happened to them and soon they were lost to sight round the point.

At length, struggling to our feet, we took our leave of the crematorium and our lost comrades, very conscious that but for the grace of God we might well have been with them. One thing at least was clear enough: never again would we come back here.

Long exposure to the groundswell of noise in the dining-room had bred in us a disregard of it. But after the peace of the hill-top, it now grated on our ears. By the time evening approached, it was necessary to seek escape, and slipping out of the main gate Johnnie and I made our way down to the beach. Not far from the village we found a boat which had been turned upside down to dry out. It was very near the water and secured by a rope to a stake further up the bank. We sat down on its hull, our ears soothed by the gentle sound of the waves of the Inland Sea lapping sleepily on the shingle. There was no one to be seen about, but our presence must have been observed for presently some children came running from the village along the beach to where we were. Some of the bigger ones had flat, expressionless faces, with high cheekbones, the mark of the typical Korean. At first they were very shy, having had no contact with prisoners before, and were content to sit on their haunches and watch us in silence. At length Johnnie hit upon an approach which could not fail to thaw their shyness.

'*Chocolado!*' he announced, taking from his pocket one or two bars of our American toffee which we had got from the B-29s. Across their faces passed little ripples of expectation.

'*Chocolado* OK!' they chirruped in unison. Breaking the bars in pieces, Johnnie distributed them among them, taking care to ensure that even the smallest of them got his share. '*Arigato! Arigato!*' (Thank you!) Their thin, treble voices rose in a little chorus of delight and gratitude.

Soon, their shyness a thing of the past, they were chatting freely. From their eagerness it seemed that they had much to tell us, and as much to ask. But what it was we were never to know, language erecting insurmountable barriers between people merely wishing to be friends. They were a most engaging band of little folk. All had sparkling, sloe-black eyes, most of the girls pretty in their simple way. When they smiled, or laughed outright (which was often), the tiny ones were quite irresistible. But their faces were pinched with starvation, and their clothing was poor and patched. In Ohama they faced the bleakest of futures. All they had to look forward to was poverty, and the unremitting toil that was necessary to keep it at bay. If they remained in Japan, the Koreans among them had to submit to a further indignity: never could they escape being branded as second-rate citizens. Yet from the bitterest of their misfortunes their tender years mercifully saved them: they were much too young to realise the nature and the extent of the calamity that had befallen their elders and their country.

At length we scrambled down from the boat and retraced our steps along the beach, the children trotting contentedly by our side. Over Moji the sun was now setting in saffron glory. It was also setting over our own empire, over which we had proudly boasted it never set. But its dissolution was to be less spectacular than that of the empire whose ruins now cumbered the earth around us. With the children and with the whispering beach we exchanged sad, little *sayonaras*. Then, passing the village, we made our way up the steep track to the camp.

At five p.m. on 13 September 1945 we took leave of Ohama for ever. The day was the twenty-ninth after the Japanese surrender and the 1,281st after our own. We mustered on the roadway beside the guard-house, the most remarkable man among us bringing up the rear, not walking like the rest of us but carried on a litter made from a couple of bamboo poles and two sacks. Cpl Gittins looked little changed from what he had been in these early days in Ohama: he had the same cadaverous body. Not once till now had he left that sick-bay. But one thing *had* changed – his eyes! Now they were radiant. He would honour that hymeneal tryst after all! The Japanese with their coffin ready next door had got it wrong!

We numbered, and found a discrepancy. Then we numbered again. Some of the Australians were missing! Surely this was a rendezvous that not even the irresponsible would want to fail. But they had just slipped out of camp without telling anyone where they were going or when they expected to be back. We could hardly march off without them. Yet if we waited any length of time for them we might well upset the arrangements for our departure. The men stood and waited, anger not far from the surface. Then someone had an idea. 'Come on boys!' he called. 'Lets' burn the bloody place down before we go!' It only needed the suggestion to be mooted for it to be taken up with enthusiasm: 'Let's burn it! Anybody got a match?' But with the defection of his men, Reg Newton already had enough. With his indignation on the point of flaring into open anger, he nipped this foolhardy and pointless suggestion in the bud. What good, he sternly told them, would a wanton act of vengeance like this do? Let them leave Ohama as they had lived in it – with some dignity.

There was hardly a man among us who did not carry away with him some memento of the place of his captivity. Samurai swords with their knotted, red-braid trappings were tied with string to some of the haversacks. From under the flap of others stuck the ends of flowery kimonos. Other trophies were of a more personal nature, the work of long hours with a knife or an old razor blade on a piece of coal or an old pit-prop; negro heads that were almost life-like; chess-boards and chessmen; miniature Hurricanes and A/A guns, the weapons they had fought with and lost. Our only survivor from the Hurricane squadrons had a flat box with a glass top strapped to his back with a piece of thin rope. He had made it himself. It contained his remarkable collection of butterflies. He had begun to collect them while still in Java, where exotic specimens are plentiful, and he had been continually adding to it since, many of his friends helping him.

Not long before we had to leave, the mine officials had organised a kind of farewell party for the officers at which they had presented each with a samurai sword. Neither my partial recovery from my illness nor inclination persuaded me to attend. The officials, however, made known their willingness to let me have a sword, but I declined the offer. It was a decision which I had cause to regret. When, later, our vessel arrived in San Francisco, it was boarded by several Americans shouting loudly, 'A couple of hundred bucks for a samurai sword!' or 'Five hundred bucks for a real, good samurai sword!' Others traded their trophies readily. At that moment of truth, sorrow's crown of sorrow was beholding sager men. Not that I was devoid of a trophy, though it belonged to a decidedly lower order of things. After the Japanese surrender I slipped unnoticed into the office and 'borrowed' the records which the Japanese kept there. They included the one we used for our morning *taiso* or physical exercises, that of the

Kimigayo, and the *Co-Prosperity Sphere March*, and *Stille Nacht* and *O du Froliche* which had been played at the pantomime. I also took a Japanese record which had a plaintive melody called *Kuni No Hana* and expressed the longing of a Japanese soldier serving in the southern regions for his homeland. I wrapped them up carefully in a shoddy towel and then packed them in a cardboard box which I now held under my arm as I waited impatiently for the return of the rene-gade Australians.

Lined up on the bank above us as we waited were the people of Ohama. Most of them had not seen much of us, apart from the daily procession of the shifts to and from the mine, but they were all eager to witness our departure. Being the tallest, the men stood at the back; before them stood their women-folk wearing their conventional blouses and *mompis*, which are unbecoming garments at best, and these were mostly well worn and patched, but invariably clean. Like the children, who were ranged along the front so that they could have a good view, they had pinched and drawn faces, hunger on them – as on us – having left its mark. It would be too much to claim that any of them had much beauty, but they had an honest dignity about them which commanded respect. At the end of the group stood Tanashe. He had often been my shift boss down the mine, and had shown me marked kindness. The cardboard box under my arms excited his curiosity.

'*Presento?*' he asked.

'*Presento nai!*' I said. '*Nippon rekordu!*'

A smile of approval lit up his face.

'*Nippon rekordu* No. 1!' he said.

Down in the camp some stealthy scurryings could be heard, and presently the missing Australians put in a belated appearance. They had chosen not to return through the main gate, where they would have encountered the blast of our reproach, but rather to slip through a secret hole in the fence at the back of the camp and tag on sheepishly at the lower end of the column. They offered neither explanation nor apology for their offence. Up at the front Reg Newton nursed his wrath, keeping it for a less public confrontation later. At last we set off. It was a moment to which, for over three long years, we had looked forward with inexpressible longing. It should have been a time for rejoicing. But it was nothing of that. Men seemed assailed by spectral anxieties and burdened by freedom. The thoughts of many, no doubt, turned to those who had been with us when we came to Ohama but would never leave it.

As we marched down the hill from the guard-house to the village, Johnnie was at my side, his samurai sword sticking up out of the corner of his pack. He had, he said, to keep it ready for that victory march through Cardiff. He was looking forward to *that*! Noting my pensiveness, he said: 'Wake up, *Rokuban*! You'll miss the boat!'

'Not on your life, Johnnie!' I said as, cocking our chins in the air, we marched on, our new American boots kicking up the red dust at our feet.

Just beyond the village a line of trucks was drawn up at the side of the road, waiting for us. It did not take us long to pile into them. When we arrived in Onada we discovered that, despite the delay caused by the missing Australians, we were still in good time. A cinema, which was still surprisingly undamaged, had been requisitioned for our use till it was time to go to the station to board the train. The men dumped their packs on the floor. Some of them went off for a stroll through the fire-blackened town; others too tired with the excitements of the day stretched themselves out on the floor and snoozed.

At seven p.m. came the order to shoulder our packs and march to the railway station. This we found had largely escaped damage. Our train was not yet in, though we were assured it was due in a minute or two. In the event it did not arrive till one o'clock in the morning.

Round about ten p.m. an elderly figure appeared on the platform. He looked awkward and ill at ease in what was obviously his best uniform. A little nervously, he moved from group to group exchanging a friendly word with the men. His English was not too easy to follow. During Kusimoto's term of office at Ohama acts of brutality had been committed, and it is difficult to absolve him of complicity, though they were never on the scale or of the nature of Fukuhara's. In Craig's case, he admitted to having had a hand, which must be remembered by those who since have made him out to be a blameless old man, the victim, as much as we, of the evil regime he served. But now, on the point of leaving Ohama and Onada, most of the men were happy to let bygones by bygones. So now they treated him courteously as he went on his last round, making his sad, awkward farewells. One thing at least was certain: we should never see him again – nor he us.

At last the train pulled in and we climbed on board. As it gathered speed out of the station we craned our necks out of the carriage windows to take our last look at Onada. But there was not much to see, apart, that is, from this old man who was holding up his hand in farewell, and looking utterly forlorn.

I woke up as the train was passing through a station. The rain was falling in sheets and, wriggling in rivulets down the carriage window, making it look like shot-silk. Peering through the watery glass, I saw a sign beside the track which read: H A M A D A. I tried to snatch another glance at it as it marched off swiftly into the rainstorm. Yes, no doubt, it *was* Hamada! But this town is on the *north* coast of Honshu and very far from the direct line to the east, which runs along the coast by the shores of the Inland Sea. What had taken them to send us off on this long detour? Never for a moment, of course, did my mind link it with the right reason: the southern route passed through, or very near to, Hiroshima, which was a place it was better for us to avoid!

So, through the wind and the sheeting rain, we chugged on along a coast that was majestic in its rugged wildness. Like that which we had passed on our trip to Shimonoseki, though on a far grander scale, this was scalloped into little bays and coves, sheltering in the lee of bold and precipitous headlands. Whipped into turbulence by the fierce wind from Manchuria, the seas surged towards the head-lands, scarfing their massive flanks with their shattered crests. The sea was dotted with islands, parts of the coast dissected by erosion. All of them were small, most of them were sugar-loaf in shape, and none was without its clump of *bonsai* pines on top, all gnarled and stunted and leaning away from the implacable wind. In the lee of the bolder of the headlands were little coves offering dubious anchor-ages to the junks and fishing boats which bobbed about in the swell, tugging at their moorings. At the back of each cove was a ramshackle village looking grey and sodden in the rain – not a fisherman in sight! The railway ran almost too close for comfort to the top of the cliffs, which here dropped sheer into the sea. On our way we crossed many bridges, catching glimpses as we passed of the rivers and streams beneath, every one of them roaring in high spate, their brown torrents leaping to rejoin their mother ocean.

Out of the rain there faintly emerged a small town. It lay between two wooded ridges, its houses stippling the shore of a sheet of water which at first I took to be an arm of the sea. But presently I realised it was a lake. Its station had a sign which read M A T S U E. Into the watery day, which was almost indistinguishable from a watery night, Matsue stalked off spectrally. But in this haunting, aqueous landscape, this was one name that struck a familiar chord in my memory. It was in Matsue that Lafcadio Hearn, that enigmatic adventurer, half Irish, half Greek, and wholly Japanese who started by being an American journalist and ended up as the eloquent apologist for everything in the Horned Isles (including his Japanese wife), finally pitched his roving tent. From us, as we passed it in the train, Matsue certainly curtained its best face. But, swaddled in rain like this, would not the most heavenly spot shed some of its allurement? But consider Matsue on a summer's day, with the fir trees on its ridges clasping emerald hands round its lake, and the sunlight splintering on its islets! Here, in his *tatami*-floored house, with his Japanese mistress beside him, Lafcadio Hearn had some cause to tune his rhapsodical lyre. Anyhow, we took leave of it – and him – but not of the rain; presently we were at Yonago, and after that came Akasaki, The next stop was Tottori.

As the train glided to a stop in the station, we could hear a girl's voice addressing us, amplified by a loudspeaker. She spoke in English – or, to be more precise, American – and she extended a welcome to us. 'I am Ja-pa-nese!' she said. 'I spend sixteen years Seattle. That explains my eccent. This town is Tottori: T-O-T-T-O-R-I. I am sorry it rains. It often rains in Tottori. The train stop here fifteen minute. I am sorry I do not make you better welcome. But we have hot water for you. Perhaps you hold your cup out of the window. We fill it with hot water for you!' From a vent in the roof of a waiting-room a water spout descended in a dazzling tube which, as it struck the flagstones, splintered into a thousand gems of sapphire light. Half in jest, someone suggested it would make a fine shower. No sooner said than done! In a trice shirts and trousers were peeled off and a shoal of pallid bodies was cavorting in the water spout with the abandon of porpoises. In Japan, especially in the landward areas, naked communal bathing never raises an eyebrow, but bleached, white bodies frisking under a water spout in a railway station are liable to engage the attention of the curious. On the opposite platform some Japanese travellers were waiting for their train, and they looked across in wonder as if asking themselves if this was the kind of activity the British would take for granted on their railway stations. But the gambolling was short-lived. Soon the fifteen minutes were up, and the men scrambled back into their carriages, and their clothes.

'I am sorry!' resumed the voice from the loudspeaker. 'Very little time in Tottori. Now you go home to your people. Tottori hope you have *bon voyage*. I think you get your destination tonight. I am sorry I have not been able to fully gratify you . . .' Whatever more she had to say was lost in a roar of ribaldry that made the very welkin ring. Happily the point of the bawdy would go over her head. Undismayed, she waited till the mirth had subsided. Then she began again, but this time it was in song. It was, I imagine, the kind of air that the spinners and knitters in the sun had sung in far-distant Illyria. But whatever the words meant, the sadness of the melody went straight to our hearts. '*Encore! Encore!*' chanted the men in ready chorus. So, generously responding to the appeal, she sang the chorus once more. Then she dropped her microphone and ran from her office out on to the platform, where she stood, her arms stretched high above her head, calling out lustily, 'Good-by-ee! Good-by-ee!' A plump, broad-faced girl, it would be fanciful to call her beautiful. But, as the men would be the first to admit, she had a heart of gold. Besides that she had a courage which matched, and finally conquered, their ridicule. As Tottori drifted backwards into the rain, they raised a cheer in her honour.

Through the unrelenting rain we carried on our way. With the approach of evening the weather seemed to get even worse. Little jagged-peaked hills drifted past in the mist. Driven by the wind, low clouds scurried across the paddy-fields at their base. But even conditions as appalling as these did not appear to deter the peasants with their invincible energy for work. Under shaggy capes and conical hats, both made of coconut fibre, they toiled, bent double, with their backs to the wind. At last night fell, its darkness merely deepening that of departing day, and into it faded the ghostly outlines of the watery landscape. During the night we must have passed through, or near to, the fabled city of Kyoto and the factory-crammed one of Osaka. This we took on trust, having failed to note them since we were at the time asleep. When dawn at last broke the train was skirting the Inland Sea. Now the rain had stopped and the landscape had a soft and delicate charm, very different from the foam-scarfed buttresses of the Matsue and the Tottori coasts.

About forty miles south of Osaka we arrived at the city of Wakayama, or rather the bleak and blackened residue of what had once been the city. We should never have recognised the station had it not been that that was where we stopped. We got out of our train and boarded a very primitive electric train whose benches were arranged cross-wise as in an early horse-wagonette. In this we travelled the short distance to Wakanoura, which once had been the port for Wakayama but had shared its fate. We stopped at what must once have been the station of Wakanoura and found a reception committee drawn up to welcome us. Prominent among them was a group of American nurses. Slim, trim, with little silk scarves over their gleaming hair and in white-coated and belted elegance, they looked very spruce and aseptic girls. They were the first white women we had seen for over three years; emboldened by the sight, a few of our men plucked up sufficient courage to speak to them. But long absence from female company had atrophied their faculty of easy conversation. Their nervousness proving infectious, soon the nurses too became tongue-tied, and the attempt at a friendly *causerie* swiftly petered out.

Nearby stood a brass band, playing martial airs. Their extreme youthfulness, allied with the very brief shorts and berets which they were wearing, suggested the Boy Scout troop at a village fête. They were, in fact, a band of the British Royal Marines, whose trumpets they were bravely sounding. Representing the

American Navy was a small group of sailors. About half of them were negroes, several being torpid Goliaths who took very little interest in us, seeming to regard our arrival as a tedious chore. To us in our starved condition they all looked over-fed and pampered. We were directed to the beach, which was very near. There we boarded an American LST in which we were taken over to the other side of the bay. We clambered ashore at the foot of a high headland, on top of which stood a rambling wooden building which vaguely looked like a hotel. On the beach, awaiting our arrival, was a detail of American sailors, beside whom were a few drums of petrol.

'Ah guess,' announced their leader, 'that you guys have been having it pretty rough. Forget about it now! From now on Uncle Sam'll look after you. Jes' strip down and dump all yah've gat in a pile and we'll burn the goddam lat!'

This was something we had not bargained for! Put everything we had – the negro heads, the chess-sets, the uniforms we had cherished and preserved through every vicissitude of fortune, the trifling mementos that had sustained sentimental links with home – put them in a pile and *burn* them? The man had lost his senses! Taking out some of their trophies, several of the men approached the despot and lodged a protest. But he was obdurate: 'You doan wanna keep *that* stuff?' he said contemptuously. 'Put it on the pile and burn it. It's junk! It's jes' goddam *junk!*' Saddened but obstinate, the men determined to accord this outrageous order no more than a token compliance. Most of them managed to retain the most precious of their treasures, making a contribution of less impor-tant items to the pyre which, fed by petrol, was soon blazing merrily.

Then they set off up the hill, led by a vast American sailor who was smirking happily as a band of Japanese children ran in front of him, sweeping the dust from the road with roughly-made birch brooms. The house on the hill had been transformed into a temporary clearing station. On our arrival we were ordered to strip, get under a shower, and scrub from our bodies the pollution of three years' captivity. Our old clothes having been taken from us – all protests ignored! – we were doused with DDT powder of which we had never heard, but whose virtues were acclaimed. A purple number was stamped on our chest to identify us, a pair of boots (no socks) were pushed on our feet to protect them from the floor, a towel was wrapped round our loins to cover our nakedness; and we were ushered into the main hall where the medical inspections were to be conducted. Round the walls was strung a line of little tables, and behind each sat a doctor. Lean, lank and crew-cut, they looked little better than schoolboys. Having been brought up in the sterner school of Scottish medicine, I found them profession-ally unimpressive. Functional, probably efficient, they dispensed entirely with what is called the bedside manner. Each prisoner had been given a sheaf of questionnaires from which each doctor extracted that which related to his field, asked the questions that were on it, and jotted down our answers opposite them. They stuck rigorously to their brief. Any personal question that a prisoner cared to ask was simply ignored.

Once the medical inspection was at an end we were handed over to the quar-termaster. To each man he issued a shirt, a singlet, a pair of underpants, and a pair of jeans, this somewhat unmartial apparel appearing to be the standard off-duty uniform of the US forces. Next we were taken to another room where we were invited to compose a telegram for dispatch to our next-of-kin. This being a unique occasion, it demanded some attempt at the lapidary phrase. A little uncertain about the length of the message, I asked the man in charge how many words we were allowed.

'Jes' as many as you like, son!' he said. 'Why limit yourself? After all, it's Uncle Sam who's paying for it!'

A venial deception! What in each case arrived home was a stereotyped message informing our next-of-kin that we had been released and were in American hands – which was just as effective as something more ambitious.

Riding at anchor in the middle of the bay were two splendid hospital ships, the *Consolation* and the *Sanctuary*. Each was of 18,000 tons and represented six that had recently been commissioned for the US Navy. They were protected by an awesome armada of over fifty ships. In the neck of the bay rode the mighty battleship *New Jersey*, lately the flagship of Admiral 'Bull' Halsey. In attendance upon her were an escort carrier, three US cruisers, and a New Zealand cruiser, the *Gambia*, while the bay was ringed by a formidable array of destroyers, both US and British, their men at constant battle-stations. As darkness fell, searchlight beams quartered the sky. What was feared was a possible suicide attack by *Kamikaze*-type Japanese fanatics, maddened by defeat.

We boarded the *Consolation*. She was scheduled to sail for Okinawa next day. But the hour passed with no sign of movement. The cause of the delay was a typhoon that was building up not far to the south, and threatening to pass directly over Wakanoura. To meet this threat all the ships were battened down and their moorings reinforced. Next day a wind of storm force howled over the bay. Under a sky that was black with menace *Consolation* rolled and strained heavily at her moorings. As the day wore on so did the fury of the wind increase. By nightfall, it was screaming above the ships like banshees. The night which followed was wild beyond belief. The vortex of the typhoon passed directly over the bay. Returning light revealed the extent of the damage the fleet had suffered. Four of the naval vessels had dragged their anchor and were aground. Six men were missing and an undetermined number injured. One of the injured was in a critical condition: the lurching of his vessel had unshipped an oil drum which had struck him on the back of the head and fractured his skull. If his life was to be saved, he would have to be brought to the *Consolation* for an immediate operation. At first it looked as if the attempts to transfer him to the hospital ship were doomed to failure. Indeed, there were fears that the launch which brought him might founder in the boiling seas. But, lashing themselves to the head of the *Consolation*'s gangway, two brawny sailors waited till a high wave brought the wounded man's stretcher within reach. For a critical moment the launch hung poised on the crest of the mighty wave; leaning far over, the men grabbed the stretcher and succeeded in dragging it to safety. The wounded man was taken to the operating theatre immediately and an emergency operation performed. At first his condition was reported to be critical, but by the time the vessel got to Okinawa we heard he was out of danger.

Despite the blackest of forecasts, the *Sanctuary* had kept to her schedule and sailed on the Saturday. Now we learned that she had run into the very eye of the typhoon and, much battered, was weltering 600 miles off course somewhere in the China seas. On the following morning *Consolation* put to sea. As she moved slowly and majestically down the bay she was given a tumultuous send-off by all the ships, but especially by the men of the *Gambia*. Passing by the *New Jersey* in the narrow channel, she entered the open sea, where a heavy swell was running. As long as she remained in the lee of the land she rode it well enough, but, getting out into more open water, she was roughly buffeted. I felt queasy, but anxious to witness our departure from Japan I climbed up to the top deck where I was surprised to find not a soul about. Making my way to the stern of the vessel, I stood for a while above the propellers as they churned out the white wake that marked our progress. The place was very exposed and I had to cling tightly to the rail to prevent myself being thrown to the deck or even jolted overboard in one of the staggering shudders as we were struck by a particularly heavy sea. In the distance loomed the coast of Japan, dwindling, as I watched it, to a thin black streak before finally vanishing beneath the surly, windswept sky.

Of Japan and the Japanese I had taken my last farewell. Henceforth, their ways would not be my ways. A numerous people, they were without doubt a great one, possessing vast energy and creative capacity. In less than a century they had heaved themselves from the Middle Ages to the forefront of modernity, humiliating in the process some of the world's greatest powers. But there was a dark side to their character. Splendid as had been their achievements, and striking their virtues, those whom it had been our misfortune to encounter during our three-and-a-half years of captivity had shown a remarkable aptitude in concealing the latter from us. Systematically upon defenceless prisoners they had practised a naked barbarity. For this, at the moment of parting, forgiveness was not much in evidence in my mind. In its place was an utter sense of relief, of thankfulness that at last it was all over. For us, the future held in its hand a glass in which we saw but darkly. But this much we could assume: at its worst, it was unlikely to be as bad as the past which had just ended. As the agent of our deliverance, and the symbol of our redemption, the *Consolation* could not have been better named.

THE RAVAGED ISLE

As the *Consolation* headed south the tail of the typhoon continued to blow fiercely and the sea heaved in grey sullen ridges, imparting to the vessel, with her high superstructure, a curious corkscrew motion which presently found all the ex-prisoners stretched prostrate on their bunks and lamenting their fate.

Apparently immune to the general nausea was the youthful army of doctors. Down in the bowels of the ship they now had time to scrutinise the sheaves of questionnaires they had collected in the house on the hill. Some of these suggested the existence of symptoms which might justify further exploration, and now a stream of summonses arrived for certain of the prostrates to bestir themselves and go for inspection. The invitation was also extended to embrace any who thought they had some ailment they would like to discuss. This was an opportunity which not even my extreme nausea could prevail upon me to neglect. Before leaving Java, and gazing fearfully into the future, I had consulted the RAF doctor about any suggestions he might have for prolonging survival in Japanese hands. 'Look here, McEwan,' he had said, somewhat testily, 'if you manage to get out of this mess with hardly a hair on your head, not a tooth in your mouth, blind as a bat but still breathing, then you can count yourself one of the lucky ones!'

The medical quarters astonished me with the lavish nature of their equipment. On all hands was stainless steel and sophisticated gadgetry on a scale I hardly imagined to exist on land, far less on a ship. Now in their natural element, the young fledgling doctors seemed to have added a cubit to their professional stature and to have assumed a *gravitas* I had not been aware of before. I was sent first to the dental clinic. Not since I had left Scotland four years before had my teeth been subjected to a dentist's inspection. In Japan we had, for a time, primitive toothbrushes with bristles made from slivers of bamboo, and for toothpaste a red-brick powder. By every reckoning my teeth should have been in a sorry state, but to my astonishment the dentist pronounced them to be in the same condition as they were in when I left home. The almost total absence of sugar from our diet had preserved them in better condition than during any similar period in my life. The vitamin deficiency in our diet had not, it seemed, impaired my eyesight. As for my blood pressure: 'That,' declared my youthful physician, 'is like a boy's!'

On the morning of Thursday, 20 September, we sighted Okinawa. The sky was still dark and lowering, the tattered residue of the typhoon still lingering, and under this scowling canopy all we could at first make out was a low coast as uninviting as the sky which frowned over it. On nearer approach we could see it was crescent-shaped, and in the large bay which its horns enclosed was anchored a vast armada of grey ships. Presently from the armada two huge battleships detached themselves and put to sea, passing very close to us. The *California* and the *Tennessee*, they had clearly been in the thick of the fighting. Their rusted hulls bore witness that they had been at sea for a long time, and they had suffered damage for we could see where metal patches had been attached to the super-structure to cover shell-holes. At the masthead of each vessel was something that looked like a rotating bed-spring, and was cause for much speculation on our part. The great advances in radar which the war had witnessed had passed us by. In the middle of the bay were anchored five aircraft carriers, vaster even than the sinister Japanese giant that had drifted eerily past Ohama during our last days in the camp. On their decks were serried rows of aircraft, their wings tucked into their sides like swallows resting during migration. In addition there were cruisers and destroyers, too numerous to reckon, as well as merchantmen lined up in their hundreds, all amorphous in their battle-grey.

Standing by the rail watching this awesome spectacle, I became aware of a crewman beside me. He said he had been here before and was familiar with the place. The bay, he said, was called Shuri, and it formed the eastern side of the island of Okinawa. What lay in front of us was a flat plain, but beyond it a ridge climbed into a range of hills that ran at right angles to the shore. These hills, said the crewman, were honeycombed with caves and tunnels, and it was in these that the Japs had made their last stand, fighting till only a handful of men remained alive in each unit. Then the survivors committed suicide, one of their number pulling the pin from a grenade he had kept for this purpose.

Forming the shore along the middle of the bay was a low cliff which seemed to drop sheer into the sea. Along this had been built an airstrip at whose northern end in particular, but also at intervals along its length, were huge piles of wrecked aircraft – Japanese, we hoped. From the strip a constant stream of aircraft, for the most part transport planes, were either landing or taking off. As at Wakanoura, the Americans were exercising a constant vigilance, an umbrella of fighters keeping up a continuous patrol above the ships in the bay. As we entered, a couple of helicopters were going on their rounds, seemingly being used as a kind of postal service delivering messages to the ships. As a means of communication it was certainly speedy and practical, and was also quite new to us.

Scarcely had we dropped anchor when a launch drew alongside and a crowd of officials boarded our vessel. Presently the air was rife with rumours. The *Queen Mary* was in Okinawan waters and would embark all British ex-prisoners. We should be taken on board an aircraft carrier and return by way of the Panama Canal in time to take part in a Victory Parade planned for New York on 21 October. Both these were wrong: the *Consolation* would herself sail round the south end of Okinawa to a place called Naha, where we should be transferred to waiting British warships for eventual repatriation. The last suggestion had the advantage that it was easily confirmed: the prisoners would have to be got off the *Consolation* forthwith – there would be nothing left on board to feed them. After serving 3,000 meals to 1,200 personnel, the chow queues, it was ominously announced, were as long as ever! Much hurried coming and going made it obvious that urgent steps were being put in train to resolve our problems. But for a further two days we remained on board, by which time famine must have stared us in the face. Then a sudden announcement dispelled the torpor: trans-shipment was to start at two p.m., and had to be completed that afternoon.

Speed and precision marked our departure from the vessel. Given a medical-card and a tally, each man had to pass through checks and counter-checks before being allowed to leave the ship. First to leave were the men, followed, at about five p.m. by the officers. Moored to the foot of the gangway was a landing craft into which we climbed. Lining the rails above our heads were the nurses, and behind them the doctors and the crewmen. Under a forest of waving hands, our hearts filled with thankfulness, we took our leave of the hospital ship. Leaning far out over the rail, her flaxen hair streaming in the wind, and golden-limbed as Aphrodite herself, was one of the nurses, seemingly on the point of taking to the element to which her angelic form declared her native. '*Bon voyage! Bon voyage!*' she called to some fortunate object of favour in the landing craft beneath her. But at that moment, avid for recognition, what harm was there in each imagining that the words were addressed to himself in particular? From the *Consolation* the landing craft then set off, zig-zagging among the thronged and towering grey shapes till it came to a large assault vessel which was called the *SS Haskell*, her decks still tightly packed with smaller landing craft. Just ahead of her lay another transport, and a little ahead again a destroyer which was to act as escort to the small convoy. Expectant, we climbed up the gangway and handed over our tabs and medical sheets to the waiting orderlies, who showed us to our quarters. No sooner was embarkation completed than the loud throb of the engines heralded our departure to sea. Hurriedly we climbed back up on deck to have a last look at Okinawa.

Here in this grey bay, now so still, and on the island beyond had been fought a bloody battle of savage intensity. Selling their lives as dearly as they could, the Japanese had fought fanatically to extermination. Yet here we were, battered and broken survivors of a brutal captivity, who a few months earlier would not have put their chances very high, still alive and sailing out to freedom! And on that dark island now lay thousands, taken in the pride of their youth. Above the low western hills, as we sailed away, the evening erupted in a banded glory of crimson, amber and gold. Nearer, and less exuberant, was a once-white shape, now gleaming gold in the sunset splendour, in which for the first time for over three years we had tasted the sweets of human kindness. One thing our restless curiosity had overlooked: this splendid ship and her five sisters had been built to accommodate the heavy casualties anticipated in the final assault on the Japanese heartland.

On the *Haskell* careful provision had been made that our diet should combine the maximum of nutrition with the minimum of demands on our stomachs, which had been weakened by long years of starvation. But to satisfy our voracious appetites even the ration of 5,000 calories a day seemed impotent, and the crisis which on the *Consolation* had been held at bay only by our speedy arrival in Okinawa threatened to renew its assault long before we could make Manila, whither we were now bound.

'Attention all personnel!' came the agitated voice of the Messing Officer over the Tannoy. 'We've issued to the PoWs on board 200 more meals than for the *entire complement* of the ship, and the chow queues are still as long as ever. Steady on, boys! Steady on! At this rate we'll be cleaned out long before we get to port!'

Two days' sailing brought us, late in the afternoon, in sight of the west coast of Luzon, the most northerly of the Philippine islands. Behind and parallel to it rose the magnificent mountains of Merivales. A wild tangle of ridges, their topmost summits were lost in the saffron and cerise cloud-banks which crowned them. At length, closing the coast of Bataan, the south-pointing peninsula which guards the entrance to Manila harbour, we made our way through the narrow strait of Corregidor. In mid-channel rose the fabled fortress. As we passed close to its northern side, it hid from us its sterner aspect. Now stretched before us was the vast and magnificent harbour at whose gate stands Corregidor as sentinel, and from this to the city of Manila itself is a distance of no fewer than twenty miles. We dropped anchor just off the naval base of Cavite, which lies just to the south of Manila, being almost a suburb of the city. Hopes of immediate disembarkation were dashed by the announcement that not before next morning would we be allowed ashore, when we would be dispatched to various camps for separation into our different nationality groups in readiness for repatriation. Among all the cities of East Asia, Manila enjoys a reputation for the exuberant splendour of its sunsets, and, as if in consolation for our being kept on board, the one which followed displayed an extravagant beauty and grandeur. Behind the towering ridges of Merivales in the west the clouds began to boil up as if tossed from an erupting crater – crimson, yellow, lurid and ever-changing – while beneath them the mountains were curiously selvaged in the brightest indigo.

Next morning was Wednesday, 26 September. Presently the *Haskell* pulled alongside a wharf which was encumbered with the débris of war, and surrounded by sunken wrecks. Their walls now roofless, the harbour installations were in total ruins, windowed by bursting shells or laid flat. The scale of the destruction left us baffled, nothing having come to our ears about Manila's having endured a savage siege. Nor had we heard of the barbarous ordeal that had been ordained for its citizens by the fanatic and suicidal Japanese naval garrison that had decided to sell their lives as dearly as possible among its ruins. Now disembarkation began. At the foot of the gangway we found an American girl waiting for us. On her arm was a basket filled with various brands of cigarettes, from which she invited us to make our choice. Though svelte and trim, she, like the *Consolation* nurses, was dressed in the uniform of the American GI: khaki shirt, trousers rolled up to the calf, very heavy boots, and a foragecap. Yet even this garb, designed to quench the last glimmer of femininity, failed, surprisingly, to dim the brightness of the eye or the smile that lit her cheek.

We lined up on the wharf, but our departure was delayed because another disembarkation was in progress from another vessel which had just docked at the other side of the wharf. This proved to be a regiment of combat troops. All the long road from New Guinea they had fought their way to Manila. Unlike ours, their uniforms were of deep-green denim, in this respect similar to those of the Dutch, though they differed from them in being liberally splotched with black and brown camouflage markings. Their faces appeared to be almost as green as their uniforms and at first I imagined they had been dyed for concealment in the jungle. But later I learned that this disguise was adventitious, a side-effect of the mepacrine they had been taking as a prophylactic against malaria; quinine, the usual antidote, whose source of supply was in Java, was denied us by the Japanese seizure of the island. This bizarre facial colouring added to their otherwise ferocious and warlike appearance. Broad of shoulder, lean in the flanks, long in the legs, and armed to the teeth, they were undoubtedly the most formidable fighting men I had ever encountered. This unexpected meeting was the occasion of a sentiment I never dreamed I would experience: I felt sympathy for the Japanese who had had to face them. We watched the battle-hardened warriors depart, gazed at in wonder by the wharf coolies. Then we climbed into the trucks which had been drawn up, and in them drove through the ruined city to the transit camp.

A huge and sprawling tented encampment, it was situated on a low plain which lay to the south of the city and stretched to the foothills of the mountain ranges which sheltered it on the east. Inevitably much of it was permanently awash, and it was criss-crossed by an elaborate system of duck-boards, to step off which in many places, involved plunging one's feet in a quagmire. It did not give the impression of being a very healthy place.

On their arrival the British contingent from the *Haskell* was assigned to the care of an Australian unit who issued us with more clothes, in particular some fine woollen sweaters which would have been regarded as a God-send in the Ohama camp winters, but were less practical in the clammy, sweltering heat of Manila. We were also given an advance against pay of forty pesos, which was the equivalent of about five pounds, with this fortune in our pockets we descended upon the PX stores whose shelves displayed an array of luxuries beyond the miser's dream. Soon from our pockets the last peso vanished and, clutching our spoils, we retired for their contemplation to our tents. But the lack of pesos did not seem to present any serious obstacle to the urge for acquisition on the part of some of the ex-prisoners, among the most insatiable of these carefree buccaneers proving to be the Indonesians. The American authorities had generously set aside a consignment of watches for purchase, at a reduced rate, by officers, whose own had been confiscated by the Japanese. But long before the needs of the officers had been met, the supply ran out. When, suspicion having been aroused by rumour, the haversacks of some of the departing Indonesians were searched, it was found that a goodly number of the missing watches had managed to be secreted in them. In addition one man, stopped while boarding a boat for Java, was found to be carrying twenty-five boots, while another's loot amounted to thirty towels and a pile of blankets.

The very thorough medical examinations to which we had been subjected on the *Consolation* were declared by the Australians to be no concern of theirs, and we were called upon to go through the whole painful process again. Now we were brusquely to learn that, in stark contrast with the ministering angels on the hospital-ship, nurses nurtured in the harsher academies of the Antipodes are a very no-nonsense breed. Jabbing a thick syringe into a cringing arm, they would silence all protest with a curt 'What's all this noise about? It's not as if we were going to *murder* you! After all, this is no more than a pin-prick. So just you pipe down!' So, submitting to the assault upon our persons, we piped down and said not a word while we were weighed, measured, had our temperature taken, and indefatigably and relentlessly vermifuged. At length, overtaken with nausea and groggy at the knees, we tottered from the medical tents into the humid twilight to seek solace for our spirit in the camp theatre.

The theatre had been dug out of one of the few hillocks in the area and took the form of a Greek amphitheatre. While the stage was covered, its seating was open to the sky. It was called the Punchbowl, or the Bowl for short. By the time we arrived, our blood thickened and impeded by the serums by which it had been invaded, a girl was on the stage. A pert sprig of American maidenhood, she sang, with great verve and charm, two songs that were new to us: *The Yankee Dollar* and *Coca Cola*. To the appeal of such a limber elf, who so base as not to yield! Under her spell we forgot the Australian nurses with their lethal syringes. Our appetite whetted with this tasty *hors-d'oeuvre*, we returned on the following evening, avid for more. There now sauntered on to the stage a gangling lad with a shock of yellow hair. Very dexterous as a raconteur, and inimitable as a mimic, he had a hilarious way of getting his tongue round comic phrases at break-neck speed. They said his name was Danny Kaye, but this meant nothing at all to us. Though an amateur, his companion was no less accomplished, but in a very different genre. He was called Leo Durocher and was the manager of some American baseball team. His forte lay in telling anecdotes about famous football players, all in an argot well-nigh unintelligible to anyone not born in the Bronx. The essence of his art lay in describing, with great suspense, situations of monumental embarrassment to which, if one took his word, baseball players were particularly susceptible, and from which they were able to extricate themselves by a unique blend of incorruptible innocence and exalted effrontery.

With this unbridled vivacity and inspired mummery, the show that was to be presented on the following night presented a bleak and melancholy contrast. Drawn from unknown retreats in the shattered city, a troupe had been collected, all of whom had been interned by the Japanese in the prison of San Tomas. Their compère turned out, surprisingly, to be a Scots girl, though how she came to be in Manila, or had been allocated this role. I was afforded no opportunity to discover. One of the singers was Chinese, and an acrobat was a mere child. Some of the singing and dancing assumed a Spanish flavour, while before the war the pianist had been a professor of music in Manila University. But this was not what the GI audience wanted, their tastes being earthy; and they showed little patience with anything that rose above this level. Not only did they withhold their acclaim, or even tolerance, but they made their restlessness felt, and their malaise inevitably communicated itself to the artistes. Mercifully some thunderclouds, piling up in the heavens, threatened to explode in a deluge, and this presented a pretext for the GIs to scurry for shelter, their flight sparing the performers an embarrassing exodus later. Might not imagination have extended to these sad sufferers and survivors from a barbarous captivity a measure of charity?

One afternoon all personnel were urgently summoned to attend in the large marquee, which served as a general assembly point for the camp. No reason was advanced for the summons apart from the cryptic aside that we were to be addressed by a *very important* person, whom we should be told about in good time. As to the identity of this visitor speculation ranged widely. Who else could it be, claimed some, than General MacArthur himself? This was stoutly disputed by others, declaring that the General was much too embroiled in more important matters. Another group whispered a secret that had just been confided to them: it was to be none other than Shirley Temple! On arriving at the marquee we found it packed with expectant prisoners, a few GIs struggling desperately to keep clear a small space just beside the back entrance. At length two American Generals entered, stony-faced and lanky men, who, apart from their caps and their shoulder-tabs, looked very much like the normal GIs. Accompanying them was a chunky, smiling British admiral. By this time few had any difficulty in recognising Sir Bruce Fraser, whose fame had preceded him, having to his toll added the *Scharnhorst* off the Norwegian coast. In the wake of this intimidating vanguard, and quite dwarfed by them, came a very self-possessed lady. Though dressed in a khaki uniform, she still contrived to retain a chic and soignée look.

At first it appeared that the Generals took for granted that she would address the troops from the humble rostrum of the earthen floor. But this she resolutely declined to do. How, she asked imperiously, were the men to see her if she occupied this lowly station? With fingers assertive and fluttering, she indicated a steel-drum that was lying on its side near the canvas, insisting that it be up-ended for her use. At her bidding the Generals were hard put to it to conceal their embarrassment, but the GIs hoisted the drum on to its end and, the Generals offering her a noticeably less than ardent hand, she clambered up on top. It would be to palter with the truth to maintain that her address brought much solace to her listeners. Witty, brittle, embracing some salty badinage when it suited her purpose, her talk borrowed too much from the manner of the music hall to satisfy all of her listeners. She said that she, as all British people, was shocked at the sordid tales she had heard of Japanese brutality to prisoners. She was flying from camp to camp in the Far East to assure the men that they were very much in the minds and hearts of their people at home, and to extend to them a word of comfort and cheer. It would not be long till we were out of the Far East and united again with our families. The performance at an end, she held out her hands to the Generals, the fingers still regal and a-flutter as before. With obvious lack of zeal, especially in full view of the troops, the Generals eased her descent from her lofty perch. Offering no assistance, Admiral Fraser merely stood smiling in the background. It was Lady Mountbatten, wife of the Supreme Commander in South-East Asia. What did we make of the show; lonely, battered men, so long denied the company of women? In truth, most of those around me felt dispirited, denied a contact they yearned for: the feminine touch, something that recalled home and the family and the simple and enduring things in life. But Lady Mountbatten's life amid the glitter and whirl of high society did not provide her with the qualifications to discharge this role.

That same afternoon I ran into Cpl Smith. In the kitchen at Ohama he had worked as a cook. He was a very capable man who had perfected a remarkable capacity for the acquisition and secret dissemination of news. Very little of importance ever escaped his prying eye. Now it was clear he had some important tidings to impart. 'Do you know anything about the background of the Hurricane pilot?' he asked, giving the man's name. I told him I had last seen him with his box of butterflies strapped on his back as we left Ohama. In fact I knew quite a lot about him, he himself having given me the information. Before the war he had worked with his father, who was a widower, on their farm near Totnes in Devon. But once the dogs of war were unleashed, he wanted to be with them, his ambition to become a fighter pilot. Eventually he succeeded in being released from his reserved farming job and joined the RAF. He had gone for training to Scone, in Scotland, and it was while he was there that he had fallen in love with, and become engaged to, a Scots girl, a farmer's daughter from Dunning. They had planned an early marriage but the Japanese war had forced the postponement of their plans, and he was posted out hurriedly to Singapore. While in captivity in Ohama he had received several postcards from the girl, all expressive of enduring fidelity.

'He's heard from her again,' volunteered Cpl Smith, and I thought I detected an ominous note in his voice.

'Not bad news?' I asked, responding to his dispirited tones.

'He's just got a telegram! I'll tell you what's in it. You can then make up your own mind. "You must not call me darling any more. You must call me mother. I've married your father!"'

Then, turning on his heels, he walked away.

Manila had long enjoyed a resplendent reputation as the Pearl of the Orient. Now it had become a city of recent and overwhelming calamity. Each one visiting these bleak ruins was presented with a horrific picture of what blind and fanatic self-sacrifice is capable of, given access to the weapons which modern technology has placed irretrievably within its grasp. In melancholy pilgrimage we visited the ancient fortifications which had been built by the Spaniards and called the Citadel. In its warren of tunnels and caverns the Japanese naval garrison, having committed unmentionable atrocities against the native population, retreated to sell their lives at a bloody and bitter price. From a murky sky, as if in accord with our dejection, the rain poured in torrents, accompanying our progress to the Chinese cemetery, its tenantry now tragically inflated. Sadly we walked the length of the Lunette, or what was recognisable as the Lunette, once the resort of fashion and beauty. From the dereliction fashion and beauty had fled, their place now usurped by desolation and the scars of conflict. For a time, the deluge still persisting, we searched for the old Spanish walled town, the Intra Muros, which had once been the heart of Manila. But no evidence survived to tell us where it was, or indeed ever had been. Sated with catastrophe, we turned our steps towards our tents in the hutted camp.

It was at this moment, when the candle of hope flickered wanly, that Fate decided to strike its cruellest blow. Some of the men in the *Consolation* had, it seemed, been considered by the Americans to be in no fit shape to undertake the journey to Manila by sea, and arrangements had been made to fly them out from Okinawa. But no regular troop-transports had been available for the job, and in consequence some ordinary large bombers had been requisitioned. These were not designed for the transport of men, and wooden platforms had been constructed and fitted into the bomb racks to provide a temporary floor on which the men were packed as tightly as possible. But one of the platforms had not been securely fitted into its rack, and, somewhere between Okinawa and Manila, it broke from its moorings, detached itself from the aircraft, and carried its load of men to their death in the sea beneath.

During my brief stay in Manila my overriding ambition was to visit Corregidor, but the fortress was over twenty miles distant from the city, the ferry-launch was erratic, and at the outset Fate seemed bent upon thwarting my purpose.

My first attempt took me as far as the wharf but faltered there when the coxswain refused to cast off as a storm was brewing. My second foundered on the outskirts of the camp when a bulldozer, slithering off the road into a ditch, effectively blocked all progress. After some delay my truck managed to edge round the vehicle in time to reach the wharf and find the launch gone. Only at the third attempt did I succeed in boarding the launch, by now crowded, and we cast off. We had not gone far when we saw a motorised barge bearing down upon us. Neither coxswain took any evasive action and the two vessels simply charged into one another. Under the severe impact the barge tilted over, whereas our launch remained upright though rocking violently. In an instant six of the seven occupants of the barge were decanted into the water. Very strong currents were running, and in their grip the men were swiftly carried away from us, all in serious danger of drowning. One of them kept calling out desperately, 'Help me! Help me! I can't swim. Somebody jump in!' While alive to his peril, no one in the launch was prepared to follow his advice and, in all probability, share his fate. By this time the sole remaining occupant of the barge, retrieving a measure of his scattered wits, began to toss boards overboard to those in the water. Our strident non-swimmer, managing to grasp one of these, clung on for dear life. Now the coxswain of our launch was spurred into action. While he wheeled his craft round in a tight circle, the men were dragged from the water. During the operation those on the launch kept up a clamour of admonition, most of it contradictory, and all of it futile. At length the last man in the water was dragged back on board. Soaking and shaking with shock, they looked a sorry lot. On our craft was an Australian doctor who examined the rescued in turn. None, he pronounced, had suffered serious injury, apart from the non-swimmer, who was waterlogged, though he should dry out in time.

Just south of Corregidor itself was a small island called Caballo, and further out in the channel a very low-lying rock called Drum. It had been razed to near the waterline, and on it had been built a concrete fort which resembled a battleship. It had been fortified by the Americans with very heavy guns. We had with us an American who said he had taken part in the recapture of the island from the Japanese. He told us that deep under the sea its rock was honeycombed with tunnels and galleries which had first been constructed by the Americans, but later extended by the Japanese. From these subterranean caverns the Japanese garrison decided that not one of them would be evicted alive. At first the problem of how to eject them defeated the ingenuity of the Americans. But in the end success was achieved by resort to a simple stratagem. Running, under cover of darkness, an oil tanker within reach of the island, they led from it a pipe to an air vent. In this way they were able to pump 2,500 gallons of gasoline into the submarine tunnels. They then ignited the fuel by means of phosphorus shells. In the ensuing holocaust not every Japanese perished. A week later, on exploring a hitherto inaccessible tunnel, a patrol of Americans found at its end an enemy. Still alive, he put up some resistance but was promptly dispatched.

On our nearer approach to the fortress I realised how wide of the mark had been my assessment, made from the deck of the *Consolation*, of its strength. Now looming up from the water ahead of us, its vertical rock walls conveyed an impression of impregnability. No sooner had our launch tied up at the jetty on the north shore than I disembarked. My first objective was the entrance to the main tunnel, which was then called Malinta Tunnel but has since been renamed Wainwright Tunnel in honour of the heroic resistance of the garrison under his command to the initial Japanese attack. It had witnessed some of the fiercest and most bloody of the fighting, both during the initial Japanese assault and, in turn, when it was recaptured by the Americans. Driven in zig-zags through the heart of the rock, it was flanked on both sides by an intricate herring-bone system of laterals which housed the control centres of the defence. All lighting had, of course, been destroyed in the fighting, and those who ventured to explore its passageways had to rely for illumination on candles. Both walls and ceiling were blackened with soot from the fires. In great heaps on the floor were stacked huge slabs of concrete, dislodged from the roof by explosions. Progress was difficult. In the flickering light from my candle, almost extinguished in the strong draughts, it looked an eerie and sinister place, much like a corridor in Hell, which it recently had been. From the floor I picked up several pages from a Japanese manual on firearms, illustrated with diagrams. I also collected some white limestone pebbles which I took home as souvenirs. Eventually, hot and dirty from my explorations, and after much scrambling over tumbled masonry, I regained the entrance.

In search of fresh air and coolness I set off to climb to the citadel, which occupied the summit of the rock. It was called Topside. There I found a row of barrack quarters, enormously long. Like everything else on the island it was roofless and its walls were raggedly windowed by shells. In this uninviting environment some GIs and nurses had set up a dubious ménage. It is not hard to understand their resentment at this unannounced invasion of their privacy by a prying Briton. Less easy to condone was the vigour and saltiness of the language in which they gave utterance to their disapproval. But they might have dispensed with all fear of unwanted publicity from me. It was wartime Corregidor that invited my curiosity, not amatory frolicking. Where I was so obviously unwanted, I had no disposition to linger. Taking my leave of them, I set off for the jetty where I found the launch, on the point of casting off; boarding it, I was soon on my way homewards, my ears lulled by the chugging of its engine. But Fate was to have its final fling. I was being driven back to camp in a military transport when, at a crossroads, a heavy truck, its driver probably drunk and ignoring other traffic, thundered across our path and missed us by inches. Jabbing his foot hard on the brake, my driver managed to stop his vehicle on the very brink of destruction.

I returned to find the camp rife with rumours. In most the *Laetitia* seemed to be involved. Other possibilities extended to Australia and America. The escort carrier *Speaker* had already left for Sydney, taking with her Reg Newton, Jack Hands, Ray Parkin and the rest of the Australians from Ohama. Almost all the remaining British troops were due, it was reported, to sail in the aircraft carrier *Glory*, destined for Vancouver. I had been bereft of companions, and companionship, and felt forlorn. This being Sunday, and in search of consolation, I attended the camp church where I found a packed congregation of American servicemen, only two seats remaining unoccupied. One of these I secured, the other being taken later by a girl, a latecomer and as far as I could see the only female in church. Utterly without self-consciousness, and very sweetly, her clear treble voice mingled and contrasted with the lusty diapason of her companions. In comparison with the restrained formality of the Anglican liturgy which I had experienced since joining the RAF, I found this American service spoke with a freshness and immediacy I had missed. Restored in spirit, I made my way to my deserted tent, a little less at odds with fate.

At 1.30 next afternoon a messenger arrived at my tent. I had expressed a preference for a return by way of the United States, and he now told me that my name had been put down for the draft for the *SS Marine Shark*, which was due to sail on the following day for San Francisco. Next morning the sky was inky-black, and from it descended a deluge. Despite this, their heads held high, the *Glory* party set off for embarkation, trudging through the rain. But with unexpected suddenness, the arrival of noon saw the departure of the rain, and when the American party set off above them arched a cloudless sky. On arriving at the docks we found the *Marine Shark*, a grey shape with a raked snout and a striped hull, rather like the submarine predator who was its namesake. As the evening closed in, we went on board. The day was 9 October.

HOMEWARD BOUND

The 3,000 service personnel who now embarked on the *Marine Shark* crowded its bunks to overflowing. Among the most noteworthy of these were seventy-eight nurses, most of whom had spent the last twenty-five months in continuous service alongside the men, sharing with them the dangers of the forward combat zone on the long and arduous march from New Guinea to Luzon. As is taken for granted in the democratic American Army, they were treated very much as fighting troops, wearing the same big boots and drill trousers as the GIs with no concessions made at all to feminine comeliness. The hard jungle life had provided these lean and trim Amazons with steel-hard limbs, but failed to extinguish their natural gaiety. They were, incidentally, and for the most part, very pretty.

It was not till eight o'clock next morning that the vessel pulled out from the wharf, and then only to tie up at a buoy in the harbour to await refuelling. About noon she cast off, moving very slowly and gracefully down the bay. In the early evening we sailed through the Boca Grande, or large channel, which separates Corregidor and Caballo from the coast of Luzon, lying to the south of them, and by the time dusk was thickening we were well down in the China Sea. In the twilight we stood about on deck and watched the fortress rock retreat and dwindle to a yellow dot, and fade slowly from sight, quite dwarfed by the dark masses of Bataan and Mt Merivales behind it. All the way south we continued to hug the Balayan coast, and by the time we entered the approaches to the Mindoro Strait, night was already spreading her cloak about the shoulders of the Luzon mountains.

Next morning the heat and humidity were oppressive, making our clothes cling to our bodies. Reluctant to disperse, the sweat collected clammily on our skin. Forsaking their cabins, men climbed to the upper deck in search of coolness but were confronted there by an air more stifling still. The cause of the trouble, we were told, was the numerous islands which clutter the channel and prevent the free passage of the sea breezes. Once we got out into the open sea, and lost sight of land, the heat and humidity would simply vanish. About noon our vessel entered the narrow channel of the San Bernardino Strait, which separates Luzon from Samar, the island lying immediately to its south-east. At its narrowest point, which is near its eastern end, the rocks on both sides approach so close together that it is surprising a large vessel can effect the passage at all.

As I stood at the rail watching closely this intricate piece of navigation, one of the ship's officers approached me. He was a very typical young American, affable and friendly with a round, smiling face and, like many of his countrymen, a frame that was notable for its length and leanness. Among all the places on the oceans of the earth I was then, he said, at one of the most remarkable. Those mountains we were looking at continued straight down into the abyss to a depth that exceeded even the height of Everest. To the uninitiated it might come as a surprise that the deepest trough on the earth's crust should occur not in mid-ocean but here near its rim. Down at the other end of Samar, he went on, was the Surigao Strait, through which Magellan sailed when he arrived in the Philippines. He was murdered on a little island called Mactan, which lies off the east coast of Cebu, and not very far from where we were standing. Though his voyage had attracted great interest and renown, the trouble which had led to his murder never found its way into the history books, though an honest assessment of the facts made it clear that some of his sailors had been making too free with the native women. Just beyond the mouth of the strait through which we were sailing was the place where Anson had lain in wait for the Spanish galleon with all her treasure from Acapulco. The action was brisk, if brief, and he captured the vessel with her cargo intact. But, the officer went on, the most remarkable feat of all had taken place here not so very long ago, and the world would not have had time to hear about it. During the battle for the Leyte Gulf the Japanese had sailed their grand fleet through this narrow channel in the dead of night with all navigational beacons extinguished, their plan to pounce from an unexpected quarter on the American troopships lying in the gulf. When this plan went awry, they promptly turned about and sailed back again by the same route in the middle of the night. In the long annals of the sea one would have to search diligently to find a feat of seamanship to match this.

Once the San Bernardino Strait was well behind us, we ran into the monsoon; and soon our vessel was weltering in a jolting swell. To add to our troubles a thick fog came down to blot out the sea. To the constant blaring of the ship's siren we made very slow progress. Most of the Ohama men became very sick. Stretched out and retching in our stifling bunks, we could derive scant comfort from the announcement over the Tannoy that our course had been altered to take us well south of the normal route; they wanted to spare us the risk of contracting pneumonia after being cooped up for years in Japanese prison camps.

A couple of days of this relentless rocking in the queasy cradle of the monsoon-swell brought us within sight of our first coral atoll. This turned out to be Ulithi, which is the most northerly group of the Caroline Archipelago. It is the experience of most on first seeing a coral atoll to be struck by the incredible depression of the reefs of which it is composed. So low, indeed, did Ulithi appear from our ship that a modest wave sweeping over it might well have carried everything on it out to sea, including the palm trees, which seemed to have their bases in the water. The atoll, however, enclosed a deep lagoon which formed a fine anchorage and it was here that some of the American forces for the invasion of the Philippines had assembled. Its important role seemed not to have diminished, for the lagoon was crowded with shipping, all grey and amorphous, which made it difficult to distinguish its features. Of the second atoll we were to encounter we saw even less for we were to pass it in the dead of night, the only evidence of its presence a solitary yellow light, gleaming across the dark sea. Endowed with a mellifluous name, Eniwetok was the most northerly of the Marshall Archipelago. How sad that a place so lonely and remote was to be forever associated in the mind of men with sinister events. But that dark fate had not as yet overtaken it.

The three days which followed our departure from Eniwetok were to be a time of great tribulation for the men, the continuing heat and humidity giving rise to a general outbreak of prickly heat. Though an irritating rather than a disabling disease, this causes constant itching and can deny its victims any rest. Once we crossed the dateline the vessel was forced to reduce speed drastically, thus losing the artificial breeze which her movement created. The cause of this reduction was, we were told, that a bearing in the engine was overheating, to which, with surprising frankness, was added the news that this was due not to mechanical but to human failure, its nature not specified. At the end of a further two days at this reduced speed the engine failed completely, and for twelve hours we were hove to. By that time the engine was sufficiently patched up to allow a resumption of the voyage. But it was limping as a cripple that, at length and just before dawn, we caught our first glimpse of the soaring mountain ridge of Oahu, blotting out the distant sky, a purple massiveness which heaved itself into the pale, amethystine heavens.

PEARL HARBOR

Pearl Harbor oddly belies the reputation which the events of 7 December 1941 have identified with infamy. From the sea a long waterway, indistinguishable from a canal, runs into the plain which forms the southern part of the island. After a time it forks into two arms to form a rough capital Y. But for a treacherous attack, nowhere could be more apt. The high mountain ridge provided a screen for raiders approaching from the north. The very narrowness of its waters restricted the movement of large capital ships, especially taking evasive action under attack, and once they had discharged their torpedoes and bombs the pilots had before them the open sea over which to escape.

From that disastrous Sunday morning much evidence of its consequences was distressingly obvious. But one thing had seen a marked change: from Pearl Harbor the last vestige of complacency had been exorcised. Warily above the basin circled a patrol of fighter aircraft, and from Hickham Field, which is just beside the anchorage, came the unbroken roar of heavy transport planes and bombers taking off or landing. Assembled on the wharf to greet our arrival were three brass bands, their repertoire proclaiming their New World origins. Two of them played strident American jazz, while the third restricted itself to the homelier melodies of the American negro. Not that it mattered much since no one on the ship paid the slightest attention to their performance: what shipboard ears hankered after was the lilting Alohas of Polynesian maidens, their feet beating out hypnotic rhythms on some palm-fringed beach. Beaches there were a-plenty, and at no great distance, but their sands were not to be sullied by feet of ours. To the east loomed the familiar sugar-loaf rock of Diamond Head, and at its foot, strewn with the detritus of countless welcoming *leis*, was Waikiki Beach. But that was to remain a haven unvisited, glimpsed only in the mind's eye from the confining rail of the *Marine Shark*.

One can, of course, sympathise with the Americans. To have unleashed, footless and feckless, on this Eden a horde of emotion-starved men would have led to a diaspora which even the most ardent military police would have been powerless to recall. So the golden-skinned temptresses in their swaying *ridis* were to remain, not only beyond our grasp but beyond our ken. Some concessions were, however, made, and not all to the approval of those to whom they were denied. What were called 'heads of services' were granted special privileges, among those favoured few being Paul Wyrill, who had been the senior British officer at Ohama. Along with a few others he was escorted ashore by a liaison officer where he was dined, wined and fêted, to be returned in due course to the ship in a blissful and befuddled coma. Numbered too, and with less justification, among the elect was Dr Perilman, an American who in Ohama had functioned amorphously in the shadow of Dr Ploegman, highly skilled in tropical medicine, from Java. Along with a companion called Gordon, who possessed the name but not the Highland physiognomy to go with it, Perilman went ashore in grand style.

Having been driven through Honolulu to Waikiki Beach, they were there entertained (they later cryptically hinted) to unimagined delights, prepared for their reception.

Now we were to learn that on board the *Marine Shark* was a man whose fame outshone all others, having among the American public been allotted a legendary role. During the first desperate American resistance on the Bataan peninsula before the withdrawal into Corregidor he had, single-handed, performed feats of unexampled gallantry against tremendous odds, earning the sobriquet of 'The One-Man Army of Bataan'. Three subsequent years spent languishing in a Japanese prison camp, mostly in Manchuria, had done nothing to sully his resplendent reputation. When the time came for this fabled figure to disembark, so widely had his fame spread that the vessel's rails were crowded with watchers, all eager to catch a glimpse of him. When at last he did appear, I was disappointed to find that his features fell short of his fame. Thick-set and low in stature, he had eyes that darted and were distrustful, and his look was generally sullen. He was, however, not alone, for on one of his arms hung an American nurse, a very pretty girl whom repute and contiguity had rendered submissive to his charms. They spent the rest of the day ashore. When they returned the girl, obviously overjoyed, grasped in one arm a gigantic teddy bear while on a finger of the other hand, which she held aloft for all to see, glistened an engagement ring, newly purchased.

Later I retreated to the top deck where in the thickening purple of evening, I sat for a time in a deckchair. Gradually the breeze, which all day long had blown down gently from the mountains, died away and the western sky kindled with lambent flame, crimson and gold, before melting into the darkening purple of the night. Along the cobalt ridges where the sugar plantations nudged the lower skirts of the forest, the lights of the villages broke out, twinkling like emergent stars, at times to be confused with them.

Next day I lingered on the upper deck, basking in the warm but not oppressive sunshine. Presently it was announced that repairs to the ship's engines had been satisfactorily completed and we would sail on schedule. Precisely at the appointed hour the gangway was hauled up; the clatter of hawsers being dropped on the quayside cobbles mingled dissonantly with the chiming of a clock on a nearby godown, and slowly the *Marine Shark* moved out into the channel. Once clear of the docks, she set her course to the east, and almost immediately, like a mettled horse given rein, the engines began to race and the vessel increased speed alarmingly. As we passed swiftly by, I cast a lingering look towards the golden sickle of Waikiki Beach. Its denial to us possibly enhanced the yearning with which we saw it retreat. High on the mountain behind us, though the night had not yet come, the village lamps began winking into life and stringing silver cobwebs about the slopes. Presently we were abreast of Diamond Head, close by on our port quarter, a bold promontory thrusting its face eastwards towards the New World, to which we were consigned. Rounding its point, we felt the wind suddenly freshen; still sailing at great speed, we headed into the rising sea.

ON THE THOROUGHFARE FOR FREEDOM

For nine more hours, till about two in the morning, the *Marine Shark* continued on her headlong, unstoppable career. Then the sullen thump-thump-thump of the engines assumed a rasping, drumming throb, and then suddenly stopped altogether, and all was silent. Helplessly, without power, we drifted on the ocean. Not till six in the morning did the engineers succeed in restoring a measure of power to the vessel, but from now on we could achieve no more than our pre-Hawaiian crawl.

Bit by bit, the explanation for these alarming events was leaked to us. The 3rd Engineer, who had been Officer-on-Watch in the engine room, had fallen asleep, drunk, and he had allowed one of the two boilers to run dry and ultimately collapse. Damage was on an extensive scale and repairs would cost, at the very least, seventy thousand dollars. Naturally the miscreant had been relieved of his duties in the engine room and was now languishing in the ship's lazaret where he had been confined, and could remain till he was summoned before a court-martial in San Francisco. With one engine permanently out of action, we were now condemned to a crippled progress across the wide waters of the Pacific. Nor was the 3rd Engineer the only delinquent whom the night's junketing would lead to a fall from grace. A couple of American officers, having taken one of the nurses out on a spree in the town, had returned to the ship deep in their cups. While trying to slip back furtively to their cabins, one of the men had fallen from an upper deck, breaking his ankle in the process. All three had barely escaped joining the 3rd Engineer in his lazaret. Also joining the casualty list, though by quite another route, was Bill Exley, one of our officers from Ohama. Troubled during the night by vague abdominal pains, he had gone down to the sick-bay in search of some digestive powder. But he was promptly laid on an operating table where his appendix was speedily and expertly removed. What might have been his fate had this happened a week or two earlier in Ohama was open to conjecture.

Two days out from Hawaii the wind, which had remained strong, freshened into a gale, and as the vessel plunged into the great troughs she creaked and groaned as if she might break her back. Serious doubts began to arise among the prisoners as to whether her remaining boiler was sufficient to ensure our passage to American shores. With astonishing frankness, the Tannoy kept us abreast of events with a litany of our tribulations. Because of very bad weather, we had been diverted to Seattle. But the weather continued no less bad on the new course, and after a further three days of battering we were told we were once again making for San Francisco, the following reasons being given for this return to our original plan: the weather was foul (which we could see); bunker oil was short (which we could imagine); food was running out (as we expected); and the ship was not seaworthy (which we feared). In any case they did not want to take ex-prisoners farther north because conditions there were very cold. If it was any consolation to us, about 250 miles north of our position there was another vessel, very similar to the *Marine Shark*, which was making for Seattle and was also in difficulties.

Day after relentless day the wind continued to howl, and the sea boiled around us. Yet still we struggled on, maimed but still afloat, heading eastwards. At length the 7,083 troubled and tempestuous miles from Manila to San Francisco dwindled to their end. Triumphantly the ship's newspaper, *The Shark's Teeth*. brought out a souvenir edition, memorably undistinguished, spanning the gamut from the patriotic to the maudlin, and on Thursday, 1 November 1945 the *Marine Shark*, her sirens at full blast, sailed under the sagging crescent of the Golden Gate Bridge. Down to the gunwale with friends and relatives of the homecoming Americans, a launch came out to greet us. On its deck was a girls' brass band, blazing away with bugles that would start the world along. With their long, shapely and sun-kissed legs, topped by flamboyant and extravagantly frogged tunics, they certainly looked much better than they sounded. It was regrettable that the ex-prisoners did not pay more attentive heed to their raucous fanfare, but who was to blame them? Their emotions were in ferment. This at last was America! This was the Land of Liberty! With their Jap mining *happi*-coats, they had shed the grimy humiliation of captivity. Presently whatever noise the girls' band was making was swallowed up and drowned in a great reverberating thunder as every ship's siren in the port added its blast to the bedlam of welcome. With the waves of sound rolling back in a deafening echo from the serried ranks of skyscrapers, we tied up at a wharf almost at their feet.

Across the wharf a stout barricade had been erected to preserve these precincts from the feet of the unsanctified, though one gangway had been kept clear for the passage of the One-Man-Army and the large crowd of reporters and photographers who now clambered on board to interview him. To enable the proceedings to be conducted with some privacy, the ship's lounge had been cleared, and strict orders had been issued that no one was to leave the vessel till the main party had disembarked. Once the ceremony was completed, and the central figure had departed, American personnel would follow. Bringing up the rear would be the British contingent. Anxious to witness the disembarkation at close quarters, I went down to secure a place beside the rail and close to the head of the gangway. Presently I was startled by the sound of loud and unrestrained sobbing; looking along the rail to discover its source, I saw that it was coming from a pretty, girlish head clasped in two distracted hands and leaning out over the varnished teak. Gazing more curiously at her, I was startled to realise that it was none other than the nurse chaperoned by the One-Man-Army who had come on board at Pearl Harbor clutching her teddybear in one arm. At length the preliminary interview was over and the centre of all interest made his entrance, followed by the retinue of ardent reporters. As he approached the gangway I saw him give a sudden start as his eyes swivelled for a moment in the direction of the nurse he had so callously betrayed. But the diversion was no more than momentary. Stony-faced and silent, he strode past her; climbing down the gangway, he stalked across to the barricade where a woman and a very pretty girl were waiting to welcome him. Their warm embrace was the occasion for much clicking of cameras. But some complained they had been unable to get a satisfactory view of the event, and he went dutifully through the ritual again. Beside me someone observed that these were his mother and his sister. Waiting for him was a cavalcade of cars, into one of which he was shepherded and swept off to civic acclaim. Of the facts of this affair there could be no question, as I had witnessed it with my own eyes – and had grieved for its victim.

When at length the general excitement had abated the American troops were, with notable lack of ceremony, disembarked and reunited with their own people at the barricade. Bringing up the rear were the British. Beside me as we lined up for numbering on the wharf was an English Red Cross girl. Trapped in Shanghai, she had spent the war years in an internment camp near that city, administering to the sick in the highest traditions of the order she served. Now there was a girl, surely, who had a story to tell! But none showed any interest in her or her story. No photographer thought that her picture in his newspaper would be of the slightest interest to its readers.

When at length the checks were completed, we were marched off to a nearby wharf. There several launches were moored and waiting for us, and eagerly we piled on board. Johnnie Probert, who had been the companion of my captive days, and my Pacific voyaging, asked the crewman at the wheel where he was taking us.

'Fort McDowell,' said the man, pointing to an island at the far end of the bay. 'It's on Angel Island.'

But Johnnie's attention had strayed to a nearer island. Rather dumpling-shaped, it had clumps of palm trees and several large orange-coloured buildings, vaguely recalling a Moorish palace.

'What's that place?' asked Johnnie.

'I thought you would have had enough of that by this time,' said the crewman, a roguish twinkle in his eye. 'But I'll take you there if you're very keen.'

'What's it called?' asked Johnnie.

'Alcatraz!' said the crewman.

The string of launches chugged on up the bay. Behind us towered the forest of skyscrapers. On our left hung the slender loop of the great bridge. To the east, behind the towns of Oakland and Berkeley, rose some yellow sun-baked ridges – nothing much in the way of vegetation there! In the bright Californian light, how much clearer everything looked! As we approached the jetty on Angel Island, the men clambered to their feet and crowded forward, causing the launch to rock alarmingly.

'Steady on, boys!' cautioned the crewman. 'Steady on! There's no need for all this mad rush; you can take your time. After all, you've got all the time in the world before you!'

Got all the time in the world before us? We, who not so long before, seemed to have *no* time in the world before us! It was almost too good to be true. From the Valley of Humiliation we had been miraculously snatched, and now before us stretched the Delectable Mountains. Our hearts were over-brimming with benediction. God bless America!

The launch tied up at the wharf, and we disembarked. Then we lined up on the road and, shouldering our packs, marched off towards Fort McDowell. The rhythmic beat of our new American boots on a free earth was sweet music in our ears.

APPENDIX 1
THE VAN DER PLOEG FAMILY

When, in March 1942, Japanese forces occupied Batavia, they promptly rounded up all able-bodied Dutch men and removed them for internment to an unknown destination. Thereafter, for a month or two, the remaining Dutch were allowed to stay on in their homes. But whatever hopes they might have entertained that this situation might be allowed to continue were rudely dissipated when they, in their turn, were assembled and dispatched in the wake of their men-folk.

For their reception the Japanese had constructed a large camp near the village of Ambarawa, which is about twenty-five miles south of Semarang on the Mageland road, familiar to me from my flight in March 1942 from the invading Japanese. There the Dutch were to linger out the remaining years of the war, continually exposed to the harassments and degradation inevitably associated with such camps run by the Japanese.

But at length two atomic bombs over the mainland of Japan brought a swift and unexpected end to Nippon domination, though it did not result in immediate liberation for the incarcerated Dutch. Round their compound now assembled a baying mob of Javanese, inflamed by what they regarded as their harsh treatment by the Dutch, and now bent on exacting a summary and bloody revenge. They began by tossing hand grenades into the camp, and there is little doubt that a general massacre would have ensued had not the murderers been thwarted from their evil purpose by the arrival on the scene of deliverers from an unexpected quarter. Arriving a little earlier at Semarang, a British relief force had learned of the plight of the captive Dutch and with all speed dispatched for their relief several lorries laden with Gurkha soldiers. Confronted with these redoubtable warriors, the homicidal ardour of the Javanese wilted; rescued on the point of death from the camp, the captives were escorted back to Semarang and thence, in due course, to Holland.

From their ordeal, release was not to erase the scars of bondage, which presently were to exact their toll. To Herr van der Ploeg were to be alloted no more than a few years of life. Growing in time to manhood, Jan became the manager of a large oil refinery in Pakistan, but, like his father, he was to succumb to similarly induced infirmities. Tineke appeared to survive captivity in better shape. Later married, she had two daughters. She still lives in Holland. In later years her mother joined a Dutch touring party on a visit to Scotland, which was the occasion for an emotional and heart-warming reunion in Edinburgh. But the years that remained to her were few.

Then after Japanese defeat, the rolling years at last numbered fifty and VJ Day was approaching. Now, on its threshold, further information came to hand which revealed the reality of captivity near Semarang in a more sombre and sinister light. Incensed, it appears, at obdurate Japanese denial of guilt – or even of any evil having taken place – some Korean women, who had been impressed by the Japanese as 'comfort women' for their armies in the field, and emboldened by the approach of VJ Day, decided to stifle their shame and, breaking their silence, let the world know of the horrors they had endured. Inspired by their bold example, several Dutch women who had been incarcerated in the camp at Ambarawa decided likewise to break their silence and reveal the harrowing reality of their treatment by their Japanese captors. Japanese officers, they now reported, entered the camp and selected the girls they wanted to gratify their lust, whereupon these were led away to a shameful fate. Nor were those who escaped this selection spared similar harassment, being exposed to continual sexual invasion by the guards.

Upon this sordid aspect of their sojourn in the camp the van der Ploeg family observed to me an inflexible silence; nor, knowing now what they witnessed and knew of, have I any regrets that nothing of these events escaped their lips. But in moments of sorrow and dejection speculation insists on breaking free from restraint. What, for instance, befell the weeping girl in the mayor's office at Djokjakarta? Or the radiant aide in the dazzling blue uniform in the General's Headquarters in Batavia? Both, one suspects, were prime candidates for degradation.

It is all a vile phantasmagoria upon which it little profits to let the mind dwell too curiously or too long – except to shed a tear for these comely and hapless victims of a lecherous soldiery.

APPENDIX 2
JAPANESE WAR CRIMINALS

After the war, those on the *Singapore Maru* held responsible were arraigned before a British war crimes court in Singapore on a charge of being 'Concerned in the ill-treatment of a draft of British prisoners-of-war, resulting in the death of sixty, and the physical suffering of many others.' They were the captain of the vessel, Shipmaster Nishimi Yoshimara, together with the Japanese OC Troops and two draft-conducting officers. I have no information about what verdicts were returned, or, if they were found guilty, what sentences were imposed.

On 12 June 1946 I received a letter from the office of the Judge Advocate General in London transmitting a request from His Majesty's representative in Tokyo for an affidavit dealing with my experiences in Ohama. Detailed information was required about the alleged beating of Sullivan by the civilian guards Yamamoto Hiowhi, Ueda Fumio, and Fujii Masaichi. 1st Lt Fukuhara, the camp commandant, who also beat Sullivan (he was, of course, the principal agent in the attack), had, it added, already been sentenced to death for atrocities committed *in another camp*.

On 21 December 1949, I was informed that sentences passed by the British Military Courts on Japanese War Criminals who were tried in connection with Ohama Camp were as follows:

Yamamoto: 10 years' imprisonment
Ueda: 5 years
Fujii: 15 years

APPENDIX 3
OHAMA REVISITED, 1970

After leaving Ohama on 13 September 1946, I never returned. I heard nothing more about it till 1970 when Reg Newton, who had been CO of Australian troops in the camp, revisited it. The following extract from a letter he wrote to me at the time will give some indication of the changes that had taken place since we left.

> I went down from Osaka by train to Gori, and changed to a private railway for Ube and Onada. The station-master at Onada was a bit hostile, as was also the police chief, when he was called. But I prevailed upon them to let me go to the main office of the Onada Cement Co., where I was sure there was somebody who could speak English. This I knew, for I had made enquiries in Tokyo. The Cement Co. people were very good, and there was no trouble after that.
>
> They took me over to Ohama – only 4½ miles away – and my feelings were rather mixed when I came to the village. The mine was closed down in 1963, through cave-in and seeping, and the pumping-out was found to be uneconomic. I found that the old camp had gone completely, and in its place quite a number of relatively new factory buildings were spreading to the south towards the village communal bath area. The old hospital had become the head office of the Mining Co., and the company was still alive and active, but in the resin and polythene fields. All of the new buildings belong to the Mining Co. The old mining area was still used for the maintenance programme in the factories, and for the Motoyama factory complex.
>
> I met only one man who was in Ohama in our days, and his name was Akira Haitani. He was the chief clerk of the Labour Dept. from November 1944 until December 1954, and is now the managing director of the Chugoku Resin Co., one of the Mining Co. subsidiaries. He remembered Paul Wyrill and myself, and particularly the Australians arriving in September 1944, and the departure of the camp in September 1945. He also remembered the hand-outs from the air drops and said that, without the additional food, they would have been in dire straits. He said that they had had trouble after we left with the Police Dept., from Yamaguchi, who had wanted to take over the stores that we had left behind, but the Mining Co. had won out at the finish because the interpreter, Tanaka, had said that the police would get into trouble from the Americans if they did not leave the Mining Co. alone. Haitani did not know what had

become of any of the Japanese Army staff of the camp, nor of Tanaka.

The whole place now appeared affluent, and all the people were well-dressed and busy. I went up to the cemetery and the small crematorium at the top of the hill, and from there the vast complex of the Onada Cement Works, running twenty-five miles to the north and round to Shimonoseki, was rather overpowering. On the eastern side, the port of Ube had increased tremendously. Over one million people now live in this area, and all is a hive of industry. The fishing village, between the mine and the cemetery along the waterfront in the next bay, is still there, although it is larger and more vessels are in operation. Similarly, a good deal of fishing of a commercial nature still takes place from Ohama and along the coast to Motoyama. The garden area at the rear of the old camp is still used as such. There are still plenty of people working in it, with *benjo* tubs still being carried as fertiliser.

INDEX